PE·Metrics™

3rd Edition

Assessing Student Performance Using the National Standards & Grade-Level Outcomes for K-12 Physical Education

SHAPE America – Society of Health and Physical Educators

Principal Authors

Stevie Chepko

Shirley Holt/Hale

Robert J. Doan

Lynn Couturier MacDonald

Library of Congress Cataloging-in-Publication Data has been applied for.

ISBN: 978-1-4925-2666-7 (print)

This book is a revised edition of *PE Metrics: Assessing National Standards 1-6 in Secondary School, First Edition,* published in 2011 by American Alliance for Health, Physical Education, Recreation and Dance (AAHPERD) and National Association for Sport and Physical Education (NASPE), and *PE Metrics: Assessing National Standards 1-6 in Elementary School, Second Edition,* published in 2010 by American Alliance for Health, Physical Education, Recreation and Dance (AAHPERD) and National Association for Sport and Physical Education (NASPE).

The web addresses cited in this text were current as of January 2018, unless otherwise noted.

Acquisitions Editor: Scott Wikgren; **Managing Editor:** Derek Campbell; **SHAPE America Editors:** Joe McGavin and Thomas Lawson; **Copyeditor:** Joe McGavin; **Permissions Manager:** Dalene Reeder; **Graphic Designer:** Sean Roosevelt; **Cover Designer:** Keri Evans; **Cover Design Associate:** Susan Rothermel Allen; **Photographs (cover):** © Human Kinetics, unless otherwise noted; the top left photo is courtesy of Jim Davis; **Photographs (interior):** © Human Kinetics, unless otherwise noted; **Photo Asset Manager:** Laura Fitch; **Photo Production Manager:** Jason Allen; **Senior Art Manager:** Kelly Hendren; **Illustrations:** © Human Kinetics, unless otherwise noted; **Printer:** Versa Press

SHAPE America – Society of Health and Physical Educators
1900 Association Drive
Reston, VA 20191
800-213-7193
www.shapeamerica.org

Printed in the United States of America   10 9 8 7 6 5 4 3 2

The paper in this book is certified under a sustainable forestry program.

Human Kinetics
P.O. Box 5076
Champaign, IL 61825-5076
Website: www.HumanKinetics.com

In the United States, email info@hkusa.com or call 800-747-4457.
In Canada, email info@hkcanada.com.
In the United Kingdom/Europe, email hk@hkeurope.com.

For information about Human Kinetics' coverage in other areas of the world,
please visit our website: **www.HumanKinetics.com**

E6761

Tell us what you think!
Human Kinetics would love to hear what we
can do to improve the customer experience.
Use this QR code to take our brief survey.

Contents

Part I: Assessment for the 21st Century

Part II: Sample Assessments for Elementary School Physical Education

Part III: Sample Assessments for Middle School Physical Education

Part IV: Sample Assessments for High School Physical Education

Preface

This book is the latest in a series of assessment resources from SHAPE America. Beginning in 2000, the National Association for Sport and Physical Education (NASPE), now SHAPE America, sponsored the development of assessment guidelines. NASPE convened K-12 teachers and administrators, teacher educators and researchers to create assessments that measured student achievement specific to the National Standards found in the first edition of NASPE's *Moving Into the Future: National Standards for Physical Education* (1995). This initial effort provided physical education teachers with general guidelines on types of assessments (e.g., check sheets, rating scales, rubrics, portfolios, written tests), examples of each assessment type and the uses for each type of assessment in physical education. In addition, NASPE defined authentic, formative and summative assessments.

Throughout the decade that followed, professionals in the discipline continued to refine assessments to measure the National Standards found in the second edition of *Moving Into the Future: National Standards for Physical Education* (NASPE, 2004). Work in the field consisted of creating performance indicators and assessments, piloting assessments and video-recording them, collecting and analyzing assessment data, revising the assessments and then repeating the cycle for both the elementary and secondary levels. This work produced the first and second editions of *PE Metrics* (NASPE, 2009, 2010, 2011). Designed to deliver a formal assessment process, the original editions of *PE Metrics* recommended strict adherence to assessment protocols, assessed students' performance relative to the National Standards, and sought to standardize assessment and data collection at the national level. The *PE Metrics* assessments under Standard 1 across all grade levels used four-level scoring rubrics that focused on motor skill performance. This in-depth analysis required teachers to video-record students' performance to afford them the observation time needed to complete the assessment using the rubrics. *PE Metrics* offered a test bank of multiple-choice questions for measuring students' knowledge under Standards 2-5. The use of video-recording increased the reliability of the assessments but made the assessments impractical for frequent use.

In 2011, NASPE's Board of Directors appointed a task force to revise the 2004 National Standards and produce a curriculum framework for teachers, which also would inform outside stakeholders, such as parents, administrators and policymakers, of the goals, outcomes and benefits of K-12 physical education. After three years of extensive review and feedback, SHAPE America (formerly NASPE), accepted the revised National Standards and published them in *National Standards & Grade-Level Outcomes for K-12 Physical Education* (2014), with the inclusion of Grade-Level Outcomes marking the most significant change in the revised standards. The outcomes added focus to what students should be able to know and do at the end of each grade. In addition, the outcomes were written in a way that facilitates the assessment and tracking of student progress over time.

The revision of the National Standards to include Grade-Level Outcomes necessitated changes in *PE Metrics'* assessment processes. As a result, this third edition of *PE Metrics* aligns with changes in the National Standards and provides sample assessments for measuring student performance against the Grade-Level Outcomes. These sample assessments focus on the holistic development of a **physically literate individual** across all three learning domains (psychomotor, cognitive and affective). They are process-focused, designed to measure multiple constructs, and provide meaningful feedback to students. At the end of each student's K-12 physical education experience, his or her teacher must be able to determine and document whether the student has the knowledge, skills and motivation to be a lifelong learner and mover.

This edition of *PE Metrics* provides guidance on the assessment process and offers sample assessments for use in elementary, middle and high school grades that align with Grade-Level Outcomes under each National Standard. You can use the sample assessments as is, modify them to fit your curriculum or use them to create original assessments that are most appropriate for your teaching environment and needs. The goal is to give you the tools you need to embed assessment into every facet of your teaching and to create assessments that are unique to your program, aligned with the National Standards for K-12 Physical Education, and provide stakeholders with evidence of your program's effectiveness in developing physically literate individuals.

Our Vision: A nation where all children are prepared to lead healthy, physically active lives.

Our Mission: To advance professional practice and promote research related to health and physical education, physical activity, dance and sport.

Our Commitment: 50 Million Strong by 2029

50 Million Strong by 2029 is SHAPE America's commitment to put all children on the path to health and physical literacy through effective health and physical education programs. We believe that through effective teaching, health and physical educators can help students develop the ability and confidence to be physically active and make healthy choices. As educators, our guidance can also help foster their desire to maintain an active and healthy lifestyle in the years to come. To learn more visit www.shapeamerica.org/50Million.

Acknowledgments

SHAPE America would like to acknowledge all the hard work that has gone into putting together this edition of *PE Metrics: Assessing Student Performance Using the National Standards & Grade-Level Outcomes for K-12 Physical Education.*

A deep and sincere note of gratitude goes out to our group of principal writers: Stevie Chepko, Shirley Holt/Hale, Lynn Couturier MacDonald, and Robert J. Doan. SHAPE America also appreciates and acknowledges the exceptional foundation for this book built by the original team of writers: Marybell Avery, Jennifer Walton-Fisette, Kevin Lorson, and Stephen Mitchell. Furthermore, this book would not have been possible without the work of previous task forces and committees and the support of the SHAPE America Board of Directors. These groups include the Assessment Task Force that created the initial editions of *PE Metrics* (Marybell Avery, Ben Dyson, Jennifer Fisette, Connie Fox, Marian Franck, Kim Graber, Judith Placek, Judith Rink, Lori Williams, Weimo Zu) and those who provided technical assistance (Marco Boscolo, Connie Fox, Pamela MacFarlane, Sara Khosravi Nasr, Youngsik Park, Eng Wah Teo, Weimo Zu). Finally, we would like to thank former SHAPE America book publications manager and editor Joe McGavin for all of his hard work on this project.

SHAPE America also appreciates the many professionals who reviewed different drafts of this book and made valuable contributions that strengthened the document.

Suggested citation for this book: SHAPE America – Society of Health and Physical Educators. (2019). *PE Metrics: Assessing Student Performance Using the National Standards & Grade-Level Outcomes for K-12 Physical Education* (3rd ed.). Champaign, IL: Human Kinetics.

SHAPE America – Society of Health and Physical Educators
Stephanie Morris, CEO
Diana Snyder, Vice President, Membership, Marketing and Publications
Thomas F. Lawson, Director of Publishing
Cheryl Richardson, Senior Director of Programs

Part I

Assessment for the 21st Century

Using *PE Metrics*

Aligning *PE Metrics* With the National Standards and Grade-Level Outcomes

Several changes in this edition of *PE Metrics* are driven by 2013 revisions to the National Standards for K-12 Physical Education and the addition of accompanying Grade-Level Outcomes for K-12 Physical Education (Society of Health and Physical Educators, 2014). The new *PE Metrics* takes advantage of the Grade-Level Outcomes to provide sample assessments for each grade, K-12, rather than selected grade bands (2, 5, 8 and high school) as in previous editions. In addition, assessments in earlier versions of *PE Metrics* were aligned with the National Standards, but in this edition, sample assessments are now aligned with both the standards and specific Grade-Level Outcomes. Appendix A contains both the National Standards and the Grade-Level Outcomes for your review.

Another change driven by modification of the National Standards was the move away from goal-based standards (2004) specific to demonstrating fitness and being physically active. The 2004 version of Standard 3 stated, "A physical educated person participates regularly in physical activity," and Standard 4 stated, "A physical educated person achieves and maintains a health-enhancing level of physical fitness." In the 2013 revision to the National Standards, SHAPE America combined those two standards into a content-based standard that focuses on what we teach in physical education. National Standard 3 now states, "The physically literate individual demonstrates the knowledge and skills to achieve and maintain a health-enhancing level of physical activity and fitness." The new focus for this standard requires a shift in how we assess student performance and knowledge under the standard. Accordingly, the assessments under Standard 3 in this book focus on students' ability to apply knowledge, as well as track and use data to develop and implement personal fitness, behavior-change and/or nutrition plans to attain self-selected goals. The intent is to ensure that students have the knowledge and skill to remain fit and active over a lifetime.

Earlier editions of *PE Metrics* also emphasized the use of research-based, scientifically valid assessments that had been field-tested with strict protocols, to which teachers were expected to adhere. Those protocols often required video-recording small groups of students for teacher review and scoring at a later time. While that process added reliability and validity to the assessment process, many teachers struggled with the practicality of implementing the protocols fully. This edition of *PE Metrics* addresses that issue by providing user-friendly sample assessments that allow teachers to measure student performance and knowledge across all five National Standards for K-12 Physical Education. While none of the assessments in this book have been field-tested, they were reviewed by practitioners and teacher educators with expertise in assessment, thereby establishing face validity. In addition, the assessment developers reviewed the assessments to ensure alignment with the National Standards and Grade-Level Outcomes and the continuity of assessments across grade levels.

Assessing 21st Century Skills in Physical Education

In recent years, educators, business leaders, academics and government agencies have identified skills that will be needed in the 21st century. These skills are linked to students' abilities to master a range of transferable competencies needed for success in a rapidly changing, digital society. While various agencies and organizations have identified an array of skills as 21st century skills, they generally agree on these four: collaboration, communication, critical thinking and creativity. Digital literacy also is included as essential for 21st century learning. All the skills included on the list are interdisciplinary in nature, allowing individuals to carry the skill set to any position, field or job, and focus on the need for students to be self-learners and innovators. It's difficult to imagine what children entering kindergarten in 2019 will need to know or the technology they will use by the time they reach their senior year of high school. The accelerating changes in information and technology mean it is more important than ever that children are given the tools they need to be lifelong learners.

For most of us, teaching for 21st century skills requires new instructional strategies, such as project-based, blended, and flipped classrooms. With a greater emphasis on applying knowledge and problem-solving skills (individual and group), teachers act as facilitators of learning. The shift to 21st century skills also necessitates changes in how we assess students for these skills as well as discipline-specific skills and knowledge. Fortunately, physical education has always provided opportunities for collaboration, critical thinking, communication and creativity. Our curriculum offers multiple opportunities to teach and assess 21st century skills in conjunction with movement, fitness and physical competency. These skills are well-represented in the National Standards and Grade-Level Outcomes (SHAPE America, 2014) and within the sample assessments in this edition of *PE Metrics*.

Throughout *PE Metrics*, 21st century skills are integrated in sample assessments designed to measure skilled performance and knowledge while keeping the focus on the key mission of developing students' physical literacy. For example, an assessment built around a grade-level outcome on developing a fitness plan also might measure students' ability to set realistic goals based on data. While the assessment's focus remains on developing a fitness plan, the rubric might contain an indicator for using critical-thinking skills to develop the plan. At the upper-elementary school level, assessments have students work with partners on movement skills such as throwing and catching. While the assessment uses a checklist or rubric to assess throwing and catching competency, it also might contain additional indicators for assessing students' ability to work together. Creativity can be assessed by projects in which students work alone or in small groups to create dances or yoga routines. In addition, many of the assessments in *PE Metrics* involve using technology to demonstrate movement and fitness competency. Others are specific to flipped classrooms, developing oral presentations, sharing projects electronically, and using video to analyze movements and/or performance. The sample assessments provide you with the tools to evaluate your students' progress toward physical literacy as well as essential life skills for today's society.

Providing Student Choice

One of the key factors in engaging students in their own learning is providing them with opportunities for choice. Choice provides students with feelings of autonomy, inserts a level of student accountability, and leads to higher levels of motivation (Bryan, Sims, Hester, & Dunaway, 2013; Hannon & Ratcliffe, 2005; Ward, Wilkinson, Graser, & Prusak, 2008: Zhang,

Solmon, Kosma, Carlson, & Gu, 2011). These choices can include selecting a partner, or the equipment or space to be used, or how to demonstrate mastery of a Grade-Level Outcome. Providing students with some choice about how to demonstrate their competency (be assessed) makes them more likely to perceive the assignment as important and to assume more personal accountability for their learning (Marzano & Pickering, 2011). Many of the samples in *PE Metrics* include lists of assignments and assessment options to allow students to select how they can demonstrate their competency in or mastery of the skills or knowledge prescribed in a particular Grade-Level Outcome. For example, you can find sample assessments that allow students (individually or in small groups) to select a skill and flip the classroom by developing an instructional video, complete a biomechanical analysis or create a narrated audiovisual presentation on a self-selected skill (Part IV: Sample Assessments for High School Physical Education). Those examples allow students to not only choose how to demonstrate their competency but also select the process of assessment that works best for their skill sets. In other assessments, students not only select the topic for the assignments but also choose whether to work alone, with a partner or in a small group. You can find an example of this type of assessment in Part II: Sample Assessments for Elementary School Physical Education, which tasks students with creating gymnastics routines within a set of parameters. The accompanying rubric allows you to assess students' skills individually, in pairs or in small groups.

Organization of This Edition of *PE Metrics*

This book is divided into four main sections. Part I includes introductory material and information on standards-based assessment. Part II of the book contains sample assessments for students in elementary school. With elementary physical education as the foundation for students' development of fundamental motor skills, the elementary-level assessments in Part II focus heavily on Standard 1. Part III of the book contains sample assessments for middle school students with a focus on Standard 2 and on teaching concepts across categories of dance and rhythms, invasion games, net/wall games, fielding/striking games, outdoor pursuits, aquatics and individual-performance activities. Part IV contains sample assessments for high school students with an emphasis on providing evidence of the knowledge and skills that students will need to remain active and fit after they leave high school.

The sample assessments in this book do not address all activities or all of the Grade-Level Outcomes. Rather, they are intended not only as practical assessments that you can use in your classes but also as guides for developing your own assessments based on your teaching environment. The assessments at all levels—elementary, middle, and high school—emphasize the importance of student learning specific to the National Standards and Grade-Level Outcomes.

All assessments under each of the five National Standards are grouped within the selected grade levels: elementary school (Part II), middle school (Part III) and high school (Part IV). Assessments within Parts II, III and IV are organized by National Standard; that is, all assessments under Standard 1 appear first in each part, followed by assessments under Standard 2, and so on. This structure helps you easily find and use the assessments appropriate to your students.

Appendices contain sample forms developed for collecting data and tracking student progress, samples of worksheets to be used with various assessments, sample knowledge tests, and samples of comprehensive assessments that measure multiple standards within one assessment. These samples will help you develop assessments for your program.

Using *PE Metrics* in Your Program

The scoring rubrics within the sample assessments are designed so that you can observe students during practice tasks, modified game play, fitness and movement activities, gymnastics or dance to determine their level of proficiency. The rubrics guide your evaluation by allowing you to assign students to one of three levels: Developing, Competent or Proficient. All rubrics include an "indicator," which is an outcome statement against which you can assess student performance using the performance criteria in each of the three levels (Developing, Competent and Proficient). For example, an indicator in a sample assessment for high school students on creating and maintaining a fitness plan, in Part IV of this book, states: "Goals meet the SMART (specific, measurable, achievable, realistic and time-bound) criteria." The indicator within that assessment's scoring rubric is intended to help teachers measure a student's ability to set and pursue personal fitness goals. At the elementary school level, Standard 1 indicators are specific to the critical elements for the skill. The indicator column states, simply, "Critical Elements," and students must demonstrate the critical elements of that particular skill to be scored as Competent in the skill. The indicators are similar to student learning outcomes, and you can think of them as an "indication" of how students demonstrate their mastery of a skill.

Each performance level in the rubric is defined by criteria linked specifically to critical elements. At the **Developing level**, students are moving toward competency and mastery of the identified critical elements. At the Developing level, then, a student's competency is emerging and needs further development. With deliberate practice, students can move from the Developing level to the **Competent level**. Students at the Competent level demonstrate all of the critical elements of the skill, exhibiting mastery of the indicator. The Competent level defines the minimal level of performance required for meeting the indicator. Students at the **Proficient level** not only demonstrate all the required critical elements of the skill during assessment, but their performance also meets additional criteria and/or displays a level of performance that goes beyond Competent. For example, a student could display all of the critical elements while throwing overhand, while another student adds the wrist snap at the end of the throw or increases their stride length to generate more power. The first student demonstrated competency while the second student demonstrated proficiency by showing a more advanced level of performance.

Throughout this book, we use the term "sample" assessment purposefully. We do not recommend any of the assessments as exemplars, but only as samples of assessments that are aligned with the National Standards and Grade-Level Outcomes. They represent SHAPE America's attempt to provide you with a way of thinking about developing assessments that is unique to your teaching environment. The purposes of assessment are to improve instruction, track student progress, and provide feedback to students on their progress toward intended outcomes. Therefore, the assessments you use must meet the needs of your students and your program.

We encourage you to modify any and all sample assessments in this book to fit your teaching environment, to use them as guidelines for developing your own assessments, and to combine or modify the assessments to align with your school or district outcomes. You will also want to modify the sample assessments to meet the needs of students with disabilities. For specific guidance in this area, we recommend *Assessment for Everyone: Modifying NASPE Assessments to Include All Elementary School Children* (Lieberman, Kowalski, et al., 2011).

While all the sample rubrics in this version of *PE Metrics* denote levels of competency and not point values for each level, you can modify the samples to assign point values and assign different weights to various indicators on the rubric. The sample assessments simply provide you with some suggestions. An example of a "rubric with weighted values" for each level can be found in Appendix B. An example of a "rubric with weighted values" for indicators can be found in Appendix C. You can change a rubric to a checklist or a checklist to a rubric if doing so better fits your needs. While the sample assessment for evaluating students' reflections or journal entries might be an analytic rubric, you might find that a general rubric works better for you. In many cases, you may want to alter a sample assessment by replacing some of the language to match the cues you have been using in your classes. That way, the assessment process and feedback from the rubric will be more meaningful to your students. Think of the sample assessments in *PE Metrics* as building blocks and tools for you to use in developing an assessment plan that is unique to your program and the needs of your students.

As you review the various samples of assessments and assignments in this book, keep in mind that you can use a single assessment to measure more than one Grade-Level Outcome, even if the outcomes are aligned under different standards. You can combine a sample assessment suggested for one National Standard and Grade-Level Outcome with another assessment for a different Grade-Level Outcome under a different National Standard to create an analytic rubric. This is particularly true for assessments under Standards 1, 4 and 5. For example, you can assess middle school students creating a line dance on their skill competency in dance & rhythms (Outcome S1.M1.8) while also assessing them on their collaboration skills (Outcome S4.M6.8) and their enjoyment of activity and their self-expression (Outcome S5.M5.8). You can assess students under all three outcomes in one assignment, using one comprehensive analytic rubric. An example of an analytic rubric assessing more than one standard can be found in Appendix D. These types of assessments have "embedded" within them opportunities to assess multiple standards. Another assessment strategy is to use a suite of assessments to provide a comprehensive and multidimensional picture of student achievement throughout a unit or school year. A suite of assessments would include several forms of assessment, including rubrics, checklists, peer and self-assessments, exit slips and worksheets. An example of a suite of assessments can be found in Appendix E.

Please note that many of the sample assessments encourage students to demonstrate their competency in specific outcomes through the use of technology. Video blogs, slide presentations, flipped classrooms and electronic postings are some of the examples provided. In addition, you might use software to track student progress, collect data and report results to various stakeholders. As physical educators, we need to be part of the digital revolution!

When the time comes to implement your assessments, you will have to think about the practicality of using a rubric while watching students who are moving. This is true especially when evaluating students in activities under Standards 1 and 2. You might want to place a streamlined copy of your rubric on a clipboard or tablet for quick reference while observing students. You can simplify the rubric by highlighting key words in the descriptors or by abbreviating the descriptors in a way that makes sense to you. After you've used the rubric a few times, it will become quite familiar and you will find yourself referring to the rubric far less frequently; it will be in your head. You also will need a simple score sheet for recording students' final scores in an efficient manner. An example of a simple score sheet for locomotor skills at the elementary level and a score sheet for backhand stroke in badminton at the middle or high school level can be found in Appendix F.

Final Thoughts

As the public demands increased accountability from all educators, physical education teachers must make a concerted effort to assess students, track their progress and report the results to administrators, parents and the public. You are limited only by your imagination in the kinds of assessments you use and how you use them. Assessments can be as informal as a check for understanding and as formal as a comprehensive examination. What is most important is that assessment becomes part of what you do every day. It must become an intrinsic component of the teaching process and a seamless extension of instruction. SHAPE America's goal in producing *PE Metrics* is to provide you with tools for incorporating assessment into your program on a practical and pragmatic level.

Assessment Essentials

The Role of Assessment in Today's Schools

With increased calls for accountability in public education and the shift to data-driven decision making, the role of assessment has evolved to take center stage in the education reform movement. Assessment can be defined as "the gathering of evidence about student achievement and making inferences about student progress based on that evidence" (Society of Health and Physical Educators, 2015). Many policymakers, parents and administrators assume that assessment occurs every day in every classroom, and that assessments produce evidence of student learning. While assessment *does* provide such evidence, student learning is only one of many roles assessment plays in education. Assessments must provide ongoing measures of student performance using more than one method, be aligned with student learning outcomes, and allow students to demonstrate competency in a variety of ways. No longer can just one assessment at one point in time provide adequate evidence of student learning. To get a complete, nuanced picture of a student's learning requires multiple assessments dispersed over time.

Purposes of Assessment

Just as the role of assessment has evolved, so have the uses of assessment. While the focus remains on measuring student learning, using assessment to provide feedback on student performance, make instruction-related decisions, and inform teaching is just as important. Assessment information and data should inform teachers and teaching in every part of the instruction process. Student performance and improvement are determined by the interaction of student learning and teachers teaching. It is part of the ongoing instruction process, just as planning learning experiences, establishing student outcomes and managing a classroom. Assessment is as multidimensional as teaching and serves multiple purposes in the instruction and learning processes.

The primary purpose of assessment in physical education is to provide stakeholders with evidence of students' learning as well as their attainment of National Standards and Grade-Level Outcomes. Collecting and reporting on data specific to outcomes allow you to document student progress, communicate your teaching effectiveness to students, parents and administrators, and make the case for additional time and funding for your program. Part of the accountability movement in education reform is data-driven decision-making. As physical educators, we must improve our ability to collect, analyze and use data for program improvement and demonstrate the use of data to ensure that all students are physically literate. Without the use of data generated by a matrix of assessments, we cannot make our case for the continued inclusion in the school curriculum.

A second purpose of assessment is to provide students with feedback on their progress. Effective assessments go beyond assigning a number, percentage or grade to student performance by providing specific, corrective feedback through the assessment itself. The most common example of providing specific feedback through an assessment is the use of **analytic**

rubrics to assess assignments or performance (see Appendix D). Well-developed analytic rubrics identify critical elements of the performance at various levels and dimensions and allow you to provide detailed feedback to students on their performance simply by having them complete the assessment. Analytic rubrics often are used when assessing complex skills, the application of knowledge, or a multipart performance or assignment. By using an analytic rubric, you can facilitate students' self-assessment of their performance, define performance expectations, and evaluate relative strengths and weaknesses for each student.

A third purpose of assessment is to gather information and data that drive instructional decision-making. All students enter your gymnasium with a wide variety of prior knowledge, experience, and skill that you must account for in designing their learning experiences. Before teaching any unit or lesson, you must determine starting points for each individual student in your class by conducting some form of **pre-assessment**. The information or data could come from records kept from the previous year, from pretest data, from observing students, or from simply asking students about their experience levels through a survey, self-assessment or even a **wordle**. For an example of a wordle as a pre-assessment, see Appendix G. In addition to determining individual starting points, pre-assessment gives you the information you need for differentiating instruction, assigning partners or groups, and setting expectations. Without assessment information or data, you are simply guessing about students' competency levels or teaching as if all students are the same, rather than teaching and assessing individuals.

Once you begin an instructional unit, assessment is key for determining your next steps, adapting or modifying learning experiences and, potentially, identifying the need to re-teach. Methods for gathering this information or data can range from peer assessments to quizzes and project updates. Assessment should occur each day in some manner and the results should always inform the next day's instruction and design, but to use the results most effectively, you need an established method for tracking assessment data. One solution is adopting one or more forms of technology, which can facilitate the gathering, analyzing, and tracking of student data, making the process much more manageable than in the past. A good resource for using technology in a physical education setting is Chapter 8 in *National Standards & Grade-Level Outcomes for K-12 Physical Education* (SHAPE America, 2014).

The final purpose of assessment is to inform your teaching. Throughout the unit of instruction, you use informal and formal assessments to make decisions about your instruction. At the end of a unit of instruction, you must review the information or data from these assessments to determine strengths and challenges for student learning. Based on a summative assessment, you can determine what skills and knowledge students have mastered and what you will need to review or repeat. You also can use data to determine what worked best during the unit of instruction and what you might need to change in the future. Assessment data allow you to self-evaluate your teaching effectiveness based on the performance of your students. Assessment and instruction are inseparable in the planning and teaching process.

While assessment data often are used for determining grades, grades and assessments have different purposes. The goal of grading is to evaluate individual students' learning and performance based on indirect and direct measures. For example, a range of indirect measures, such as attendance, participation and effort, often have been part of the grading process. While those constructs are important, they are not direct measures of learning. Paul Dressell from the Michigan State University describes a grade "as an inadequate report of an imprecise judgment of a biased and variable judge of the extent to which a student has attained an undefined level of mastery of an unknown proportion of an indefinite amount of materials" (Miller, Imrie & Cox, 1998, p. 24). While grading can play a role in assessment, assessment is a much broader measure of student learning and includes many ungraded measures, such as worksheets, discussion and concept maps. A grade is one data point, not linked to any particular learning outcome, and it does not allow for any systematic examination of learning. A matrix of assessments (formal and informal) allows you to examine data to determine learning patterns and guide instructional decision-making.

Using Observation for Assessment

As in any performance-based discipline, you will rely on your observation skills to complete most of the assessments in this book. The first step in this process is to identify the critical elements of the skill or skills to be assessed. To help you with this task, we have included the appropriate critical elements with each sample assessment under Standard 1. At the elementary school level, we provide suggested critical elements for all fundamental movement patterns: running, skipping, sliding, jumping, kicking, throwing and striking. At the middle school and high school levels, we provide suggested critical elements for sport-specific skills, such as tennis forehand and backhand, various types of passes, and various yoga poses and dance steps. To help you observe and score at the same time, we have included abbreviated versions of the critical elements in the scoring rubrics for those assessments.

Once you have identified the critical elements of a particular skill, you must look for each of them as you scan your class. That doesn't mean that you will check off each critical element for each student as you scan the class or groups of students. Instead, you should look holistically at the skill and the total movement pattern, and not individual parts. The individual critical elements are part of the whole and should be evaluated based on their impact on the overall effectiveness of the movement. Throughout the assessments in *PE Metrics*, the focus is on the process of the movement and not the product. The assumption is that you are creating a mastery-oriented learning environment where students are focused on effort and their own improvement. Your observation should then focus on how well students are demonstrating competency in the holistic process of the skill or movement.

To make the process even more challenging, you probably have to assess 20 or more moving students and record their scores! This is a challenge that is unique to physical education, which features lots of moving parts and bodies. The first step is to place the rubric or checklist on a clipboard (virtual or real) so that you have easy access to a list of the critical elements for the skill or technique as you complete your direct observation of students. Because it's not practical to record each student on a separate checklist or rubric, you will need to create a score sheet (see Appendix F). Here are some tips for creating a score sheet on which to record your observations.

- If you are using a checklist to assess, create a score sheet with a "Yes" and a "No" column for each student. Then, check the appropriate column (yes or no) for each student as you evaluate the skill.

- If you are using a rubric to assess, create a score sheet with four columns, one for each performance level on the rubric (Developing, Competent and Proficient, for example, or 1, 2 and 3), plus one column labeled "NO" for "No opportunity to observe." Mark this column for students who are absent so that you know to check their skill levels at a later time. Use the score sheet to record the level of performance for each student. Remember, if you use numbers for the rubric headings, they do not represent a value. For a rubric, the number simply tells students the level at which they performed for that skill. Students should know that the level recorded is intended to provide them with feedback on their performance based on the critical elements identified for that level.

- Use an electronic score sheet. You can create an electronic score sheet that works on most tablets or computers by using Google Docs, spreadsheets or a district-based gradebook. Most electronic tools allow you to use a touch screen to record students' performance levels, which are entered automatically into a spreadsheet. Recording student scores in this way will allow you to analyze and interpret the results later. If you don't have access to such electronic tools, you can record the scores on a paper score sheet and analyze them later.

- At the beginning of the marking period, upload your class list into your score sheets. Many school districts can do this for you with a gradebook or score sheet template of some kind. You also might be able to cut and paste the class list into your school spreadsheet.

- Limit the number of skills that you assess to keep the process manageable. For example, don't try to assess each fundamental movement skill every year. For guidance on which skills to assess, see *National Standards & Grade-Level Outcomes for K-12 Physical Education* (SHAPE America, 2014). The Grade-Level Outcomes will provide guidance on which grade level you should expect students to demonstrate a mature pattern (i.e., skill performance using all of the critical elements).

Once you have your score sheet in place, you can begin the process of direct observation of student competency. Here are some tips for using direct observation in a performance-based environment.

- Perform your direct observation in an authentic environment. Skills patterns are more "true" when they are observed during practice tasks, modified games, or warm-up or cool-down.

- Scan the class regularly during various learning experiences that incorporate the skill or technique to be evaluated.

- As you scan the class, note and assess students who display deficiencies in one or more of the critical elements. These students usually are easy to spot. On your score sheet, mark these students as 1, or Developing.

- Scan the class again and note students who demonstrate all of the skill's critical elements, as well as the other elements listed in the rubric under the Proficient level. Again, these students will be easy to spot. On the score sheet, mark these students as 3 or Proficient.

- After scoring those students, you can assume that the rest of the students fall into the Competent level: they demonstrate all of the critical elements, but they don't display the other elements identified in the rubric under the Proficient level.

- On your score sheet, you can make Competent the default score, meaning that you won't have to record a score for these students. That will save you valuable time in the process of assessing students and using the data for guiding your instruction.

- Assessment should occur every day, so plan to assess skills over multiple days. You can assess students any time that they're using or practicing the skill. If you follow this practice, you can take a second look at students whose skill performance bordered on Competent or Proficient. You can change a score as you evaluate over time. The key is to assess on an ongoing basis, not set aside a single day for "testing."

Assessment is of no value unless you take the time to interpret and analyze the results. Review your score sheets regularly to determine what competencies students have mastered, what competencies you will need to review or require more practice time, and what competencies you might need to reteach. These ongoing assessments will provide a road map for ensuring that all students are physically literate and provide you with evidence of your teaching competency and your program's effectiveness.

Categories of Assessments

Assessments fall into categories based on their intent. One broad category contains informal and formal assessment. **Informal assessment** is a way to gather information on your students in an authentic setting using non-standardized instruments. The goal of informal assessment is to collect information in real time that allows you to improve student learning and your instruction. These are in-process measures based on specific assignments or tasks that allow students to demonstrate their competency. The sample assessments in *PE Metrics* are informal and are designed to take place as a normal and ongoing part of the teaching and learning process. Samples of informal assessments include measures such as checks for understanding, worksheets, rubrics, exit slips and any measures that are performance- and content-driven.

Formal assessments are standardized measures of selected constructs or outcomes with pre-decided criteria. These measures follow a particular testing protocol, assign a score or grade to the student, and have data supporting the conclusions made from the test. Data from formal assessments are computed and summarized mathematically. The most common formal assessment in physical education is FitnessGram, from The Cooper Institute. FitnessGram comes with set protocols, with mathematically computed bands of competency levels based on a national or state database.

Some assessments are categorized by when they occur in the unit of instruction, such as pre-assessment and post-assessment, and formative or summative assessments. **Pre-assessments** are given at the beginning of a unit to determine students' baseline knowledge and/or performance. Pre-assessments are used to make instruction-related decisions at the beginning of the unit and to determine impact on student learning at the end of the unit. Pre-assessments include activities such as teacher observations, surveys of prior experience, formal skill pretests and/or review of assessment data from the previous year. This information allows you to formulate a picture of where students are at the beginning of a learning sequence or unit of instruction. This edition of *PE Metrics* provides numerous samples of pre-assessments.

Summative assessments occur at the end of a unit of instruction and provide information on student performance and mastery of outcomes. These assessments allow you to summarize each student's progress at the end of the unit by identifying both strengths and weaknesses and providing guidance on next steps for continuous improvement. Comparing summative data with pre-assessment data provides evidence regarding the unit's impact on student learning. Many of the sample assessments provided in *PE Metrics* are summative. For example, the fundamental movement skill assessments found among the elementary school assessments are summative, as are the tactics and strategy measures for middle school students and the fitness portfolio for high school students. By using summative assessments, you can collect tangible evidence of students' mastery of the Grade-Level Outcomes for K-12 Physical Education (SHAPE America, 2014).

In between the pre-assessment and summative assessment lie formative assessments, which are ongoing. Assessment is not a one-and-done task, but a continuous process of gathering information and data on students and their learning.

Assessment Tools

Various tools are available for gathering data on student knowledge and performance. Selecting the appropriate tool depends on the tool's ability to provide evidence specific to the outcome and the identified performance criteria. Each of the tools that follow vary in the specificity that they provide on student performance:

- **Checklist:** Identifies whether individual performance criteria are present or absent using a simple "Yes" or "No." For example, the presence of a criterion such as "steps in opposition on the overarm throw" during a student performance of the skill would be judged either "Yes" or "No." While this provides information on the criteria identified, it does not provide any guidance on how well the student met the criteria (the quality of the response). Checklists are simple to design, easy to use and are useful as peer assessments or when determining whether a student has submitted all parts of an assignment. Checklists provide limited feedback on the quality of the knowledge or skill performance. See Figure 1 for an example.

- **Rating scale:** Similar to a checklist, with added information on the extent to which a criterion behavior is met. To be effective, individual criterion behaviors must be easily observable and scored independently. Also, performance levels must be clearly and precisely differentiated among levels. That is done by using a gradation of criteria across as few as three levels and as many as five levels. For rating scales, one common definition is used for each of the levels for all criteria being assessed. For example, Level 1 might be defined as "does not demonstrate the criterion behavior," with Level 3 being "demonstrates the criterion behavior more than 25 percent of the time but less than 50 percent of the time," and Level 5 being "demonstrates the criterion behavior more than 75 percent of the time but less than 100 percent of the time." This same definition for each level applies to all criteria listed. Because the definition remains the same no matter the criterion identified, rating scales provide limited feedback to students regarding each criterion. Rating scales often are used to measure the frequency of a behavior, but they can be used for assessing to what extent a criterion is demonstrated. See Figure 2 for an example.

- **Holistic rating scale:** Maintains the use of gradation of criteria across levels, but differentiates among levels by using holistic descriptions for each of the levels. This requires you to define and describe observable behaviors for each level. Judgments are based on all the criteria being met in the holistic description at that level. Holistic rating scales often are used to evaluate the overall competence of the student's performance while providing him or her with more specific feedback on their performance. See Figure 3 for an example.

- **Rubrics:** Unique assessment tools that define performance criteria for each level of performance. The criteria identified at each level are specific to the criterion (called an indicator) to be measured. This allows you to match students' performances to well-defined criterion behaviors and delineates the degree to which the criterion is met at that level. Identified criterion behaviors at each level (strong, middle and weak levels of performance) are specific to assignments or learning tasks and aligned with outcomes, and are used to evaluate performance.

   Rubrics outline expectations for learners by identifying "indicators" of competent performance. Once these indicators are developed, descriptors are written that communicate expectations for the level and define "what counts" at that level. By defining "what counts" at each level, you provide students with feedback specific to their performance. This feedback provides students with detailed guidance on what they need to improve to move to the next level. By providing specific, corrective and detailed feedback through an assessment, you enhance student learning and skill development.

   These two types of rubrics are the most commonly used as assessments. **Holistic rubrics** assign a level of performance based on multiple criteria and performance as a whole. Individual levels are defined holistically. The focus of the rubric at each level is on the overall quality of the performance and not the evaluation of individual parts of the movement or skill performance. The student is assigned a level based on a single description on a scale. Using a holistic rubric allows you to evaluate students' performances quickly and provides an overview of their performance. Students receive generalized feedback on their performance based on the holistic descriptors at each level. See Figure 4 for an example.

   Analytic rubrics divide assignments, tasks and skills into independent components, with criterion behaviors defined for each of the parts as well as across levels of competency. Independent evaluation of each component allows for extensive and specific feedback to students. Analytic rubrics often are used with complex assignments or performances with multiple parts. Because analytic rubrics allow for measures of independent components, they allow you to evaluate more than one outcome under more than one standard using the same assessment tool. See Table 1.

Name of performer: _____

Name of observer: _____

For each line on the check sheet, use one of these codes:

A = The movement is absent or some of the criteria are executed poorly

P = The movement is present and meets all criteria

Checklist for pivot:

- Weight on balls of feet _____
- Feet shoulder-width apart _____
- Pivot foot remains on ground without sliding, while the body turns or rotates _____
- Pivot with preferred leg _____
- Pivot with nonpreferred leg _____

Figure 1   Sample peer checklist for offensive skills (pivot, fake, jab step).

Rating scale key:

0 = Not active: no participation in physical activity on a weekly basis

1 = Active occasionally: once or twice a week

2 = Somewhat active: twice a week on a semi-regular basis

3 = Active regularly: at least three times a week on a regular basis

4 = Active daily: five days or more a week on a regular basis

Based on the scale above, rate your participation in activities designed to increase your cardiorespiratory endurance.

0   1   2   3   4

Based on the scale above, rate your participation in activities designed to increase your flexibility.

0   1   2   3   4

Figure 2   Pre-assessment activity level survey.

Rating 1	Log is incomplete, missing data and with few or no details provided. Selected activities do not align with fitness goals.
Rating 2	Log is complete, but limited detail is provided. No supporting documentation to support perceived exertion score (e.g., step count, heart rate monitor, Fitbit, weight, number of repetitions).
Rating 3	Log is complete, with sufficient detail and supporting documentation on perceived exertion provided (e.g., step count, heart rate monitor, Fitbit, weight, number of repetitions).

Figure 3   Holistic rating for participation log.

Level 1	Reflection describes only the activity, without a personal response to the experience. Does not connect participation to personal health and wellness.
Level 2	Reflection describes the activity and includes some general comments on personal response to the experience. Indirect connections made to personal health and wellness.
Level 3	Reflection describes the activity and includes detailed and insightful statements on personal response to the experience. Direct connections made to personal health and wellness.

Figure 4   General holistic rubric for reflections.

Table 1 Analytic Scoring Rubric for Galloping

INDICATOR	DEVELOPING	COMPETENT	PROFICIENT
Critical Elements Galloping	Demonstrates fewer than 5 of the critical elements for galloping	Demonstrates all 5 critical elements for galloping: • Trunk faces in forward direction • Lead leg lifts and moves forward • Lead foot closes quickly • Lead leg lifts • Arms in front, slightly bent	Demonstrates all 5 critical elements for galloping using both the preferred and nonpreferred feet as lead
Rhythm	Moves with erratic rhythm	Moves with steady rhythm	Moves with steady rhythm
Continuity	Cannot maintain a mature pattern in a continuous sequence (at least 5 times in a row)	Maintains a mature pattern in a continuous sequence (at least 5 times in a row), with preferred foot as lead	Maintains a mature pattern in a continuous sequence (at least 10 times in a row), with both the preferred and nonpreferred feet as leads

Other forms of assessment used in physical education include quizzes, examinations, projects and portfolios. Examinations and quizzes provide evidence specific to students' knowledge of skills, tactics or strategies, rules, etiquette, biomechanical and physiological principles, concepts and application of concepts. You can assess any knowledge component appropriately using quizzes or examinations. Project assignments or portfolios usually are assessed using a rubric or a suite of assessments. For guidance on creating and selecting assessments, see Chapter 8 in *National Standards & Grade-Level Outcomes for K-12 Physical Education* (SHAPE America, 2014).

Assessing Complex Assignments (Projects or Portfolios)

Multipart assignments or projects require more complex assessments. Evaluating students' work on these complex assignments or projects often requires the use of an analytic rubric or a suite of assessments. An analytic rubric allows you to assess each part of the assignment or project separately. For example, if the assignment or project is to flip a classroom by developing an instructional video, an analytic rubric allows you to assess the assignment or project across multiple components. One component might be specific to the accuracy of the content, with another specific to the quality of the video, another specific to oral communication competency demonstrated in the video and another specific to the quality of the analysis of the skill. Within one analytic rubric, you can assess multiple outcomes under different standards.

You can use a suite of assessments for complex assignments or projects as well, but they are used more commonly for assessing a portfolio. A portfolio is a systematic collection of student work and related materials (e.g., worksheets, logs) that demonstrate competency in a range of skills across a number of outcomes and/or standards. The example provided in this book is a fitness portfolio, which documents the stages of learning and provides a progressive record of student growth. Various types of assessments are used for individual components of the portfolio over time.

Because portfolios are completed in stages, you can use different assessments at different stages. For example, the first task in a fitness portfolio might be to set personal fitness goals based on one's FitnessGram scores. The assessment for the first part of the assignment might be a checklist that denotes that the student completed the fitness assessment and has submitted her or his scores. The second part of the assignment, setting fitness goals based on the SMART (specific, measurable, achievable, realistic, time-bound) formula, might require using an analytic rubric. Based on their fitness scores and their personal goals, students next would develop a plan for improving self-selected areas of fitness, and you might assess each plan using an analytic rubric. Once students implement their plans, they would submit participation logs that document their plans' implementation. You could use a checklist to note that submission. Another part of the portfolio might require students to reflect on their progress in implementing their plans. These reflections might be assessed using a holistic rubric. Also, peer assessments could provide feedback on other parts of the portfolio. For components where students may be working together, encourage them to use Google Docs to make document sharing simple and accessible. Such a combination or suite of assessments for the fitness portfolio would be based on your description of the portfolio assignment and would provide you with multiple data points to use to determine student progress.

Both analytic rubrics and a suite of assessments allow you to provide feedback at various stages of the learning process, which is critical for a progressive assignment such as a portfolio. By evaluating each stage of the assignment, you can identify students' mistakes or misconceptions early on so those errors can be corrected before the final product is submitted. This approach also has the advantage of spreading out your assessment of the portfolio over time. Waiting to assess the entire portfolio at the end could be overwhelming.

Developing an Assessment Plan

All assessments for your program must align with your selected student outcomes, must be appropriate for your teaching environment (e.g., space, number of students, availability of equipment) and must meet the needs of your students. SHAPE America's *National Standards & Grade-Level Outcomes for K-12 Physical Education* provides you with a road map of student outcomes by grade level, but a road map is not a mandate. When reviewing the sample assessments in this book, remember the context of your teaching environment and the goals of your program. Select, modify or create assessments that fit your program and that provide you with the most robust information on what your students know and can do. Here are some tips for developing an assessment plan that works best for you:

- Inventory the current assessments in use in your program. Evaluate their strengths and weaknesses, identify the type of assessments in place and determine if gaps exist in your assessment process.

- Review sample assessments provided in sources such as this book, educational websites, programs in your district or other resources available to you. You don't need to reinvent the wheel; create a catalog of existing assessments that you can modify to meet your needs.

- Create student learning outcomes (SLOs) for your program by reviewing standards and outcomes used in your district as a guide. Once you have established your SLOs or have decided to adopt selected outcomes:

  » Determine which outcomes are to be assessed each year. Don't try to assess students under every outcome every year. Be selective on which outcomes are most important at each grade level.

  » Determine when to assess each outcome. By determining that, you will have a clearer picture of the time and resources needed.

  » Determine what type of assignment or performance you will use to provide evidence of student achievement. This will determine what artifacts or evidence you will collect.

  » Select an appropriate assessment tool to evaluate the assignment or performance. You must align the assessment tool with the intent of the assignment and the assignment with the intent of the identified SLO.

  » Once you select the assessment tool, determine how you will analyze and collect the assessment information or data. You must have a data gathering process in place. This includes determining when and where assessment data will be collected and stored.

- Once you have collected data from various assessments, determine how you will analyze and summarize results. Utilize the results to make instructional decisions and curriculum changes and to determine if your SLOs have been met. Most school districts have data management systems that can be used to manage and analyze data.

- Determine how you will share your results with students, colleagues, parents and administrators and make that a regular component of your communication plans.

Summary

This edition of *PE Metrics* provides samples of a range of assessments that align with and measure SHAPE America's *National Standards & Grade-Level Outcomes for K-12 Physical Education* (2014). The goal is to provide you with a road map on how to select, develop, modify and/or create assessments that are appropriate for your teaching environment and are aligned with National Standards and Grade-Level Outcomes. These assessments should all be part of a cohesive assessment plan, which ties teaching and learning together. The plan should include all the assessments in your toolbox, a focus on the process, providing students with feedback on their progress and guiding instructional and program decision-making.

Part II

Sample Assessments for Elementary School Physical Education

Standard 1 Sample Assessments

Standard 1. The physically literate individual demonstrates competency in a variety of motor skills and movement patterns.

The sample assessments for Standard 1 are written as **summative assessments** and are designed to measure elementary school students' progress toward SHAPE America's Grade-Level Outcomes for K-12 Physical Education (2014). For most of the psychomotor skills under Standard 1, the summative assessments are at the grade level in which students are expected to demonstrate a **mature pattern**, that is, demonstrating all of the skill's **critical elements**. However, each of these assessments also can serve as a **formative assessment**, with a focus on the critical elements of that skill and the subsequent charting of students' progress in the development of that skill toward a mature pattern. Formative assessments within instructional physical education provide students with a personal review of their progress in skill development, provide teachers with feedback for refining instruction and re-visiting skills and concepts, and offer both teacher and students a way to measure student growth.

You will not find an assessment for every skill at each grade level just as you will not find an assessment for every Grade-Level Outcome under Standard 1. That does not mean assessment should not take place for each skill or each outcome at that grade level. Refer to the *National Standards & Grade-Level Outcomes for K-12 Physical Education* for expected focus and critical elements for the different grade levels. Those outcomes and critical elements provide the focus for your formative assessment at each grade level.

The assessments for Grade 3 students illustrate how you can use the assessments for formative measurement of student growth. Students in Grade 3 are in a period of transition—moving from the foundational skills of K-2 into the more advanced skills and combinations of skills that await them in Grade 4 and beyond. As you will note in Appendix A none of the Grade-Level Outcomes under Standard 1 for Grade 3 stipulate that students are expected to demonstrate a mature pattern in any of the manipulative skills, yet this year of development is critical for the maturation of these skills in Grade 4. With that in mind, we encourage you to use the Grade 4 manipulative assessments as formative assessments in Grade 3, noting the critical elements leading to mastery in Grade 4.

Grade 5 presents only one summative assessment for a manipulative skill, i.e., striking with a long implement. With a mature pattern expected prior to Grade 5 for almost all of the fundamental skills of physical education, Grade 5 has an assessment focus on combination skills and beginning tactics. You will find sample assessments for combination skills in gymnastics and dance, as well as combinations and tactics in the games environment. It is important to note that while the majority of fundamental skills have an expectation of a mature pattern by the end of Grade 4, not all children will attain that level of skill development by the end of Grade 4. Thus, Grade 5 continues as a developmental progression for many students; the assessments in Grade 4 will serve well for those students.

Assessments for Measuring Elementary School Students' Skills and Knowledge

The assessments in this section are samples of possible assessments and not exemplars. The intent is not to provide specific assessments to be used by all programs but to provide you with "samples" that you can modify or adapt to your unique teaching environment. You are encouraged to use the sample assessments as a starting point for developing or adapting assessments that meet the needs of your program and students.

The three-level rubrics in these samples use a standard set of terms with common definitions, which is important for providing consistent feedback to students. The **Developing level** denotes students moving toward competency, but these students have not yet mastered all the identified critical elements or components specific to the indicator. Students at the **Competent level** demonstrate all of the critical elements aligned with the indicator. The Competent level defines the minimum level of performance required for meeting the indicator. Students at the **Proficient level** not only demonstrate all the required critical elements of the indicator, but their performance also meets additional criteria and/or displays a level of performance that goes beyond Competent. These three terms are used in the same manner in each of the rubric samples. Rubric indicators are not for the purpose of dividing the assessment into percentages for grading but to delineate the components within the assessment. The focus of assessments for elementary students is not student scores, e.g., accuracy to target, number of catches; the focus is on gaining information to assist teachers in maximizing student learning in our physical education programs.

If you have students with disabilities in your classroom, many of the assessments will need to be modified and adapted. For specific guidance in this area, we recommend *Assessment for Everyone: Modifying NASPE Assessments to Include All Elementary School Children* (Lieberman, Kowalski, et al., 2011).

Note: This section includes no formal assessments of skills under Standard 1 for kindergarten students. Instead, we recommend employing formative, ongoing assessment to inform your teaching as these younger students practice locomotor, nonlocomotor and manipulative skills. This informal assessment will provide feedback to you as a teacher and guide continued task selection for student growth.

Hopping   Grade 1

Grade-Level Outcome

Hops, gallops, jogs and slides using a mature pattern. (S1.E1.1)

Assessment Task

Explore hopping for critical elements of a mature pattern.

Guidelines

- Students perform locomotor movements in small groups as you observe for individual assessments.
- Observe for assessment during a warm-up activity, instant activity, Corner to Corner (Holt/Hale & Hall, 2016), or as a station.
- Focus on the identified critical elements and score students based on critical elements of the skill.
- Observe more than one time for the assessment; a single observation may not provide a true assessment of skill, especially for younger students.

Setup

- Students in scattered formation, with at least 3 square feet per student for hopping
- Sufficient general space for hopping, galloping, jogging, and sliding

Note: *Hopping is very tiring for young children. Keep the movement intervals brief for an accurate assessment.*

Critical Elements for Hopping

- Take off and land on same foot
- Use ankle and knee flexion to push upward and to absorb the shock upon landing
- Arms push up and down to lift and for balance
- Knee seldom straightens fully

Scoring Rubric for Hopping, Grade 1

INDICATOR	DEVELOPING	COMPETENT	PROFICIENT
Critical Elements Hopping	Demonstrates fewer than 4 of the critical elements for hopping	Demonstrates all critical elements when hopping on preferred foot: • Take off and land on same foot • Ankle and knee flexion to push upward and to absorb shock upon landing • Arms push up and down to lift and for balance • Knee seldom straightens fully	Demonstrates all critical elements for hopping on both preferred and nonpreferred foot
Rhythm and Continuity	• Erratic rhythm • Cannot maintain continuous hopping sequence (at least 5 consecutive hops)	• Steady rhythm • Maintains continuous hopping sequence (at least 5 consecutive hops) on preferred foot	• Steady rhythm • Maintains continuous hopping sequence (at least 5 consecutive hops) on both the preferred and nonpreferred foot

Grade-Level Outcome

Hops, gallops, jogs and slides using a mature pattern. (S1.E1.1)

Assessment Task

Explore sliding for critical elements of a mature pattern.

Guidelines

- Students perform locomotor movements in small groups as you observe for individual assessments.

- Observe for assessment during a warm-up activity, instant activity, Corner to Corner (Holt/Hale & Hall, 2016), or as a station.

- Focus on the identified critical elements and score students based on critical elements of the skill.

- Observe more than one time for the assessment; a single observation may not provide a true assessment of skill, especially for younger students.

Setup

- Students in scattered formation

- Sufficient general space for sliding

Critical Elements for Sliding

- Trunk faces forward, head turned sideways in direction of travel

- Lead leg lifts and moves sideways to support weight

- Rear foot closes quickly to supporting foot

- Body is momentarily airborne

- Arms are lifted and extended to the sides

Scoring Rubric for Sliding, Grade 1

INDICATOR	DEVELOPING	COMPETENT	PROFICIENT
Critical Elements Sliding	Demonstrates fewer than 5 of the critical elements	Demonstrates all critical elements with preferred lead foot • Trunk faces in forward direction, head turned in direction of travel • Lead leg lifts and moves sideways • Rear foot closes quickly • Body momentarily airborne • Arms lifted and extended to sides	Demonstrates all critical elements for sliding using preferred foot and nonpreferred foot as lead
Rhythm and Continuity	• Erratic rhythm • Cannot maintain mature pattern in a continuous sequence (at least 5 times in a row)	• Steady rhythm • Maintains consecutive slides (at least 5 times in a row) with mature pattern on preferred lead foot	• Steady rhythm • Maintains consecutive slides (at least 10 times) using either foot as lead

Galloping | Grade 1

Grade-Level Outcome

Hops, gallops, jogs and slides using a mature pattern. (S1.E1.1)

Assessment Task

Explore galloping for critical elements of a mature pattern.

Guidelines

- Students perform locomotor movements in small groups as you observe for individual assessments.

- Observe for assessment during a warm-up activity, instant activity, Corner to Corner (Holt/Hale & Hall, 2016), or as a station.

- Focus on the identified critical elements and score students based on critical elements of the skill.

- Observe more than one time for the assessment; a single observation may not provide a true assessment of skill, especially for younger students.

Setup

- Students in scattered formation

- Sufficient general space for galloping

Critical Elements for Galloping

- Trunk faces forward

- Lead leg lifts and moves forward to support weight

- Rear foot closes quickly to supporting foot

- Lead leg lifts to repeat action

- Arms are in front, bent slightly

Scoring Rubric for Galloping, Grade 1

INDICATOR	DEVELOPING	COMPETENT	PROFICIENT
Critical Elements Galloping	Demonstrates fewer than 5 of the critical elements for galloping	Demonstrates all critical elements for galloping • Trunk faces forward • Lead leg lifts and moves forward • Rear foot closes quickly • Lead leg lifts • Arms in front, slightly bent	Demonstrates all critical elements for galloping when using both the preferred and nonpreferred foot as lead
Rhythm and Continuity	• Erratic rhythm • Cannot maintain mature pattern in a continuous sequence (at least 5 times in a row)	• Steady rhythm • Maintains mature pattern in a continuous sequence (at least 5 times in a row) with preferred lead foot	• Steady rhythm • Maintains mature pattern in a continuous sequence (at least 10 times in a row) with both the preferred and nonpreferred foot as lead

Grade-Level Outcome

Skips using a mature pattern. (S1.E1.2)

Assessment Task

Explore skipping for critical elements of a mature pattern.

Guidelines

- Students perform locomotor movements in small groups as you observe for individual assessments.

- Observe for assessment during a warm-up activity, instant activity, Corner to Corner (Holt/Hale & Hall, 2016), or as a station.

- Focus on the identified critical elements and score students based on critical elements of the skill.

- Observe more than one time for the assessment; a single observation may not provide a true assessment of skill, especially for younger students.

Setup

Sufficient space for skipping in general space

Critical Elements for Skipping

- Step and hop on one foot and then on the other foot

- Arms move in opposition to feet

- Arm and leg lift on hopping action

- Lead foot alternates

Scoring Rubric for Skipping, Grade 2

INDICATOR	DEVELOPING	COMPETENT	PROFICIENT
Critical Elements Skipping	Demonstrates fewer than 4 of the critical elements	Demonstrates all critical elements • Step and hop on one foot and then on the other foot • Arms move in opposition to feet • Arm and leg lift • Lead foot alternates	Demonstrates all critical elements • Varies speed or direction
Rhythm and Continuity	• Erratic rhythm • Cannot maintain mature pattern in a continuous sequence (at least 5 times in a row)	• Steady rhythm • Maintains mature pattern in a continuous sequence (at least 5 times in a row)	• Steady rhythm • Maintains mature pattern in a continuous sequence (at least 10 times in a row)

Running

Grade 2

Grade-Level Outcome

Runs with a mature pattern. (S1.E2.2a)

Assessment Task

Explore running for critical elements of a mature pattern.

Guidelines

- Students perform running as a class or in small groups as you observe for individual assessments.
- Observe for assessment during a warm-up activity, instant activity, or as a station.
- Focus on the identified critical elements and score students based on critical elements of the skill.

Setup

Sufficient space for running safely

Note: *Assessing students' running skills requires adequate general space for students to run safely without fear of collisions. To provide space, consider having practice and completing the assessment outdoors.*

Critical Elements for Running

- Arm-leg opposition maintained throughout action
- Toes point forward
- Foot lands heel to toe
- Arms swing forward and backward without crossing the midline
- Trunk leans slightly forward

Scoring Rubric for Running, Grade 2

INDICATOR	DEVELOPING	COMPETENT	PROFICIENT

Critical Elements
 	
Running
	• Demonstrates fewer than 5 of the critical elements for running
	  » Demonstrates in- or out-toeing
	  » Arms and/or legs cross the midline resulting in an excess of rotation (waddle motion)
	• Cannot stop in balanced position
		• Demonstrates all critical elements for running
		  » Arm-leg opposition
		  » Toes point forward
		  » Foot lands heel to toe
		  » Arms swing forward and backward without crossing midline
		  » Trunk leans slightly forward
		• Stops within one step, in balanced position
			• Demonstrates all critical elements for running, with fluid, rhythmic movement
			• Stops within one step, in balanced position

Stride	Runs with short, choppy steps	Stride length is beginning to lengthen (50% of height)	• Legs push and extend for elongated stride (beyond 50%) • Demonstrates full range of motion with both arms and legs • Demonstrates changes in speed for jogging and sprinting upon command (S1.E2.2b)

Grade-Level Outcome

Throws underhand using a mature pattern. (S1.E13.2)

Assessment Task

Use an underhand throwing pattern to send a ball forward through the air to a large target.

Guidelines

Focus on student performance of the critical elements, not on accuracy to target.

Setup

- 10-by-10-foot square target on wall, 3 feet from the floor, with throwing line 15 feet from the target

- Students in pairs, one who throws and one who retrieves the ball

- Partner stands a safe distance (5 feet) behind thrower to retrieve ball as needed

- Partners switch roles after thrower completes 5 attempts

Equipment

- 10-by-10-foot target on wall (paper, plastic)

- 5 "no-bounce" tennis-size balls, 5 softball-size balls (student choice for assessment)

Note: *Weight of ball affects flight—not too heavy, not too light*

Critical Elements for Throwing Underhand

- Face target in preparation for throwing action

- Arm back in preparation for action

- Step with opposite foot as throwing arm moves forward

- Release ball between knee and waist level

- Follow through to target

Scoring Rubric for Throwing With an Underhand Pattern, Grade 2

INDICATOR	DEVELOPING	COMPETENT	PROFICIENT
Critical Elements Throwing Underhand	Demonstrates fewer than 5 of the critical elements • Steps forward on the same side as throw • Release of ball too early or too late resulting in an inaccurate throw or lack of distance	Demonstrates all critical elements • Face target in preparation for throwing • Arm back in preparation • Step with opposite foot as throwing arm moves forward • Release ball between knee and waist level • Follow through to target	Demonstrates all critical elements • Step and throw well-timed resulting in smooth motion with lead foot pointing to target • Consistent release point is used resulting in beginning distance accuracy • Shifts weight from back foot to front foot, fluid, well-timed motion • Step and throw with smooth motion consistently

Jumping Rope   Grade 2

Grade-Level Outcome

Jumps a self-turned rope consecutively forward and backward with a mature pattern. (S1.E27.2a)

Assessment Task

Jump a short rope consecutively both forward and backward.

Guidelines

- You can assess jump rope skills easily within station practice for students, with one station designated as teacher assessment.

- Watch for student fatigue, which can affect performance, as consecutive jump practice can be tiring for youngsters.

- Remind students of the assessment task: consecutive jumps forward, consecutive jumps backward. This assessment is not for tricks and fancy moves.

Setup

- Students in scattered formation, each with enough personal space to turn rope and allowing for slight movement within personal space (minimum of 6 square feet).

- Students jump a self-turned short rope with forward and backward turns using either a single bounce, double bounce, or step jump.

- Allow students 3 attempts for consecutive jumps forward and 3 attempts for consecutive jumps backward.

- Stop each student after 10 consecutive jumps forward and/or backward.

Equipment

Appropriate length rope for each student

Critical Elements for Jumping Rope (short)

- Proper grip and posture

- Two-foot jump or step jump, landing on balls of feet

- Knees slightly bent

- Rope swings in a steady rhythm

- Rope swings in continuous motion

Scoring Rubric for Jumping Rope (Short), Grade 2

INDICATOR	DEVELOPING	COMPETENT	PROFICIENT
Critical Elements Short Jump Rope	Demonstrates fewer than 5 of the critical elements	Demonstrates all critical elements for jumping rope • Proper grip and posture • Two-foot or step jump, landing on balls of feet • Knees bend slightly • Rope swings in steady rhythm • Rope swings in continuous motion	Demonstrates all critical elements with both a two-foot and a step jump
Rhythm and Continuity	• Turns of rope and jumps ill-timed, with stops between jumps • Cannot complete 5 consecutive jumps using forward and backward turns without at least one break	• Turns of rope and jumps are well-timed and rhythmic • Completes at least 5 consecutive jumps using both forward and backward turns	• Turns of rope and jumps are well-timed and rhythmic • Completes at least 10 jumps using both forward and backward turns
Difficulty		• Demonstrates forward jumping only OR • Demonstrates backward jumping only	Demonstrates forward and backward jumping with both a single and a double bounce

Leaping   Grade 3

Grade-Level Outcome

Leaps using a mature pattern. (S1.E1.3)

Assessment Task

Leap with preferred foot leading.

Guidelines

Remind students to be aware of safety when leaping in general space with others involved in the same movement pattern.

Note: *Leaping requires a large space for students to move freely, combining travel and leaping action; an area that is too small will result in possible injury and incorrect assessment of the skill.*

Setup

- Sufficient assessment space for traveling and leaping.

- Students travel with personal rhythm for leaping (e.g., run, run, run, leap).

- Assess students individually while others are involved in practice tasks at a safe distance from assessment area.

Critical Elements for Leaping

- Takeoff is on one foot, with landing on opposite foot

- Legs extend for height and distance

- Arms extend and lift for airborne time

- Knee bends to absorb force on landing

Scoring Rubric for Leaping, Grade 3

INDICATOR	DEVELOPING	COMPETENT	PROFICIENT
Critical Elements Leaping	Demonstrates fewer than 4 of the critical elements for leaping • Lands on foot used for takeoff • Takes only a long step with no elevation	Demonstrates all critical elements for leaping on preferred foot • Takeoff is on one foot with landing on opposite foot • Legs extend for height and distance • Arms extend and lift • Knee bends on landing	Demonstrates all critical elements • Demonstrates full range of motion (full extension of arms and legs with lift) • Combines travel and leaps in consecutive movement pattern
Difficulty		Leaps either for height or distance	Leaps for height and for distance

Grade-Level Outcome

Jumps and lands in the horizontal plane using a mature pattern. (S1.E3.3)

Assessment Task

Jump forward, using a two-foot takeoff and a two-foot landing.

Guidelines

You can complete this assessment easily in station setup, with other stations for practice tasks, one of which is jumping for distance.

Setup

- Students stand behind one line, with parallel lines 3 feet and 4 feet away as targets.
- Jump forward from a stationary position using two-foot takeoff and two-foot landing.
- Complete 3 jumps forward for distance.

Critical Elements for Jumping and Landing in a Horizontal Plane

- Arms back and knees bend in preparation for jumping action
- Arms extend forward as body propels forward
- Body extends and stretches slightly upward while in flight
- Hips, knees and ankles bend on landing
- Shoulders, knees and ankles align for balance after landing

Scoring Rubric for Jumping and Landing in a Horizontal Plane, Grade 3

INDICATOR	DEVELOPING	COMPETENT	PROFICIENT
Critical Elements Jumping and Landing in a Horizontal Plane	Demonstrates fewer than 5 critical elements for jumping and landing in a horizontal plane	• Demonstrates all critical elements of jumping and landing in a horizontal plane in 2 of the 3 attempts: » Arms back and knees bend in preparation » Arms extend forward as body propels forward » Body extends and stretches upward in flight » Hips, knees and ankles bend on landing » Shoulders, knees and ankles align after landing • Demonstrates critical elements with a mechanical rather than a fluid motion	Demonstrates all critical elements of jumping and landing in a horizontal plane in all 3 attempts
Distance	Jumps in a high arching motion rather than forward, resulting in very little distance	Demonstrates an appropriate but limited extension of arms and legs that contributes to distance of the jump	Demonstrates a full extension of arms and legs that contributes to the distance of the jump
Landing	Lands in an off-balance position causing a fall forward/backward	Lands and maintains a balanced position	Arm and leg extensions well timed and coordinated with smooth execution and balanced landing

Jumping and Landing – Vertical Plane
Grade 3

Grade-Level Outcome

Jumps and lands in the vertical plane using a mature pattern. (S1.E4.3)

Assessment Task

Jump upward, using a two-foot takeoff and a two-foot landing.

Guidelines

You can complete this assessment easily in station setup, with other stations for practice tasks, one of which is jumping for height.

Setup

- Jump upward from a stationary position using two-foot takeoff and two-foot landing
- Complete 3 vertical jumps

Critical Elements for Jumping and Landing in a Vertical Plane

- Hips, knees and ankles bend in preparation for jumping action
- Arms extend upward as body propels upward
- Body extends and stretches upward while in flight
- Hips, knees and ankles bend on landing
- Shoulders, knees and ankles align for balance after landing

Scoring Rubric for Jumping and Landing in a Vertical Plane, Grade 3

INDICATOR	DEVELOPING	COMPETENT	PROFICIENT
Critical Elements Jumping and Landing in a Vertical Plane	Demonstrates fewer than 5 critical elements for jumping and landing in a vertical plane	Demonstrates all critical elements of jumping and landing in a vertical plane in 2 of the 3 attempts • Hips, knees and ankles bend in preparation • Arms extend upward as body propels upward • Body extends and stretches upward while in flight • Hips, knees and ankles bend on landing • Shoulders, knees and ankles align for balance after landing	Demonstrates all critical elements of jumping and landing in a vertical plane in all 3 attempts
Height	Arm swing and jump mistimed leading to a poorly coordinated jump	Demonstrates an appropriate but limited extension of arms, legs and trunk, limiting height of jump	Demonstrates full extension of arms, legs and trunk, contributing to height of jump
Landing	Lands in an off-balance position, causing a fall forward or backward	Lands and maintains balanced position	Arm and leg extensions well timed and coordinated with smooth execution and balanced landing

Grade-Level Outcome

Balances on different bases of support, demonstrating muscular tension and extensions of free body parts. (S1.E7.3)

Assessment Task

Balance on different bases of support, i.e., gymnastics balances.

Guidelines

- Remind students to maintain spatial awareness and personal space to ensure safety in all gymnastics practice or work.

- A "no touching others" policy reinforces safety and maintains a safe environment for both practice and assessing.

Setup

- Students in scattered formation with personal space of at least 3 square feet.

- Students explore balances with different bases of support, shapes, and levels on teacher signal.

- Students perform 3 balances for assessment.

Equipment

Sufficient mats, large or small, for students to work safely

Critical Elements for Balance

- Alignment of body parts over base of support, i.e., center of gravity over base of support

- Stillness maintained for at least 3 seconds

- Extension of free body parts for balance and counterbalance

- Tight muscles on balances for stillness

Scoring Rubric for Balance in Gymnastics, Grade 3

INDICATOR	DEVELOPING	COMPETENT	PROFICIENT
Critical Elements Balance in Gymnastics	• Demonstrates fewer than 4 of the critical elements for balance » Holds stillness for less than 3 seconds » Limited extension of free body parts • Cannot demonstrate different bases of support for balances	• Demonstrates all critical elements in less than 3 balances: » Center of gravity over base of support » Stillness maintained for at least 3 seconds » Extension of free body parts » Tight muscles • Maintains stillness in all balances for 3 seconds • Full extension of free body parts • Maintains muscular tension in all base of support body parts	• Demonstrates all critical elements in all balances » Maintains stillness in all balances for 3 seconds » Full extension of free body parts and muscular tension for all balances • Demonstrates smooth transitions between balances with stretching, curling, and twisting actions (S1.E10.3)

Transferring Weight in Gymnastics   Grade 3

Grade-Level Outcome

Transfers weight from feet to hands for momentary weight support. (S1.E8.3)

Assessment Task

Transfer weight from feet to hands and then back to feet.

Guidelines

- Remind students to maintain spatial awareness and personal space to ensure safety in all gymnastics practice or work.

- A "no touching others" policy reinforces safety and maintains a safe environment for both practice and assessing.

Setup

- Students in scattered formation with personal space of at least 6 square feet.

- Students perform 3 assessments of weight transfer from feet to hands and back to feet.

Do not attempt this assessment with any student who cannot support his or her weight on hands momentarily.

Equipment

Sufficient mats for students to work safely

Critical Elements for Weight Transfer

- Weight momentarily supported on hands only

- Hands maintain stationary contact with the floor for transfer from feet to hands

- Feet return to starting position on floor without loss of balance

- Extension and lift of leg for momentary balance on hands

- Muscular tension/tightness in core throughout transfer

Scoring Rubric for Weight Transfer in Gymnastics, Grade 3

INDICATOR	DEVELOPING	COMPETENT	PROFICIENT
Critical Elements Weight Transfer in Gymnastics	Demonstrates fewer than 5 of the critical elements for weight transfer • Loss of balance upon landing	Demonstrates all critical elements for weight transfer • Weight momentarily supported on hands only • Hands maintain stationary contact with floor for transfer from feet to hands • Feet return to starting position without loss of balance • Extension and lift of leg for balance on hands • Tight muscles in core and extended legs	Demonstrates all critical elements for weight transfer • Toes pointed, full extension through core
Alignment Over Base	Does not extend lift leg	Extends and elevates lift leg	Extends and elevates both legs over base of support
Duration	Weight not transferred to hands	Maintains weight on hands for fewer than 3 seconds	Maintains weight on hands for at least 3 seconds

Grade-Level Outcome

Throws overhand using a mature pattern in a nondynamic environment [closed skills]. (S1.E14.4a)

Assessment Task

Use an overhand throwing pattern to throw a ball to a large wall target from a distance of 25 feet.

Note: *Focus the assessment on critical elements of overhand throw, with the target as visual focus only.*

Guidelines

You can complete assessments of manipulative skills easily in station setup, with other stations for practice tasks, one of which is the skill being assessed.

Setup

- Students in pairs, one who throws and one who retrieves the ball.

- Partner stands a safe distance (5 feet) behind thrower to retrieve ball as needed.

- Partners switch roles after thrower completes 5 attempts.

Equipment

- 5 tennis-size balls that do not bounce, 5 softball-size balls (student choice for assessment)

- Large square target (6 feet × 6 feet) on wall (or several large geometric shapes), 3 feet from the floor with the throwing line 25 feet from the target(s)

Critical Elements for Throwing Overhand

- Hip and spine rotate side to target in preparation for throwing action

- Arm back and extended, and elbow at shoulder height or slightly above in preparation for action; elbow leads

- Opposite foot steps forward as throwing arm moves forward

- Hip and spine rotate as throwing action is executed

- Arm follows through toward target across body

Scoring Rubric for Throwing Overhand, Grade 4

INDICATOR	DEVELOPING	COMPETENT	PROFICIENT
Critical Elements Throwing Overhand	Demonstrates fewer than 5 critical elements	Demonstrates all critical elements • Hip and spine rotate in preparation for throwing action • Arm back and extended, elbow at shoulder height or above in preparation; elbow leads • Step with opposite foot as throwing arm moves forward • Hip and spine rotate as throw is executed • Follow through toward target and across body	Demonstrates all critical elements • Stride elongated and well-timed
Throwing Arm	Holds elbow below shoulder height in preparation for action	Full extension of arm in preparation and follow through	Full extension of arm in preparation and follow through with a wrist snap upon release
Force	• Forward step on the same side as throwing arm • No forward step or mistimed forward step, arm action only for throw • No hip/spine rotation	• Forward step/weight shift is timed with hip/spine rotation • Forward stride is toward target with lead foot toes pointed forward	Forward step/weight shift, hip/spine rotation, and forward stride are well-timed
Distance or Accuracy	• Lack of distance • Lack of accuracy (fails to consistently hit the wall)	• Throws for distance • Throws with reasonable accuracy (hits wall at least 60% of time)	Throws for distance and accuracy (hits target 80% of time)

Grade-Level Outcome

Catches a thrown ball above the head, at chest or waist level, and below the waist using a mature pattern in a nondynamic environment [closed skills]. (S1.E16.4)

Assessment Task

Catch a thrown ball using both above and below the waist catching patterns.

Guidelines

- You can complete an assessment of manipulative skills easily in station setup, with other stations for practice tasks, one of which is the skill being assessed.
- Sufficient space for pairs of students to practice throwing and catching skills safely, as well as for the assessment station.
- Throws to catchers may be either underhand or overhand for accuracy above the head, at the chest, and below the waist.
- Pause after each 5 attempts to remind students what kind of catch is to be assessed.

Note: *The catcher is only as good as the thrower for this assessment. To ensure accurate assessment of catching skills, the thrower must be a skilled thrower or the teacher.*

Setup

- Distance of 15 feet for throws to catcher
- 5 attempts at catching a high throw (above catcher's head)
- 5 attempts at catching a medium-height throw (at catcher's chest)
- 5 attempts at catching a low throw (below catcher's waist)

Equipment

Softball-sized balls, with sufficient weight to travel to different levels of height at a distance of 15 feet

Critical Elements for Catching

- Extend arms outward to reach for the ball (thumbs in for a catch above the waist, thumbs up for a catch at the waist, thumbs out for a catch below the waist)
- Watch the ball all the way into the hands
- Catch with hands only
- Pull the ball into the body as catch is made
- Curl the body slightly around the ball (specific only to certain catches)

Scoring Rubric for Catching, Grade 4

INDICATOR	DEVELOPING	COMPETENT	PROFICIENT
Critical Elements Catching	Demonstrates fewer than 5 of the critical elements for catching • Fear reaction evident (head turned to side and eyes away from the ball) • Hands close late or not at all resulting in ball bouncing off hands	Demonstrates all critical elements for catching • Extend arms to reach for the ball • Hand position matched to level of catch • Watch ball into hands • Catch with hands only • Pull ball to the body • Curl the body	Demonstrates all critical elements for catching at all 3 levels • Makes adjustment of body and hand positions based on flight of the ball • Hands begin closure during flight of ball in anticipation of contact
Success	Catches are not successful	Completes fewer than 3 of the catches successfully at each level	Successfully completes catches at all 3 levels

Dribbling With Hands   Grade 4

Grade-Level Outcome

Dribbles in self-space with both the preferred and the nonpreferred hands using a mature pattern. (S1. E17.4a)

Assessment Task

Dribble a ball continuously in self-space with preferred hand; repeat with nonpreferred hand.

Guidelines

- Students may perform dribbling tasks in small groups as teacher observes.

- Assessment observation may be completed as a warm-up activity, instant activity, or as a station.

Note: *Grouping students in designated spatial zones will help you observe individual students.*

Setup

- Students in scattered formation with personal space of at least 3 square feet.

- Students dribble for 1 minute with preferred hand as you observe small group; repeat with focus on each group until assessment is completed.

- Students dribble for 1 minute with nonpreferred hand as you observe small group; repeat with focus on each group until assessment is completed.

Equipment

6- to 8-inch balls with good bounce (e.g., playground balls), 1 per student

Critical Elements for Dribbling

- Knees slightly bent

- Opposite foot forward when dribbling in self-space

- Contact ball with finger pads

- Firm contact with top of ball

- Eyes looking "over", not down at the ball

Scoring Rubric for Dribbling With Hands, Grade 4

INDICATOR	DEVELOPING	COMPETENT	PROFICIENT
Critical Elements Dribbling With Hands	• Demonstrates fewer than 5 of the critical elements for dribbling 　» Uses palm of hand upon contact 　» Head down, looking at the ball • Lacks control of the ball • Unable to continuously dribble in self-space	• Demonstrates all critical elements for dribbling with both preferred and nonpreferred hands 　» Knees slightly bent 　» Opposite foot forward 　» Finger pads for contact 　» Firm contact, top of ball 　» Head up, looking over the ball • Maintains a rhythm with preferred hand while continuously dribbling in self-space	• Demonstrates all critical elements for dribbling with both preferred and nonpreferred hands 　» Can switch hands for the dribble with opposite foot forward for each hand 　» Maintains a steady rhythm while continuously dribbling for at least 1 minute in self-space with preferred and nonpreferred hands

Grade-Level Outcome

Kicks along the ground and in the air, and punts using mature patterns. (S1.E21.4)

Assessment Task

With a running approach, kick a stationary ball with enough force to send it 30 feet along the ground.

Guidelines

- You can complete an assessment of manipulative skills easily in station setup, with one station for the assessment and the other stations for practice tasks.

- Sufficient space for students to complete assessment task and the practice station safely.

Note: *If possible, complete this assessment outdoors, as the outdoor surface encourages kickers to use maximum force.*

Setup

- Assessment space marked with a 4- to 6-foot approach area and 30-foot distance marked to assess distance traveled by kick.

- Students in pairs facing partners on parallel lines 30 feet apart.

- Kicker behind starting line for approach to stationary ball, receiver behind receiving line at distance of 30 feet.

- Kicker attempts 5 kicks along the ground; receiver collects balls and retains them until kicker completes assessment; kicker and receiver switch roles and positions after 5 attempts.

Note: *For safety, maintain distance of 30 feet between kicker and receiver during all kicking for distance assessments.*

Equipment

5 slightly deflated playground balls or plastic balls (6 to 8 inches in diameter)

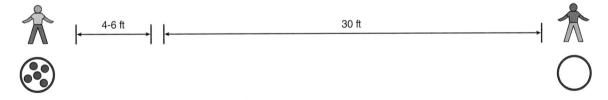

Critical Elements for Kicking Along the Ground

- Arms extend forward in preparation for kicking action

- Contact with ball is made directly behind center of ball

- Contact ball with top of foot (shoelaces) for kicking action

- Trunk leans back slightly in preparation for kicking action

- Follow through with kicking leg and foot extending forward and upward toward target

Scoring Rubric for Kicking Along the Ground, Grade 4

INDICATOR	DEVELOPING	COMPETENT	PROFICIENT
Critical Elements Kicking Along Ground	Demonstrates fewer than 5 of the critical elements • Arms at sides, not extended • Ball contacted below center resulting in airborne ball • Ball contacted with toes and not top of foot • Ball travels in extreme right or left direction	Demonstrates all critical elements for kicking along the ground • Arms extended forward • Contact directly behind center of ball • Contact with shoelaces • Trunk leans back slightly in preparation • Follow through with extension toward target • Slight deviation from straight pathway to receiver	Demonstrates all critical elements for kicking along the ground • Kicks each ball in a straight pathway to receiver
Force	Little or no follow-through resulting in punching action	Kick is through the ball allowing for additional power	Swing of leg through the ball is well-timed allowing for increased force production
Distance	Unable to kick a distance of 30 feet	Kicks targeted distance with reasonable accuracy	Kicks targeted distance with accuracy

Grade-Level Outcome

Kicks along the ground and in the air, and punts using mature patterns. (S1.E21.4)

Assessment Task

With a running approach, kick a stationary ball with enough force to send it 30 feet through the air.

Guidelines

- You can complete an assessment of kicking skills easily in station setup, with one station for assessment and other stations for practice tasks.

- Sufficient space for students to complete the assessment task and the practice stations safely.

Setup (same as for kicking along the ground)

- Assessment space marked with at least 30-foot distance for ball to travel, 4- to 6-foot distance for approach.

- Students in pairs facing partners on parallel lines 30 feet apart.

- Kicker behind starting line for approach to stationary ball, receiver behind receiving line at distance of 30 feet.

- Kicker attempts 5 kicks in the air; receiver collects balls and retains them until kicker completes assessment; kicker and receiver switch roles and positions after 5 attempts.

Equipment

5 slightly deflated playground balls or plastic balls (6 to 8 inches)

Critical Elements for Kicking in the Air

- Arms extend forward in preparation for kicking action

- Contact with ball is made directly below center of ball

- Ball contacted with top of foot (shoelaces) for kicking action

- Trunk leans back slightly in preparation for kicking action

- Follow through with kicking leg and foot extending upward and forward toward target

Scoring Rubric for Kicking in the Air, Grade 4

INDICATOR	DEVELOPING	COMPETENT	PROFICIENT
Critical Elements Kicking in the Air	Demonstrates fewer than 5 of the critical elements for kicking in the air • Arms at sides and not forward • Ball is contacted with toe and not top of foot (shoelaces) • Ball contacted behind center, resulting in ball traveling on ground • Ball travels in extreme right or left direction	Demonstrates all critical elements for kicking in the air • Arms extended forward • Contact directly below center of ball • Contact with shoelaces • Trunk leans back slightly in preparation • Follow through with extension toward target • Slight deviation from straight pathway to receiver	Demonstrates all critical elements for kicking in the air • Swing of leg through the ball well-timed allowing for increased force production and height on kick • All kicks in straight aerial pathway to receiver
Force	Limited leg swing resulting in very little power	Kick through the ball allowing for additional power	Kicker adjusts force so ball travels desired distance to receiver
Distance	Unable to kick a ball 30 feet through the air	Kicks ball through the air with reasonable distance accuracy	Kicks ball through the air with distance accuracy

Grade-Level Outcome

Kicks along the ground and in the air, and punts using mature patterns (S1.E21.4).

Assessment Task

Punt a ball with enough force to send it a distance of at least 30 feet.

Guidelines

- You can complete an assessment of kicking skills easily in station setup, with other stations for practice tasks and one station for assessment.

- Sufficient space for students to complete the assessment task and the practice stations safely.

Note: *Assessment of punting is best completed outdoors, with enough space for aerial kicks and for other students to be actively engaged in practice stations.*

Setup

- 2 parallel lines marked at a distance of 30 feet

- Students in pairs, with partners facing each other behind parallel starting and receiving lines

- Kicker is behind starting line, receiver is behind receiving line at distance of 30 feet.

- Kicker attempts 5 punts; receiver collect balls and retains them until kicker completes assessment.

- Kicker and receiver switch roles and positions after 5 attempts.

Equipment

5 slightly deflated playground balls or plastic balls (6 to 8 inches)

Critical Elements for Punting

- Kicker step-hops forward, body becoming airborne momentarily

- Arms extend forward, drop ball as kicking leg moves forward

- Kicking leg and foot extend; top of foot (shoelaces) contacts ball for punting action

- Trunk leans backward in preparation for punting action

- Follow through with kicking leg and foot extending forward and upward, just beyond waist level

Scoring Rubric for Punting, Grade 4

INDICATOR	DEVELOPING	COMPETENT	PROFICIENT
Critical Elements Punting	Demonstrates fewer than 5 of the critical elements • Kicker remains on the ground (no step-hop approach) • Tosses ball up and not dropped resulting in lack of control • No contact with ball for punting action • Aerial pathway of ball is to extreme right or left	Demonstrates all critical elements • Step-hop approach, momentarily airborne • Arms extend forward, ball dropped for kick • Kicking leg extends, contact with shoelaces • Trunk leans back in preparation • Kicking leg extends forward and upward, just below waist level • Slight deviation from straight aerial pathway	Demonstrates all critical elements • All punts in 45-degree aerial pathway • Flight pathway straight
Force	Limited range of motion in leg resulting in a lack of power and distance	Kick through the ball allowing for additional power	• All critical elements are well-timed allowing for increased force production and proper angle of height on punt • Kicker adjusts force so ball travels desired distance
Distance	Unable to punt a distance of 30 feet	Punts with reasonable distance accuracy	Punts with distance accuracy

Grade-Level Outcome

Volleys underhand using a mature pattern in a dynamic environment (e.g., 2 square, 4 square, handball). (S1.E22.4)

Assessment Task

Using a one-hand underhand pattern, volley the ball to the wall for consecutive hits.

Guidelines

- You can complete an assessment of the underhand volley easily in station setup, with other stations for practice tasks, one of which is the skill being assessed.

- Sufficient space for assessment, including to the sides and behind the student performing the volley.

Note: *Remind students that the ball must bounce one time between volleys, and it must bounce inside of the floor boundary and above the wall target line.*

Setup

- Tape line on wall approximately 3 feet above floor; tape line on floor, approximately 8 feet from wall

- Clear wall space for assessment station

- Student stands in ready position just inside the 8-foot line; on signal begins underhand volley.

- 3 attempts to complete 5 consecutive volleys

- If student reaches 10 consecutive volleys, stop the sequence.

- Ball must bounce one time between each volley.

Equipment

Lightweight 8-inch ball, appropriate size and weight for students

Critical Elements for Volleying With an Underhand Pattern

- Face the target in preparation for volley

- Opposite foot forward

- Flat surface of hand contacts ball

- Contact with ball between knee and waist level

- Hand and arm follow through upward and to target

Scoring Rubric for Volleying With an Underhand Pattern, Grade 4

INDICATOR	DEVELOPING	COMPETENT	PROFICIENT
Critical Elements Volleying Underhand	Demonstrates fewer than 5 of the critical elements • Ball contacted above waist level, sending it upward rather than forward • Side arm swing rather than forward, backward	Demonstrates all critical elements • Face the target • Opposite foot forward • Flat surface for contact • Contact between knee and waist level • Follow through upward and to target	Demonstrates all critical elements for volleying underhand in all 3 attempts
Force	• Hits ball with insufficient force to travel to the wall • Ball does not stay within boundaries for wall or floor	Adjusts force to keep ball within boundaries for floor and wall	Adjusts force to keep ball within boundaries for floor and wall
Success	• Unable to complete 5 consecutive hits • Volleys ball after 2 bounces or with no bounce	Completes 5 consecutive hits for only 1 or 2 attempts	Completes 5 consecutive hits for each of the 3 attempts
Ball and Body Position	Does not move into position behind ball	Slight hesitancy in moving into position behind the ball	Moves quickly to be in position behind the ball for each volley

Striking With Short-Handled Implements, Sidearm Pattern · Grade 4

Grade-Level Outcome
Strikes an object with a short-handled implement while demonstrating a mature pattern. (S1.E24.4a)

Assessment Task
Use a short-handled paddle or racket (sidearm pattern) to strike a ball to the wall for consecutive hits.

Guidelines
- You can complete an assessment of short-implement striking skills easily in station setup, with other stations for practice tasks, one of which is the skill being assessed.
- Remind students that the ball must bounce inside boundaries (back, sides) and above tape line on wall.

Note: *Ensure students' safety by allowing adequate space for skill-practice stations and for assessment.*

Setup
- Students in pairs
- Tape line on wall approximately 3 feet above floor; tape line on floor, approximately 8 feet from wall.
- Student stands in ready position just behind the 8-foot line; on signal begins striking.
- 3 attempts to complete 5 consecutive hits
- Ball must bounce one time between each hit.
- If student reaches 10 consecutive hits, stop the sequence.
- Student being assessed will complete 3 attempts for consecutive hits. Other partner is positioned a safe distance behind and to the side to retrieve balls if needed. Striker and retriever will switch roles and positions after 3 attempts.

Equipment
- Short-handled paddle, pickle balls, Wiffle balls, or low-compression tennis balls
- Clear wall space for assessment station

Critical Elements for Striking With Short-Handled Implement (Sidearm Pattern)
- Racket back in preparation for striking
- Coil and uncoil the trunk in preparation (side to target) and for execution of the striking action
- Step on opposite foot as contact is made with ball
- Racket or paddle swings low to high
- Follow-through for completion of striking action

Scoring Rubric for Striking With Short-Handled Implement (Sidearm Pattern), Grade 4

INDICATOR	DEVELOPING	COMPETENT	PROFICIENT
Critical Elements Striking With Short-Handled Implement	Demonstrates fewer than 5 of the critical elements	Demonstrates all critical elements • Racket back in preparation • Coil and uncoil • Step on opposite foot • Swing low to high • Follow through	• Demonstrates all critical elements for all 3 attempts • Well-coordinated and well-timed unified motion resulting in smooth striking motion
Force	• Unable to strike with sufficient force to send ball to wall target • Unable to control force resulting in ball landing outside boundaries	• Cannot consistently adjust force within boundaries • Cannot consistently strike above tape line on wall	Consistently adjusts force to strike ball within boundaries and to wall target
Success	• Cannot complete consecutive hits • Strikes ball after 2 bounces or with no bounce	Completes 5 consecutive hits on only 1 or 2 of the attempts	Demonstrates 5 or more consecutive hits on all attempts
Ball and Body Position	Does not move into position behind ball	Slight hesitancy in moving into position behind the ball	• Moves quickly to be in position behind the ball for each volley • Alternates hits with a partner over a low net or against a wall (S1.E24.4b)

Grade-Level Outcome

Strikes a pitched ball with a bat using a mature pattern. (S1.E25.5a)

Assessment Task

Strike a pitched ball with a bat, sending it forward through the air.

Guidelines

- Adequate space for student safety. This assessment is best conducted outdoors.

- Assessment requires 4 students in various positions; the remainder of the class should be engaged in practice tasks, preferably related to the assessment (e.g., catching, throwing underhand, and striking with a long-handled implement).

- A variety of age-appropriate balls and bats for the assessment and for skill practice.

Setup

- Students to be assessed in groups of 4: batter, pitcher, outfielder, and catcher.

- Pitcher throws with a gentle underhand throw.

- Batter completes 3 attempts to strike the ball, sending it forward in an aerial pathway.

- After batter completes 3 attempts, players rotate positions for next assessment. Procedure continues until all 4 students have been assessed.

Equipment

- 3 age-appropriate balls, e.g., Wiffle balls

- Rubber base

- Age-appropriate bat (plastic, oversized)

Note: *Remember that, for this assessment, the batter is only as good as the thrower. You might want to serve as the pitcher to ensure accurate pitches for batters to swing at during the assessment.*

Critical Elements for Striking With a Long-Handled Implement

- Bat up and back in preparation for striking action

- Step forward on opposite foot as bat swings through hitting zone

- Trunk coils and uncoils in preparation for and execution of striking action

- Bat swings in horizontal plane

- Wrist uncocks on follow-through for completion of striking action

Scoring Rubric for Striking a Pitched Ball With a Long-Handled Implement, Grade 5

INDICATOR	DEVELOPING	COMPETENT	PROFICIENT
Critical Elements Striking a Pitched Ball With a Long-Handled Implement	Demonstrates fewer than 5 of the critical elements for striking with a long-handled implement • Swing is downward with chopping action (not in horizontal plane) • Faces forward in preparation for swing	Demonstrates all critical elements for striking with a long-handled implement • Bat up and back in preparation • Step on opposite foot • Coil and uncoil the trunk • Swing in a horizontal plane • Wrist uncocks	Demonstrates all critical elements for striking with a long-handled implement • Preparation and follow-through demonstrate a full range of motion contributing to power
Success	Does not make contact with ball on any attempt	Makes contact on 1 or 2 of the attempts	• Ball travels through the air for all 3 attempts • Batter purposely adjusts force for changes in distance (S2.E3.5b)

53

Grade-Level Outcome

Combines balance and transferring weight in a gymnastics sequence or dance with a partner. (S1.E7.5)

Assessment Task

Design and perform a partner gymnastics sequence on mats with 5 balances and 4 weight transfers.

Guidelines

- You can complete assessment of gymnastics sequences as other students are developing and practicing their work.

- Student choice for observation by class during the assessment of partner sequence.

Note: *Remind students to include in their sequences only those gymnastics balances and weight transfers that they have mastered already.*

Setup

- Students in pairs (student choice)

- Assessment area with mats and free floor space for partners to perform sequence

- Requirements for each sequence: 5 balances, 4 weight transfers, beginning shape, and ending shape

- Student choices: partner relationship (mirror, side by side, follow the leader), travel, and/or movement concepts (e.g., bases of support, transfers, shapes)

- Remind students of the importance of practice and memorization, as they will perform the sequence only once for the assessment

Equipment

- Sufficient mats and floor space for all students to work safely with partners in gymnastics

- Paper, pencil for recording sequences

Critical Elements for Balances and Transfer

Balances

- Body parts (i.e., center of gravity) aligned over base of support

- Stillness maintained for at least 3 seconds

- Free body parts extend for balance and counterbalance

- Muscles tighten for stillness on balances

Weight Transfer

- Transfers of weight to hands:

  » Sufficient strength to maintain weight on hands only

  » Ability to transfer back to feet safely

  » Extension of legs, alignment over base of support

- Transfers of weight by rolling:
  - » Tucking of head to chin
  - » Back curls
  - » Push with hands
- Transfers of weight by curling, twisting, stretching:
  - » Sufficient strength in new base of support to support weight
- Sustained or free flow of transfers

Scoring Rubric for Balances and Weight Transfer in a Gymnastics Sequence, Grade 5

INDICATOR	DEVELOPING	COMPETENT	PROFICIENT

Critical Elements
 	
Balances and Weight Transfer
	• Unable to demonstrate all of the critical elements for combined balance and weight transfer
	• Sequence lacks required components
		Demonstrates all critical elements for combined balance and weight transfer
		• **Balance**
		  » Alignment
		  » Stillness
		  » Extension
		  » Tight muscles
		• **Weight Transfer**
		  » Sufficient strength to support weight and for transfer
		  » Tucked body for roll
		  » Flow of transfers
			Demonstrates all critical elements of balance and weight transfer

Balances	Unable to hold stillness in balances	Completes all balances on same base of support	• At least one balance has narrow base of support • At least one inverted balance • Sequence has variety in shapes, levels, and bases of support (S2.E1.5)
Transfers	No transfers between balances	All weight transfers are identical	• Sequence has variety in weight transfers • Smooth transitions between balances
Sequence	• Sequence not memorized • Sequence incomplete	Sequence memorized and performed as written	• Sequence choreographed between partners from beginning to ending shape • Sequence accurately recorded with pictographs and descriptions as needed

Grade-Level Outcome

Combines locomotor skills and movement concepts (levels, shapes, extensions, pathways, force, time, flow) to create and perform a dance with a group. (S1.E11.5)

Assessment Task

Design and perform a group dance, combining locomotors and movement concepts.

Guidelines

- Review movement concepts before students begin work in creating dances.
- Students working together in self-selected groups is an important component of physical education. (Standard 4: S4.E2.5a, 5b; S4.E4.5)
- Depending on the unit of study, the dance project may center around creating a dance from components of cultural dances studied; a focus on concepts (e.g., space, force); a study of rhythm; or dance to tell a story or portray emotions.

Setup

- Length of dance 1 ½ - 2 minutes
- No fewer than 3, no more than 6 in the group
- Requirements of dance: incorporate 3 movement concepts (space, force, time, flow, levels, shapes, directions, pathways); 2 locomotors; beginning shape and ending shape
- Student choices: partner relationship (mirror, side by side, follow the leader), travel, movement concepts; and selection of story, emotion, rhythm, etc. within unit of dance study
- Remind students of importance of practice and memorization, as they will perform the sequence only once for the assessment

Equipment

- Music or rhythmic accompaniment
- Paper and pencils for recording choreography of dance

Scoring Rubric for Combining Locomotors and Movement Concepts in Dance, Grade 5

INDICATOR	DEVELOPING	COMPETENT	PROFICIENT
Dance Requirements	Dance requirements incomplete	Demonstrates all the requirements of the dance • 2 locomotors • 3 concepts • length of dance • beginning and ending shape	Demonstrates all the requirements of the dance • Dance flows smoothly from beginning to ending shape
Locomotors and Concepts	Locomotors and/or movement concepts not demonstrated correctly	Correct demonstration of movement concepts and locomotors	Includes a variety of concepts and locomotors, all performed correctly
Choreography	• Not all members of the group are actively involved • Dance not memorized	• Actively involves all members of group • Choreographed and memorized	Dance choreographed and recorded with pictographs and/or descriptions for all members of the group
Focus	Dance does not convey intended focus	Dance conveys intended focus—emotion, rhythm, story, etc.	Dance conveys intended focus

Passing and Receiving With Feet   Grade 5

Grade-Level Outcomes
- Passes with the feet using a mature pattern as both partners travel. (S1.E19.5a)
- Receives a pass with the feet using a mature pattern as both partners travel. (S1.E19.5b)

Assessment Task
Move the ball the length of the field, sending passes to and receiving passes from a partner, using the feet.

Guidelines
Assessing these skills requires adequate space for student safety. This assessment is best conducted outdoors.

Setup
- Partners dribble with feet, sending and receiving passes, to move the ball the length of the field. Partners must complete at least 4 passes. (You might need to adjust the assessment setup depending on the amount of outdoor space available.)
- Position partners at least 10 feet from each other for travel.
- Position tall cones at intervals within the passing and receiving area.
- Each set of partners completes 4 attempts at the assessment task.
    - » Partners complete attempts 1 and 2 without cones in the travel area.
    - » If partners are successful on attempts 1 and 2, position tall cones as "stationary defense" at equal intervals on the field, and partners complete attempts 3 and 4 with cones in place.
    - » If unsuccessful on attempts 1 and 2, partners complete attempts 3 and 4 without cones.

Equipment
- 8-inch, slightly deflated playground ball or soccer ball
- 6 tall cones

Critical Elements for Passing and Receiving With Feet

Tap/Dribble
- Tap ball gently with inside and outside of feet
- Adjust force to maintain 2-3 feet distance between body and ball

Passing
- "Check" momentum before passing
- Pass ahead of the moving receiver

Receiving
- "Give" with foot to receive the pass
- Receive the pass while continuing to travel

Scoring Rubric for Passing and Receiving With Feet, Grade 5

INDICATOR	DEVELOPING	COMPETENT	PROFICIENT
Critical Elements Passing and Receiving With Feet	Does not demonstrate all the critical elements • Stops to pass and/or stops to receive pass • Fails to execute a lead pass to receiver	Demonstrates all the critical elements • Tap/dribble with inside and outside of feet • Maintains 2-3 feet distance of ball and body • Checks momentum before passing • Passes ahead of partner • Gives to receive pass • Receives pass without stopping	Demonstrates all the critical elements • Successfully completes assessment without and with cones
Force	Insufficient force to send ball to partner OR inaccurate passes to partner	Matches force of pass to distance of partner	Adjusts pathways, force, directions without cones, with cones, against 2v2 defense
Success	Completes less than 4 successful attempts of passing and receiving, moving the ball down the field (with or without cones)	Successfully completes all 4 assessment attempts without cones	Successfully completes passing and receiving with partner against 2v2 defense

Standard 2 Sample Assessments

Standard 2: The physically literate individual applies knowledge of concepts, principles, strategies and tactics related to movement and performance.

The assessments in Part II are written to evaluate students' **functional understanding** of concepts related to movement—that is, the combination of cognitive understanding of movement concepts and the ability to demonstrate the concepts in movement. The goal of all skill development is that students can combine those two areas of learning into competence that leads to their being able to apply, analyze, and create sequences and strategies in dance, gymnastics, and game environments.

Young children often attain cognitive understanding of a concept before they can demonstrate the concept in the performance of a skill. Two cautions arise when teaching for cognitive understanding with young children:

- Be sure the child understands the vocabulary when asked to perform a skill. The child might be able to perform the skill without knowing the associated vocabulary.

- Some children will be able to identify a concept, such as pathways, when they see it in a diagram or performed by others, but are not yet able to perform the skill.

As with all teaching of children, it's important that you're sure there is a match between cognitive understanding and performance ability if the two areas of learning are presented in a single task.

Students in Grades K-2 learn movement concepts to develop their functional understanding. Students in Grades 3-5 apply movement concepts in their performance of locomotor, nonlocomotor, and manipulative skills. The assessment samples that follow are built on this progression from understanding of movement concepts to applying them. The assessments for Grades K-2 include a cognitive measurement as well as an observation measurement embedded within a performance assessment. The assessments for students in Grades 3-5 are built upon a functional understanding of the movement concepts learned in Grades K-2 and therefore reflect combinations of skills and concepts as well as beginning strategies and tactics.

Grade-Level Outcome

Differentiates between movement in personal (self-space) and general space. (S2.E1.Ka)

Assessment Tasks for Space Awareness

- Show me your self-space/your personal space within the boundaries of our movement area.

- Travel throughout general space; on signal, stop in your self-space.

Assessment Tasks for Levels

- **Check for Understanding:** Tell your neighbor the 3 levels we studied today. If you heard high, medium, low, give your neighbor a "thumbs up."

- **Exit Slip:** Match the figure in the illustration to the correct level: high, medium, low. (See Appendix H for examples of an exit slip.)

- **Teacher Observation:** In self-space show me high level; show me medium level; show me low level. Travel in general space at a low level; travel at a medium level; travel at a high level. (S2.E2.1a)

Guidelines

- Assess a movement concept with travel only after students have a functional understanding of personal and general space (i.e., the ability to move safely without interfering in the movement of others).

- Exploration of general and self-space presents excellent opportunities for students to develop an understanding of movement concepts. For example:

  » Exploration of self-space is an ideal time for introduction, mastery, and assessment of levels

  » The practice of locomotors in general space is an ideal time for introducing directions and pathways

- Assess cognitive understanding of a movement concept with an exit slip or with students' demonstration during closure (tell a partner).

- Assess performance understanding, as well as checks for understanding, during the practice of locomotors.

- You can use this type of assessment for each of the movement concepts that kindergarten students are studying (e.g., pathways, levels, directions, speed).

Setup

Depending on choice for cognitive assessments: exit slip procedures, closure discussion (tell your neighbor) or teacher observation during class activity

Equipment

Exit slip diagram of high, medium and low levels, pencils (See Appendix H for exit slip examples.)

Scoring Rubric for Space Awareness, Kindergarten

INDICATOR	DEVELOPING	COMPETENT	PROFICIENT
Self-Space	Unable to demonstrate an understanding of self-space in relation to others	Identifies and describes self-space and general space	Demonstrates understanding of self-space when combined with travel
Self-Space and General Space	Unable to differentiate between self- and general space	Demonstrates differentiation of movement in self-space and in general space	Demonstrates self- and general space, maintaining body control and avoiding collisions

Scoring Rubric for Traveling With Levels, Kindergarten

INDICATOR	DEVELOPING	COMPETENT	PROFICIENT
Identifying Levels	Unable to identify levels in illustrations or when demonstrated by others	Identifies levels correctly in 2 of the 3 venues—diagram, observation of others, performance	Identifies levels correctly in all 3 venues—diagram, observation of others, performance
Demonstrating Levels	Unable to demonstrate levels on teacher signal	Demonstrates all 3 levels correctly on teacher signal	• Demonstrates a functional understanding of levels: cognitive and performance • Demonstrates levels correctly in self-space and when traveling in general space (S2.E2.1a)

Grade-Level Outcome

Travels in 3 different pathways. (S2.E2.K)

Assessment Tasks

- **Check for Understanding:** Tell your neighbor the 3 pathways we traveled today. If you heard straight, curved, zigzag, give your neighbor a "thumbs up."

- **Exit Slip:** Match the illustration to the correct pathway: straight, curved, or zigzag. (See Appendix H for an example.)

- **Teacher Observation:** Travel in general space using a straight pathway, travel with a curved pathway, travel with a zigzag pathway.

Setup

Depending on choice of cognitive assessment: exit slip procedures, closure discussion (tell your neighbor) or teacher observation during class activity

Equipment

- Exit slip diagram of pathways

- Pencils

Scoring Rubric for Pathways, Kindergarten

INDICATOR	DEVELOPING	COMPETENT	PROFICIENT
Identifying Pathways	Unable to identify pathways in illustrations or when demonstrated by another student or the teacher	Identifies pathways correctly in 2 of the 3 venues—diagram, observation of others, performance	Identifies pathways correctly in all 3 venues—diagram, observation of others, performance
Demonstrating Pathways	Unable to demonstrate 3 pathways on teacher signal	Demonstrates all 3 pathways correctly on teacher signal	• Demonstrates a functional understanding of pathways: cognitive and performance • Travels in straight, curved and zigzag pathways (S1.E1.K)

Embedded assessment within Standard 1, locomotors (S1.E1.K). See Appendix D for an example of an embedded assessment.

Embedded assessment: These indicators could be added to the rubric specific for locomotors under Standard 1. By adding them to an existing rubric, you can assess both locomotors and the movement concept relative to the travel at the same time. See Appendix D for examples of embedded assessments.

Directions   Grade K

A prerequisite to Directions, Grade 3 (S2.E3.3)

Assessment Tasks

- **Check for Understanding:** Teacher demonstration of 6 directions; forward, backward, right, left, up and down. Students tell neighbor directions in which the teacher is moving.

- **Teacher Observation:** Students travel in general space, changing directions on teacher signal.

Scoring Rubric for Directions, Kindergarten

INDICATOR	DEVELOPING	COMPETENT	PROFICIENT
Identifying Directions	• Unable to name 6 directions • Unable to identify directions when demonstrated by another student or teacher	Identifies 6 directions correctly either by observation of direction or by demonstration of direction on signal • Forward • Backward • Right • Left • Up • Down	Identifies 6 directions plus clockwise and counterclockwise either by demonstrating on teacher signal or when observing teacher
Demonstrating Directions	Unable to demonstrate directions correctly on teacher signal	Demonstrates directions correctly on teacher signal	• Demonstrates a functional understanding of the 6 directions, plus clockwise and counterclockwise • Demonstrates directions correctly when traveling using different locomotors in general space

Embedded assessment within Standard 1, locomotors (S1.E1.K). See Appendix D.

*You could add these indicators to the scoring rubric for locomotors under Standard 1, Outcome S1.E1.K to assess, at the same time, students' locomotor skill performance and their understanding and application of movement concepts related to pathways.

Grade-Level Outcome

Travels demonstrating low, middle and high levels. (S2.E2.1a)

Assessment Task

Travel in general space at a low level, at a medium level, at a high level.

Guidelines

- Assess performance understanding during the practice of locomotors.

- Assess any movement concept with travel only after students have demonstrated a functional understanding of personal and general space (i.e., the ability to move safely without interfering in the movement of others).

Scoring Rubric for Levels With Travel, Grade 1

INDICATOR	DEVELOPING	COMPETENT	PROFICIENT
Demonstrating Levels	Unable to demonstrate levels on teacher signal	Demonstrates the 3 levels correctly on teacher signal while traveling in general space	• Demonstrates a functional understanding (cognitive and performance) of levels • Demonstrates levels correctly in self-space and when traveling with different locomotors in general space

Speed With Travel   Grade 1

Grade-Level Outcome

Differentiates between fast and slow speeds. (S2.E3.1a)

Assessment Tasks

- **Check for Understanding:** Class discussion, led with focused questions from teacher.

- **Teacher Observation:** Students travel in general space, moving at a fast speed; travel in general space moving at a slow speed.

Guidelines

- Students exploring self- and general space present an excellent opportunity for developing an understanding of movement concepts.

    » Practice of locomotors in general space is an ideal time for introduction and students' mastering (appropriate for Grade 1) different speeds of movement.

- Assess cognitive understanding of concepts such as speed during closure with teacher-led discussion of the concept, as well as how the concept is used in movement activities.

- Assess performance understanding during the practice of locomotors.

Note: *Assessment of fast and slow speeds with travel should be conducted only after students have a functional understanding of personal and general space, i.e., the ability to move safely without interfering in the movement of others.*

Scoring Rubric for Speed With Travel, Grade 1

INDICATOR	DEVELOPING	COMPETENT	PROFICIENT
Demonstrating Speed	No change in speed with teacher signal	• Demonstrates differentiation between fast and slow speeds OR • Correctly performs changes in speed with teacher signal	• Correctly matches speed of running with teacher signal • Correctly identifies fast and slow speeds • Identifies movement tasks/activities for fast speed and tasks for slow speed • Travels with differentiation between jogging and sprinting (S1.E2.2b)

Grade-Level Outcome

Differentiates between strong and light force. (S2.E3.1b)

Assessment Task

Cognitive understanding of strong and light force via teacher questions, sharing with neighbor.

Guidelines

- Young children often equate the concept of force with size (e.g., strong is large, light is small). Discussing the concept of force and providing multiple examples will assist children's understanding.

- When using imagery to provide examples, remind children to focus on the force component, not the pantomime of the image created.

- Provide examples from dance, gymnastics and games and sports to help children relate the concept of force to their movement (e.g., the difference in force needed for a bunt and a homerun; a dribble that is waist high versus a dribble that goes above the head).

Setup

Cognitive understanding of force as a movement concept: discussions, leading questions by teacher, followed by "tell your neighbor..."

Note: *At the Grade 1 level, cognitive understanding of force is the only assessment. Functional understanding will come later as students engage in the sequences of games and gymnastics, as well as the strategies of games.*

Combining Shapes, Levels, Pathways in a Sequence | Grade 2

Grade-Level Outcome

Combines shapes, levels and pathways into simple travel, dance and gymnastics sequences. (S2.E2.2)

Assessment Tasks

- **Travel Sequence:** Create a sequence of 3 locomotors, with changes in levels and pathways. Don't forget beginning and ending shapes.

- **Gymnastics Sequence:** Create a sequence of 3 locomotors and 2 shape balances, in addition to the required beginning and ending shapes.

- **Dance Sequence:** Create a sequence of shapes and levels, or locomotors and pathways as if you are explaining the movements without words (i.e., A Dance Without Words).

Guidelines

- Assessment of movement sequences begins in Grade 2. Students will need guidance in understanding the components of the sequence, the choices they have, and the requirements given by the teacher.

- The assessment of movement concepts within a sequence is a measure of students' functional understanding (i.e., cognitive and performance understanding).

- Students may design in combination with locomotors, with balance and transfers in gymnastics, or as a simple sequence of dance. We recommend that you select the venue (travel, gymnastics, or dance) for Grade 2 students.

Setup

- Adequate space for children to work independently on sequences with travel

- Posted guidelines for sequence: requirements, choices

Scoring Rubric for Combining Shapes, Levels and Pathways in a Sequence, Grade 2

INDICATOR	DEVELOPING	COMPETENT	PROFICIENT
Components	• Sequence incomplete • Sequence does not demonstrate levels, shapes, or pathways	Sequence contains all the required components plus a beginning and an ending shape	• Sequence contains all the required components, beginning and ending shapes, plus additional shapes, levels or pathways • Sequence flows from beginning to ending shape with smooth transitions between movements or between movements and stillness (balances)
Memorization	Sequence not memorized	Sequence memorized and can be repeated with minimum prompting	Sequence memorized and repeated without prompting

Note: *The goal of Standard 2, combined with Grade-Level Outcomes for Kindergarten, Grade 1 and Grade 2, is the development of a functional understanding of movement concepts by the end of Grade 2. Not all students attain that understanding of concepts at the benchmark Grade level, however, just as not all students master fundamental skills at the same rate. Grade 2 is an excellent time to review the basic movement concepts (space awareness, directions, levels, pathways, force, speed/time, shapes) and to conduct a summative assessment in readiness for application of those concepts and their use in combination with skills in movement performance.*

Grade-Level Outcome

Recognizes the concept of open spaces in a movement context. (S2.E1.3)

Assessment Task

Travel in general space, combining pathways and speed, to move to open spaces.

Guidelines

- Assessment of movement concepts in Grade 3 places the emphasis on understanding of the concepts within a movement context; that is, applying the concepts and using them in combination with skills and/or other concepts.

- Assess functional understanding of movement concepts in a dynamic environment, combining the locomotor or manipulative skill with the concept to be assessed.

Setup

Sufficient space for students to travel safely in general space

Scoring Rubric for Traveling to Open Spaces Using Pathways and Speed, Grade 3

INDICATOR	DEVELOPING	COMPETENT	PROFICIENT
Traveling to Open Space	Travels in general space, unable to move to open spaces	Travels in general space, repeatedly moving to open spaces	Travels in general space, seeing open spaces and moving quickly to them
Changes in Speed and Pathways	Travels to open space, but without changes in pathways or speeds	Travels in general space with changes in pathways or speed to move to open spaces	• Uses changes in speed and pathways to move to open spaces • Combines speed, pathways to move to open spaces, with consistent awareness of the space of self and others

Identifying Locomotors in a Physical Activity   Grade 3

Grade-Level Outcome

Recognizes locomotor skills specific to a wide variety of physical activities. (S2.E2.3)

Assessment Task

Identify the locomotor skills in dance, gymnastics or games/sports activities.

Note: *Select physical activities from dance, gymnastics and games/sports skills of previous lessons.*

Guidelines

- Assessment of movement concepts in Grade 3 places the emphasis on the understanding of skills and concepts in a movement context; that is, applying concepts and using the concepts and skills in dance, gymnastics, and games environments.

- You can use checks for understanding and "tell your neighbor" throughout participation in different physical activities for students to 1) identify the locomotor skills in the activity and 2) describe how the particular locomotor skill is used in the activity. For example:

  » Skill: jumping

    - Jumping high to receive a pass

    - Jumping for a rebound

    - Jump stop in basketball

    - Split step in tennis

    - Jumping in ballet, cultural, creative dance

    - Jumping in gymnastics, mounts and dismounts, in relation to mats and apparatus

- Exit slips and journal entries with "complete this sentence" provide assessments of students' understanding of the concepts in different activities.

Setup

- Assess during station work, with one station devoted to journal entry

- Exit slips for a brief written assessment at end of class

- "Tell your neighbor," with responses from each set of partners posted by teacher

Equipment

- Pencils, paper for exit slips, journals for entries

- See Appendix I for worksheet on Identifying Locomotors in Physical Activities

Scoring Rubric for Identifying Locomotors in a Physical Activity, Grade 3

INDICATOR	DEVELOPING	COMPETENT	PROFICIENT
Identifying Locomotors	Unable to identify locomotors within teacher-designated physical activities	Correctly identifies locomotors within teacher-designated physical activities	• Correctly identifies locomotors within physical activities of dance, gymnastics, and games/sports • Identifies the specific skill of the locomotor • Identifies the movement concepts as well as locomotors as directed by the teacher (S2.E3.3)

Grade-Level Outcomes

- Applies the concept of open spaces to combination skills involving traveling (e.g., dribbling and traveling). (S2.E1.4a)
- Dribbles in general space with changes in direction and speed. (S2.E1.4c)

Assessment Task

On signal, begin dribbling the ball in general space, combining pathways, directions and changes in speed to dribble to open spaces.

Guidelines

- This assessment of movement concepts continues the emphasis on understanding the concept in a movement context, applying the concept, and using it in combination with skills and/or other concepts.
- Assess functional understanding of concepts in a dynamic environment, combining the concepts to be assessed with a locomotor or manipulative skill.

Setup

Sufficient space for students to travel and dribble safely in general space

Equipment

6- to 8-inch balls that bounce (e.g., playground), 1 per student

Scoring Rubric for Applying Concepts to Dribbling – Open Spaces, Grade 4

INDICATOR	DEVELOPING	COMPETENT	PROFICIENT
Traveling to Open Spaces While Dribbling	Travels and dribbles in general space, unable to move to open spaces	Travels and dribbles in general space, moving to open spaces with control of ball and body	Travels and dribbles in general space, with mature pattern, seeing open spaces and moving quickly to them
Traveling to Open Spaces With Changes in Speed and Direction	Unable to dribble in general space with control of ball and body	Travels and dribbles to open spaces, changing pathways, directions and speed	Travels and dribbles to open spaces, changing pathways, directions and speed with consistent awareness of the space of self and others

Applying Concepts of Direction and Force When Striking With a Short-Handled Implement

Grade 4

Grade-Level Outcomes

- Applies the concepts of direction and force when striking an object with a short-handled implement, sending it toward a designated target. (S2.E3.4b)

- In connection with Standard 1: Strikes an object with a short-handled implement while demonstrating a mature pattern. (S1.E24.4a)

Note: *Assess students' application of direction and force in combination with striking only if students have attained competency or proficiency in striking with a short-handled implement.*

Assessment Task

On signal, bounce the ball, striking it with the racket, sending it to the wall inside the designated "target" area, with the rebound bounce landing inside the striking boundary tape line on the floor.

- Right-handed student, strike ball to center 5 times, to left of center area 5 times.

- Left-handed student, strike ball to center 5 times, to right of center area 5 times.

- Remember: single hits (bounce, hit, bounce, catch), not continuous hits.

Guidelines

- The combination of movement concepts with mature pattern skills is the beginning stage of skills in dynamic situations within the games environment.

- The control of direction and force with the skill of striking leads to purposeful placement of objects for future offensive tactics and strategies.

- This assessment is an advancement of striking with a racket, demonstrating a mature pattern. (S1. E24.4a)

Setup

- Horizontal tape on wall, height of 3 feet; vertical tape lines on wall, designating 3 areas: center, right, and left of student in position for striking (each area 6-8 feet wide)

- Student in ready position for striking, behind tape line on floor, 10 to 12 feet from wall; second student at safe distance behind hitter to retrieve balls after each assessment attempt

- Balls placed out of striking area, in readiness for each striking attempt

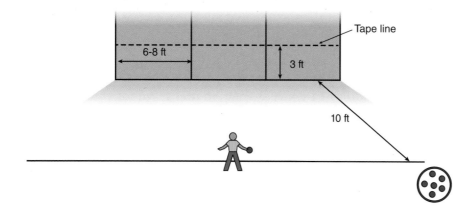

Equipment

- Short-handled racket

- 10 tennis-size balls appropriate for striking with rackets (e.g., low-compression tennis balls, high-density foam balls) OR balls suited for striking indoors

Scoring Rubric for Applying Concepts of Direction and Force When Striking With a Short-Handled Implement, Grade 4

INDICATOR	DEVELOPING	COMPETENT	PROFICIENT
Force and Direction	Unable to contact ball for striking action	Successfully strikes ball to designated target, adjusting force and direction as needed	Successfully strikes ball with mature striking pattern, to designated target, with adjustment in force and direction as needed
Success	Completes striking action with no control of force or direction • Ball does not travel to designated target area • Rebound bounce is not within assessment boundary	Completes attempts with reasonable accuracy • Target area • Rebound bounce within boundary	Completes attempts with accuracy • Target area • Rebound bounce within boundary

Applying Movement Concepts to Strategy in Game Situations   Grade 5

Grade-Level Outcomes

- Applies movement concepts to strategy in game situations. (S2.E3.5a)

- In connection with Standard 1: Passes and receives with the feet using a mature pattern as both partners travel. (S1.E19.5a, 5b)

Note: *Movement concepts for strategy and tactics are combined with skills as Grade-Level Outcomes for students in Grade 5. This assessment task combines passing with feet using a mature pattern as both partners travel (S1.E19.5a) and receiving a pass with feet using a mature pattern as both partners travel (S1.E19.5b). See sample rubric in Appendix J for assessing students' performance against all three Grade-Level Outcomes and embedding assessments across standards. (S2.E3.5c)*

Assessment Task

Move the ball the length of the field, sending and receiving passes, to and from a partner, with the feet.

Guidelines

- Conduct the assessment with passive defense (cones as defenders) and active defense (2 v 2).

- The assessment should focus on the student's ability to select movement concepts and apply them strategically to complete the task successfully.

Note: *Assessment of sending and receiving with the feet requires adequate space for student safety, especially for older students. This assessment is best conducted outdoors.*

Setup

- In pairs, students dribble with feet, sending and receiving passes, to move the ball the length of the field; completing a minimum of 4 passes. (You may need to adjust the assessment setup based on amount of outdoor space available.)

- Position partners at least 10 feet from each other for travel.

- Position tall cones at intervals within the passing and receiving area.

- Each set of partners complete 4 attempts at the assessment task.

  » Partners complete the first two attempts without cones in the travel area.

  » If partners are successful on attempts 1 and 2, position tall cones as "stationary defense" at equal intervals on the field. Complete attempts 3 and 4 with cones in place.

  » If partners are unsuccessful on attempts 1 and 2, continue attempts 3 and 4 without cones.

Equipment

- 8-inch, slightly deflated playground ball or soccer ball
- 6 tall cones

Scoring Rubric for Applying Movement Concepts to Strategy in Game Situations, Grade 5

INDICATOR	DEVELOPING	COMPETENT	PROFICIENT
Applying Movement Concepts	No application of movement concepts when passing and receiving with feet, partners traveling	Applies movement concepts when passing and receiving with reasonable success in moving the ball the length of the field • Pathways • Force • Directions • Speed	• Adjusts pathways, force, directions and speed against passive and active defense • Successfully completes passing and receiving with partner against 2 v 2 defense, applying a variety of movement concepts

See Appendix J for an example of an embedded assessment.

Grade-Level Outcomes

Applies the concepts of direction and force to strike an object with a long-handled implement. (S2.E3.5b)

Note: *This assessment will only be given after students have attained the competency level or above for striking with a long-handled implement, i.e., the implement in the assessment. (S1.E25.5b)*

Assessment Tasks

- **Applying the concept of force:** Strike a ball from a batting tee, sending it a short distance to the target zone and sending it a long distance beyond the target zone.

- **Applying the concept of directions:** Strike a ball from the batting tee, sending it in a forward direction to the left of target zone and to the right of the target zone.

- Assessing students' ability to strike an object with a long-handled implement requires adequate space for ensuring student safety. This assessment is best conducted outdoors.

Note: *Based on movement space and equipment, this assessment is easily adapted for striking with hockey sticks and/or long-handled rackets.*

Guidelines

- Applying movement concepts adds breadth to students' use of manipulative skills and provides opportunities for them to demonstrate competencies specific to tactics and strategies.

- The assessment of applying force and direction to striking with a long implement can serve as a formative assessment, with students being assessed over time as they practice the skill. As such, you may conduct the assessment tasks for applying force and direction separately.

- Peer assessment facilitates the assessment procedures as well as the recording of results.

- The assessment requires 4 students in various positions. The remainder of the class should be engaged in practice tasks, preferably related to the assessment (e.g., striking with a long implement, striking a gently pitched ball, underhand throwing and catching with a partner).

Equipment

- Developmentally appropriate softballs (6)

- Container for holding balls

- Developmentally appropriate bat

- 4 indoor/outdoor bases positioned at distances of 30 feet to 40 feet from one another (or existing baseball/softball area on playground)

- Batting tee

Setup

- Students to be assessed in group of 4: batter, 2 outfielders, 1 student to record accuracy to designated target

- Assessment 1:

  » Batter completes 3 attempts to send the ball forward in an aerial pathway with force so the ball lands beyond second base. Then batter completes 3 attempts to send the ball forward with necessary force for it to land inside the bases.

» Fielders collect balls and return them to container; peer records accuracy scores.

- Assessment 2:
    - » Batter announces to peer recorder the target zone into which he or she will hit the ball (e.g., to the left, to the right, forward).
    - » Batter completes 3 attempts to send the ball to the designated target. Batter then completes 3 attempts to send the ball to a second target zone. (Batter is assessed on 2 directional zones only.)
    - » Fielders collect balls and return them to container; peer records accuracy scores.

- After 6 attempts (3 and 3) at targeted "force" zones and 6 attempts (3 and 3) at targeted "directional" zones, players rotate positions for next student assessment. Assessment continues until all 4 students are assessed.

- See Appendix K for an example of Peer Assessment for Striking With Force and Direction.

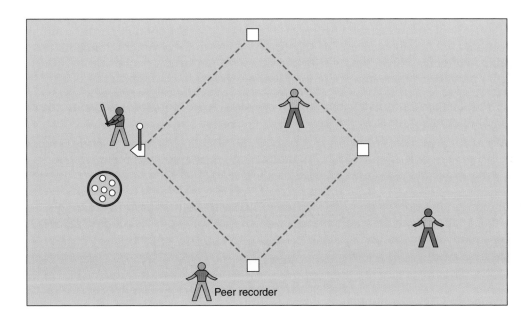

Peer recorder

Scoring Rubric for Applying Concepts of Force and Direction to Striking With a Long-Handled Implement, Grade 5

INDICATOR	DEVELOPING	COMPETENT	PROFICIENT
Striking Pattern	Does not demonstrate mature striking pattern with long implement	Mature pattern of striking with selected long implement	Mature pattern of striking with selected long implement
Force	Unable to adjust force or direction for targeted zones OR adjusts force in only 1 completion of batting	Successfully completes 2 of 3 attempts at adjusting force	Successfully completes all attempts at adjusting force
Direction	Adjusts direction in only 1 completion of batting	Successfully completes 2 of 3 attempts at directional changes	• Successfully completes all attempts at directional changes • Batter successfully applies changes in force and direction with ball pitched from another student and/or teacher

Grade-Level Outcome

Combines spatial concepts with locomotor and nonlocomotor movements for small groups in gymnastics, dance and games environments. (S2.E1.5)

Assessment Task

Design and perform a group dance, combining spatial concepts with locomotor and nonlocomotor movements.

Guidelines

- Movement concepts rarely are studied in isolation at the Grade 5 level; they are studied, applied, and assessed in combination with skills.

- The assessment for movement concepts in dance is embedded within the rubric for Grade-Level Outcome S1.E11.5, which combines locomotor skills and movement concepts (levels, shapes, extensions, pathways, force, time, flow) to create and perform a dance with a group (see p. 56). You will note movement concepts embedded in the rubric.

- Movement concepts are used in combination with locomotor and nonlocomotor skills in dance to convey the intended focus of the dance.

- Student selection of the dance composition, acceptance of differing abilities, and active involvement of all group members are important components of physical education (Standard 4: S4.E4.5). They are added to the assessment rubric.

- Depending on the unit of study, the dance project may center around creating a dance from components of cultural dances studied; a focus on spatial concepts (directions, pathways, levels, extensions); a study of rhythm; or dance to tell a story or portray emotions.

Setup

- Dance length = 1 ½ - 2 minutes

- No fewer than 3, no more than 6 in the group

- Requirements for dance: 2 spatial concepts, 3 locomotors, 1 nonlocomotor, beginning shape, ending shape

- Student choices: group relationship (mirror, side by side, follow the leader), travel, movement concepts, selection of story, emotion, rhythm, etc. within unit of dance study

- Remind students of the importance of practice and memorization, as they will perform the sequence only 1 time for the assessment

Equipment

- Music or rhythmic accompaniment

- Paper and pencils for recording choreography of dance

Scoring Rubric for Combining Spatial Concepts With Locomotor and Nonlocomotor Movements in Dance, Grade 5

INDICATOR	DEVELOPING	COMPETENT	PROFICIENT
Dance Requirements	• Dance requirements are incomplete • Prompting required for completion of dance	• Demonstrates all the requirements of the dance » 3 locomotors » 1 nonlocomotor » 2 spatial concepts » Beginning and ending shape » Length of dance • Choreographed, recorded and memorized	• Dance exceeds requirements of concepts and locomotors • Dance recorded accurately with pictographs and/or descriptions for all members of the group
Spatial Concepts	Spatial concepts are not correctly demonstrated	Correct demonstration of spatial concepts and locomotors	• A variety of movement concepts, locomotors and nonlocomotors, all performed correctly • Dance flows smoothly from beginning to ending shape
Focus	Dance does not convey intended focus	Dance conveys intended focus—emotion, rhythm, story, etc.	• Dance conveys intended focus with locomotors, movement concepts and shapes • Dance has aesthetic appeal
Respect for Others (S4.E4.5)	Not all members of the group are actively involved	Actively involves all members of the group	Dance portrays individual differences and strengths in performance of skills and concepts

Grade-Level Outcome

Combines movement concepts with skills in small-sided practice tasks in game environments, gymnastics and dance with self-direction. (S2.E2.5)

Assessment Task

Create a gymnastics sequence of balances, weight transfers, and movement concepts; you may choose to create the sequence alone, with a partner, on mats or equipment.

Guidelines

- Movement concepts are rarely studied in isolation at the Grade 5 level; they are studied, applied, and assessed in combination with skills.

- Movement concepts are used in combination with the skills of balance and transferring weight, stillness and travel, in gymnastics to add breadth and richness to sequences.

Remind students to include in their sequences only gymnastics balances and weight transfers that they have mastered already.

Setup

- Assessment area with mats and free floor space for partners to perform sequence.

- Requirements of sequence: 5 balances, 4 weight transfers, 3 movement concepts, beginning shape, ending shape.

- Student choices: alone or with partner, sequence on mats or equipment, travel, movement concepts (bases of support, levels, inversion, extensions, shapes, sudden or sustained movement), transition actions (twisting, curling, stretching).

- Remind students of the importance of practice and memorization as they will perform the sequence only 1 time for the assessment.

Critical Elements for Balances and Weight Transfer

Balances

- Body parts (i.e., center of gravity) aligned over base of support

- Stillness maintained for at least 3 seconds

- Free body parts extend for balance and counterbalance

- Muscles tighten for stillness on balances

Weight Transfer

- Transfer of weight to hands

  » Strength applied sufficient enough to maintain weight on hands only, then transfer back to feet safely

  » Legs extend

» Center of gravity aligned over base of support

- Transfer of weight by rolling

    » Head tucks to chin

    » Back curls

    » Hands push

- Transfer of weight by curling, twisting, stretching

    » Strength applied in new base of support sufficient enough to support weight

- Sustained or free flow of transfer

Equipment

- Sufficient mats and floor space for all students to work safely alone or with partners, proper spacing and surface for equipment

- Paper, pencil for recording sequences

Scoring Rubric for Combining Movement Concepts With Skills in Gymnastics, Grade 5

INDICATOR	DEVELOPING	COMPETENT	PROFICIENT
Balance and Weight Transfer	Unable to demonstrate all of the critical elements for combined balance and weight transfer	Demonstrates all critical elements of balance and weight transfer	Sequence exceeds requirements in balances, weight transfers, and movement concepts
Sequence Requirements	Sequence partially meets requirements	Sequence is complete with all the requirements • 5 balances • 4 weight transfers • 3 movement concepts • beginning and ending shapes	• Combines travel with balances and weight transfers • Includes a variety of movement concepts • Stretching, curling, twisting actions are used for transitions • Balances on different bases of support
Movement Concepts	Limited use of movement concepts in sequence	Sequence has a variety of movement concepts	Sequence contains a variety of movement concepts, balances, and transfers as well as travel
Choreography and Memorization	Sequence not memorized OR not recorded	• Sequence accurately recorded on paper • Sequence memorized and performed as written with balances, transfers, and movement concepts • Sequence choreographed from beginning to ending shape	Sequence choreographed and accurately recorded with pictographs and descriptions as needed
Self-Direction	Frequent reminders for completion of sequence and/or written work	Occasional prompts for completion of sequence and/or written work	Sequence portrays individual strengths in skills and concepts, creativity in composition

Standard 3 Sample Assessments

Standard 3: The physically literate individual demonstrates the knowledge and skills to achieve and maintain a health-enhancing level of physical activity and fitness.

While the value of regular participation in physical activity is unquestioned and physical education is viewed as a favorite part of the day for elementary school children, physical fitness has not always been viewed positively. Fitness for young children, pre-K to Grade 2, brings images of weightlifters, marathon runners, and being the fastest in the class. Upper elementary students, Grades 3 to 5, associate being physically fit with "no pain, no gain", heavy perspiration and formal exercises. For many students, fitness assessment is viewed as an unpleasant experience connected with feelings of failure and embarrassment, and charts of school records on the gymnasium wall.

Health-related fitness is a vital component of an elementary physical education program and is recognized as such in the National Standards. Fitness assessment is essential to the students' overall understanding of their progress toward living a healthy lifestyle. However, the purpose of fitness assessment in the elementary school is not the assessment itself. Fitness assessment is only as valuable as what the teacher does with the assessment. Knowledge of the results, as is true with all assessment, receives its value in its contribution to improved teaching and student learning.

For young children the focus of fitness assessment is on recognizing the importance of being healthy, being active on a daily basis, and choosing physical activity as a personal habit. At an early age students begin to assess opportunities for physical activity in their neighborhoods, safe play spaces for after-school physical activity, and their participation in activity. Students in Grade 3 identify the components of health-related fitness and informally assess their personal levels of fitness. Grade 4 students begin a formal assessment of health-related fitness and the selection of strategies for addressing areas for remediation. Grade 5 students analyze personal fitness assessments and design personal fitness plans leading toward the goal of healthy lifestyles.

Fitness assessments for students at the elementary level focus not on athletic fitness, not on being the strongest or the fastest, but on health-related fitness, the "good health balance" of activity and nutrition, and the importance of being physically active.

Grade-Level Outcomes

- Discusses the benefits of being active and exercising and/or playing. (S3.E1.1)

- Actively participates/engages in physical education class. (S3.E2.K, S3.E2.1)

- Recognizes that when you move fast, your heart beats faster and you breathe faster. (S3.E3.K)

- Identifies the heart as a muscle that grows stronger with exercise, play, and physical activity. (S3.E3.1)

Assessment Tasks

- **Teacher Observation:** During physical education activities, note any students not actively engaged in the lesson. If the pattern of non-participation continues, privately discuss the importance of being physically active for good health with the student.

- **Check for Understanding:** At intervals during different activities, stop the activity and ask the students to place their hands over their hearts. Ask the following questions:

  » Can you feel your heart beating?

  » Have you ever been able to hear your heart beating?

    Engage the students in 60 seconds of running very fast in self-space. Repeat the questions.

  » Can you feel your heart beating?

  » Can you hear your heart beating?

  » What happens to the heart when you play really hard? Is this good or bad for you? (S3.E3.1)

- **Exit Slip:** Diagram of couch potato, person jumping rope, age-appropriate person sitting with video game engaged. Have students circle the diagram that will help the heart grow stronger. Example of exit slip found in Appendix L (S3.E3.K).

Guidelines

Fitness for young children should be about being active and enjoying movement, not calisthenics and formal exercises; therefore, the focus of assessment is on class discussions and observation of participation.

- Teacher observation during physical activity will provide information on those students not actively engaged as well as those not moving with enjoyment.

- Class discussion and "tell your neighbor" during closure will provide information on understanding the benefits of being active and the role of physical activity for a healthy heart.

Equipment

- Exit slips

- Pencils

Fitness Knowledge   Grade 2

Grade-Level Outcomes
- Identifies physical activities that contribute to fitness. (S3.E3.2b)
- Recognizes the "good health balance" of nutrition and physical activity. (S3.E6.2)

Assessment Tasks
- **Teacher Observation:** During physical education activities, note any students not actively engaged in the lesson. If the pattern of non-participation continues, privately discuss the importance of being physically active for good health with the student.

- **Check for Understanding:** Teach students to "check the pulse", not for an accurate count but to feel the differences when active and non-active. At intervals during different activities, stop the activity and ask the students to check their pulse.

    Purposely choose activities that cover the range from low cardiorespiratory to very vigorous, with students checking the pulse. Use the pulse count to lead into discussion of activities that contribute to fitness. (S3.E3.2b)

- **Paper and Pencil:** Have the students draw a picture of a person they think is physically fit. Under the picture write one sentence to answer the question, "What makes this person healthy and fit?"
    - » A review of the drawings and answers will lead to class discussions: "Can you tell if a person is healthy and fit by looking at them? What makes a person healthy and fit?"
    - » Lead into discussion of the "good health balance" and the importance of both nutrition and physical activity. (S3.E6.2)

Note: *The "good health balance" of nutrition and physical activity presents excellent opportunities for collaboration with classroom teachers, cafeteria dieticians, and parent organizations (PTA, PTO).*

Guidelines
- Fitness for young children should be about being active and enjoying movement, not calisthenics and formal exercises; therefore, the focus of assessment is on understanding the importance of being active and the relationship between fitness and health.

- Teacher observation during physical activity will provide information on those students not actively engaged as well as those not moving with enjoyment.

- Class discussion and checks for understanding will provide information on understanding the benefits of being active and the role of physical activity in being healthy.

- Young children checking their pulse does not always reveal an accurate pulse count; for purposes of the assessments in Grade 2, an accurate count is not essential, just that children can experience the differences in the pulse with vigorous and less vigorous activities.

- Checking the pulse is easiest for young children with two fingers of each hand placed beside the esophagus; remind children not to use the thumbs for checking the pulse.

Equipment
- Blank paper
- Pencils

Grade-Level Outcome

Describes the concept of fitness and provides examples of physical activity to enhance fitness. (S3.E3.3)

Assessment Tasks

- **Peer Assessment:** Tell your neighbor a physical activity that will enhance fitness. How will that activity help you improve fitness? Give your neighbor a "high five" if you agree with the answer and the reasons for choosing that activity to improve fitness. Share answers with the class. Chart them on the wall.

- **Exit Slip:** As different components of health-related fitness are introduced throughout the year, have students complete an open-ended phrase relating that component of fitness to a physical activity that enhances that component, e.g., "A physical activity I can do at home to improve my flexibility is..."

- **Check for Understanding:** "Thumbs up, thumbs down" if the physical activity I name will improve muscle strength in my upper body (cardiorespiratory endurance, flexibility, etc.).

- **Journal Entry:** Write a short paragraph describing the concept of fitness. You may illustrate your writing with a pictograph if you choose to do so.

Guidelines

- Grade 3 is the beginning of the introduction of health-related fitness and the various components of health-related fitness. The concept of fitness is reviewed from previous experiences in Grade 2, leading to students' understanding of fitness as more than bulky muscles and running for speed and distance.

- Grade 3 fitness for cognitive understanding is distributed throughout the year with class discussions and checks for understanding. With the learning experiences for each fitness component, discussions will include examples of physical activity to enhance that component of health-related fitness.

Equipment

- Student journals

- Pencils

- Prepared exit slips

Pre-Assessment of Fitness Knowledge   Grade 3

Grade-Level Outcome

Demonstrates, with teacher direction, the health-related fitness components. (S3.E5.3)

Assessment Task

Assessment of health-related fitness components—FitnessGram

Guidelines

- Assessment of the health-related fitness components begins in Grade 4. Their introduction in Grade 3 is a natural follow-up of the discussion of each of the components and serves as preparation for the official assessment in Grade 4.

- Fitness assessment in Grade 3 is for learning purposes only; no scores are sent home to parents, no formal summative reports completed for students.

- Assessment of each of the fitness components may be introduced when each component is the lesson focus (i.e., distributed throughout the year), or the assessments may be introduced after all the components have been taught.

- A station format works well for a summative assessment with a station for each fitness component.

- "With teacher direction" is the key to assessment of health-related fitness as a learning experience for students in Grade 3. The proper technique for each fitness component will be a critical part of the teaching for each assessment task.

Setup

Refer to the *FitnessGram Administration Manual* for proper testing procedure, as well as setup and equipment, for each of the health-related fitness components.

Grade-Level Outcome

Analyzes opportunities for participating in physical activity outside physical education class. (S3.E1.4)

Assessment Tasks

- **Tell Your Neighbor:** Following class discussion of opportunities for physical activity participation beyond the school day, have students "tell your neighbor" 1) a safe place for play that exists in your neighborhood/near your home, and 2) the physical activities you enjoy at that play space.

- **Journal Entry:** Have students record in their journal the opportunities for physical activity in their neighborhood, near their home, and at extended locations with drives by parents (sports, gymnastics, dance, swimming). Which one is your favorite? Why?

Note: *Remember to read each journal and respond. You will learn of the opportunities and lack of opportunities for physical activity that exist for the children you teach.*

Guidelines

- Analyzing opportunities for physical activity follows class discussion and the identification of types of physical activity beyond recess and physical education at school.

- Depending on the community in which the school is located, physical activity opportunities will vary greatly for schools and for students within the school. What is important is discovering what opportunities are available for students outside the school environment. This analysis presents opportunities for discussion of healthy, safe environments for physical activity as well as presentations by community recreational leaders, etc.

Equipment

- Student journals
- Pencils

An example of a self-assessment of physical activity patterns outside of physical education class is in Appendix M.

Fitness Assessment – Knowledge

Grade 4

Grade-Level Outcomes

- Identifies the components of health-related fitness. (S3.E3.4)

- Completes fitness assessments (pre- & post-). (S3.E5.4a)

Assessment Task

Completion of health-related fitness component assessment in fall and spring using FitnessGram

Guidelines

- Grade 4 is the first official assessment of health-related fitness for children, based on guidelines from FitnessGram.

- With the Grade 3 introduction to the fitness components and its assessments (S3.E5.3), Grade 4 students will have a basic understanding of health-related fitness components and the assessment of each.

- All assessments should be conducted in an environment that does not intimidate or embarrass the lesser-skilled students.

- Assessment scores should be recorded in private, either with paper and pencil, electronically, or by communication between student and teacher.

- A formative assessment can be conducted with a station setup and personal recording of scores, serving to inform both student and teacher of fitness level relative to each health-related component.

- A summative fitness assessment is conducted after distributed teaching and practice throughout the year.

Setup

Refer to *FitnessGram Administration Manual* (The Cooper Institute, 2017) for proper testing procedure, as well as setup and equipment, for assessing each of the health-related fitness components.

Grade-Level Outcome

Identifies areas of needed remediation from personal test and, with teacher assistance, identifies strategies for progress in those areas. (S3.E5.4b)

Assessment Tasks

- **Journal Entry:** After students receive their fitness assessment scores/printout, have each student choose one area of fitness they want to improve and record it in his or her journal.

  » Students with one or more areas below the "Healthy Fitness Zone" choose one of those areas for improvement.

  » Students with all scores in the "Healthy Fitness Zone" or above will choose an area for improvement based on personal choice.

    Record in your journal the area of fitness you choose to improve. From the strategies we have discussed throughout the year (list on the wall chart), choose one strategy for improving that area of fitness. Each of you will record the strategy in your journal.

- **Take-Home Event Task:** The above can easily be adapted for a student-and-parent project by sending home the students' assessment scores for family suggestions of activities and strategies for improvement.

Note: *Students are often unrealistic with their strategies for improvement. Individual discussions and gentle suggestions for realistic strategies will lead to student growth. Be available to talk with students about strategies that will lead to improvement. Respond to each student's journal entry.*

Guidelines

- Fitness assessment is only as valuable as what we as teachers do with the assessment; thus, the focus of fitness assessment is on individual students and providing them the tools for good health.

- Discussion of fitness components, prior to and after the assessment, should focus on why that fitness component is important for good health, what activities promote that area of fitness, and general strategies for improving the area of fitness.

- Following the completion of all components of the fitness assessment, students should be provided privacy for viewing their test results.

- Class discussions should address remediation in general, never with a recall of an individual student's scores.

Equipment

- Students' journals

- Pencils

- Blank paper

Scoring Rubric for Using Fitness Assessment Results to Identify Improvement Strategies, Grade 4

INDICATOR	DEVELOPING	COMPETENT	PROFICIENT
Areas for Improvement	• Fitness assessment and/or plan incomplete • Unable to identify fitness component for remediation and/or unable to identify physical activity to improve component	Identifies one area of fitness for improvement	Identifies one or more areas of fitness for maintenance or improvement
Strategies	Does not select a strategy for improvement of fitness	• Records selected fitness component and strategy • Identifies a physical activity/strategy for improvement of the selected fitness component	Strategies selected appropriate for student's physical activity opportunities (home, community, school)
Alignment of Selected Activity	Selected physical activity not aligned with area for improvement	Selected physical activity correctly matches fitness area for improvement	Selected physical activities/strategies match fitness areas for maintenance or improvement

Grade-Level Outcome

Differentiates between skill-related and health-related fitness. (S3.E3.5)

Assessment Tasks

- **Check for Understanding:** Tell your neighbor the difference between skill-related and health-related fitness. (After students share responses with the class, discuss and summarize the difference in the two types of fitness to reinforce student understanding.)

- **Exit Slip:** Why is our focus on health-related fitness rather than skill-related?

Note: *The combination of these two assessments will give you as the teacher an indication of the students' understanding of the difference between skill- and health-related fitness.*

Guidelines

- The differences in skill-related and health-related fitness become increasingly important as students begin to assume responsibility for their personal fitness; the focus of the assessment is their understanding of that difference and the reason for its importance.

    » Skill-related: speed, agility, balance, coordination, power and reaction time

    » Health-related: cardiorespiratory endurance/aerobic capacity, muscular strength & endurance, flexibility, body composition

- Assessment for Grade 5 students focuses on students understanding the two types of fitness (health and skill related). Leave comparisons of the specific components of each type of fitness to middle and high school.

Note: *Remember to use language that Grade 5 students can understand easily.*

Equipment

- Prepared exit slip

- Pencils

Designing a Personal Fitness Plan　　　　Grade 5

Grade-Level Outcomes

- Analyzes results of fitness assessment (pre- & post-), comparing results with fitness components for good health. (S3.E5.5a)

- Designs a fitness plan to address ways to use physical activity to enhance fitness. (S3.E5.5b)

Assessment Tasks

- **Analysis of Fitness Data:** You have completed all the assessments for health-related fitness. Compare your fitness scores with the "Healthy Fitness Zones" (FitnessGram) to determine which areas of health-related fitness need improvement and which are within, or above, the Healthy Fitness Zones.

    In Grade 4, you selected one area of fitness for improvement or an area for maintaining a healthy level of fitness; you then selected a physical activity strategy for that fitness area. This year you will analyze each component* of your fitness assessment (cardiorespiratory, muscular strength, muscular endurance, flexibility) in order to design a personal fitness plan for good health, a plan that addresses all areas of your fitness.

- **Design of Fitness Plan:** After you have analyzed your fitness assessment in comparison to the Healthy Fitness Zones, use that information to design a personal fitness plan that you can use throughout the school year or throughout the summer. Your plan will include the following:

    » One strategy/physical activity for improving or maintaining fitness for each of the health-related components

    » The location for the physical activity: home, neighborhood park, school environment

    » A goal in one component of fitness for you to reach by spring testing (or summer). Your goal might be a target for improvement or keeping all of your scores within or above the Healthy Fitness Zone. Record your goal on your personal fitness plan.

- **Extra Credit:** One physical activity that involves the entire family

*Note: *Body composition scores, if collected, should not be reported directly to or discussed with students. Many school districts have enacted policies for reporting body mass index (BMI) scores to students and their parents. Check with your administration before proceeding with BMI assessment, data collection, and the reporting of results.*

Note: *After students complete their personal fitness plans, have the classroom teacher or a parent sign them, followed by your signature. Students then can choose to keep their plans in their backpacks or posted at home for easy reference.*

Guidelines

- The Grade 5 outcomes pertaining to analysis of fitness assessment and the design of a fitness plan are a natural progression from Grade 4 completion of fitness assessment and identification of strategies to address areas of needed remediation. (S3.E5.4a,4b)

- With the foundation of Grade 4 assessment of health-related fitness, students in Grade 5 should be ready to analyze their personal test results in comparison to the fitness components for good health (FitnessGram) and design strategies/select physical activities to address areas of remediation.

- Have students design their personal fitness plan after they complete pre-assessments in the fall. After the spring fitness assessment, they can create an updated fitness plan for the summer.

- Although students created a mini-version of a fitness plan in Grade 4, the design of a fitness plan that matches physical activities and fitness components can be overwhelming; remind the class that your assistance is always available.

- The ultimate goal is for students to design a personal plan for enhancing their fitness, involving remediation, improvement, and maintenance.

Equipment

- Personal Fitness Plans forms

- Pencils

- Printouts from FitnessGram indicating standards for Healthy Fitness Zones

- Printout of individual student scores

An example of a personal fitness plan worksheet is in Appendix N.

Scoring Rubric for Designing a Personal Fitness Plan, Grade 5

INDICATOR	DEVELOPING	COMPETENT	PROFICIENT
Fitness Plan Requirements	Fitness assessment and/or plan incomplete	Designs a personal fitness plan that includes required components and strategies	Personal plan exceeds requirements with more than one strategy for each fitness component
Areas for Improvement	Unable to identify fitness component for remediation and/or unable to identify physical activity to improve	• Identifies a physical activity/ strategy for improvement and/or maintenance of each of the fitness components • Sets a personal goal for 1 area of fitness	• Identifies a physical activity/ strategy for improvement and/or maintenance of each of the fitness components • Sets a personal goal for more than 1 area of fitness
Alignment of Strategies	Selected physical activity not aligned with area for improvement	Selected physical activity correctly matches fitness area for improvement	• Strategies correctly match fitness components • Strategies appropriate for student's physical activity opportunities (home, community, school)

Note: *While important, assessing a student's fitness plan is secondary to the student's commitment to the plan, as well as your ongoing positive feedback.*

Note: *The Grade-Level Outcomes under Standard 3 that address nutrition (Outcome S3.E6.K-5) provide excellent opportunities for collaborating with classroom teachers in health and nutrition units. Plan with the classroom teacher for cooperative activities and reinforcement of student learning.*

Standard 4 Sample Assessments

Standard 4: The physically literate individual exhibits responsible personal and social behavior that respects self and others.

The importance of personal and social responsibility as well as respect for self and others is often overlooked in our teaching of elementary physical education. Our time with students is often limited, and typically our focus is on skill acquisition. However, Standard 4 is critical to all teaching and learning. Don Hellison, author of *Teaching Personal and Social Responsibility* (2011) and creator of the "Five Levels of Responsibility", has said, "If students do not respect themselves, their peers, and you as their teacher, there will be no teaching and no student learning" (personal conversation, 1995, 2004). You cannot assume students' acceptance of responsibility; you must build assessment of responsibility and respect for self and others into your lesson plans for physical education.

The Grade-Level Outcomes for K through Grade 2 focus on personal responsibility (e.g., safety, protocols, self-direction) and an awareness of others. Pre-kindergarten and kindergarten children are still in the ego stage of child development and as a result work *beside*, not necessarily *with*, others. Beginning in Grade 2, the skills of social responsibility, working with others and accepting others, emerge as Grade-Level Outcomes. In Grade 3, children begin to move beyond the focus on self and personal ego, with more of a focus on partners and cooperative endeavors within the physical education environment. For students in Grades 4 and 5, respect for self in physical activity settings and respect for, as well as acceptance of, others regardless of skill level are important benchmarks in preparation for physical activity within and outside the school setting.

The sample assessments for Standard 4 focus on personal and social responsibility. The best way to assess students' performance of these outcomes is through observation of their behaviors in a variety of activities. You can assess students while they participate in lessons that address the skills and knowledge stipulated in Standards 1 and 2. The sample assessments under Standard 4 are embedded within the assessments for Standards 1 and 2. Rubrics within those sample assessments contain a component that focuses on personal and social responsibility. For some of those assessments, there is an additional rubric for measuring student performance of the Grade-Level Outcomes under Standard 4. You can enrich students' development of these important skills and knowledge by collaborating with the classroom teacher and/or guidance counselor to enhance student learning of these outcomes throughout the curriculum. Many elementary schools emphasize character development, self-responsibility, and personal growth within their school goals.

Note: Assessing skills under Standard 4 is not a "checklist" to be completed in a single observation. Assessing these important skills should occur throughout the year and in all activity settings.

Grade-Level Outcomes

- Shares equipment and space with others. (S4.E4.K)

- Accepts personal responsibility by using equipment and space appropriately. (S4.E1.1)

- Works independently with others in a variety of class environments (e.g., small & large groups). (S4.E4.1)

Assessment Tasks

- Travel throughout general space; on signal, stop in your self-space. (page 60)

- Explore hopping (galloping, jogging, sliding) in general space. (page 25)

- Travel in general space, combining locomotors with directions, levels, pathways, and speed.

Guidelines

- For many young children school brings their first experiences of sharing with others—space, equipment, attention; physical education presents the ideal environment for this important learning.

- Assessment of sharing is focused heavily on teacher observation, distributed over time, and in a variety of venues.

- Teacher observation/assessment of personal responsibility and working independently with respect for others is conducted as children practice locomotors and movement concepts.

- Assessment of sharing, accepting personal responsibility, and working independently are embedded within the movement experiences provided for young children; children are rarely aware the assessment is taking place.

Setup

Sufficient general space for performance of locomotors

Scoring Rubric for Personal Responsibility, Embedded With Space Awareness, Grades K-1

INDICATOR	DEVELOPING	COMPETENT	PROFICIENT
Self- and General Space (S2.E1.1)	• Unable to demonstrate self-space in relation to others • Unable to differentiate between self- and general space	• Identifies self-space and general space • Demonstrates movement in self-space and in general space	• Demonstrates a functional understanding of levels: description and performance • Demonstrates self-space correctly when combined with travel
Personal Responsibility (S4.E1.1)	Unable to travel in general space without multiple collisions with others	Travels in general space with no collisions	Demonstrates traveling in general space with control of body and no collisions

Personal and Social Responsibility – Working With a Partner   Grade 2

Grade-Level Outcomes

- Works independently with others in partner environments. (S4.E4.2)
- Accepts responsibility for class protocols with behavior and performance actions. (S4.E2.2)
- Works safely in physical education and with equipment. (S4.E6.2a,2b)

Assessment Tasks

- Conduct this assessment in conjunction with the assessment for Throwing With an Underhand Pattern, Grade 2, on page 30.
- Partner A uses an underhand throwing pattern to send a ball through the air to a large target. Partner B stands a safe distance (5 feet) behind the thrower to retrieve the balls as needed. Partner B is the focus of this assessment.

Guidelines

- Conduct observation and/or assessment of personal responsibility and working independently with respect for others as children practice locomotors, movement concepts, and manipulative skills.
- Accepting personal responsibility and working independently with others are embedded within the movement experiences provided for young children; the assessment of those important skills is also embedded within the learning experiences.
- Grade 2 students benefit from class discussions during closure regarding working with others, selecting partners, safety, and accepting responsibility.

Setup and Equipment

Refer to Standard 1, Grade 2 (S1.E13.2), page 30 for Equipment and Setup

Scoring Rubric for Working With a Partner During Assessment, Grade 2

INDICATOR	DEVELOPING	COMPETENT	PROFICIENT
Acceptance of Partner	Negative acceptance of partner	Positive selection of partner or acceptance of partner assignment	• Positive acceptance of partner • Provides positive feedback to partner on throwing assessment
Personal Responsibility	Frequent reminders necessary to stay in safe space and/or retrieve balls	Accepts responsibility for independently retrieving balls as needed and staying in safe space throughout partner's throwing assessment	Accepts responsibility for independently retrieving balls as needed and staying in safe space throughout partner's throwing assessment

Note: *Practice tasks in station format for the underhand throwing pattern will provide excellent opportunities for observing and assessing students against the Standard 4 outcomes listed at the top of the assessment. (S4.E4, E2, E6) You can enhance students' practice of the task by having partners provide feedback on the critical component that is the focus of the practice station.*

Grade-Level Outcomes

- Exhibits personal responsibility in teacher-directed activities. (S4.E1.3)
- Works independently for extended periods of time. (S4.E2.3)
- Works independently and safely in physical activity settings. (S4.E6.3)

Assessment Task

Balance on different bases of support, i.e., gymnastics balances (page 36)

Guidelines

- Students' working independently in educational gymnastics presents an ideal environment for the assessment of Standard 4; the teaching of educational gymnastics is dependent on the students' exhibiting responsible personal behavior.
- Educational gymnastics provides the environment for the assessment of skills, knowledge, and responsible personal and social behavior as students work on individual tasks within group settings.
- The assessment of personal responsibility and working safely will be a formative assessment throughout the gymnastics unit of study.

Setup and Equipment

Refer to Standard 1, Grade 3, (S1.E7.3) for Equipment and Setup, page 36

Scoring Rubric for Balancing in Gymnastics Combined With Responsible Personal and Social Behavior, Grade 3

INDICATOR	DEVELOPING	COMPETENT	PROFICIENT
Balances (S1.E7.3)	• Demonstrates fewer than 4 of the identified critical components » Holds stillness for less than 3 seconds » Limited extension of free body parts • Inability to balance on different bases of support for each balance	• Demonstrates all critical components in fewer than 3 balances » Center of gravity over base of support » Stillness maintained for 3 seconds in all balances » Extension of free body parts » Tight muscles • Maintains stillness in all balances for 3 seconds • Full extension of free body parts • Maintains muscular tension in all base of support body parts	• Demonstrates all critical components in all balances • Maintains stillness in all balances for 3 seconds • Full extension of free body parts and muscular tension for all balances • Demonstrates 3 balances with smooth transitions between stretching, curling, twisting actions (S1.E10.3)
Personal Responsibility (S4.E1.3, S4.E2.3)	• Unable to work independently on gymnastics tasks; frequent teacher reminders needed • Demonstrates lack of respect for work and space needs of others	• Demonstrates personal responsibility with respect for the work and space needs of others in gymnastics • Works independently for extended periods of time on assigned gymnastics tasks	• Demonstrates personal responsibility with respect for the work and space needs of others • Works independently for extended periods of time • Provides positive feedback to others while respecting their space and their work in gymnastics
Safety (S4.E6.3)	Does not demonstrate awareness of safety for self and others in the gymnastics setting	Demonstrates awareness of safety for self and others in the gymnastics setting	Assists others with safety awareness in the gymnastics setting

Note: *Personal responsibility and working safely are critical in all educational gymnastics (all students, all grade levels); formative assessment of such should be ongoing throughout gymnastics units of study.*

Personal Responsibility – Safety   Grade 3

Grade-Level Outcomes

- Exhibits personal responsibility in teacher-directed activities. (S4.E1.3)
- Works independently and safely in physical activity settings. (S4.E6.3)

Assessment Task

Travel in general space, combining pathways and speed, to move to open spaces (page 68).

Guidelines

- Grade 3 assessments of Standards 1 and 2 provide excellent opportunities for teacher observation of students' acceptance of personal responsibility as displayed in respect for self and others.
- The combination of locomotors and movement concepts provides the environment for the assessment of skills, knowledge, and responsible personal and social behavior.

Setup

Refer to Standard 2, Grade 3 (S2.E1.3) for Setup, page 68

Scoring Rubric for Open Spaces Combined With Responsible Personal and Social Behavior, Grade 3

INDICATOR	DEVELOPING	COMPETENT	PROFICIENT
Travels to Open Space (S2.E1.3)	Travels in general space, unable to move to open spaces	Travels in general space, repeatedly moving to open spaces	Travels in general space, seeing open spaces and moving quickly to them
Changes in Speed and Pathways	Travels to open space, but without changes in pathways or speeds	Travels in general space with changes in pathways or speed to move to open spaces	Uses changes in speed and pathways to move to open spaces
Personal Responsibility and Safety (S4.E1.3, S4.E6.3)	Travels to open spaces with seemingly no regard for others (i.e., collisions and near-misses)	Travels to open spaces with no collisions; responds to teacher instruction with correct performance	• Changes speed and/or pathways to accommodate others while traveling to open spaces • Combines speed, pathways to move to open spaces, with consistent awareness of the space of self and others

Grade-Level Outcomes

- Exhibits responsible behavior in independent group situations. (S4.E1.4)
- Works safely with peers and equipment in physical activity settings. (S4.E6.4)
- Accepts players of all skill levels into the physical activity. (S4.E4.4b)

Assessment Task

Using a short-handled paddle or racket (sidearm pattern) strike a ball to the wall, alternating hits with a partner (page 50)

Note: *Station format for practice of skills provides excellent opportunities for teacher observation and assessment of students' exhibiting personal responsibility in independent group situations: working safely, respecting space and practice of others. A simple three-part rubric will serve for recording the observations.*

Guidelines

- Students in Grades 4 and 5 are increasingly involved in partner and group activities; respect for self and others plays a major role in the success of these activities.
- Acceptance of personal and social responsibility cannot be assumed; it must be assessed.
- Opportunities for assessing personal and social behaviors are embedded within the performance and assessments of Standards 1 and 2.

Setup and Equipment

Refer to Standard 1, Grade 4 (S1.E24.4a) for Equipment and Setup, page 50

Scoring Rubric for Striking With Short Implement Combined With Responsible Personal and Social Behavior, Grade 4

INDICATOR	DEVELOPING	COMPETENT	PROFICIENT
Critical Elements Striking (S1.E24.4a)	Demonstrates fewer than 5 of the critical elements for striking with a short implement	Demonstrates all critical elements for striking with a short implement • Racket back in preparation • Coil and uncoil • Step on opposite foot • Swing low to high • Follow through	• Demonstrates all critical elements for striking with a short implement on all 3 attempts • Well-coordinated and well-timed unified motion resulting in smooth striking motion
Force	• Unable to strike with sufficient force to send ball to wall target • Unable to control force resulting in ball landing outside boundaries	• Cannot consistently adjust force within boundaries • Cannot consistently strike above tape line on wall	• Consistently adjusts force to strike ball within boundaries and to wall target • Alternates hits with a partner (S1.E24.4b)
Success	• Cannot complete consecutive hits • Strikes ball after 2 bounces or with no bounce	Completes 5 consecutive hits on only 1 or 2 of the attempts	Demonstrates 5 or more consecutive hits on all attempts
Critical Elements Ball and Body Position	Does not move into position behind the ball	Slight hesitancy in moving into position behind the ball	Moves quickly to be in position behind the ball for each volley
Responsible Personal and Social Behavior (S1. E24.4b, S4.E1.4, S4.E6.4, S4.E4.4b)	• Does not graciously accept partner • Does not alternate hits with partner • Frequent teacher reminders needed for focus on task	• Works willingly with assigned and/or chosen partners • Alternates hits with partner • Practices skills with partner without teacher reminders	• Provides feedback to partner for success • Alternates hits with partner without teacher reminders • Praises partner's striking skills

Personal Responsibility　　　　　　　　　　　　Grade 4

The following Standard 1 and 2 assessments provide additional opportunities for the assessment of Standard 4.

Grade-Level Outcome

Exhibits responsible behavior in independent group situations. (S4.E1.4)

Assessment Task

On signal, begin dribbling in general space, combining pathways, directions and changes in speed to dribble to open spaces (page 70).

Scoring Rubric for Personal Responsibility (While Dribbling to Open Spaces), Grade 4

INDICATOR	DEVELOPING	COMPETENT	PROFICIENT
Personal Responsibility	Dribbles and travels to open spaces with seemingly no regard for others—frequent collisions and/or loss of control of ball	• Dribbles and travels to open spaces with no collisions • Dribbles and travels with control of ball and body	• Combines speed, pathways to dribble and travel to open spaces, with consistent awareness of the space of self and others • Changes speed and/or pathways to accommodate others as they dribble and travel to open spaces

Grade-Level Outcomes

- Works safely with peers and equipment in physical activity settings. (S4.E6.4)

- Accepts players of all skill levels into the physical activity. (S4.E4.4b)

Assessment Tasks

- Catch a ball using both above and below the waist catching patterns (page 40).

- Approach a stationary ball with a running approach and kick with enough force to send it approximately 30 feet along the ground (page 42) and through the air (page 44).

- Punt a ball with enough force to send it a distance of approximately 30 feet (page 46).

Scoring Rubric for Personal and Social Responsibility, Partner Catching, Grade 4

INDICATOR	DEVELOPING	COMPETENT	PROFICIENT
Social Responsibility	Does not accept partner	Positive selection of partner or acceptance of partner assignment	• Positive acceptance of partner • Provides positive feedback to partner on catching assessment
Personal Responsibility	Does not provide "gentle" throws to designated level	Accepts responsibility for "gentle" throws to designated level for partner's catching assessment	Accepts responsibility for "gentle" throws to all 3 designated levels

Scoring Rubric for Personal and Social Responsibility – Safety, Partner Kicking, Grade 4

INDICATOR	DEVELOPING	COMPETENT	PROFICIENT
Social Responsibility	Does not accept partner	Positive selection of partner or acceptance of partner assignment	• Positive acceptance of partner • Provides positive feedback to partner on kicking assessment
Personal Responsibility, Safety	Frequent reminders necessary to stay in safe space and/or retrieve balls	Accepts responsibility for retrieving balls or for staying in safe space throughout partner's kicking assessment	Accepts responsibility for retrieving balls and staying in safe space throughout partner's kicking assessment

Note: *Standards 1 and 2 are filled with Grade-Level Outcomes that focus on partner and small group work in educational gymnastics, dance, and games environments. These interactions provide rich opportunities for the assessment of personal and social responsibility, respect for self and others that can be embedded within the skills rubric found in Standards 1 and 2. Sample Grade-Level Outcomes include S1.E11.4, S1.E14.4b, S1.E15.4, S1.E19.4a, S1.E19.4b, S1.E20.4, S1.E22.4, S1.E24.4b, S1.E26.4.*

Personal and Social Responsibility   Grade 5

It all comes together in Grade 5, the scaffolding of standards for maximizing student learning. Standards are combined for assessment, each building on previous student learning and the assessment of that learning. The following assessments for Grade 5 demonstrate the combining of Standards 1, 2, and 4 for striking with a long implement, a gymnastics sequence, dance design, and games strategy.

Grade-Level Outcomes

- Engages in physical activity with responsible interpersonal behavior (e.g., peer to peer, student to teacher, student to referee). (S4.E1.5)

- Exhibits respect for self with appropriate behavior while engaging in physical activity. (S4.E2.5b)

- Accepts, recognizes, and actively involves others with both higher and lower skill abilities into physical activities and group projects. (S4.E4.5)

Assessment Tasks

- Strike a pitched ball, sending it forward through the air (page 52).

- Strike a ball off a batting tee, sending it a short distance to the target zone; sending it a long distance beyond the target zone (page 74).

- Strike a ball off the batting tee, sending it in a forward direction; sending it to the left target zone (to the right target zone) (page 74).

Guidelines

Class discussions and journal entries will also assist in the teacher's understanding of students' receiving and giving respect for self and others.

Equipment and Setup

Refer to Standards 1 and 2 (S1.E25.5a, S2.E3.5a, 5b) for additional guidelines, equipment needs, and setup for Striking With a Long Implement (pages 52 and 74).

Scoring Rubric for Personal and Social Responsibility, Striking With a Long-Handled Implement, Grade 5 (in combination with S1.E25.5a and S2.E3.5a, 5b)

INDICATOR	DEVELOPING	COMPETENT	PROFICIENT
Social Responsibility	Does not accept member(s) of the group	• Acceptance of members of the group • Includes all members of the group in discussions and "chatter" prior to, during, and after assessment	• Positive acceptance of all members of the group • Includes all members of the group in *all* discussions and "chatter" prior to, during, and after assessment
Personal Responsibility	• Does not accept responsibility for assigned position and/or expectations in the assessment • Does not accept personal batting score and makes excuses	• Accepts responsibility for assigned position and expectations in the assessment • Exhibits personal responsibility upon completion of batting attempts; does not berate self or brag about scores	• Provides positive feedback to batter and praise upon completion of assessment • Accepts personal batting score with satisfaction, neither bragging nor berating self

Gymnastics Sequence   Grade 5

Grade-Level Outcomes

- Engages in physical activity with responsible interpersonal behavior (e.g., peer to peer, student to teacher, student to referee). (S4.E1.5)

- Exhibits respect for self with appropriate behavior while engaging in physical activity. (S4.E2.5b)

- Accepts, recognizes, and actively involves others with both higher and lower skill abilities into physical activities and group projects. (S4.E4.5)

Assessment Tasks

- Design and perform a partner gymnastics sequence on mats with 5 balances and 4 weight transfers (page 54).

- Create a gymnastics sequence of balances, weight transfers, and movement concepts; you may choose to create the sequence, alone, with a partner, on mats or equipment (page 78).

Setup and Equipment

Refer to Standards 1 and 2 (S1.E7.5, S2.E2.5) for additional guidelines, equipment needs and setup for Gymnastics Sequence, pages 54 and 78

Scoring Rubric for Personal and Social Responsibility, Respect for Others (Gymnastics Sequence), Grade 5 (in combination with S1.E7.5 and S2.E2.5)

INDICATOR	DEVELOPING	COMPETENT	PROFICIENT
Respect for Others	• Unable to design gymnastics sequence with partner • Controls sequence composition with no input from partner • Disregards abilities of partner when developing sequence	• Sequence designed with input from both partners • Partners work cooperatively in practice of sequence • Balances and weight transfers selected demonstrate safety for both partners • Sequence components correctly matched to skill level of each partner	• Sequence choreographed between partners from beginning to ending shape (S1.E7.5) • Sequence portrays individual strengths in skills and concepts, creativity in composition (S2.E2.5)

Grade-Level Outcomes

- Engages in physical activity with responsible interpersonal behavior (e.g., peer to peer, student to teacher, student to referee). (S4.E1.5)

- Exhibits respect for self with appropriate behavior while engaging in physical activity. (S4.E2.5b)

- Accepts, recognizes, and actively involves others with both higher and lower skill abilities into physical activities and group projects. (S4.E4.5)

Assessment Tasks

- Design and perform a group dance, combining locomotors and movement concepts (page 56).

- Design and perform a group dance, combining locomotors, nonlocomotors, and spatial concepts (page 76).

Setup and Equipment

Refer to Standards 1 and 2 (S1.E11.5, S2.E1.5) for additional guidelines, equipment needs and setup for Design and Performance of Group Dance, pages 56 and 76

Scoring Rubric for Personal and Social Responsibility, Interpersonal Behavior (Group Dance), Grade 5 (in combination with S1.E11.5 and S2.E1.5)

INDICATOR	DEVELOPING	COMPETENT	PROFICIENT
Social Responsibility, Design	Not all members of the group actively involved in the design of the dance	Actively involves all members of the group in design of dance	Design and performance portrays individual strengths in skills, concepts, creativity
Social Responsibility, Performance (S1.E11.5)	Not all members of the group actively involved	Actively involves all members of group	• Dance choreographed for all members of the group • Dance portrays individual differences and strengths in performance of skills and concepts (S2.E1.5)

Games Strategy

Grade 5

Grade-Level Outcomes

- Engages in physical activity with responsible interpersonal behavior (e.g., peer to peer, student to teacher, student to referee). (S4.E1.5)

- Exhibits respect for self with appropriate behavior while engaging in physical activity. (S4.E2.5b)

- Accepts, recognizes, and actively involves others with both higher and lower skill abilities into physical activities and group projects. (S4.E4.5)

Assessment Task

Move the ball the length of the field, sending and receiving passes, to and from a partner, with the feet (pages 57 and 73). Assessment will be completed with passive defense (cones) and with active defense (2v2).

Setup and Equipment

Refer to Standards 1 and 2 (S1.E19.5a, 5b, S2.E3.5a) for additional guidelines, equipment needs and setup for Games Strategy, pages 57 and 73

Scoring Rubric for Social Responsibility, Interpersonal Behavior (Games Strategy), Grade 5 (in combination with S1.E19.5a, 5b and S2.E3.5a)

INDICATOR	DEVELOPING	COMPETENT	PROFICIENT
Acceptance and Respect for Others	• Unable to cooperate with partner for completion of assessment • Journal entry or exit slip reveals not happy with partner selection	Successfully completes passing and receiving with partner in both passive and active defense situations	• Compliments partner upon completion of assessment • Discusses strategy with partner prior to assessment; cooperatively designs strategy
Alignment of Skill to Partner	• Execution does not match skill for passing ahead of moving partner • Execution does not match skill for adjusting force when passing to partner	• Passes ahead of partner (S1.E19.5a,b) • Matches force of pass to distance of partner (S2.E3.5a,b)	• Adjusts pathways, force, directions, and speed against passive and active defense (S2.E3.5a,b) • Successfully completes passing and receiving with partner against 2 v 2 defense, applying a variety of movement concepts (S2.E3.5a,b)

Standard 5 Sample Assessments

Standard 5: The physically literate individual recognizes the value of physical activity for health, enjoyment, challenge, self-expression and/or social interaction.

All the practice and mastery of skills and all the fitness knowledge are of little worth unless the individual chooses to use the skills and knowledge in being physically active and living a healthy lifestyle. Thus, Standard 5, the recognition of the value of physical activity, becomes the foundation for all other standards in physical education. The contributions of physical activity to health, enjoyment, challenge, self-expression and social interaction lead to a lifestyle of healthful physical activity, which is the goal of physical literacy. Chuck Corbin (2001) said, "Motor skill learning, feelings of enjoyment in activity, and intrinsic motivation are all-important early goals" (p. 353). Young children delight in movement; it is their primary mode of learning. We as teachers seek to maintain that joy in movement as children develop and master the foundational skills of physical education.

The assessment of enjoyment, challenge, self-expression, and social interaction within physical education as well as the recognition of the contribution of physical activity to health begin early for elementary students and continue throughout elementary physical education. Standard 5 assessments are not about performance scores or "correct" answers. The sample assessments that follow are written to provide insight into children's perceptions. The assessment responses are personal; thus, no evaluation rubrics are provided.

Kindergarten and Grade 1 assessments center on class discussions and sharing with others. Students in Grades 2 and 3 complete exit slips and personal entries into journals. Grade 4 students have a homework assignment and completion of rating forms. Student projects are the focus of assessments in Grade 5, providing students with a variety of assessment options and the choice of working alone, with a partner, or in a small group. All the assessments are designed for personal reflection on the value of physical activity.

Grade-Level Outcomes

- Identifies physical activities that are enjoyable. (S5.E3.Ka)

- Discusses personal reasons (i.e., the "why") for enjoying physical activities. (S5.E3.1b)

Assessment Tasks

- **Class Discussion**

  » What was your favorite physical education activity today? Why was that your favorite part of physical education today? What part of class today made you smile?

  » What is your favorite physical activity for recess? What makes that your favorite activity for recess?

  » What did we learn in physical education today? Can you practice this at home, in your neighborhood, with friends, with your family?

- **Tell Your Neighbor:** Tell your neighbor the physical education activities you enjoyed in class today. Then tell your neighbor why those were favorites. After you share with each other, we will share as a class and post them on a wall chart for everyone to see.

- **Bulletin Board:** Have the children draw a picture of their favorite physical activity: physical education class, playground, in the neighborhood. Create a collage of the drawings for a "Favorite Physical Activities" bulletin board in the hallway outside physical education.

Guidelines

- During closure of each physical education lesson, children enjoy relating their favorite activity of the day, what they learned during physical education, and what was challenging. These discussions provide teachers with valuable information for planning future lessons for student learning.

- A portion of the discussion can lead to identifying activities that are enjoyable outside of physical education class: recess, before and after school, in the neighborhood.

- Some children are comfortable sharing in the large group setting; others prefer sharing with a partner, while still others prefer to write or draw by themselves as their way of sharing.

Equipment

- Large chart paper

- Colorful markers

- Drawing paper for individual illustrations

Enjoyment, Challenge   Grade 2

Grade-Level Outcome

Compares physical activities that bring confidence and challenge. (S5.E2.2)

Assessment Tasks

- **Exit Slip:**
    - » Have students complete an open-ended phrase, "My favorite part of physical education class today was…." "The biggest challenge for me in today's lesson was…."
    - » Distributed throughout the year at the completion of a unit of study:
        - My favorite physical education activities are…
        - The activities that are my least favorites are…
        - Why my favorites? Why my least favorites?

- **Journal Entries:**
    - » Have students write a paragraph about their favorite physical activity, identifying the activity and answering the "why" question.
    - » Have students write a paragraph about the physical activity that brings them the biggest challenge and answering the "why" question. Follow this one with the question, "How can I help you with this activity?"

Guidelines

- Children who have confidence in their skills are often eager to join in a discussion of those skills and why they enjoy them; children who are challenged in the skills of physical education are often less eager to share their challenges.

- Students who are less confident in sharing verbally often enjoy writing about their challenges, their feelings in the activities of physical education. Their writings will provide valuable information for interaction, feedback, and their needs in future lessons.

- It is important to respond to journal entries, especially when asking students to share their feelings.

Equipment

- Prepared exit slips
- Student journals
- Pencils

Grade-Level Outcomes

- Discusses the challenge that comes from learning a new physical activity. (S5.E2.3)

- Reflects on the reasons for enjoying selected physical activities. (S5.E3.3)

Assessment Tasks

- Class discussion of the challenge that comes from learning a new skill, the feelings associated with being skilled at an activity and not being skilled; share with neighbor, share with group.

- **Journal Entry - Challenge:**

  » "My biggest challenge in physical education....." followed by:

  » "I would like my teacher to help me with....."

- **Journal Entry - Enjoyment:** Have the students reflect on their favorite physical activities, both inside physical education and outside physical education. With each activity identified the children are to describe their reason(s) for selecting that activity (e.g., skill, play with friends, being part of a team, being outside, etc.). Remind the class that reflection takes a few minutes; it is not a single "one and done" activity.

- Class sharing (optional) may lead to a wall chart of reasons for enjoyment of activity as well as a listing of the many physical activities children are engaged in, both inside and outside the school environment.

Note: *Remind the students that challenge is a part of all new learning: music, art, sports, classroom, etc.*

Guidelines

- **Journal Entry - Challenge**

  » Sharing challenges is not always easy for students; teacher personal sharing of challenges in physical activity helps children realize they are not alone in the challenges of learning new skills.

  » For some children sharing challenges in other areas of learning (e.g., music, art, academics, etc.) helps students realize everyone has strengths and everyone has challenges.

  » End the discussion of challenges with student suggestions for overcoming the challenges.

- **Journal Entry - Enjoyment**

  » Reflection is a skill to be developed in children. Some students will begin writing quickly and finish very quickly; others will sit quietly for several minutes and then begin writing. Be sure to give directions for "when you finish" so others are not disturbed.

  » While some students are eager to share in class discussions, others are very hesitant to verbalize. Journal writing provides all students the means of expressing feelings, joys, and challenges associated with participation in physical activity and learning new skills.

  » Remember to respond to all journal entries.

Note: *If your teaching area does not facilitate the use of student journals (e.g., storage), a single sheet of paper per student will serve the same purpose.*

Equipment

- Student journals

- Notebook paper

- Pencils OR student access to computers

Examining Health Benefits and Social Interaction in Physical Activity

Grade 4

Grade-Level Outcomes

- Examines the health benefits of participating in physical activity. (S5.E1.4)

- Describes & compares the positive social interactions when engaged in partner, small-group and large-group physical activities. (S5.E4.4)

Assessment Tasks

- **Homework Assignment:** Have the students find one artifact (article, research, etc.) relating to physical activity and health.

- Class discussion of articles, research focused on physical activity for good health—beyond just fitness and physical health.

- **Rating Scale:** Have the students complete a rating scale of engaging in partner, small-group, and large-group activities with a listing of the activities and the social interaction each activity provides.

Guidelines

- **Class Discussion**

  - » From their work on health-related fitness, students in Grades 3 and 4 are aware of the components of fitness and activities that contribute to each of those components. Lead the discussion into all health benefits of physical activity (i.e., enjoyment, social interaction, self-confidence, etc.).

  - » Grade 4 students are beginning to develop serious habits of physical vs. sedentary activities, indoor vs. outdoor time after school, active vs. non-active time at recess—in general, active vs. non-active choices. Discussion of the health benefits beyond fitness is very important in this formative stage; the class discussion should be non-threatening with positive information in support of activity.

  - » Children see adults "exercising" for the purpose of losing weight, often leading them to view physical activity as a negative experience. The focus on this discussion is not on losing weight but on the health benefits of physical activity for all children.

  - » Be sensitive to the overweight students in physical education and their feelings during discussions of health and physical activity.

- **Rating Scale**

  - » The purpose of this assessment is for students to evaluate their social interaction and enjoyment within partner, small-group, and large-group activities.

  - » Each assessment is personal in nature and represents the student's perception of the social interaction and enjoyment offered through the activity.

  - » Student engagement in partner, small-group, and large-group activities will need to have taken place before the assessment.

Equipment

- Provide each student with a rating scale and enough personal space to complete the rating.

- Pencils

For an example of a social interaction rating scale see Appendix O.

Grade-Level Outcomes

- Analyzes different physical activities for enjoyment and challenge, identifying reasons for a positive or negative response. (S5.E3.5)

- Expresses (via written essay, visual art, creative dance), the enjoyment and/or challenge of participating in a favorite physical activity. (S5.E2.5)

Assessment Tasks

- **Analysis of Physical Activities:** Listed on the white board are all the physical education activities we have studied this year. Some of them you enjoyed greatly; others were a challenge for you. On your personal worksheet record your response to each of these activities.

  » Column 1 is a listing of the physical education activities.

  » Column 2 is your response to the activity: negative or positive. Place a "plus" or a "minus" sign in the column beside the activity.

  » Column 3 is for you to identify the reasons for your positive or negative response to the activity. You may choose a one- to three-word description for the reaction (e.g., fun, not fun, difficult, fun with friends, challenge, challenge with mastery, etc.) or write a sentence.

    (There are no right or wrong answers; just record your feelings about each activity.)
    The bottom of the worksheet provides space for you to list "out of school" physical activities (e.g., sports, gymnastics, dance, etc). You may add those to your critique of physical activities. For an example of an analysis of physical activities see Appendix P.

- **Welcome to Physical Education:** Pretend a new student has arrived at our school. This student has never had physical education and knows nothing about the things you have been learning in class. Your task is to prepare a presentation to this student that leaves them excited about coming to physical education. You may choose a written "essay" (with or without illustrations), a visual representation of your favorite activity (e.g., sculpture, painting, clay), a finger-puppet show, or a creative dance.

- **Creative Project - Forever Favorite:** This is your last year of physical education at our school. You have learned many things, and hopefully have the joy and confidence to be active forever. Your assignment is this: Choose your favorite activity from all the things you have learned in physical education. Write an essay, create a dance or gymnastics sequence, create a finger-puppet show, create a visual representation (e.g., drawing, sculpture, painting) that shows your favorite activity in physical education, compose a rap or a song. Your presentation may show enjoyment of an activity, practice and mastery, challenge, enjoyment with challenge, or components of physical education you found most valuable to you. If you choose, we will display them in the school hallway for everyone (parents, visitors, other students) to see the special things we do in physical education.

Guidelines

- **Analysis of Physical Activities**

  » This assessment is a continuation of the Grades 3 and 4 assessments:

    - Reflects on the reasons for enjoying selected physical activities. (S5.E3.3)

    - Describes & compares the positive social interactions when engaged in partner, small-group and large-group physical activities. (S5.E4.5)

» Identifying the "why" for a positive or negative reaction provides the teacher with valuable information regarding the reasons for students' positive or negative reactions to physical activity. Your reflection on these responses can provide valuable information for curriculum planning as well as individual student interaction.

» Remind students that analysis, like reflection, takes time. Do not rush their completion of this assessment.

» Remember, prepare in advance for what students will do after they finish the assignment while others are still working.

- **Creative Project - Forever Favorite**

  » Grade 5 students are capable of student projects that extend beyond a single class period, often extending into the classroom and at home. These assessments are examples of student projects, opportunities for students to express recognition of the value of physical education, and the skills they have learned in a very personal project.

  » Students may choose to work alone, with a partner, or in a small group for completion of the assessment.

  » Remind the students they are welcome to involve art, music, and their classroom teacher in their project as well as their parents. While they showcase their favorite learning, others receive a lesson in the value of physical activity for youngsters.

Setup and Equipment

- **Analysis of Physical Activities**

  » Prepared worksheet

  » Pencils

  » Personal space for completion of assessment

- **Creative Project - Forever Favorite**

  » Project paper

  » Pencils

  » Equipment for digital recordings

  » Communication with other teachers regarding the projects and possible requests from students for supplies

Part III

Sample Assessments for
Middle School Physical Education

Standard 1 Sample Assessments

Standard 1: The physically literate individual demonstrates competency in a variety of motor skills and movement patterns.

The Grade-Level Outcomes under Standard 1 for middle school students (Grades 6-8) focus on **applying** motor skill patterns acquired during the elementary school years to sport, dance and physical activities. To enhance student progress in meeting the outcomes, consider developing a mastery-oriented learning environment that emphasizes student improvement and effort. The practice tasks should progress from controlled environments to less-controlled environments that simulate actual game or activity conditions. For games and sports, that means **small-sided** or **modified games**: traditional full-sided game play is not recommended. Students need as many practice opportunities for skill development as possible, and that is more likely to occur in smaller, skill-specific learning experiences than in traditional game play. To improve skill transfer, you can offer instructional units based on content categories (invasion, net/wall, target and fielding/striking games, dance, outdoor pursuits and individual-performance activities), rather than sport-specific units. Many of the games or activities in each category have the same types of fundamental skills or knowledge, so you can draw students' attention to those similarities to enhance the learning process. For example, the forehand strike in pickleball has a similar movement pattern as in other racket sports, such as badminton and tennis.

This section includes sample **assessments** for measuring students' skills and knowledge in games (invasion, net/wall, and fielding/striking), dance, outdoor pursuits and individual-performance activities. While the sample assessments are written for measuring particular skills, you can adapt them for other skills within the category. You can modify the **rubrics** easily to fit similar games or activities. Likewise, you can use the assessments as **formative**, **summative** or peer assessments. **Pre-assessment** is an important component of the assessment process, providing information about your students' skill levels before you plan or implement any learning experiences. Data from the pre-assessment should help you determine entry levels for instruction and practice tasks, as well as providing baseline information for students to set realistic goals for improvement.

Each assessment under Standard 1 includes suggested modifications for applying the task or tool to the outcomes at other grade levels. For example, an assessment written for a particular outcome for Grade 7 includes suggestions for modifying it for Grades 6 or 8. Pay attention to **critical elements** addressed in the outcome when developing your own assessments.

Assessments for Measuring Middle School Students' Skills and Knowledge

The intent of the assessments in this section is to provide you with "samples" that you can modify or adapt to your unique teaching environment. They should not be considered exemplars to be used by all programs as written. You are encouraged to use the sample assessments as a starting point for developing or adapting assessments that meet the needs of your program and students.

The three-level rubrics in these samples use a standard set of terms with common definitions, which is important for providing consistent feedback to students. The **Developing level** denotes students moving toward competency, but these students have not yet mastered all the identified critical elements or **critical components** specific to the indicator. Students at the **Competent level** demonstrate all of the critical elements or components aligned with the indicator. The Competent level defines the minimum level of performance required for meeting the indicator. Students at the **Proficient level** not only demonstrate all the required critical elements or components of the indicator, but their performance also meets additional criteria and/or displays a level of performance that goes beyond Competent. These three terms are used in the same manner in each of the rubric samples.

If you have students with disabilities in your classroom, many of the assessments will need to be modified and adapted. For specific guidance in this area, we recommend *Assessment for Everyone: Modifying NASPE Assessments to Include All Elementary School Children* (Lieberman, Kowalski, et al., 2011).

Throwing in Invasion and Fielding/Striking Games   Grade 6

Grade-Level Outcome

Throws with a mature pattern for distance or power appropriate to the practice task (e.g., distance = outfield to home plate; power = 2nd base to 1st base). (S1.M2.6)

Assessment Task

Throw a hand-size ball for distance or power with a mature throwing pattern.

Pre-Assessment

Throwing a ball using a mature pattern that incorporates all of the skill's critical elements is essential for ensuring student success in many games and activities. Simple passing and catching activities in most invasion or fielding/striking sports can verify a student's ability to perform the overhand throw correctly. It's important to pre-assess students' throwing pattern before asking them to throw for distance and/or power. Any pre-assessment of students' overhand throwing pattern should require students to throw for distance without an accuracy requirement.

Guidelines

- Conduct the assessment during a practice task

- Give special attention to the force and distance required for the type of game and to students' developmental levels

- The purpose is to show whether the student can throw for distance or with power while maintaining a mature throwing pattern

Setup

- To measure distance, have students simulate a throw either from the outfield to home or from second base to home. To measure power, have them simulate a throw from second base to first base.

- Judging distance should be individualized

- Change throwing distances according to developmental level

Modifications for Other Grade Levels

You can modify the assessment task to measure Grade 7 or Grade 8 outcomes. The outcome for Grade 7 (S1.M2.7) requires the task to be performed in a dynamic environment. You can do that by having the thrower move to field the ball and then throw with a mature throwing pattern for distance or power. The Grade 8 outcome (S1.M2.8) requires the task to be performed in a small-sided game, which still allows you to use the rubric that follows.

Critical Elements for Throwing Overhand

- Approach step (e.g., crow hop, shuffle step, etc.) in preparation for throwing action

- Throwing arm takes a downward circular pattern and throwing hand drops below the waist

- Steps with the opposite foot

- Length of the step is greater than half of the student's standing height

- Hips rotate simultaneously with step forward and prior to shoulder rotation

- Forearm is laid back in an L position as hips start to rotate toward target

- Throwing hand points to target in follow-through

- Movements well-coordinated and timed

Scoring Rubric for Throwing in Invasion and Fielding/Striking Games, Grade 6

INDICATOR	DEVELOPING	COMPETENT	PROFICIENT
Critical Elements Mature Throwing Pattern	One or two critical elements not demonstrated: • No approach step • Backswing upward or not in a circular pattern • Steps with same foot as throwing arm • Slight or no hip rotation • Delay or missing L position • No follow-through	Demonstrates all critical elements: • Uses an approach step • Backswing throwing arm takes a downward circular pattern • Appropriate length of step forward • Proper hip rotation • Forearm in L position • Appropriate follow-through	Demonstrates all critical elements • Motion crisp with steady rhythm • Full range of motion
Critical Elements *Distance	• Trajectory too high or too low to reach target • Timing poor or disjointed	• Throw uses a medium trajectory (45 degrees) and reaches target • Movements well-coordinated and timed	• Throw to target with one or no bounces • Smooth and flowing execution
Critical Elements Power	• Throw uses a medium or high trajectory • Arm dominated pattern	• Step ½ length of height • Legs used for push-off	• Elongated step • Well-timed release

*Note: When measuring throwing for distance, it is important to consider power as well. Power can be defined as the combination of strength and speed—the ability to exert maximum force in a quick, explosive burst. Using this concept, it is important to remember that the trajectory of the throw will be different if the objective is distance as opposed to power. In most invasion games, the power of the throw is equally as important as how far the object must travel.

Passing and Receiving   Grade 6

Grade-Level Outcome

Passes and receives with hands in combination with locomotor patterns of running and change of direction & speed with competency in modified invasion games such as basketball, flag football, speedball, or team handball. (S1.M4.6)

Assessment Task

In pairs or groups of three, students pass and receive a ball while moving down the court or field in a modified game. Have students vary their speed and change directions while in motion. If defenders are used, they should be semi-passive.

Guidelines

- Conduct the assessment during a modified invasion game

- Add modification such as using semi-passive defenders, points for crossing boundaries instead of shots on goal, relaxed dribbling rules, etc. Focus students' attention on passing and receiving while in motion, as well as on changing direction and speed, not the game's outcome

- Play each game 3-5 minutes

Setup

- Use a quarter of a football field or a full basketball court

- Students or teacher choose the type of equipment the students will pass and receive

- Students given a choice on such things as the size of the space, partners to play with, defense or no defense

Modifications for Other Grade Levels

You can modify the assessment task to address the relevant outcomes for Grades 7 and 8. Outcome S1.M4.7 requires students to pass and receive with feet. Outcome S1.M4.8 requires they pass and receive using an implement. You can use the rubric that follows for assessing those skills by changing the activity to soccer or speedball for Outcome S1.M4.7 and to floor, field, or ice hockey for Outcome S1.M4.8.

Critical Elements for Passing, Receiving, and Receiving While Running

Chest Pass

- Hands grip ball on the sides, with thumbs directly behind ball

- Elbows bent

- Student steps toward target

- Arms are extended fully when releasing the ball

- Thumbs point down in follow-through

- Pass thrown to a point 1-2 steps ahead of the moving receiver, at a catchable height

Bounce Pass

- Hands grip ball on the sides, with thumbs directly behind ball
- Elbows bent
- Student steps to target
- Arms extended down and out, palms rotating outward
- Bounce is at 2/3rd distance between passer and receiver
- Pass thrown at catchable height

Overhead Pass

- Hands grip ball on sides, with thumbs directly behind ball and fingers spread
- Student steps to target
- Body weight transfers toward front foot
- Arms bent slightly, then brought forward sharply
- Wrist snaps to release the ball
- Pass thrown to a point 1-2 steps ahead of the moving receiver, at a catchable height

Receiving

- Fingertips are spread to receive ball
- Hands only contact the ball, not the body
- Body maintains balance, hands control the ball

Receiving While Running

- Changes direction while running to pass or receive the ball
- Varies speed to pass or receive the ball

Scoring Rubric for Passing and Receiving, Grade 6

INDICATOR	DEVELOPING	COMPETENT	PROFICIENT
Critical Elements Chest Pass	One or two critical elements not present: • Uses improper hand grip • Takes no steps • Limited extension of arms during ball release • Limited follow through • Pass uncatchable	Demonstrates all critical elements: • Proper hand grip • Elbows bent • Steps to target • Arms extended during ball release • Proper follow through • Pass is at a catchable height	Demonstrates all critical elements • Throws pass with appropriate force • Pass catchable at receiver's waist level
Critical Elements Bounce Pass	One or two critical elements not present: • Improper hand grip • No step • Limited extension of arms or no rotation of palms • Pass uncatchable	Demonstrates all critical elements: • Proper hand grip • Elbows bent • Steps to target • Arms extended down and out • Rotation of palms outward • Pass catchable	Demonstrates all critical elements • Pass thrown with appropriate force • Pass catchable at the receiver's chest/waist level
Critical Elements Overhead Pass	One or two critical elements not present: • Improper hand grip • No step • Limited weight transfer • No wrist snap • Pass uncatchable	Demonstrates all critical elements: • Proper hand grip • Steps to target • Weight transfer to front foot • Arms brought forward sharply • Snap of the wrist • Pass catchable	Demonstrates all critical elements • Pass thrown with appropriate force • Pass catchable at the receiver's chest/waist level
Critical Elements Receiving	One or two critical elements not present: • Uses body to help with the catch • Loses balance or does not control the ball	Demonstrates all critical elements: • Receives ball with fingers spread • Catches with hands only • Maintains balance and control	Demonstrates all critical elements • Moves fluidly after receiving ball either to move up court or pass to teammate
Critical Elements Receiving While Running	One or two critical elements not present: • Varies speed and direction for fewer than half the receiving attempts	Demonstrates all critical elements: • Changes direction while running • Varies speed to receive ball	Demonstrates all critical elements • Varies speed and direction to receive pass in majority of attempts • Uses changes in speed and direction to help create open receiving lanes

Note: Many invasion games have multiple ways to pass. This rubric uses a chest pass, but you could use it to assess different types of passes in any invasion games by substituting the appropriate critical elements.

Grade-Level Outcomes

- Performs pivots, fakes and jab steps designed to create open space during practice tasks. (S1.M6.6)

- Executes at least 1 of the following designed to create open space during small-sided game play: pivots, fakes, jab steps. (S1.M6.7)

- Executes at least 2 of the following to create open space during modified game play: pivots, fakes, jab steps, screens. (S1.M6.8)

Assessment Task

This assessment includes multiple offensive skills such as pivots, fakes, and jab steps during a practice task. Each offensive skill should be performed 5 times during the practice task. Students will dribble or run to one of the cones, stop, and demonstrate a pivot, fake, or jab step. Remind students there are many types of fakes. Some of the more common fakes are shot fake, pass fake, look away, jab step, shoulder shrug, and head bob. Students will perform a fake at the cone.

Guidelines

- Performs the assessment during a practice task

- Performs each skill 5 times

Setup

Use a 10-yard by 10-yard grid on the basketball court or outdoor field, depending on the activity. See figure.

Grid Activities

Grid activities are used for small-sided and modified games to keep students focused on the learning objectives and to maximize practice time for each student. The activity that follows is a simple example that you can modify easily to fit your students' needs.

Set up a square with cones. For small groupings, 10 yards by 10 yards usually works well, but you can adjust the size to fit the number of players and the goal of the learning experience. Conduct these types of practice tasks for a set amount of time or number of successful passes to keep players focused.

In this 2 v 1 example, the player with the ball passes to a teammate at the corner, then moves to an open cone. The defender is semi-active, which means he or she may block the passing lane but may not strip the ball from offensive players.

This drill encourages the offensive player to fake before passing and to move to open space. The defender practices recognizing the passing lanes and closing space. When time has elapsed (e.g., 2 minutes), players switch roles.

There are endless variations of grid activities, which are efficient ways of practicing tactics and skills while maximizing the number of practice attempts for each player.

Modifications for Other Grade Levels

You can modify this assessment task to align with the companion Grade 7 and 8 outcomes. Outcome S1.M6.7 for Grade 7 has students execute at least one of the offensive moves in a small-sided game. You can use the same checklist by changing the task to be a 5-minute 2 v 2 game. Outcome S1.M6.8, for Grade 8, has students execute at least two of the offensive moves in a small-sided game. Encourage students to use the offensive skills during game play, and you can use the same rubric.

125

✍ *Peer Checklist for Offensive Skills (Pivot, Fake, and Jab Steps), Grades 6, 7, 8*

Name of performer: _____

Name of observer: _____

For each line on the check sheet use one of the following codes:

A = the movement is absent or some element of the criteria is poorly executed

P = the movement is present and meets all criteria

Checklist for Pivot

- Weight on balls of feet _____
- Feet shoulder-width apart _____
- Pivot foot remains on ground without sliding while the body turns or rotates _____
- Pivots with preferred leg _____
- Pivots with nonpreferred leg _____

Checklist for Fakes

- Ready position on balls of feet with shoulders facing target _____
- Fakes are crisp _____
- Student can perform 2 or more different types of fakes _____

Checklist for Jab Steps

- Ready position on balls of feet with shoulders facing target _____
- Establishes a pivot foot and jab-step foot _____
- Moves jab-step foot and not pivot foot after catching the ball _____
- Stands in an athletic position (not straight up and down) _____

Provide two specific examples of how the performer used the technique effectively:

Make two specific suggestions for how the performance could be improved:

Frequency Counts

List the number of times that you see the skill performed during the activity.
Keep track by putting a hash mark each time you see the skill.

Pivot _____

Fake _____

Jab Step _____

Comments:

_____

Offensive Skills in Invasion Games   Grades 6-8

Grade-Level Outcomes

- Performs the following offensive skills without defensive pressure: pivot, give & go, and fakes. (S1.M7.6)

- Performs the following offensive skills with defensive pressure: pivot, give & go, and fakes. (S1.M7.7)

- Executes the following offensive skills during small-sided game play: pivot, give & go, and fakes. (S1.M7.8)

Assessment Tasks

This assessment includes multiple offensive skills, including pivot, give & go, and fakes during a practice task.

- Pivot – Student dribbles or runs to one of the cones, stops, and demonstrates a pivot.

- Give & go – Student starts on one cone, passes the ball to a partner, and runs quickly to another cone to receive a return pass from the partner.

- Fakes – Student performs a fake at the cone. Remind students that they can use many types of fakes, including shot fake, pass fake, look away, jab step, shoulder shrug, and head bob.

Guidelines

- Perform the assessment during a practice task

- Perform each skill 5 times

Setup

Use a 10-yard by 10-yard grid on the basketball court or outdoor field, depending on activity

Modifications for Other Grade Levels

You can modify this assessment task to align with the companion outcomes for Grades 7 and 8. Outcome S1.M7.7 includes defensive pressure, so you can use the same setup with a semi-passive defender included in the assessment. Outcome S1.M7.8 requires the assessment to occur in a small-sided game. You can use the same rubric by changing the task to a 5-minute 2 v 2 small-sided game. Encourage students to use the offensive skills during game play, while you use the same rubric.

Critical Elements for Offensive Skills in Invasion Games, Grades 6-8

Pivot

- Weight on ball of feet

- Feet shoulder-width apart

- Pivot foot remains on ground without sliding while the body turns/rotates

- Pivot with the preferred leg

Give & Go

- Pass to partner is crisp and catchable

- Moves immediately and quickly to a new spot on the court or field

- Looks for and calls for the ball

- Receives pass with correct form

Fakes

- Ready position, on balls of feet, with shoulders facing target

- Fakes are crisp and convincing

- Uses multiple fakes or combinations

Scoring Rubric for Offensive Skills in Invasion Games, Grades 6-8

INDICATOR	DEVELOPING	COMPETENT	PROFICIENT
Critical Elements Pivot	One or two critical elements not present: • Stands flat-footed or weight on heels • Feet not shoulder-width apart • Pivot foot lifts or slides during rotation of the other foot	Demonstrates all critical elements: • Weight on ball of feet • Feet shoulder-width apart • Pivot foot remains on ground • Body turns or rotates • Pivots with the preferred foot	Demonstrates all critical elements • Can pivot with both the preferred and non preferred foot
Critical Elements Give & Go	One or two critical elements not present: • Throws uncatchable pass • Does not move immediately after the pass • Does not move quickly to the new spot • Eyes not toward partner • Does not call for the ball • Does not catch partner's pass	Demonstrates all critical elements: • Pass crisp and catchable • Moves quickly • Calls for the ball • Receives pass with correct form	Demonstrates all critical elements • Moves fluidly to create passing lane
Critical Elements Fakes	One or two critical elements not present: • Performs 1 or no fakes • Fakes not crisp	Demonstrates all critical elements: • Ready position • Fakes crisp • Performs at least 2 different forms of fakes	Demonstrates all critical elements • Performs more than 2 different forms of fakes

Dribbling and Passing With Foot in Invasion Games   Grades 6-7

Grade-Level Outcome

- Passes and receives with feet in combination with locomotor patterns of running and change of direction and speed, with competency in modified invasion games such as soccer or speedball. (S1. M4.7)

- Foot-dribbles or dribbles with an implement with control, changing speed and direction in a variety of practice tasks. (S1.M9.6)

Assessment Task

Demonstrate a combination of dribbling and passing with foot in a practice task. Students dribble throughout the field looking to pass to a stationary teammate. After passing, passer becomes stationary, and the receiver looks to pass to a different stationary teammate.

Guidelines

Conduct the assessment during a practice task

Setup

- Students in groups of 4

- Place 3 hula hoops per group spread throughout an open field

- Each group has 2 soccer balls

- Every student without a soccer ball stands in a hula hoop (stationary player)

- Students with soccer balls should be spread across the field

Critical Elements for Dribbling and Passing With Feet

Dribble With Inside of Foot

- Body directly behind the ball

- Grounded foot behind and to the inside of the ball while the other foot is slightly off the ground for contact

- Contact with the ball: the toe of the contact foot is pointed out; knee out, foot slightly off the ground, and sole parallel to the ground

- Continuous running action, with repetitive contacts with the ball by either foot

Passing With Foot

- Grounded foot toward target and positioned on side of the ball (approximately 6-12 inches)

- Contact foot raised with toe pointing out, knee pointing out, and ankle joint locked at 90-degree angle

- Leg is drawn backward from the hip in a straight line

- Slight bend in the knee with leg drawn back

- Leg has an appropriate level swing for the amount of force needed for the pass

- Ball contacted with inside of the foot facing the approaching ball

- Ball contacted near its midline

- Passer completes pass with leg follow-through appropriate to the distance of the pass

Scoring Rubric for Foot Dribbling and Passing, Grades 6-7

INDICATOR	DEVELOPING	COMPETENT	PROFICIENT

Critical Elements
Dribbling With Foot
	• One or two critical elements not present:
	  » Improper body position
	  » Improper foot position
	  » Contact with ball not with the instep
	  » No foot alternation
	• Dribbling not controlled
		• Demonstrates all critical elements:
		  » Proper body and foot position
		  » Contacts ball with instep and knees pointed out
		  » Continuous running action
		  » Contacts ball with repetitive contacts from both feet
		• Dribbles in a controlled manner
			Demonstrates all critical elements
			• Continuous running action throughout the task
			• Dribbling controlled and explored with different speed and pathways

Critical Elements Passing	One or two critical elements not present: • Improper foot position • Limited or non-straight backswing • Ball contacted on the sides (instead of midline) • Pass too hard or soft for the distance • Limited follow through • Pass receivable	Demonstrates all critical elements: • Proper foot position • Leg swing straight and fully extended back • Ball contacted on the midline • Pass completed with the appropriate force • Leg follows through to the target • Pass easily controlled by the receiver	Demonstrates all critical elements • Pass with appropriate force • Pass leads receiver and easy to control

Invasion Games – Shooting on Goal   Grade 8

Grade-Level Outcome

Shoots on goal with a long-handled implement for power and accuracy in modified invasion games such as hockey (floor, field, ice) or lacrosse. (S1.M10.8)

Assessment Task

Shoot on goal with power and accuracy in a modified game.

Guidelines

- Perform assessment during a modified 3 v 3 floor hockey game. Modifications include changes in rules, playing space, number of players, etc.

- Purpose is to show whether students can shoot with power and maintain accuracy

- Accuracy judged by how many times the ball goes into goal (without a goalie)

Setup

- To measure distance, use a shooting line that is the same distance as the free throw line to the baseline on a basketball court. Without a shooting line, you will find it difficult to assess student's power.

- Distance of shot changes according to developmental level.

Modifications for Other Grade Levels

The assessment task may be modified for Grade 6 and 7 outcomes. The Grade 6 Outcome S1.M10.6 requires the task to be in a dynamic environment and to only focus on power. This can be captured by having the shooter move to get the ball and then shoot with power without measuring accuracy. The Grade 7 Outcome S1.M10.7 requires the task to be in a small-sided game, which allows the same rubric to be used.

Scoring Rubric for Shooting on Goal, Grade 8

INDICATOR	DEVELOPING	COMPETENT	PROFICIENT
Critical Elements Power and Accuracy	One or two critical elements not present: • Ball or puck shot with a medium speed • Shoots within the goal less than 50% of the time	Demonstrates all critical elements: • Ball or puck shot with a high speed • Shoots within the goal 50% or more of the time	Demonstrates all critical elements • Shoots toward corners or top of goal • Shoots within the goal 70% or more of the time

Grade-Level Outcome

Maintains defensive ready position with weight on balls of feet, arms extended, and eyes on midsection of the offensive player. (S1.M11.6)

Assessment Task

Defensive ready position assessed during a modified invasion game. Students should have their weight on balls of the feet, arms extended, and eyes on the midsection of the offensive player. In groups of 3 or 4, students play a modified invasion game.

Guidelines

- Perform assessment during a modified invasion game

- Modifications include playing boundaries and number of players to ensure capturing the critical elements

- Played for three to five minutes

Setup

- Use a quarter of a football field or a full basketball court

- Type of invasion game used for the assessment determined by teacher or students

Modifications for Other Grade Levels

Grade 7 and 8 outcomes can be assessed using similar guidelines and setup. The rubrics for these outcomes are included on the next two pages.

Critical Elements of the Defensive Ready Position

- Weight on balls of feet

- Arms extended in front of body

- Eyes on midsection of the offensive player

Scoring Rubric for Defensive Ready Position, Grade 6

INDICATOR	DEVELOPING	COMPETENT	PROFICIENT
Critical Elements Ready Position	One or two critical elements not present: • Weight on the heels • Arms not extended • Eyes not on the midsection of the offensive player • Critical elements observed less than half the assessment	Demonstrates all critical elements: • Weight on balls of feet • Arms extended • Eyes on midsection of the offensive player • Critical elements observed the majority (70%) of the assessment	Demonstrates all critical elements • Reacts out of the ready position quickly • Anticipates player or pass direction

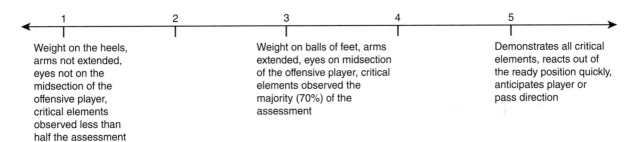

1 — Weight on the heels, arms not extended, eyes not on the midsection of the offensive player, critical elements observed less than half the assessment

3 — Weight on balls of feet, arms extended, eyes on midsection of the offensive player, critical elements observed the majority (70%) of the assessment

5 — Demonstrates all critical elements, reacts out of the ready position quickly, anticipates player or pass direction

Invasion Games – Defensive Skills   Grade 7

Grade-Level Outcome

Slides in all directions while on defense without crossing feet. (S1.M11.7)

Assessment Task

Defensive sliding assessed during a modified invasion game. Students should have their weight on balls of the feet, arms extended, and eyes on the midsection of the offensive player. In groups of 3 or 4, the students play a modified invasion game.

Critical Elements of the Defensive Slide

- Slide feet sideways without crossing them

- Weight on balls of feet

- The steps should be quick and short

- Hips (torso) facing offensive player

- Hips back and knees bent

- Hands up

- Eyes on midsection of the offensive player

Scoring Rubric for the Defensive Slide, Grade 7

INDICATOR	DEVELOPING	COMPETENT	PROFICIENT
Critical Elements Defensive Slides	One or two critical elements not present: • Crosses feet • Weight on heels • Steps slow or too large • Hips turned away from offensive player • Knees straight • Hands down • Eyes on head of offensive player • Critical elements observed less than half the assessment	Demonstrates all critical elements: • Feet do not cross • Weight on balls of feet • Quick and short steps • Hips (torso) facing offensive player • Hips back and knees bent • Hands up • Eyes on midsection of the offensive player • Critical elements observed the majority (70%) of the assessment	Demonstrates all critical elements • Reacts quickly • Able to stay in front of the offensive player • Anticipates player or pass direction

Grade-Level Outcome

Drop-steps in the direction of the pass during player-to-player defense. (S1.M11.8)

Assessment Task

Drop-step assessed during a modified invasion game. Students should have their weight on balls of the feet, arms extended, and eyes on the midsection of the offensive player. In groups of 3 or 4, the students play a modified invasion game.

Critical Elements of the Drop-Step

Ready Position

- Back perpendicular to baseline
- Feet shoulder-width apart
- Weight on balls of feet
- Knees slightly flexed
- Back straight but leaning forward slightly

Drop Step

- Pivot foot (foot farthest from offensive player) points to half court
- Hips open to sideline
- Weight shifts to outside foot (moving toward baseline)
- Pivot foot moves closer to the outside foot

Finish

- Weight shifts back to outside foot
- Pivot foot moves closer to baseline in one giant step

Scoring Rubric for Defensive Drop-Step, Grade 8

INDICATOR	DEVELOPING	COMPETENT	PROFICIENT
Critical Elements Drop-Step	One or two critical elements not present: • Improper ready position • Feet or hips not angled correctly • No weight shift • Small step with pivot foot	Demonstrates all critical elements: • Starts in proper ready position • Weight shifts with pivot foot moving closer to other foot • Giant step with pivot foot toward baseline • Weight moves back to center of feet	Demonstrates all critical elements • Reacts quickly • Stays with offensive player during the assessment

Net/Wall Games – Striking   Grade 7

Grade-Level Outcome

Executes consistently (at least 70% of the time) a legal underhand serve to a predetermined target for net/wall games such as badminton, volleyball or pickleball. (S1.M12.7)

Assessment Task

Perform a legal underhand serve over a net to hit a target on the floor. The goal is for the serve to land within the hula hoop.

Guidelines

- Perform the assessment during a practice task

- 10 attempts per student (taking a break to rest after 5)

Setup

- Use a full badminton, volleyball, or pickleball court

- A hula hoop is placed in each of the back corners of the court for racket sports

- 4-foot by 4-foot grid used for volleyball

- Challenge higher skilled students by placing a poly spot in the hula hoop for racket sports or a small hula hoop for volleyball

Modifications for Other Grade Levels

The assessment task may be modified for Grade 6 outcomes. The Grade 6 Outcome S1.M12.6 requires the student to perform a legal serve without the accuracy requirement. You can use the same rubric but only assess using the first indicator row.

Scoring Rubric for Striking With Consistency and Accuracy, Grade 7

INDICATOR	ATTEMPT 1	ATTEMPT 2	ATTEMPT 3	ATTEMPT 4	ATTEMPT 5
Legal Serve Executes a legal serve					
Accuracy Serve hits the floor inside the hula hoop					
Comments:					

INDICATOR	ATTEMPT 6	ATTEMPT 7	ATTEMPT 8	ATTEMPT 9	ATTEMPT 10
Legal Serve Executes a legal serve					
Accuracy Serve hits the floor inside the hula hoop					
Comments:					

Grade-Level Outcome

Strikes with a mature overhand pattern in a dynamic environment for net/wall games such as volleyball, handball, badminton or tennis. (S1.M13.7)

Note: *The forearm pass is a sport-specific striking skill, not an overhand pattern. For the purpose of this sport-specific assessment, ignore "overhand" in the outcome.*

Assessment Task

Perform a mature forearm pass during a dynamic task.

Guidelines

- Tosser stands on grid opposite passer
- Ball tossed to one of the corners of the grid (unpredictable). Passer will need to move to the corner of the grid and pass the volleyball to tosser.
- For higher skilled students, the tosser can move to a corner of the grid (forcing the passer to pass to a moving player).
- 10 attempts per student (taking a break to rest after 5).

Setup

8-foot by 8-foot grid used for the assessment

Modifications for Other Grade Levels

The assessment task may be modified for Grade 6 and 8 outcomes. The Grade 6 Outcome S1.M13.6 requires the student to perform a mature overhand pattern in a nondynamic environment. You can use the same rubric, but make the tosses predictable or do not make the passer move. The Grade 8 Outcome S1.M13.8 requires the student to perform a mature overhand pattern in a modified game. The same rubric can be used by having the student play a modified volleyball game.

Critical Elements for Volleyball Forearm Pass

- Feet shoulder-width apart in stagger stance
- Body weight forward on the inside front half of each foot with heels slightly off the ground
- Knees flexed approximately 90 degrees
- Hands connected with thumbs even and level (not crossed)
- Grip relaxed with hands extended downward
- Arms in front of body with elbows rotated inward (exposing forearms)
- Forearms parallel
- Ball contact on the fleshy part of the forearm
- Force applied by absorption and a slight shoulder shrug to pass the ball to target (no big arm swings)

Scoring Rubric for Striking, Grade 7

INDICATOR	DEVELOPING	COMPETENT	PROFICIENT
Critical Elements Forearm Volleyball Pass	One or two critical elements not present: • Improper foot and body position • Improper hand and arm position • No shoulder shrug • Ball contacted with hands instead of forearms • Pass not at a medium height and to target	Demonstrates all critical elements: • Proper foot and body position • Proper hand and arm position • Contact with forearms • Shoulder shrug and ball absorption • Pass at appropriate height	Demonstrates all critical elements • Pass with appropriate force • Ability to redirect pass

Net/Wall Games – Forehand and Backhand　　Grade 8

Grade-Level Outcome

Demonstrates the mature form of forehand and backhand strokes with a short- or long-handled implement with power and accuracy in net games such as pickleball, tennis, badminton or paddleball. (S1.M14.8)

Assessment Task

Strike using forehand and backhand strokes with either a short- or long-handled implement for power and accuracy. Students will strike the ball or shuttlecock for power and accuracy by hitting the space within a 4-foot by 4-foot target.

Guidelines

- Perform the assessment during a practice task

- Perform each skill 10 times (taking a break to rest after 5)

- Type of instrument (short or long handled) selected by student or teacher

Setup

- Use a 15-foot by 15-foot grid on the basketball court

- A hula hoop placed in each of the back corners of the court for racket sports

- 4-foot by 4-foot target for volleyball or tennis

- Challenge higher skilled students by placing a poly spot in the hula hoop for racket sports or a hula hoop in the grid for volleyball or tennis

Modifications for Other Grade Levels

The assessment task may be modified for Grade 6 and 7 outcomes. The Grade 6 outcome S1.M14.6 measures the mature form of the forehand and backhand strokes with a short-handled implement. The Grade 7 Outcome S1.M14.7 measures the mature form of the forehand and backhand strokes with a long-handled implement. Use the rubric without assessing for power and accuracy for both the Grade 6 and 7 outcomes.

Note: *Racket sports such as pickleball and tennis could use critical cues specific to the forehand and backhand swings with minor modifications.*

Critical Elements for Forehand and Backhand Clear

Forehand and Backhand Ready Position

- Bend slightly at knees with feet shoulder-width apart

- Weight on balls of feet

- Head up with shoulders parallel to net

- Racket edge parallel to ground

- Racket at waist level

Forehand Overhead Clear

- Grip
    - » Handshake with racket using preferred hand
    - » "V" formed by thumb and forefinger is on top of grip
    - » Throat of racket supported lightly with nonpreferred hand

- Backswing
  - » Turn with preferred foot dropping back (pivot on nonpreferred foot)
  - » Racket brought back behind the shoulders in a "back-scratching" position: arm bent, elbow parallel to the floor
  - » Lead shoulder facing net
  - » Weight on back foot
- Forward swing
  - » Contact shuttle at the highest point possible
  - » Contact shuttle slightly in front of body
  - » Moment of contact
    - Forearm rotates outward
    - Wrist snaps quickly, racket head faces slightly upward at contact
  - » Shift weight from back to front foot
  - » Turn with hips creating torque
- Follow through
  - » Racket arm crossing body in the direction of the non-racket side
  - » Square shoulders to the net
  - » Return to ready position with weight on balls of feet

Backhand Overhead Clear

- Grip
  - » "V" formed with thumb and forefinger is a quarter turn from forehand grip
  - » Preferred palm on top of racket handle
  - » Throat of racket supported lightly with nonpreferred hand
- Backswing
  - » Turn with preferred foot stepping forward (pivot on nonpreferred foot)
  - » Lead shoulder facing net
  - » Weight on back foot
  - » Twist racket arm inward to raise elbow and drop the hand
  - » Uncoil the arm by performing an external rotation of the upper arm and supination of the forearm
- Forward swing
  - » Tighten grip by pressing with the thumb
  - » Contact shuttle slightly in front of body
  - » Shift weight from back to front foot by stepping toward the net
  - » Keep racket edge parallel to ground throughout swing
- Finish
  - » After hitting shuttle, immediately stop the racket and let it rebound back
  - » Return to ready position with weight on balls of feet

Scoring Rubric for Forehand, Grade 8

INDICATOR	DEVELOPING	COMPETENT	PROFICIENT
Critical Elements Grip	One or two critical elements not present: • Palm on top of handle • Baseball grip with no "V" with thumb and forefinger	Demonstrates all critical elements: • Handshake with racket using preferred hand • "V" formed by thumb and forefinger on top of grip • Throat of racket supported lightly with nonpreferred hand	Demonstrates all critical elements • Grip relaxed without unnecessary tension
Critical Elements Backswing	One or two critical elements not present: • Shoulders remain facing net • Pivot disconnected from turn • No backswing or preparation observed	Demonstrates all critical elements: • Turn with preferred foot dropping back (pivot on nonpreferred foot) • Back-scratching technique used • Lead shoulder facing net and weight on back foot	Demonstrates all critical elements • Back-scratching technique used to its fullest • Well-timed backswing with pivot
Critical Elements Forward Swing	One or two critical elements not present: • Contact with arm bent • Ball contacted off back foot • No weight shift or weight shift badly timed • Weak wrist snap on contact	Demonstrates all critical elements: • Contact at highest point possible • Contact shuttle slightly in front • Shift weight from back to front • Forearm rotates and wrist snaps quickly on contact	Demonstrates all critical elements • Well-coordinated and well-timed unified motion • Demonstrates a full range of motion resulting in both power and accuracy
Critical Element Follow-Through	One or two critical elements not presents: • Abbreviated follow-through • Shoulders remain sideways to net • Ready position not evident	Demonstrates all critical elements: • Follow-through • Square shoulders to the net • Return to ready position with weight on balls of feet	Demonstrates all critical elements • Full range of motion on follow-through • Achieves ready position with weight on balls of feet and racket forward
Critical Elements Power and Accuracy	One or two critical elements not present: • Shuttle hit with a medium or high trajectory (above 15 degrees) • Lands within hula hoop less than 50% of the time	Demonstrates all critical elements: • Shuttle hit with a low and hard trajectory (15 degrees) • Lands within the hula hoop 50% or more of the time	Demonstrates all critical elements • Lands within the hula hoop 70% or more of the time

Scoring Rubric for Backhand, Grade 8

INDICATOR	DEVELOPING	COMPETENT	PROFICIENT
Critical Elements Grip	One or two critical elements not present: • Thumb and forefinger not a quarter turn from forehand grip • Preferred palm on the side or below the racket handle	Demonstrates all critical elements: • "V" formed with thumb and forefinger in a quarter turn from forehand grip • Preferred palm on top of racket handle • Throat of racket supported lightly with nonpreferred hand	Demonstrates all critical elements • Grip relaxed without unnecessary tension
Critical Elements Backswing	One or two critical elements not present: • Shoulders remain facing net • No backswing or preparation observed • Elbow down and hand up (very common)	Demonstrates all critical elements: • Turn with preferred foot stepping forward (pivot on nonpreferred foot) • Turn with hips creating torque • Elbow up and hand down • Lead shoulder facing net	Demonstrates all critical elements • Full range of motion evident in backswing
Critical Elements Forward Swing	One or two critical elements not present: • Loose grip • Wrist not firm during the swing • Shuttle contacted parallel to body • No weight shift • No torque	Demonstrates all critical elements: • Tighten grip by pressing with the thumb • Wrist kept firm while swinging • Contact shuttle slightly in front of body • Shift weight from back to front foot	Demonstrates all critical elements • Well-coordinated and well-timed unified motion • Full range of motion resulting in both power and accuracy
Critical Elements Follow-Through	One or two critical elements not present: • Full follow-through • Ready position not evident	Demonstrates all critical elements: • After contacting shuttle, immediately stop the racket and let it rebound back • Return to ready position with weight on balls of feet • Weight on back foot	Demonstrates all critical elements • Full range of motion on follow-through • Assumes ready positon with weight on balls of feet and racket forward
Critical Elements Power and Accuracy	One or two critical elements not present: • Shuttle hit with a medium or high trajectory (above 15 degrees) • Lands within hula hoop less than 50% of the time	Demonstrates all critical elements: • Shuttle hit with low and hard trajectory (15 degrees) • Lands within hula hoop 50% or more of the time	Demonstrates all critical elements • Lands within the hula hoop 70% or more of the time

Net/Wall Games – Weight Transfer   Grade 6

Grade-Level Outcome

Transfers weight with correct timing for the striking pattern. (S1.M15.6)

Assessment Task

Evaluated on weight transfer using a short- or long-implement racket in a net/wall activity. A student will toss the ball or hit the shuttlecock while the partner will strike it using proper weight transfer.

Guidelines

- Perform the assessment during practice tasks
- 10 attempts per student (taking a break to rest after 5)
- Use assessment criteria only with specific grade-level outcome
- Student chooses forehand or backhand in 6th grade assessment
- Students or teacher chooses what type of short-handled implement to use for the 7th grade assessment
- Students or teacher chooses what type of long-handled implement to use for the 8th grade assessment

Setup

Use a 15-foot by 15-foot grid

Modifications for Other Grade Levels

The Grade 7 and 8 outcomes can be assessed using the same guidelines and setup. The rubrics for these outcomes are included on the next two pages.

Scoring Rubric for Weight Transfer With Implement, Grade 6

INDICATOR	DEVELOPING	COMPETENT	PROFICIENT
Critical Elements Weight Transfer	Timing of weight transfer early or late limiting power	Transfers weight with correct timing	Transfers weight with correct timing and optimizing power

Grade-Level Outcome

Transfers weight with correct timing using low-to-high striking pattern with a short-handled implement on the forehand side. (S1.M15.7)

Scoring Rubric for Weight Transfer, Short-Handled Implement, Grade 7

INDICATOR	DEVELOPING	COMPETENT	PROFICIENT
Critical Elements Weight Transfer With Short-Handled Implement	Timing of weight transfer early or late, limiting power	Transfers weight with correct timing using low-to-high striking pattern	Transfers weight with correct timing and optimizes power applied in the low-to-high striking pattern

Net/Wall Games – Weight Transfer   Grade 8

▩ Grade-Level Outcome

Transfers weight with correct timing using low-to-high striking pattern with a long-handled implement on the forehand and backhand sides. (S1.M15.8)

Scoring Rubric for Weight Transfer, Long-Handled Implement, Grade 8

INDICATOR	DEVELOPING	COMPETENT	PROFICIENT
Critical Elements Weight Transfer With Long-Handled Implement	Timing of weight transfer is early or late, limiting power in the striking pattern	Transfers weight with correct timing using low-to-high striking pattern	Transfers weight with correct timing and optimizes power applied in the low-to-high striking pattern

Grade-Level Outcome

Performs consistently (70% of the time) a mature pattern with accuracy and control for 1 target game such as bowling or bocce. (S1.M18.8)

Assessment Task

Perform a mature underhand throw with accuracy and control to a target according to the sport or activity.

Guidelines

- 10 attempts per student (taking a break to rest after 5)

- Target determined by the activity (example: pins for bowling, the pit and pole for horseshoes, etc.)

Setup

Use a full or modified court or field depending on equipment and resources

Critical Elements of the Underhand Throw

Ready Position

- Weight evenly distributed on both feet in the stance

- Step off on opposite foot

- Knees bent

- Eyes on target

- Shoulders square to target

Swing

- Lean forward slightly

- Keep arm straight and let it fall down and back

- Retrace the same arc on the forward swing

- Pitch smooth and rhythmic

Release

- Extension of body and arm resulting in proper lift

Modifications for Other Grade Levels

The assessment task may be modified for Grade 6 and 7 outcomes. The Grade 6 Outcome S1.M18.6 requires the student to perform a mature throw without accuracy requirements. You can use the rubric by eliminating the accuracy indicator. The Grade 7 Outcome S1.M18.7 requires students to perform the mature throw with 70% consistency. Use the modified Grade 6 rubric and document the number of successful (mature throwing pattern) throws (see second rubric). The percentage can then be calculated.

Note: *Cornhole was used for the rubric, but any critical elements for the underhand throw can be inserted in the rubric.*

Scoring Rubric for Underhand Throw, Grade 8

INDICATOR	DEVELOPING	COMPETENT	PROFICIENT
Critical Elements Ready Position	One or two critical elements not present: • Weight not distributed evenly • Step with same foot • Straight legs • Shoulders not squared with target	Demonstrates all critical elements: • Weight evenly distributed on both feet in the stance • Step off on opposite foot • Knees bent • Eyes on the target • Shoulders square to target	Demonstrates all critical elements • Ready position relaxed
Critical Elements Swing	One or two critical elements not present: • Leaning back or no lean • Arm bends during swing • Pitch motion choppy	Demonstrates all critical elements: • Lean forward slightly • Keep arm straight and let it fall down and back • Retrace the same arc on the forward swing • Pitch smooth and rhythmic	Demonstrates all critical elements • Full range of motion evident
Critical Elements Release	One or two critical elements not present: • No extension	Demonstrates all critical elements: • Extension of body and arm resulting in proper lift	Demonstrates all critical elements • Well-coordinated and well-timed unified motion • Full range of motion resulting in both power and accuracy
Critical Elements Power and Accuracy	One or two critical elements not present: • Beanbag lands on the board less than 70% of the time	Demonstrates all critical elements: • Beanbag falls on the board at least 70% of the time	Demonstrates all critical elements • Beanbag falls on the board 70% or more of the time • Beanbag goes through the hole 25% of the turns

Modified Scoring Rubric to Check for Consistency, Grade 8

INDICATOR	1	2	3	4	5	6	7	8	9	10
Demonstrates all critical elements of ready position, swing, and release										
Accuracy Underhand throw lands on board										

Check (√) to indicate if critical elements of performance were met.

Comments:

Grade-Level Outcome

Strikes a pitched ball with an implement for power to open space in a variety of small-sided games. (S1.M20.8)

Assessment Task

Strike a hand-sized pitched ball for power during a modified fielding and striking game (Wiffle ball, softball, etc.). After striking the ball, the hitter should run back and forth between the pitcher's plate and home plate as many times as possible before the ball is returned to home plate.

Guidelines

- Perform the assessment during a small-sided game
- Small-sided game consists of 3 students (fielder, pitcher, and batter)
- 10 swings per student, rotating after 2 swings
- Power judged by a hard swing and the ball traveling past pitcher
- Students or teacher chooses type of striking activity used

Setup

- A cone or base set up for a pitcher plate and home plate
- Distance between pitcher plate and home plate based on the type of ball being thrown and developmental level of the students

Modification for Other Grade Levels

The Grade 6 and 7 outcomes can be assessed using similar guidelines and setup. The Grade 6 Outcome S1.M20.6 requires the student to hit with force during a practice task. This can be accomplished with a task where students pair up and pitch the ball to each other (use the same checklist but do not assess for power and open space indicators). The Grade 7 Outcome S1.M20.7 requires the student to strike the ball into open space, so the same checklist can be used without the power indicator. For an example of frequency count assessment see Appendix Q.

✍ *Scoring Checklist for Striking a Pitched Ball With Power and to Open Space, Grade 8*

Name of student: _____

Contacts the ball with sweet spot of bat (last 1/3rd of bat)	Yes	No
Hit ball travels fast past the pitcher	Yes	No
Hit ball travels to open space	Yes	No

Outdoor Pursuits   Grade 8

▇ Grade-Level Outcome

Demonstrates correct technique for basic skills in at least 2 self-selected outdoor activities. (S1.M22.8)

▇ Assessment Task

Demonstrate correct outdoor pursuit skills during a practice trial or modified activity. Geocaching and pedaling (mountain bike) rubrics are provided as examples.

▇ Guidelines

- Perform assessment during a practice task or modified activity

- Depending on the activity, attempts (10 trials) or time (5 minutes) should be used

▇ Setup

Depending on the outdoor pursuit activity, you should observe skills from a distance, where you can observe skills in their entirety.

▇ Modifications for Other Grade Levels

The assessment task may be modified for Grades 6 and 7. The Grade 6 Outcome S1.M22.6 requires the student to perform basic skills from one outdoor pursuit. You can use one (not both) of the rubrics provided. The Grade 7 Outcome S1.M22.7 requires a variety of skills from one self-selected outdoor activity. As an example, you could use the pedaling rubric and add braking or lifting wheels as two skills from mountain biking.

Scoring Rubric for Geocaching, Grade 8

INDICATOR	DEVELOPING	COMPETENT	PROFICIENT
Critical Elements Uses GPS	One or two critical elements not present: • Difficulty using basic features of the GPS • Difficultly creating coordinates and/or waypoints • Cannot find more than 1 waypoint	Demonstrates all critical elements: • Uses features of the GPS to find waypoints • Creates coordinates and waypoints in the GPS • Finds 2-3 waypoints using the GPS	Demonstrates all critical elements: • Uses all the features of the GPS • Creates multiple coordinates and waypoints in the GPS • Finds more than 3 waypoints using the GPS

Scoring Rubric for Pedaling – Mountain Bike, Grade 8

INDICATOR	DEVELOPING	COMPETENT	PROFICIENT
Critical Elements Pedals	One or two critical elements not present: • No pushing down but using a circular motion with pedal stroke • Hips not driven forward • Spine leaned forward or back	Demonstrates all critical elements: • Pushing down with pedal stroke • Hips driven forward toward handlebars • Spine straight up	Demonstrates all critical elements • Rapid pedal rotation

Grade-Level Outcome

Demonstrates correct technique for basic skills in at least 2 self-selected individual-performance activities. (S1.M24.8)

Assessment Task

Demonstrate the correct individual-performance skill during a practice trial or modified activity. In-line skating and track and field are provided as examples.

Guidelines

- Perform assessment during a practice task or modified activity
- Depending on the activity, attempts (10 trials) or time (5 minutes) should be used

Setup

- Depending on the outdoor pursuit activity, you should observe skills from a distance, where you can observe skills in their entirety.
- For the shot put, a modified shot or softball is used.

Modifications for Other Grade Levels

The assessment task may be modified for Grades 6 and 7. The Grade 6 Outcome S1.M22.6 requires the student to perform basic skills in one individual-performance activity. You can use one (not both) of the rubrics provided. The Grade 7 Outcome S1.M22.7 requires a variety of skills from one self-selected individual-performance activity. As an example, you could use the shot-put rubric and add any of the other track and field events as two activities from track and field.

Scoring Rubric for In-Line Skating – Jumping and Landing, Grade 8

INDICATOR	DEVELOPING	COMPETENT	PROFICIENT
Critical Elements Jump and Land for In-Line Skating	One or two critical elements not present: • Stands straight before and after movement • Feet not in a V or T position • No use of arms for balance • Difficulty maintaining balance • No use of brake when needed	Demonstrates all critical elements: • Maintains a slightly crouched position before and after movement • Feet begin in a V or T position • Use arms for balance • Bend knees to land softly and regain balance immediately • Brakes to regain balance	Demonstrates all critical elements • Maintains rhythm while jumping and landing

Critical Elements for the Shot Put

Grip and Shot Placement

- Weight of the shot placed where fingers meet the palm of the hand
- Shot held against the neck, under the jaw bone, and underneath the ear

Starting Position

- Putter stands at back of circle
- Preferred foot in the 11 o'clock position on the line of direction
- Eyes focused on a focal point in back of circle
- Non-throwing arm and shoulder kept square and held back

Glide

- Putter drops down over the dominant leg, raising the other leg
- Nonpreferred leg makes a swinging motion toward throwing direction
- Dominant leg pushes across circle
- Putter uses a ball-to-heel motion glide
- Preferred leg snaps underneath thrower
- Preferred leg ends in a 9 o'clock position
- Nonpreferred leg ends in a 5 o'clock position
- Backswing

Throwing Position

- Putter feet and hips turned to the left side of the circle
- Head faces the back of circle
- Body weight over the preferred leg
- Knees bent
- Non-throwing elbow thrust back toward middle
- Hips lead the shoulder to throw
- Throwing arm extends
- Wrist snaps forward

Scoring Rubric for Shot Put, Grade 8

INDICATOR	DEVELOPING	COMPETENT	PROFICIENT
Critical Elements Grip and Shot Placement	One or two critical elements not present: • Improper hand placement of shot • Improper shot placement	Demonstrates all critical elements: • Proper hand and finger placement • Shot against neck under jaw bone	Demonstrates all critical elements: • Grip and shot placement well-coordinated
Critical Elements Starting Position	One or two critical elements not present: • Improper starting position • Improper foot placement • Non-throwing arm and shoulder not squared	Demonstrates all critical elements: • Proper starting position • Proper foot placement • Eyes on a focal point • Non-throwing arm and shoulder kept square	Demonstrates all critical elements: • Putter coil position to increase torque
Critical Elements Glide	One or two critical elements not present: • No drop to initiate glide • Limited leg swing and push • Incorrect ending glide position • Shot putter uses a hopping or jumping movement	Demonstrates all critical elements: • Shot putter first drops down • Nonpreferred leg swings toward the throwing direction • Leg push evident • Ball-to-heel motion glide used • Dominant leg ends in a 9 o'clock position • Legs end in 9 and 5 o'clock positions	Demonstrates all critical elements: • Shot putter glide well-timed with unified motion
Critical Elements Release Position	One or two critical elements not present: • Improper feet and hips position • Head facing wrong direction • Knees not bent • Limited thrust of non-throwing elbow • Arm leads throw instead of shoulder • No arm extension or wrist snap	Demonstrates all critical elements: • Shot putter feet and hips placement • Weight over the preferred leg • Knees bent • Non-throwing elbow thrust evident • Hips lead the shoulder • Extension of throwing arm • Wrist snaps forward	Demonstrates all critical elements: • Shot putter release is well-coordinated with a unified motion

Grade-Level Outcome

Demonstrates correct rhythm and pattern for 1 of the following dance forms: folk, social, creative, line or world dance. (S1.M1.6)

Assessment Task

Perform either a folk, social, creative, line or world dance using correct rhythm and pattern.

Pre-Assessment

A basic rhythm identification task can be conducted before teaching traditional dances. Clapping or dribbling a basketball to a beat can help identify the ability to stay on a beat. Other rhythmic activities include rhythm sticks, Lummi stick routines, jump roping, and drumming fitness.

Guidelines

- Dance selected by teacher or student
- Review dance steps and sequence before assessment
- Assessment completed individually or in small groups
- Dance performed with music and in its entirety

Setup

- No more than 6-8 students in a group
- Enough space to move freely
- Space available for both individual and group practice/rehearsal

Modifications for Other Grade Levels

The assessment task may be modified to fit Grade 7 Outcome S1.M1.7 by having students perform a dance from two different categories.

Dance is a form of expression in which many movement concepts and skills are performed. Moving to a rhythm can come easily to some but can be harder for others. Many students might cringe at the thought of being assessed on dance, but it is an important component of any physical education program. The Grade-Level Outcomes do not provide a set of specific dances. It is important to choose an appropriate dance form or dance that best fits students' needs.

The critical elements listed below are general dance assessment indicators for dance technique and execution. They are readily transferrable to different forms of dance. You may add specific criteria such as the number of steps, shapes, or other skills to the rubric as needed.

Critical Elements for Dance

Technique/Line

- Uses correct posture
- Vertical alignment of body while still and moving
- Body alignment maintained during transitions
- Turns, head spot
- Agility and coordination in execution of combinations
- Full extension of body parts

- Shapes clear with correct orientation and alignment

- Space – space occupied by body including direction, size, pathways, levels and shapes

- Time – relationship of one movement to another including pulse, tempo, rhythm and phrases

Timing/Memorization

- Correct count maintained

- Accurate in beat and tempo

- Changes in tempo and pacing

- Steps and sequences memorized and executed with precision

Performance

- Uses entire dance area

- Communicates emotions and ideas through movement

- Demonstrates creativity by using prop(s) and/or costuming, unique combinations/shapes/transitions

- Demonstrates focus, projection, and energy

- Choice of music enhances performance

- Demonstrates a variety of motion/body movements such as percussive, sustain, swing, collapse, suspend, and/or vibratory

Scoring Rubric for Dance and Rhythms, Grade 6

INDICATOR	DEVELOPING	COMPETENT	PROFICIENT
Critical Elements Technique/Line	• Vertical alignment and posture weak with loss of control • Difficulty remaining in balance while moving and holding poses (still movements) • Limited flexibility with reductions in extensions with spine, legs, and/or shoulders • Movements lack flow and coordination with hesitations or missteps throughout • Multiple technique mistakes evident	• Maintains posture with occasional lapses (less than 20% of the time) • Vertical alignment maintained while still and/or moving • Demonstrates flexibility 　» Spine 　» Legs 　» Shoulders • Shapes clear with correct orientation or alignment • Agility and coordination with combinations	• Maintains posture throughout • Vertical alignment maintained while still and moving • Shapes clear with correct orientation and alignment • Agility and coordination with combinations, transitions, beginning and ending of phases
Critical Elements Timing/Memorization	• Difficulty with maintaining count, beat, and/or tempo • Seems lost with evident missteps • No changes in tempo and pace • Obvious sequence mistakes and reliance on following others • Little or no precision in movements	• Correct count with accurate beat/tempo with only minor variations (less than 20% of the time) • Changes in tempo and pace evident • Steps and sequence memorized with only minor hesitations evident • Steps and movements executed with precision	• Correct count with accurate beat/tempo • Unique changes in tempo and pace evident • Steps and sequence executed with confidence and no hesitations • Steps and movements executed with precision and full extensions
Critical Elements Performance	• Limited use of dance area, which restricts the exploration of space and time • Lacks creativity with limited variety of motions/body movements • Same motions/body movements/steps repeated throughout • Low energy, limited projection and focus	• Explores relationships of space and time • Uses all four corners of dance area • Demonstrates creativity using at least two from list below: 　» Props or costumes 　» Unique combinations 　» Unique shapes 　» Unique transitions 　» Choice of music • Communicates emotions/ideas • Demonstrates focus, projection, and energy	• Demonstrates unique exploration of space and time • Uses entire dance area • Demonstrates creativity using at least four from list below: 　» Props or costumes 　» Unique combinations 　» Unique shapes 　» Unique transitions 　» Choice of music

Standard 2 Sample Assessments

Standard 2: The physically literate individual applies knowledge of concepts, principles, strategies and tactics related to movement and performance.

Learning experiences and assessments in middle school (Grades 6-8) should integrate the application of skills and knowledge. Students are expected to learn the how, when and why of **tactics** and **strategies**. The cognitive aspect of physical education content may increase student motivation to learn by increasing the level of challenge that students experience. You should incorporate decision-making in learning experiences and practice tasks to help students make the connection between the outcomes in Standard 2 and the sports and physical activities in the curriculum.

Most of these sample assessments are rubrics, **checklists**, and projects but traditional quizzes, worksheets, and exams can also be used to assess outcomes. Like the Standard 1 assessments, many of the Standard 2 assessments can be used with different physical activities within the content category by modifying the critical elements or components in the rubric. Within each game category (invasion, fielding/striking, target, net/wall), the tactics, skills, and strategies are common, so the rubrics will only need minor changes to be relevant to different games within the same category. Focusing on these common tactics and strategies enables students to make connections among the different sports in the curriculum and facilitates the transfer of learning. For example, creating open space in team handball is very similar to creating open space in any invasion game. With the limited time available to many physical education programs across the country, it is important to have contextual transfer throughout the physical education curriculum.

When assessing Standard 2, it may be helpful to evaluate performance in a sport or activity with lower technique requirements so that learners focus more on strategies and tactics rather than on executing Standard 1 skills. Many of the Standard 2 assessments are generic, so students may choose a sport or activity they are more confident in to demonstrate Standard 2 outcomes. While the primary emphasis of Standard 2 assessments is cognitive (the how, what and why), skill acquisition can be a secondary function of these assessments.

Grade-Level Outcome

Opens and closes space during small-sided game play by combining locomotor movements with movement concepts. (S2.M1.8)

Assessment Task

Use a combination of locomotor movements and movement concepts to open and close space in a small-sided game.

Pre-Assessment

Any of the critical components for creating or reducing space can be practiced and assessed before placing students in a small-sided game. The physical skills can be assessed, and a short written quiz or video skill analysis assignment also can be helpful before using this assessment. Students should learn and be assessed on why and how the locomotor movements and movement concepts are important in creating and reducing space in invasion games as well as the actual movement skills.

Guidelines

- Perform the assessment during a small-sided game

- Select and/or modify any invasion game

- Participate in practice tasks or modified game for 5-8 minutes

- Create and reduce space throughout the game

- Ensure field or course dimensions are not too large or too small

- Adjust field or court size as necessary

Setup

4-yard by 4-yard space (increased or decreased depending on the game and/or available space)

Modifications for Other Grade Levels

The assessment task may be modified for Grade 6 and 7 outcomes. The Grade 6 Outcome S2.M1.6 measures the ability to create space by combining locomotor movements with movement concepts. Use only the creating space indicators and have the students perform the assessment in a practice task or small-sided game. The Grade 7 Outcome S2.M1.7 measures the ability to reduce space by combining locomotor movements with movement concepts. Use only the reducing space indicators and have the students perform the assessment in a practice task or small-sided game.

Critical Components of Creating or Reducing Space With Movement

Creating Space

- Varies pathways while walking/running

- Changes or varies speed

- Changes direction quickly

- Uses fakes, pivots, changes of pace

Reducing Space

- Changes body shape or size

- Reduces the angle in space

- Reduces distance between players or goal

✍ *Peer Checklist for Creating and Reducing Space With Movement, Grade 8*

Name of performer: _____

Name of observer: _____

For each line on the checklist use one of the following codes:

A = the movement is absent or some element of the criteria is executed poorly

P = the movement is present and meets all criteria

Checklist for Creating Space

- Varies pathways while walking/running _____
- Changes or varies speed _____
- Changes direction quickly to create space _____
- Uses fakes, pivots, changes of pace _____

Checklist for Reducing Space

- Changes body shape or size _____
- Reduces the angle in space _____
- Reduces distance between players or the goal _____

Provide one example of how a player created open space during the game and what the result was:

Provide one example of how a player closed open space during the game and what the result was:

Frequency Counts

In this section, place a hash mark for each time you see the player use the skill during the practice task or modified game.

Varies pathways _____

Varies speed _____

Changes direction _____

Uses fakes, pivots, changes of pace _____

Changes body shape or size _____

Reduces angles _____

Reduces distance between players or the goal _____

Comments:

_____

Scoring Rubric for Creating Space With Movement, Grade 8

INDICATOR	DEVELOPING	COMPETENT	PROFICIENT
Creates Space	One or two critical components not present: • Uses the same pathway throughout game • One speed at all times • Routinely uses the same direction • No fakes, pivots or change of pace • Creates open space less than 50% of the time	Demonstrates all critical components: • Changes pathways • Varies speed • Changes direction • Fakes, pivots, or change of pace • Creates open space at least 51% of the time	Demonstrates all critical components • Movements quick and unpredictable • Fakes, pivots, and change of pace
Reduces Space	One or two critical components not present: • Does not change body size or shape • Limited use of reducing angles and/or distance • Demonstrates reducing space movements less than 50% of the small-sided game	Demonstrates all critical components at least once: • Changes body size or shape • Reduces angles • Reduces distance • Reduces space movements the majority of the small-sided game	Demonstrates all critical components two or more times

Invasion Games – Creating Space With Offensive Tactics   Grade 8

Grade-Level Outcome

Executes at least 3 of the following offensive tactics to create open space: moves to create open space on and off the ball; uses a variety of passes, fakes and pathways; give & go. (S2.M2.8)

Assessment Task

Use a combination of tactics to create open space.

Pre-Assessment

Any of the tactics for creating space can be practiced and assessed before students perform the assessment. Many of the physical elements of the tactics were taught and assessed using Standard 1 assessments, but the how and why should be assessed as well. Exit slips, video analysis of invasion game play focusing on when players used or did not use the tactics, quizzes, etc. can all be used to help students learn or provide feedback to students on the use of tactics in invasion games.

Guidelines

- Perform the assessment during a small-sided game
- Any invasion game or modified invasion game used for assessment
- Participate in practice tasks or modified game for 5-8 minutes
- Use multiple tactics throughout the game

Setup

4 v 4 game play with reduced boundaries (half of the basketball court or a quarter of a soccer field depending on sport)

Modifications for Other Grade Levels

The assessment task may be modified for Grade 6 and 7 outcomes. The Grade 6 Outcome S2.M2.6 measures the ability to use at least one of the tactics while the Grade 7 Outcome S2.M2.7 measures the ability to use at least 2 of the tactics. To assess the Grade 6 and 7 outcomes, you can use the same assessment and assessment task but only measure the frequency required in the outcome.

✍ Exit Slip for Pass Selection

Exit Slip: List the criteria for selecting each of the passes during modified game play.

- Chest pass –
- Bounce pass –
- Overhead pass –
- Head fake –
- Shot fake –
- Give & go –

Scoring Rubric for Using Offensive Tactics to Create Open Space, Grade 8

INDICATOR	DEVELOPING	COMPETENT	PROFICIENT
Pivot and Fakes	One or two critical components not present: • No or only one or two pivot and fakes • Uses the same fake or pivot throughout • Limited (less than 3) use of fakes throughout assessment	Demonstrates all critical components: • Multiple (2 or more) pivots and fakes • Selected pivot or fake creates open space	Demonstrates all critical components: • Uses a variety of pivot and fakes when appropriate and with success
Give & Go	One or two critical components not present: • Give & go performed incorrectly • Give & go mistimed resulting in a turnover • Limited (less than 3) uses of the give & go	Demonstrates all critical components: • Give & go performed correctly • Give & go well timed • Uses a give & go multiple times (more than 3 times)	Demonstrates all critical components • Combines give & go with accurate passing and receiving
Passes	One or two critical components not present: • Incorrect pass form • Passes to stationary player or pass inaccurate • Limited use of different types of passes	Demonstrates all critical components: • Passes are performed correctly • Accurate passes • Lead passes • Uses a variety of passes throughout assessment	Demonstrates all critical components: • Passes used when appropriate and with success • Varies speed or pace of pass
Tactic Use	Executes less than 3 offensive tactics	Executes at least 3 offensive tactics	Executes more than 3 offensive tactics

TACTIC	FREQUENCY 1	FREQUENCY 2	FREQUENCY 3	FREQUENCY 4
Passes: • Overhead • Chest • Bounce • Hook • Shovel • Ground • Jump • Sidearm				
Fakes and Pathways: • Shot fake • Pass fake • Look away • Jab step • Shoulder shrug • Head bob • Straight pathway • Curved pathway • Zigzag pathway				
Give & Go: • Successful give & go				
Check (√) to indicate successful performance. Comments:				

Note: Although the rubric is written for team handball, many invasion games use the same tactics. Any of the invasion games could be use by substituting the critical components specific to the skill into the rubric.

Invasion Games – Transitions   Grade 8

Grade-Level Outcome

Transitions from offense to defense or defense to offense by recovering quickly, communicating with team-mates and capitalizing on an advantage. (S2.M6.8)

Assessment Task

Students execute transitions in an invasion game.

Guidelines

- Students perform the assessment during a modified game

- Any invasion game can be modified and used for this assessment

- Participate in practice tasks or modified game for 5-8 minutes

Setup

3 v 2 or 4 v 3 game play with reduced boundaries (half of the basketball court or a quarter of a soccer field depending on sport)

Modifications for Other Grade Levels

The assessment task may be modified for Grade 6 and 7 outcomes. The Grade 6 Outcome S2.M6.6 measures recovering quickly in transitions. The Grade 7 Outcome S2.M6.7 measures the ability to communicate with teammates during transitions. To assess the Grade 6 and 7 outcomes, you can use the same assessment and assessment task but only use the indicators that are relevant to the outcome.

Scoring Rubric for Transitions, Grade 8

INDICATOR	DEVELOPING	COMPETENT	PROFICIENT
Recovers Quickly	One or two critical components not present: • Slow to react to change of possession • Stays in the middle when transitioning on defense • Keeps head down • Loses track of offensive player or ball	Demonstrates all critical components: • Moves quickly after change of possession • Spreads out while returning • Keeps eye contact with ball and opposing players	Demonstrates all critical components • Recovers quickly and forces ball to sideline
Communicates With Teammates	One or two critical componets not present: • Limited or no verbal communication • Limited or no physical communication • Communicates less than 70% of transitions	Demonstrates all critical components: • Verbally communicates with teammates during transitions • Physically communicates (hand gestures, head nod, etc.) with teammates during transitions • Communicates 70% of transitions	Demonstrates all critical components • Verbal and physical communications used successfully
Capitalizes on an Advantage	One or two critical components not present: • Not spread out for both offensive and defensive transitions • Does not capitalize on advantage situations	Demonstrates all critical components: • Stays spread on offense and defense • Identifies and uses open player	Demonstrates all critical components • Scores on multiple advantage situations

Grade-Level Outcome

Creates open space in net/wall games with either a long- or short-handled implement by varying force or direction or by moving opponent side to side and/or forward and back. (S2.M7.8)

Assessment Task

Students create open space with either a long or short implement.

Guidelines

- Perform assessment during a practice task or modified game
- Any net/wall game or modified net/wall game
- Participate in practice tasks or modified game for 5-8 minutes

Setup

- Use a full badminton, volleyball, or pickleball court
- Tape the court into 4 or 8 equal square quadrants

Modifications for Other Grade Levels

The assessment task may be modified for Grade 6 and 7 outcomes. The Grade 6 Outcome S2.M7.6 measures varying force and direction using a short-handled implement. The Grade 7 Outcome S2.M7.7 measures varying force and direction as well as moving the opponent from side to side using a long-handled implement. Use the same assessment and assessment task but include only the critical indicators that are relevant to the outcome.

Scoring Rubric for Using Tactics and Shots, Grade 8

INDICATOR	DEVELOPING	COMPETENT	PROFICIENT
Varying Force and Direction	One or two critical components not present: • Uses the same force • Hits directly to the opponent • No pace on object	Demonstrates all critical components: • Varying force of a shot • Hits in a direction away from an opponent • Changes the force and direction of shots by hitting in different quadrants	Demonstrates all critical components • Varies pace, trajectory, and placement
Moving Opponent	One or two critical components not present: • Shots do not consistently move opponent to quadrants side to side	Demonstrates all critical components: • Shots move opponent to different quadrants side to side • Shots move opponent to different quadrants front and back • Moves opponent to different quadrants 70% of the time	Demonstrates all critical components • Varies force and direction to move opponent side-to-side and back and forth

For an example of a peer assessment for shot selection and location see Appendix R.

Target Games – Shot Selection   Grade 8

Grade-Level Outcome

Varies the speed, force and trajectory of the shot based on location of the object in relation to the target. (S2.M9.8)

Assessment Task

Students participate in a target game. Target games require players to show judgment concerning what shot to play and how to play it. For example, in golf a player must select the appropriate club based on the distance of the ball from the hole. In bowling a player must locate the ball over the correct direction arrow to hit the pins. In shuffleboard a player must decide whether or not to play a shot that stays in the scoring zone or one that knocks an opponent out of the scoring zone. For the assessment, students vary the speed, force and trajectory of a shot depending on the relation of object to target.

Guidelines

- Perform assessment during a practice task or modified game

- Any target game can be modified and used

- Participate in practice tasks or modified game for 5-8 minutes

Setup

Use a full or modified court/field depending on activity

Modifications for Other Grade Levels

The assessment task may be modified for Grade 6 and 7 outcomes. The Grade 6 Outcome S2.M9.6 requires the selection of an appropriate shot and/or club based on location of the object in relation to the target. You can use a simple written assignment in golf, where the student would identify which club to use for different distances or areas of a golf course. The key point with the Grade 6 outcome is identification of the type of shot or the club to use. Students do not actually have to perform the skill, which comes later in the Grade 7 and 8 outcomes. The Grade 7 Outcome S2.M9.7 measures the student's ability to vary the speed and/or trajectory of the shot based on location of the object in relation to the target. You can use the Grade 8 assessment but only evaluate the relevant indicators in the outcome.

Scoring Rubric for Shot Selection, Grade 8

INDICATOR	DEVELOPING	COMPETENT	PROFICIENT
Varying Force and Direction	One or two critical components not present: • Uses the same force for all shots • Limited direction with shots	Demonstrates all critical components: • Varying the force of a shot to hit closer to target • Varying direction of a shot to hit closer to target • Varying force and direction of shots to get closer to target 70% of the time	Demonstrates all critical components • Adjust direction and force of shot in varying environmental conditions (wind, uneven surface, etc.)
Varying Speed	One or two critical components not present: • Uses the same speed for all shots	Demonstrates all critical components: • Varying speed of the ball because of the conditions of the course (green vs fairway in golf) • Varying speed of the ball to attempt to knock an opponent's ball away (bocce, croquet, etc.) • Varying speed when appropriate 70% of the time	Demonstrates all critical components • Adjust speed of shot in varying environmental conditions (wind, uneven surface, etc.)
Varying Trajectory	One or two critical components not present: • Uses the same trajectory for all shots	Demonstrates all critical components: • Varying trajectory depending on the distance of the object • Varying trajectory to match throwing technique (multiple throwing techniques in horseshoes or beanbag toss) • Varying trajectory when appropriate 70% of the time	Demonstrates all critical components • Adjust trajectory of shot in varying environmental conditions (wind, uneven surface, etc.)

Fielding/Striking Games – Reducing Space   Grade 8

Grade-Level Outcome

Reduces open spaces in the field by working with teammates to maximize coverage. (S2.M11.8)

Assessment Task

Work as a team to cover defensive territory.

Guidelines

- Perform the assessment during a modified game

- Assessment requires observation of fielding team only

Setup

Use a full or modified infield

Modifications for Other Grade Levels

The assessment task may be modified for Grade 6 and 7 outcomes. The Grade 6 Outcome S2.M11.6 identifies the correct defensive play while the Grade 7 Outcome S2.M11.7 selects the correct defensive play based on the situation. This can be measured by a simple written assignment with different questions related to baserunners and balls hit to different areas. Students select the appropriate base to throw to (an example is with a runner at second base, a ground ball hit to shortstop). The fielder looks to see if the runner was going, but if not, he/she would throw to first for the force out. If the runner is running to third, the fielder would tag the runner. The important point with the Grade 6 and 7 outcomes is that students are identifying or selecting the correct defensive play based on the situation. They do not actually have to perform the skill.

Scoring Rubric for Reducing Space, Grade 8

INDICATOR	DEVELOPING	COMPETENT	PROFICIENT
Communication: Shortstop/Second Base	One or two critical components not present: • Limited or no pre-pitch communication	Demonstrates all critical components before pitch: • Bag on steals • Cut-off throws hit to different part of the outfield • Play up to throw runner out at home or play back for a double play • Number of outs communicated	Demonstrates all critical components • Executes correctly one of the critical components communicated
Communication: First, Third, Pitcher, Catcher	One or two critical components not present: • Limited or no pre-pitch communication	Demonstrates all critical components before pitch: • Bunt coverage • To play up or back • To hold the runner or not • Number of outs communicated	Demonstrates all critical components • Executes correctly one of the critical components communicated

Grade-Level Outcome

Describes and applies mechanical advantage(s) for a variety of movement patterns. (S2.M12.8)

Assessment Task

Complete a video analysis project of a movement pattern or skill.

Guidelines

- Select a specific skill or sequence of movements and provide a movement analysis of the movement or sequence. This can include such things as:
    - » Mechanical advantages
    - » Critical elements
- Video-tape an individual-performance or dance and rhythm activity
- Analyze a peer performance of the skill or sequence using the critical elements sheet provided by the teacher
- Based on this analysis, write a summary of the performance strengths and weaknesses. Make recommendations for future practice tasks designed to improve performance
- Task can be completed individually or in small groups (no more than 3)

Setup

Video recording devices to film peer's performance (phone or iPad)

Modifications for Other Grade Levels

The assessment task may be modified for Grade 7 Outcome S2.M12.7, which identifies and applies Newton's laws of motion to various dance or movement activities. The same guidelines can be used with the focus on Newton's laws of motion instead of mechanical advantages.

Critical Elements of the Long Jump

Run Up

- Stride length increases indicating the runner is applying greater force
- Rear leg is fully extended at push-off
- Heel is tucked close to the buttocks
- Thigh comes parallel to the ground before foot strike
- Recovery leg is swung forward in a tuck position
- Runner eliminates lateral leg movements so that forces are kept in the forward-backward plane
- The runner eliminates out-toeing and narrows the base of support
- Support leg flexes at the knee as the body's weight comes over the leg
- Trunk rotation increases to allow for a longer stride and better arm-leg opposition
- Trunk leans slightly forward
- Arms swing forward and back, with the elbows approaching right angles and moving in opposition to the legs

Takeoff

- Takeoff leg (usually the one that stays on the ground when you kick a ball)
- Heel comes up first
- Rolling action of the foot
- Ankle bridge (flexion at the ball of the foot), ankle remains at 90 degrees
- Knees extend
- Body leans forward
- Arms extend
- Takeoff with foot at front of mat at 45-degree position
- Lifting effect should not be seen until the body's center of mass is over/past takeoff foot

Flight

- Thrust the free leg in front of the body as long as possible
- The takeoff leg will follow suit in the same positon
- Bring arms forward and reach for your toes
- As high and far as you can
- Posture – upright torso

Landing

- Bring heels up
- Upright torso
- Extension of legs in front of the body
- Keep head down toward the knees
- Fall forward or sideways (not backward)

Scoring Rubric for Mechanical Advantage, Grade 8

INDICATOR	DEVELOPING	COMPETENT	PROFICIENT
Demonstrates the Ability to Analyze and Apply Mechanical Advantages to a Movement Skill/ Sequence	• Concepts/principles inappropriate for analysis or not related to critical elements • Critical elements incorrect for skill/sequence • Recommendations not aligned with analysis • Summary incomplete	• Identifies concepts/principles appropriate to the skill/sequence • Critical elements correctly identified • Analysis includes general principles • Recommendations align with analysis • Summary accurate and based on analysis	• Identifies the most important concepts/principles for skill/ sequence • Critical elements identified and illustrated • Analysis includes general principles with specific examples • Specific recommendations made that align with analysis • Summary accurate, based on analysis, and includes specific examples

Grade-Level Outcome

Makes appropriate decisions based on the weather, level of difficulty due to conditions or ability to ensure safety of self and others (S2.M13.6)

Assessment Task

Research and describe appropriate decisions based on the weather, level of difficulty, or ability to ensure safety of self and others during an outdoor pursuit's activity.

Guidelines

- Select an outdoor activity and research the appropriate decision needed to stay safe. This can include such things as weather and level of difficulty due to conditions of environment or skill of the student.

- Level of difficulty due to conditions of environment or skill of student.

- Based on the research, write a summary of the safety considerations needed for the activity.

- Material presented in a presentation software or poster.

- Task completed individually or in small groups (no more than 3).

Setup

Access to computer and presentation software, if applicable

Research

- At least 3 different credible sources cited that support the analysis

- At least 5 of the following must be discussed and applied to the movement or sequence:

  » Appropriate footwear

  » Use of map and compass/GPS

  » Water safety tips (drinking water)

  » What food to use and how to keep food safe

  » What clothing is needed with the different climates/season

  » What safety items are needed: lights, whistle, etc.

  » What needs to be in the first aid kit

  » What equipment is needed

  » Other (approved by teacher)

Writing and Grammar for Presentation in a Software Program or Poster

- Well-organized, focused, and clearly outlined major points

- Minor spelling or grammar errors

Presentation Software or Poster

Prepare a poster or a presentation in a software program of your choice with at least 5 slides.

- Include pictures or diagrams that illustrate the analysis to add interest

- Content should be sequential and well-organized

- Each slide illustrates just a single point

- Letters are legible

- Contrast between lettering and background on slide adds clarity

- Use no more than 2 font styles

- Avoid complete sentences – use outline format

- Keep design basic and simple

Scoring Rubric for Outdoor Pursuits, Grade 6

INDICATOR	DEVELOPING	COMPETENT	PROFICIENT
Synthesis of Safety Considerations	• Less than 3 credible articles/sources reviewed and submitted • 4 or fewer safety considerations included	• At least 3 credible articles/sources reviewed and submitted • At least 5 safety considerations included	• More than 3 articles/sources reviewed and submitted • 6 or more safety considerations included
Application of Safety Considerations	• Safety considerations inappropriate for the outdoor activity • Provides only a holistic analysis of the safety consideration without identifying key points • No pictures, illustrations, or diagrams included	• Identified safety considerations appropriate to the outdoor activity • Pictures and/or illustrations for each safety consideration • At least 2 diagrams and illustrations including both correct and incorrect safety habits • Safety considerations accurately applied and presented with clarity	• Identified the most important safety considerations appropriate to the outdoor activity • Key safety considerations identified and illustrated • 3 or more diagrams and illustrations including both correct and incorrect technique • Safety considerations accurately applied and presented with clarity
Competency in Oral Communication	• Content not sequential, making it difficult to determine accuracy of analysis • Poster or slides crowded with text presenting multiple points • 3 or more fonts used	• Poster or slides sequential and well-organized • Each slide presents a single point • Text legible with contrast between text and background • No more than 2 fonts in presentation • Pictures, illustrations, and/or diagrams add clarity to presentation	• Slides sequential, well-organized with multiple pictures, diagrams, and/or illustrations • Each slide presents a single point with pictures, illustrations or diagrams • Text legible with contrast between text and background increasing visual appeal • No more than 2 fonts used in presentation

Standard 3 Sample Assessments

Standard 3: The physically literate individual demonstrates the knowledge and skills to achieve and maintain a health-enhancing level of physical activity and fitness.

Standard 3 for middle school (Grades 6-8) integrates the psychomotor and cognitive domains, which provides students with educational experiences that best prepare them to be physically active outside of school now and throughout their lives. Middle school students are expected to understand how fitness, physical activity and nutrition can influence an individual's performance and overall health. They are also expected to develop and implement their own basic fitness and nutrition plans. The sample assessments for Standard 3 evaluate students' knowledge and at the same time provide practice opportunities that reinforce important concepts for physically active lifestyles.

We have provided a wide range of sample assessments for Standard 3. Some of the assessments are the traditional quizzes or worksheets, but many are comprehensive in nature and will take some time to complete. For example, in the remediation plan, the students are asked to complete a fitness test and then develop a fitness plan to help improve their health. Students should complete a fitness assessment early in the semester so they can begin to design their fitness plan based on their fitness test results. At the middle school level, some teachers integrate fitness and physical activity over the course of the curriculum, have Fitness Fridays, or offer a specific unit on fitness. There is no right or wrong way to offer fitness and physical activity content; however, you want to be strategic when you are providing this instruction because these assessments will take time to complete.

Grade-Level Outcomes

- Develops a plan to address 1 of the barriers within one's family, school, or community to maintaining a physically active lifestyle. (S3.M1.8)

- Identifies the 5 components of health-related fitness (muscular strength, muscular endurance, flexibility, cardiorespiratory endurance, body composition) and explains the connections between fitness and overall physical and mental health. (S5.M1.8)

Assessment Task

Create a video blog identifying the 5 components of health-related fitness and explain the connections between fitness and overall health (e.g., physical activity and stress; physical activity and heart disease; flexibility and injury prevention; physical activity and weight control).

Guidelines

- Complete research on:

    » components of health-related fitness

    » how fitness and overall physical and mental health connect with the components of health-related fitness

- The assignment can be adjusted to focus on just one or more components of health-related fitness instead of all five, depending on the readiness of the students.

- Create a narrated blog based on your research.

- Create a video blog of the narrated version. The final video blog will be posted on the physical education website for others to view or use.

Setup

- Video recording devices to film blog

- Computer access to research content

Modifications for Other Grade Levels

The assessment task may be modified for Grade 6 and 7 outcomes. The Grade 6 Outcome S3.M1.6 describes how being physically active leads to a healthy body. The Grade 7 Outcome S3.M1.7 identifies barriers related to maintaining a physically active lifestyle and seeks solutions for eliminating those barriers. Both outcomes can be assessed by adjusting the scoring rubric and the instructions for the assessment task to fit the content of the outcomes. For example, the indicator about applying health-related fitness concepts could be changed to an indicator about barriers to a physically active lifestyle (Grade 7) or an indicator about the relationship of physical activity and a healthy body (Grade 6).

Critical Components for Video Blog Health-Related Fitness Project

Specific requirements for the assignment are below:

Research

- At least 3 different credible sources cited that support the connections between health and fitness.

- All 5 health-related fitness components need to be discussed and applied to both fitness and overall physical and mental health.

- Cited articles are appropriate to the topic.

Content Requirements

- All health-related fitness components accurately applied and presented with clarity

- A clear connection between health-related fitness components and physical and mental health presented

Writing and Grammar

- Video blog narrative well-organized, focused, and major points clearly outlined

- Concepts logically arranged to present a sound argument

- Normal conventions of spelling and grammar followed with only minor errors

- Minor errors in spelling and grammar do not impact readability

Video Blog

- Prepare a video blog of at least 2 to 3 minutes based on your research.

- Presentation of video blog assessed on:

  » Direct eye contact with camera

  » Seldom use of notes

  » Speak with fluctuation in volume

  » Use appropriate vocabulary

  » Accurate content

Scoring Rubric for Video Blog, Grade 8

INDICATOR	DEVELOPING	COMPETENT	PROFICIENT
Use of Sources	• Less than 3 sources • Cited work misaligned to content • Less than 5 health-related fitness components discussed • Information from sources not correctly analyzed and/or explained	• At least 3 sources • Cited work aligned to content • All 5 health-related fitness components discussed • Information from sources correctly analyzed and explained	• More than 3 sources used • Cited work directly aligned to content • All 5 health-related fitness components discussed in detail • Information from sources correctly analyzed and explained in depth
Application of Health-Related Fitness Concepts	Limited connections between health-related fitness and overall health	Clear connections between health-related fitness and overall physical and mental health	Integration of health-related fitness components to specific physical and mental health benefits
Written Narrative	• Poorly organized narrative with gaps • Errors in spelling and grammar negatively impact readability	• Narrative well-organized, logically arranged • Only minor errors in grammar and/or spelling that do not interfere with readability	• Narrative well-organized, logically arranged, and directly supports analysis • Errors in grammar and/or spelling rare and do not impact readability
Oral Communication	• Video blog poorly sequenced, making it difficult to follow • Video blog does not meet time requirements • Inconsistent eye contact • Monotone voice throughout • Uses slang or non-content-related language • Large pauses between content areas	• Video blog sequential and well-organized • Video blog meets time requirements • Direct eye contact with camera • Infrequent use of notes • Speaks with fluctuation in tone • Uses appropriate vocabulary • Smooth transitions between content areas	• Video blog is sequential, well-organized, and cites specific resources • Eye contact and body language reinforce content • Voice inflection enhances presentation • Transitions smooth and built off previous content

Grade-Level Outcome

Participates in physical activity 3 times a week outside of physical education class. (S3.M2.8)

Assessment Task

Participate in and log physical activity at least 3 times a week outside of physical education class.

Guidelines

Participates and logs in physical activity performed outside of physical education class

Setup

Distribute activity logs

Modifications for Other Grade Levels

The assessment task may be modified for Grade 6 and 7 outcomes. The Grade 6 Outcome S3.M2.6 has students participate in a self-selected physical activity outside of physical education class. The Grade 7 Outcome S3.M2.7 has students participate in a physical activity twice a week outside of physical education class. Both outcomes can be assessed by modifying the questions on the self-assessment task (see below) to address the different components in the outcomes. For an example of a physical activity log specific to time recording see Appendix S.

✍ Sample Middle School Physical Activity Log

Write down the activity and add the amount of time each day:

ACTIVITY	MONDAY	TUESDAY	WEDNESDAY	THURSDAY	FRIDAY	SATURDAY	SUNDAY
Before school Yoga (example)	15 minutes			20 minutes			
During school (not physical education class)							
After school							
Comments:							

Engages in Physical Activity   Grades 6-8

Grade-Level Outcomes

- Participates in a variety of aerobic-fitness activities such as cardio-kick, step aerobics and aerobic dance. (S3.M3.6)

- Participates in a variety of strength- and endurance-fitness activities such as Pilates, resistance training, bodyweight training and light free-weight training. (S3.M3.7)

- Participates in a variety of self-selected aerobic-fitness activities outside of school such as walking, jogging, biking, skating, dancing and swimming. (S3.M3.8)

Assessment Task

Participate in physical activity in or outside of physical education class.

Guidelines

Participate and log in physical activity performed in or outside of physical education class according to the outcome

Setup

- Distribute physical activity logs.

- Data collection completed through applications like Google Docs or an app on a device or computer station. This will make the management of the data much easier and get students in the habit of using technology to track and monitor their physical activity.

Modifications for Other Outcomes and Grade Levels

This activity log can be easily modified for Grade-Level Outcomes S3.M4 and S3.M5 by changing the activities to match the content of the outcomes (e.g., aerobic fitness using technology, strength and endurance, lifetime activities). For an example of a physical activity log specific to step count see Appendix T.

✍ Sample Physical Activity Log

PHYSICAL ACTIVITY	DATE	AMOUNT OF TIME
Aerobic – fitness		
• Cardio-step		
• Step aerobics		
• Aerobic dance		
• Other: _____		
Strength and endurance – fitness		
• Pilates		
• Resistance training		
• Body weight training		
• Light free-weight training		
• Other: _____		
Aerobic – fitness		
• Walking		
• Jogging		
• Biking		
• Skating		
• Dancing		
• Swimming		
• Other: _____		

Grade-Level Outcome

Compares and contrasts health-related fitness components. (S3.M7.8)

Assessment Task

Complete an online journal activity that compares and contrasts the health-related fitness components.

Guidelines

- Complete the journal activity as homework
- Uses Google Classroom or another form of web resource

Setup

Computer access

Modifications for Other Grade Levels

The assessment task may be modified for Grade 6 and 7 outcomes. The Grade 6 Outcome S3.M7.6 has students identifying the components of skill-related fitness. The Grade 7 Outcome S3.M7.7 has students distinguish between health-related and skill-related fitness. Both outcomes can be assessed by the journal activity or could be measured by a quiz or exit slip.

Critical Components for Journal Activity

Specific requirements for the assignment are below:

Content Requirements

- Compare the health-related fitness components
- Contrast the health-related fitness components

Writing and Grammar

- Journal entry is well-organized, focused, and clearly outlines major points
- Concepts were logically arranged to present a sound argument
- Normal conventions of spelling and grammar were followed with only minor errors
- Minor errors in spelling and grammar did not interfere with the readability of entry

Scoring Rubric for Journal Activity, Grade 8

INDICATOR	DEVELOPING	COMPETENT	PROFICIENT
Compares and Contrasts Various Components or Concepts	• Not all health-related fitness components compared • Inaccurate information	• All health-related fitness components accurately compared and contrasted • Accurate information	• Compares and contrasts health-related fitness components • Accurate information • Relates components to specific physical and mental wellness
Writing and Grammar	• Poorly organized journal • Gaps in entries • Errors in spelling and grammar negatively impact readability	• Well-organized and logically arranged journal entries • Required number of entries present • Only minor errors in grammar and/or spelling that do not interfere with readability	• Entries well-organized, logically arranged, and directly support conclusions • Required number of entries present • Less than 5 errors in grammar and/or spelling with no impact on readability • Transitions effective and aid in comprehension

Note: Many outcomes can be assessed using a journal assignment. The assessment and scoring guide can be modified to fit the critical components of the selected outcome.

Fitness Knowledge   Grade 7

Grade-Level Outcome

Describes and demonstrates the difference between dynamic and static stretches. (S3.M9.7)

Assessment Task

Create stations that demonstrate the differences between the stretches. Students must develop visuals and explanations for each station with specific instruction for station activities/exercises. When station cards are complete, students rotate through each station.

Guidelines

- In small groups, create stations and station cards that demonstrate the difference between the two types of stretches

- Assignment completed in class or at home

Setup

- Students work in groups of four

- Access to materials to make station cards

Modifications for Other Grade Levels

The assessment task may be modified for Grade 6 and 8 outcomes. The Grade 6 Outcome S3.M9.6 has students only performing correct techniques and methods of stretching. The Grade 8 Outcome S3.M9.8 has students employ a variety of static-stretching techniques for all the major muscle groups. Students can demonstrate the components of the outcomes using the station assignment.

Critical Components for Station Assignment

Specific requirements for the assignment are below:

Content Requirements

- How each type of stretch is performed

- The critical elements of each stretch and why it is important to maintain them

- When to use each type of stretch

- Differences between the two types of stretches

- Movements should be broken down into stages

Stretches

- Dynamic – performed before workout (but still have some type of movement)

- Static – performed after athletic activity

- Stretches are performed in complete control (no bouncing) and to full extension

- Hold stretch for 15-30 seconds

- Minimal balance issues

- Constant breathing pattern

- Movements are slow and sure

Scoring Rubric for Station Assignment, Grade 7

INDICATOR	DEVELOPING	COMPETENT	PROFICIENT
Station Cards	• Inaccurate information • Missing information on types of stretches and performance criteria • Lack visuals or graphics	• Accurate information • Performance criteria identified • Visuals accurate and easy to interpret	• Accurate and detailed information • Performance criteria and cues • Visuals accurate, easy to interpret, and attractive
Critical Elements Proper Stretching Technique	• Stretches cold muscles without any type of warm-up • Confuses dynamic and static stretches • Bounces when stretching • Holds stretch for less than 15 seconds • Loses balance frequently • Holds breath during stretch • Movements rushed and unsure	• Dynamic and static stretches performed at an appropriate time • Performed in complete control and to full extension • Holds stretch for 15-30 seconds • Minimal balance issues • Constant breathing pattern • Movements slow and sure	• Performs stretches in control • Full range of motion • Holds stretch without losing balance • Breathing free and natural • Movements slow and sure with correct alignment

Fitness Knowledge   Grade 6

Grade-Level Outcome

Identifies each of the components of the overload principle (FITT formula: frequency, intensity, time & type) for different types of physical activity (aerobic, muscular fitness, and flexibility). (S3.M11.6)

Assessment Task

Identify the components of the overload principle in the quiz provided.

Guidelines

- Quiz completed in class, online, or at home

- Quiz modified into a worksheet that can be completed in pairs or small groups

Setup

Paper and pencil or link on school's physical education website

Modifications for Other Grade Levels

The assessment task may be modified for the Grade 7 outcome. The Grade 7 Outcome S3.M11.7 has students describing the overload principle (FITT formula) for different types of physical activity, the training principles on which the formula is based, and how the formula and principles affect fitness. The quiz can be modified with specific questions added to address these additional components of the outcome.

✍ *Quiz on FITT and Overload Formulas*

Use the sample fitness training log to answer questions 1-5. Each questions is worth 1 point.

The following is a sample student fitness training log. Examine the data and answer the questions that follow.

TRAINING SESSION	DAY	MACHINE TYPE	LEVEL ON MACHINE	TOTAL CALORIES (KCAL) BURNED	TIME IN MINUTES
1	Monday	Treadmill	4	135	20
2	Wednesday	Elliptical	4	155	25
3	Friday	Treadmill	4	200	30
4	Monday	Treadmill	5	155	20
5	Wednesday	Elliptical	5	175	25
6	Friday	Treadmill	5	200	30
7	Monday	Treadmill	6	325	50
8	Wednesday	Elliptical	6	195	25
9	Friday	Treadmill	6	240	30
10	Monday	Treadmill	7	180	20
11	Wednesday	Elliptical	7	215	25
12	Friday	Treadmill	7	260	30

1. According to the FITT formula, what is the frequency for this person's training?

2. According to the FITT formula, is there evidence of increasing intensity? Why or why not?

3. If this person is following the FITT formula, what is the time (range)?

4. According to the FITT formula, what is the type?

5. On what training day do you see overload the most?

Fitness Knowledge   Grade 6

Grade-Level Outcome

Identifies major muscles used in selected physical activities. (S3.M14.6)

Assessment Task

Identify the major muscle groups used in activities listed on the worksheet.

Guidelines

Worksheet completed in class or at home

Setup

Paper and pencil or link on school's website

Modifications for Other Grade Levels

The assessment task may be modified for Grade 7 and 8 outcomes. The Grade 7 Outcome S3.M14.7 has students describing how muscles pull on bones to create movement in pairs by relaxing and contracting. The Grade 8 Outcome S3.M14.8 has students explaining how body systems interact with one another (e.g., blood transports nutrients from the digestive system, oxygen from the respiratory system) during physical activity. The worksheet can be modified with specific questions added to meet the different components of these outcomes.

Student name: _____   Score:_____/15

Quadriceps   Hamstrings   Calves   Chest

Back   Shoulders   Triceps

Biceps   Forearms   Trapezius   Abs

✍ Worksheet on Major Muscles and Physical Activities

Directions: Write down all the major muscle groups used in the physical activities listed below. You will use the muscle groups more than once and may have more than one muscle group in each activity. Each question is worth 1 point.

1. Rolling a bowling ball

2. Throwing a softball

3. Riding a stationary bike

4. Lunges

5. Running

6. Badminton overhead clear

7. Basketball chest pass

8. Treading water

9. Push-ups

10. Yoga – chair pose

11. Skateboarding for speed

12. Cross-country skiing

13. Cardio kickboxing

14. Line dancing – electric slide

15. Golf putt

Assessment and Program Planning

Grade-Level Outcome

Designs and implements a program of remediation for 3 areas of weakness based on the results of health-related fitness assessment. (S3.M15.8)

Assessment Task

Design and implement a program of remediation for at least 3 areas of weakness based on health-related fitness scores.

Guidelines

- Select at least 3 areas of health-related fitness and develop a program of improvement
  - » Set goals for improvement plan based on pre-assessment fitness scores
  - » Develop and implement the plan for improvement
- The number of remediation areas can be modified to meet the readiness of the students

Setup

- Access to pre-assessment data
- Access to physical education website

Modifications for Other Grade Levels

The assessment task may be modified for Grade 6 and 7 outcomes. The Grade 6 Outcome S3.M15.6 has students designing and implementing a program of remediation for one area of weakness on the results of the health-related fitness assessment. The Grade 7 Outcome S3.M15.7 has students designing and implementing a program of remediation for two areas of weakness. The assignment can be modified by meeting the criteria of the outcome.

Critical Components for Remediation Plan

Specific requirements for the assignment are below:

Pre-Assessments

- Provide students with their health-related fitness scores
- Students analyze fitness scores to identify 3 areas of weakness

Goals

- Set at least 3 goals for areas of weakness
  - » Goals follow the SMART format of Specific (S), Measurable (M), Achievable (A), Realistic (R), and Time bound (T)

Plan

- Describe fitness activities designed to improve performance
  - » Selected fitness tasks align with goals
  - » Fitness tasks sequential and progressive
  - » Determine how often and how long you will participate in each fitness task

- Develop a month-long calendar as part of your plan for improvement
  - » Plan includes 5 days with 2 days for rest
  - » Identify the fitness tasks for each day
    - Number of repetitions or length of time for each
    - Identify one warm-up activity for each day
    - Sample calendar available on physical education website

Implementation

- Maintain a daily activity log
  - » Activity log must include the following:
    - Date
    - For each fitness task, number of repetitions OR amount of time
    - Perceived exertion identified
    - Location/other participants
  - » Activity log is turned in on Friday of each week

Reflection

- Complete a weekly reflection that includes
  - » Your successes
  - » Your challenges
  - » What you would change in your plan moving forward
- Each of the above questions supported with specific examples or data
- Progress or lack of progress based on pre-, mid-, and post-assessments
- Reflection due each Friday

Scoring Rubric for Remediation Plan Project, Grade 8

INDICATOR	DEVELOPING	COMPETENT	PROFICIENT
Sets, Tracks Progress, and Achieves Goals	• 2 or less goals set • Goals lack alignment to areas of weakness • Goals missing at least one of the following criteria: » Specific » Measurable » Achievable » Realistic » Time bound	• Minimum of 3 goals set for areas of weakness • At least 2 goals align with area of weakness • Goals meet the SMART criteria: » Specific » Measurable » Achievable » Realistic » Time bound	• 3 or more goals set • All goals align with areas of weakness • Goals meet the SMART criteria: » Specific » Measurable » Achievable » Realistic » Time bound
Creates a Performance-Based Improvement Plan	• Fitness tasks inappropriate for goals • Fails to identify specific fitness tasks • Plan not daily • Number of repetitions or length of time not identified • No warm-up activity	• Selected fitness tasks: » Appropriate for goals » Sequential and progressive • Develops a month-long plan to include » Daily plans consisting of specific fitness tasks » Number of repetitions or length of time identified » One warm-up activity identified for each day	• Selected fitness tasks: » Appropriate for goals » Sequential and progressive » Include physical activities in plan as well as fitness tasks • Develops a month-long plan to include » Daily plans consisting of specific fitness tasks » Number of repetitions or length of time for each identified » One warm-up activity identified for each day » Fitness activities varied and challenging
Implements a Plan and Tracks Progress	Daily activity incomplete • No data for some days • Number of repetitions or length not identified • Perceived exertion not identified • Location/other participants missing	Maintain a daily activity log to include • Date • Number of repetitions or length of time • Perception of intensity level • Location/other participants	Maintain a daily activity log to include • Date • Number of repetitions or length of time • Perception of intensity level • Location/other participants • Daily formative assessments
Reflects and Analyzes Progress in Meeting Goals	• Reflections lack specificity with only general observations included • Reflections fail to be supported by data or specific examples	• Reflects on the following: » Successes » Challenges • Reflections supported by assessment data • Reflections include specific examples • Analysis of pre-, mid- and post-assessments	• Reflects on the following: » Successes » Challenges » Modifications • Reflections supported by data and specific examples • Analysis of pre-, mid- and post-assessments

Standard 4 Sample Assessments

Standard 4: The physically literate individual exhibits responsible personal and social behavior that respects self and others.

Standard 4 focuses primarily on personal and social responsibility. These behaviors are typically assessed through observation during a variety of learning activities designed for Standards 1, 2 and 3. Embedded within these standards are numerous opportunities to observe and evaluate students' personal and social behaviors. Behaviors associated with personal responsibility at the middle school level include such things as safety, class protocols, self-direction, and following class rules. Behaviors associated with social responsibility include working in pairs and small or large groups, providing feedback to peers, or being a quality teammate. Specific **indicators** for Standard 4 can be added to existing rubrics for Standards 1, 2 and 3 or separate assessment tools can be created for Standard 4. If you elect to add an indicator for Standard 4 to an existing rubric for Standard 1, you have created an **analytic rubric** with an "embedded" assessment for another standard. This allows you to measure the achievement of outcomes across standards using a single analytic rubric. An example is provided below with the assessment of the bounce pass in combination with the assessment of teamwork skills.

INDICATOR	DEVELOPING	COMPETENT	PROFICIENT
Critical Elements Bounce Pass	One or two critical elements not present: • Improper hand grip • No step • Limited extension of arms or no rotation of palms • Pass uncatchable	Demonstrates all critical elements: • Proper hand grip • Elbows bent • Steps to target • Arms extended down and out • Rotation of palms outward • Pass catchable	Demonstrates all critical elements • Pass thrown with appropriate force • Pass catchable at the receiver's chest/waist level
Teamwork	• Passes/offensive skills do not account for performance differences • Demonstrates frustration with teammates through comments or actions • No encouragement • Feedback negative	• Passes/offensive skills based on teammates' movements/abilities • All teammates involved • Comments encouraging and positive • Feedback constructive and positive	• Passes/offensive skills modified for teammates' movements/abilities • All teammates equally involved • Comments encouraging, positive, and frequent • Feedback constructive and positive

As with all outcomes, you must identify your expectations to your students and teach specifically to these outcomes. First-time users of the assessments should focus their attention on one behavior at a time or one behavior per lesson. If you have more experience, the focus can expand to multiple behaviors in one class or activity. Standard 4 assessments provide many opportunities for students to self-reflect, work with peers, and participate in a range of peer evaluations. Students can be involved by setting behavior expectations before engaging in an activity or identifying ways they want to hold classmates responsible for their actions. Standard 4 allows students to engage in guided discussions about personal and social responsibility, which are the foundation for a supportive learning environment.

Many of the assessments provided can be modified according to the activity or the personal and social responsibility level of students. Make sure students have a voice in suggesting rules or guidelines, ethical scenarios to act out, and other personal and social responsibility elements to assess. You should feel free to use peer- and self-assessments throughout teaching and assessing Standard 4.

Grade-Level Outcome

Cooperates with a small group of classmates during adventure activities, game play, or team-building activities. (S4.M5.6)

Assessment Task

Cooperate with teammates during practice tasks or modified game play.

Guidelines

- Partner or teammates selected by student or teacher
- Assessment occurs during practice tasks or modified game play
- Works with a partner or two others

Setup

- Grid activities
- Modified game play

Critical Components for Teamwork

- Works with partner/teammate to ensure success
- Provides assistance and/or encouragement to others
- Demonstrates inclusive behaviors

Scoring Rubric for Teamwork, Grade 6

INDICATOR	DEVELOPING	COMPETENT	PROFICIENT
Teamwork	• Passes/offensive skills do not account for performance differences • Demonstrates frustration with teammates through comments or actions • No encouragement • Feedback negative	• Passes/offensive skills based on teammates' movements/abilities • All teammates involved • Comments encouraging and positive • Feedback constructive and positive	• Passes/offensive skills modified for teammates' movements/abilities • All teammates equally involved • Comments encouraging, positive, and frequent • Feedback constructive and positive

Working With Others
Grade 8

Grade-Level Outcome

Responds appropriately to participants' ethical and unethical behavior during physical activity by using rules and guidelines for resolving conflicts. (S4.M4.8)

Assessment Task

Given an ethical scenario, students role play an appropriate response by using rules and guidelines for resolving the conflict.

Guidelines

- List of ethical and unethical behaviors provided
- Student choice on behaviors to act out
- Two behaviors acted out
- Every student participates
- Skit 1.5-3 minutes in length

Setup

- Provide appropriate time and space to practice
- 3 or 4 students in a group

Examples of Ethical Scenarios

- Knowing the ball was not caught when the teacher/referee called it a clean catch
- Knowing the score is incorrect
- Cheating on fitness scores
- Use of performance-enhancing drugs
- Classmates are sending inappropriate messages or teasing classmates
- Teacher leaves the final exam out on accident
- Student-suggested scenarios

Critical Components for Role Play Assignment

Specific requirements for the assignment are below:

Practice/Collaboration With Peers

- Communicates ideas and feelings with group
- Supports the contributions of others
- Actively engages in the practice of skit

Content Requirements

- At least 2 unethical and ethical scenarios acted out by group
- Scenarios direct with a clear problem being resolved or controlled for
- Use rules and guidelines in response to ethical scenarios

Performance

- Voice clearly audible

- Uses props in a highly imaginative or creative way

- Clearly and unmistakably interprets the ethical scenario with rules and guidelines

- Skillfully and confidently adapts tone of voice, facial expression, gestures, and vocabulary

- Sustains engagement throughout the skit and encourages the involvement of others

- Stays on topic

- Presentation is 1.5-3 minutes long

Scoring Rubric for Ethics, Grade 8

INDICATOR	DEVELOPING	COMPETENT	PROFICIENT
Practice/Collaborate With Peers	• Communicates inappropriately with classmates (raises voice, overbearing the conversation, etc.) • Does not offer support to classmates' thoughts and suggestions • Lacks physical or mental engagement in practice	• Communicates appropriately with classmates • Supports classmates' thoughts and suggestions • Engages in practice	• Leads verbally or by example during practice sessions • Communication enhances practice sessions • Builds practice ideas off of others
Applies Content Requirements	• Less than 2 scenarios • Scenario vaguely resolves problem • Limited or no rules or guidelines	• At least 2 unethical and ethical scenarios used • Scenarios directly resolve problem • Uses rules and guidelines in response to scenarios	• Uses more than 2 scenarios • Scenarios directly resolve problem • Multiple rules and guidelines
Performance of Students' Skit	• Voice unclear or quiet • No use of props • Lacks creativity • Interpretations unclear • Does not adapt either the tone of voice, facial expression, gestures, or vocabulary • Loses focus • Off topic in skit • Presentation less than 1.5 minutes	• Voice clearly audible • Uses props in a highly imaginative or creative way • Interpretations clear • Skillfully and confidently adapts either the tone of voice, facial expression, gestures, or vocabulary • Sustains engagement • Stays on topic • Presentation is 1.5-3 minutes	• Voice clearly audible • Uses props in a highly imaginative and creative way • Interpretations clear and direct • Skillfully and confidently adapts tone of voice, facial expression, gestures, and vocabulary • Sustains engagement • Injects humor in creative ways

Personal Responsibility   Grade 6

Grade-Level Outcome

Exhibits personal responsibility by using appropriate etiquette, demonstrating respect for facilities, and exhibiting safe behaviors. (S4.M1.6)

Assessment Task

During practice tasks, students are assessed using a personal responsibility checklist.

Guidelines

- Review rubric before the start of the school year or unit
- Teacher will observe over multiple class periods

Setup

Students perform practice task

> **Note:** *Assessment checklist and critical components can be modified for specific activities or situations.*

Critical Components for Personal Responsibility Behaviors

Specific requirements for the assignment are below:

Appropriate Etiquette

- Promotes and uses positive talk with classmates
- Complies with instructions
- Claps or wishes luck to opposition/opponent
- Shows respect for injured player by providing space and encouragement
- If appropriate, acknowledges an opposition player's major game or skill achievement
- Shakes hand with peers after competition
- Retrieves equipment for peers
- Updates score or practice trials throughout game or task
- Sports specific etiquette (waiting to start bowling approach until opponent has completed their turn, not talking during a golf swing, roll the ball under the net in volleyball, etc.)

Respect for Facilities/Equipment

- Uses the equipment as intended (not kicking a volleyball)
- Always wears the correct footwear for physical education space
- Does not slam or throw equipment
- Does not leave equipment out
- Does not have open bottles of water in physical education space
- Always treats facilities and equipment with respect

Exhibiting Safe Behaviors

- Does not run with equipment unless instructed to by teacher
- Controls body in personal and general space
- Performs task at appropriate skill and developmental level

✍ Personal Responsibility Checklist, Grade 6

Name of performer: _____

Name of observer: _____

For each line on the check sheet use one of the following codes:

(+) = the behavior was observed in the class period

(-) = the behavior has potential to be a problem

Checklist for Appropriate Etiquette

- Promotes and uses positive talk with classmates _____
- Complies with instructions _____
- Claps or wishes luck to opponent _____
- Shows respect for injured player by providing space and encouragement _____
- If appropriate, acknowledges an opposition player's game or skill achievement _____
- Shakes hand with peers after competition _____
- Retrieves equipment for peers _____
- Updates score or practice trials throughout game or task _____
- Sports specific etiquette:_____ _____

Checklist for Respect for Facilities/Equipment

- Uses the equipment as attended _____
- Wears the correct footwear for physical education space _____
- Does not slam or throw equipment _____
- Does not leave equipment out _____
- Does not leave open bottles of water in physical education space _____

Checklist for Exhibiting Safe Behaviors

- Does not run with equipment unless instructed to by teacher _____
- Controls body in personal and general space _____
- Performs task at appropriate skill and developmental level _____

Provide two specific examples of how the performer effectively showed personal responsibility:

Make two specific suggestions on how personal responsibility could be improved:

Comments: _____

Rules and Etiquette   Grade 8

Grade-Level Outcome
Applies rules and etiquette by acting as an official for modified physical activities and games and creating dance routines within a given set of parameters. (S4.M6.8)

Assessment Task
Officiate a small-sided game applying rules fairly.

Guidelines
- Review rules and officiating signals with class before activity
- Provide information sheet of calls/rules and signals used while officiating
- Modify scoring rubric for a variety of games and sports

Setup
- Small or modified games with 1 or 2 students officiating
- Use small-sided games (two or three players) and reduce space
- Officiating team includes two line judges, a referee, and score keeper

Note: *Students refereeing contests and keeping score are put in situations where they make judgments and decisions to which competitors react. All of these situations have the potential to create tension, disagreement, and even confrontation.*

Critical Components of Officiating Small-Sided Game (Volleyball)

Rules to Be Officiated
- In/out
- Net faults
- Caught or thrown balls
- 4 contacts
- Center line faults
- For highly skilled classes, doubles

Application and Comportment
- Applies rules accurately
- Assures player safety throughout match
- Gives appropriate signals
- Demonstrates accurate judgment
- Demonstrates poise and control
- Demonstrates proper emphasis on call and signals

Scoring Rubric for Officiating (Volleyball), Grade 8

INDICATOR	DEVELOPING	COMPETENT	PROFICIENT
Application and Comportment of Rules to Be Officiated	• Applies rules inaccurately • Multiple safety hazards during play • Improper signals • Inaccurate or inconsistent judgment • Lack of emphasis on call or signal	• Applies rules accurately 70% of the match • Assures player safety • Appropriate signals • Demonstrates accurate judgment 70% of the match • Demonstrates poise and control • Appropriate emphasis on call and signals	• Applies rules accurately 100% of the match • Assures player safety • Appropriate signals • Demonstrates accurate judgment 100% of the match • Demonstrates poise and control • Appropriate emphasis on call and signals

The indicator below can be added to the scoring rubric if you wish to evaluate the participants' respect for the officials during modified game play.

Scoring Rubric for Respect for Officials, Grade 8

INDICATOR	DEVELOPING	COMPETENT	PROFICIENT
Fair Play	Disrespectful to officials by doing any of the following behaviors: • Not following officials' rulings • Outbursts after officials' calls • Little effort in playing by the rules	Respects the officials by: • Following rulings • Showing self-control • Effort in playing by rules	Respects the officials by: • Following the rules • Showing self-control and helping others • Encouraging others • Thanking officials

Standard 5 Sample Assessments

Standard 5: The physically literate individual recognizes the value of physical activity for health, enjoyment, challenge, self-expression and/or social interaction.

Middle school students are experiencing a period of immense change, both physically and socially. One of the most significant changes is that peers are replacing adults as the most influential people in students' lives. You, as a middle school teacher, will need to convince students of the value of physical activity in their lives and help them focus on the opportunities for joy, challenge, self-expression and social interaction provided through movement. Middle school students need to explore all the options for physical activity available to them and begin to seek out the activities they find most rewarding. While skill competency is still the focus, embedded in all physical activity are opportunities for students to reflect on the challenges presented, the many possibilities for social interaction, and the sheer joy and self-expression found in human movement. The emphasis in Standard 5 is on the students reflecting on these values and the role physical activity can play in their long-term health and fitness.

The Standard 5 outcomes lie in the affective domain, where alternative forms of assessment are more appropriate than traditional tests or assignments. These assessments focus on what students are feeling and what they value in physical education. Letters, bulletin boards, student-created flyers, websites, etc. can all be creative ways to increase awareness of the importance of physical activity and help students recognize its worth.

Grade-Level Outcome

Identifies different types of physical activities and describes how each exerts a positive impact on health. (S5.M1.7)

Assessment Task

Complete an online journal activity that connects specific physical activities with health benefits.

Guidelines

- Complete the journal activity for homework
- Use Google Classroom or another form of web resource

Setup

Computer access

Modifications for Other Grade Levels

The assessment task may be modified for Grade 6 and 8 outcomes. The Grade 6 Outcome S5.M1.6 has students describing how being physically active leads to a healthy body. The Grade 8 Outcome S5.M1.8 has students identifying the health-related fitness components and their relationship to physical and mental health. Both outcomes can be assessed by changing the critical components of the assessment task and the rubric indicators to specifically match the components of the outcomes.

Critical Components for Journal Activity

Specific requirements for the assignment are below:

Content Requirements

- Identify different types of physical activities
- Explain the connection between the activities and possible positive health impact
- Identify any value you may have found in participation in the activity (challenge, joy, social interaction, self-expression)

Writing and Grammar

- Journal entry well-organized, focused, and clearly outlines major points
- Concepts logically arranged to present an effective argument

Scoring Rubric for Journal Activity, Grade 7

INDICATOR	DEVELOPING	COMPETENT	PROFICIENT
Connects Physical Activity With Positive Health Impact	Connections unclear between the selected activities and positive health impact	Clear connection between selected activities and positive health impact	Clear and detailed connections between selected activities and positive health impact
Organization	• Journal entry poorly organized • Lack of support for conclusions	• Journal entry well-organized • Connections logically aligned and supporting health benefits	• Journal entry well-organized • Connections logically aligned and supporting health benefits • Conclusions support value of physical activity

Note: *Many outcomes within Standard 5 can be assessed using a journal assessment. The assessment and scoring guide can be modified to fit the critical components of the outcome desired.*

Challenge

Grade 8

Grade-Level Outcome

Develops a plan of action and makes appropriate decisions based on that plan when faced with an individual challenge. (S5.M3.8)

Assessment Task

Identify an individual challenge and develop a plan of action to make an appropriate decision the next time the challenge presents itself.

Guidelines

- Complete worksheet for homework

- Provide a list of possible challenges

Setup

Provide students with worksheet

Modifications for Other Grade Levels

The assessment task may be modified for Grade 6 and 7 outcomes. The Grade 6 Outcome S5.M3.6 has students recognizing individual challenges and ways to cope with them in a positive way. The Grade 7 Outcome S5.M3.7 has students generating positive strategies and providing possible solutions when faced with group challenges. Both outcomes can be assessed by changing the critical components of the assessment task and worksheet to match the specific components of the outcomes.

✍ *Plan for Success Against Individual Challenges*

List the individual challenge you have:

What are some barriers that make this challenge difficult to overcome?

What specific decisions need to be made that are related to overcoming the challenge?

List multiple ways or strategies you can use to overcome the challenge:

Track the Specific Events You Made to Overcome the Challenge

DATE	WAYS YOU HAVE TAKEN STEPS TO OVERCOME THE CHALLENGE

Critical Components for Challenge Worksheet

Specific requirements for the assignment are below:

Content Requirements

- Identifies at least 1 individual challenge

- Provides multiple barriers that relate to difficulty of overcoming the challenge

- Lists multiple positive ways or strategies to overcome the challenge

- Discusses decisions needed to be made to overcome the challenge

- Tracks multiple personal events to work toward overcoming the challenge

Scoring Rubric for Challenge Worksheet, Grade 8

INDICATOR	DEVELOPING	COMPETENT	PROFICIENT
Plan to Overcome an Individual Challenge	• Individual challenge not specific to the individual • Provides less than 2 barriers and/or positive ways or strategies to overcome challenge • Limited discussion • Less than 3 events listed or the events not related to overcoming challenge	• Identifies at least 1 individual challenge • Provides 2-3 barriers • Lists 2-3 positive ways or strategies • Multiple decisions discussed • Lists at least 3 events related to overcoming challenge	• Identifies multiple individual challenges • Provides more than 3 positive ways or strategies to overcome challenge

Note: *Many outcomes within Standard 5 can be assessed using a worksheet assessment. The assessment and scoring guide can be modified to fit the critical components of the outcome desired.*

Self-Expression and Enjoyment   Grade 8

Grade-Level Outcome

Discusses how enjoyment could be increased in self-selected physical activities. (S5.M4.8)

Assessment Task

Write letters to a school or local official expressing enjoyment of physical activity.

Guidelines

- Complete a worksheet OR

- Create a word cloud using guidance on worksheet

Setup

Provide a worksheet to guide letter or word cloud

Modifications for Other Grade Levels

The assessment task may be modified for Grade 6 and 7 outcomes. The Grade 6 Outcome S5.M4.6 has students describe how moving competently in a physical activity setting creates enjoyment. The outcome can be assessed by changing the critical components of the assessment task and letter. The Grade 7 Outcome S5.M4.7 has students identify why self-selected physical activities create enjoyment. The students can fill out the graphic organizer without writing the letter.

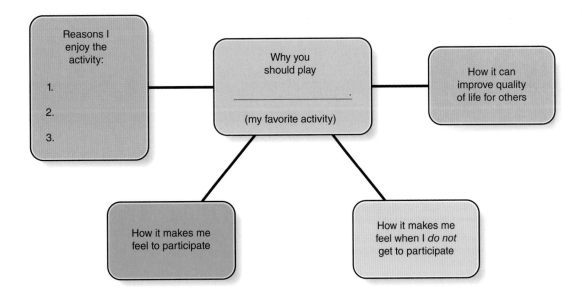

Create outline of letter below:

Critical Components for Letter

Specific requirements for the assignment are below:

Content Requirements

- Identifies at least 1 physical activity

- Provides multiple reasons participating in the activity is enjoyable

- Describes multiple ways of how the student feels participating or not participating in the activity

- Describes multiple ways participating in the activity can improve the quality of life for others

Writing and Grammar

- Outline lists major points to be discussed in the paper

- Letter is well-organized, focused, and clearly outlines major points

- Letter follows correct letter-writing mechanics

- Concepts were logically arranged to present a sound argument

- Normal conventions of spelling and grammar were followed with only minor errors

- Minor errors in spelling and grammar did not interfere with the readability of entry

- Transitions were effectively used to ensure comprehension

Scoring Rubric for Letter, Grade 8

INDICATOR	DEVELOPING	COMPETENT	PROFICIENT
Discusses Enjoyment of Participating in Physical Activity	Identifies a physical activity but: • Does not identify reasons physical activity is enjoyable OR • Does not describe feelings from participating or not participating in the activity OR • Does not discuss how participation will improve quality of life	• Identifies at least 1 physical activity • Provides 2-3 reasons activity is enjoyable • Describes feelings from participating or not participating in the activity • Lists at least 2 ways participation will improve quality of life	• Identifies multiple physical activities • Provides at least 3 reasons activity is enjoyable • Describes multiple feelings from participating or not participating in the activity in detail • Lists at least 3 ways participation will improve quality of life
Writing and Grammar	• Poorly organized letter with gaps • Errors in spelling and grammar negatively impact readability • Lacks transitions from content to content and sentence to sentence	• Letter well-organized, logically arranged • Letter and outline written in correct form • Only minor errors in grammar and/or spelling that do not interfere with readability • Transitions effectively used to ensure comprehension	• Letter well-organized, logically arranged, and directly supports overall idea • Errors in grammar and/or spelling are rare and do not impact readability • Transitions effective and aid in comprehension

Part IV

**Sample Assessments for High
School Physical Education**

Standard 1 Sample Assessments

Standard 1: The physically literate individual demonstrates competency in a variety of motor skills and movement patterns.

The Grade-Level Outcomes for high school students focus on personal choice in lifetime and fitness activities. By high school, students have begun to select fitness and physical activities they are likely to pursue into adulthood. Those choices are related to students' skill competency or their perceived skill competency, their individual interests, and the availability of opportunities to participate in the activities. At this level, students should participate in units of instruction that are longer (15-16 lessons) than those in middle school, allowing students more opportunities to improve their physical literacy in self-selected activities. These longer units help high school students build on fundamental movement and fitness competencies they developed in elementary and middle school by refining their skills in the activities of their choice. Developing competency in one or more activities is paramount if students are to continue engaging in physical activity, with competent students most likely to continue to participate (Barnett et al., 2008; Stodden et al., 2009; Stuart et al., 2005). As a high school physical educator, you will need to establish a climate of skill mastery to ensure that your students graduate as physically literate individuals, especially in their self-selected lifetime or fitness activities.

Assessments

The sample assessments in this part of the book address skill competency in lifetime and fitness activities, which are the focus of the Standard 1 Grade-Level Outcomes. The samples include **formative** and **summative assessments**, **pre- and post-assessments** for determining students' entry and exit points, as well as peer and self-assessments, such as **checklists**. Peer assessments allow students to work with one another and to provide feedback to classmates on their performance. Summative assessments require building **analytic rubrics** that address outcomes under several National Standards through one comprehensive instrument (see Appendix D). The analytic rubrics take an additive approach. Assessments that address outcomes under Standard 1 include indicators that are specific to skill competencies detailed in those outcomes. Assessments that address outcomes under Standard 2 include **indicators** that are specific to analysis of movement. For assessments that address each lifetime or fitness activity, the analytic rubrics contain added indicators that are specific to Grade-Level Outcomes under Standards 3, 4 and 5. Samples of complete analytic rubrics for selected lifetime or fitness activities appear in the Appendix.

When beginning each unit of instruction, you will want to conduct a pre-assessment to establish students' baseline competency levels in the skills and knowledge to be covered in the unit. That allows you to group students by ability, differentiate your instruction based on students' individual competency levels, and determine each student's progress over time. You also should conduct assessments throughout the unit to determine how well students are progressing and whether you need to modify your instruction or practice tasks. Finally, conduct post-assessments to determine students' exit competency levels and to track their skill improvement over time. This sequence of assessments provides you with the data for making instructional decisions.

Assessments for Measuring High School Students' Skills and Knowledge

The assessments in this section should be considered samples of possible assessments and not exemplars. The intent is not to provide specific assessments to be used by all programs but to provide you with "samples" that you can modify or adapt to your unique teaching environment. You are encouraged to use the sample assessments as a starting point for developing or adapting assessments that meet the needs of your program and students.

The three-level rubrics in these samples use a standard set of terms with common definitions, which is important for providing consistent feedback to students. The **Developing level** denotes students moving toward competency, but these students have not yet mastered all the identified **critical elements** or components specific to the indicator. Students at the **Competent level** demonstrate all of the critical elements or components aligned with the indicator. The Competent level defines the minimum level of performance required for meeting the indicator. Students at the **Proficient level** not only demonstrate all the required critical elements or components of the indicator, but their performance also meets additional criteria and/or displays a level of performance that goes beyond Competent. These three terms are used in the same manner in each of the rubric samples.

If you have students with disabilities in your classroom, many of the assessments will need to be modified and adapted. For specific guidance in this area, we recommend *Assessment for Everyone: Modifying NASPE Assessments to Include All Elementary School Children* (Lieberman, Kowalski, et al., 2011).

Lifetime Activity – Tennis

Level 1

Grade-Level Outcome

Demonstrates competency and/or refines activity-specific movement skills in 2 or more lifetime activities (outdoor pursuits, individual-performance activities, aquatics, net/wall games or target games). (S1.H1.L1)

Assessment Task

Demonstrate the tennis forehand and backhand during practice tasks or game play.

Pre-Assessment

For most racket sports, wall-volley tests are easy to conduct and provide baseline performance data for determining students' entry-level skills, planning for differentiated instruction, grouping students by ability, and tracking students' progress over time. For tennis, placing a line on a flat wall 3 feet from the floor allows you to measure students' entry-level skills for both forehand and backhand strokes. Students hit a tennis ball into the wall for 30 seconds and try to return it against the wall using both forehand and backhand strokes. The hitter must remain behind the restraining line (20-30 ft from the wall) for the groundstroke to count. A second student counts the number of successful attempts, while a third student feeds balls to the hitter if the hitter loses control of the groundstroke. Use the same wall-volley assessment to check students' progress at the midpoint of the unit and as a post-assessment. These assessments are formative and should not be used to determine student grades. You can use the same type of pre-assessment, with some modifications, for pickleball and racquetball.

Guidelines

- Assess skill competency during the practice task, modified game play or game play
- Using both formative and summative measures, assess skill competency over time
- Base evaluations on students' performance of the skill's critical elements

Setup

- Use wall or backboard for pre-assessment
- Participate on regulation courts in either singles or doubles format
- Enough equipment available to ensure maximum practice opportunities
- Access to 10 or more tennis balls per student
- Use full-size tennis rackets

Critical Elements for Tennis Forehand and Backhand

Forehand and Backhand Ready Position

- Bend slightly at knees with feet shoulder-width apart
- Shift weight onto balls of feet
- Keep head up, with shoulders parallel to net
- Hold racket edge parallel to ground
- Hold racket at waist level

Forehand

- Grip*

- » Make handshake with racket, using preferred hand
- » Form a "V" with thumb and forefinger on top of grip
- » Place palm of preferred hand on end of racket handle
- » Support throat of racket lightly with nonpreferred hand
- Backswing (closed stance)**
  - » Turn with preferred-side foot dropping back (pivot on nonpreferred foot)
  - » Racket back on turn at waist height in preparation
  - » Stand with lead shoulder facing net (unless hitting with an open stance)
  - » Shift weight to back foot
- Forward swing
  - » Keep wrist firm while swinging
  - » Contact ball well in front of body
  - » Shift weight from back foot to front foot by stepping toward the net
  - » Turn, with hips creating torque
  - » Keep racket edge parallel to ground throughout swing
  - » Swing through the ball with a low-to-high swing
- Finish
  - » Follow through to opposite shoulder
  - » Square shoulders to the net
  - » Return to ready position with weight on balls of feet

Note: *If you teach other grips, such as the semi-western or western, adjust critical elements accordingly.*

****Note:** *If you teach open stance, adjust critical elements accordingly.*

Backhand
- Grip
  - » Form a "V" with thumb and forefinger a quarter turn to the nonpreferred side from forehand grip
  - » Place palm of preferred hand on the end of the racket handle
  - » Support throat of racket lightly with nonpreferred hand
  - » If using a two-handed backhand, add nonpreferred hand on handle in front of dominant hand
- Backswing
  - » Turn with preferred-side foot stepping forward (pivot on nonpreferred foot)
  - » Bring racket back on turn at waist height in preparation
  - » Stand with lead shoulder facing net
  - » Keep weight on back foot
- Forward swing
  - » Keep wrist firm while swinging
  - » Contact ball in front of body

» Shift weight from back foot to front foot by stepping toward the net

» Turn, with hips creating torque

» Keep racket edge parallel to ground throughout swing

» Swing through the ball with a low-to-high swing

• Finish

» Follow through

» Square shoulders to net

» Return to ready position with weight on balls of feet

Note: *For students using two-hand forehands and backhands, adjust critical elements accordingly.*

Scoring Rubric for Forehand and Backhand, Level 1

INDICATOR	DEVELOPING	COMPETENT	PROFICIENT
Critical Elements Grip	One or more critical elements of forehand or backhand grip not present • Palm on top of handle • Uses baseball grip with no "V" with thumb and forefinger • Uses incorrect positioning for alternate grips • Uses same grip for forehand and backhand	Demonstrates all critical elements of forehand and backhand grips: • Handshake with racket using preferred hand (forehand – eastern) • Uses correct alternate grip • Forms "V" with thumb and forefinger (backhand) • Supports throat of racket lightly with nonpreferred hand • Places palm of preferred hand at end of racket • Keeps both hands firmly on racket handle (for two-handed backhand)	Demonstrates all critical elements of forehand and backhand grips • Grip relaxed without undue tension
Critical Elements Backswing	1 or 2 critical elements not present • Shoulders remain facing net • Pivot disconnected from turn • Racket remains below waist • No backswing or preparation observed	Demonstrates all critical elements: • Pivots with preferred foot dropping back (forehand) and nonpreferred foot stepping forward (backhand) unless using open stance • Brings racket back on turn at waist height in preparation • Lead shoulder facing net and weight on back foot	Demonstrates all critical elements • Holds racket parallel to ground throughout backswing • Full range of motion evident in backswing • Backswing well-timed with pivot
Critical Elements Forward Swing	1 or 2 critical elements not present: • Contacts ball off back foot • Little or no rotation with hips • No weight shift or weight shift badly timed • Racket face either too open or too closed • Swings at ball, not through it	Demonstrates all critical elements: • Keeps wrist firm while swinging • Contacts ball well in front of body • Shifts weight from back to front foot by stepping toward net • Turns, with hips creating torque • Keeps racket edge parallel to ground throughout swing • Swings through ball with low-to-high swing	Demonstrates all critical elements • Swings with well-coordinated and well-timed, unified motion • Full range of motion, resulting in both power and accuracy • Applies topspin to ball
Critical Elements Finish	1 or 2 critical elements not present: • Follow-through abbreviated • Shoulders remain sideways to net • Ready position not evident	Demonstrates all critical elements: • Follows through • Squares shoulders to net • Returns to ready position with weight on balls of feet	Demonstrates all critical elements • Full range of motion on follow-through • Assumes ready position with weight on balls of feet in center of court

Note: *You could use critical cues for the forehand and backhand swings, with minor modifications, for other racket sports, such as pickleball and badminton.*

✍ *Sample Formative Assessment: Peer Checklist for Tennis Forehand/Backhand*

Name of performer: _____

Name of observer: _____

For each line on the checklist use one of the following codes:

A = The movement is absent or some of the criteria are executed poorly

P = The movement is present and meets all criteria

Checklist for Tennis Forehand

Performer Demonstrates:

- Ready position with shoulders facing net and weight on balls of feet _____
- Proper grip – handshake with "V" formed with thumb and forefinger (or alternate grip) _____
- Well-timed and smooth pivot and turn – preferred foot dropping back _____
- Shoulder sideways to net, racket back, step-turn with torque (or open stance) _____
- Ball contact well in front of lead foot _____
- Swing is through the ball, with low-to-high arc _____
- Follow-through with swing and return to ready position _____

Checklist for Tennis Backhand

Performer Demonstrates:

- Ready position with shoulders facing net and weight on balls of feet _____
- Proper grip with quarter turn (or alternative grip) _____
- Well-timed and smooth pivot turn, as preferred foot steps forward _____
- Shoulder sideways to net, racket back, step-turn with torque _____
- Ball contact in front of lead foot, swing through ball _____
- Swing through ball, with low-to-high arc _____
- Follow-through and return to ready position _____

Lifetime Activity – Tennis

Level 1

Grade-Level Outcome

Demonstrates competency and/or refines activity-specific movement skills in 2 or more lifetime activities (outdoor pursuits, individual-performance activities, aquatics, net/wall games or target games). (S1.H1.L1)

Assessment Task

Demonstrate overhand serve in tennis.

Guidelines

- Offer units of instruction 15 to 16 classes in length
- Assess skill competency through practice tasks or game play
- Assess skill competency over time with both formative and summative assessments
- Evaluate students' skills based on critical elements

Setup

- Regulation courts
- Enough equipment available to ensure maximum practice opportunities
- Use full-size tennis rackets
- Evaluate skill based on process and not outcome

Critical Elements for Tennis Overhand Serve

Stance

- Stand sideways to net, nonpreferred foot forward (see photo *a*)
- Point lead foot toward opposite service post
- Place back foot parallel to baseline
- Align toes of back foot with heel of front foot

Grip

- Hold racket with edge perpendicular to surface
- Form "V" with thumb and forefinger up the edge of racket
- Spread fingers in a loose grip

Toss

- Toss ball up gently and slightly in front of body (see photo *b*)
- Toss as high as full extension of arm and racket
- Toss consistent with a fluid motion and straight arm
- Release ball around eye level and follow through with tossing motion

Backswing and Contact

- Bring racket behind body as you toss the ball

- Bend knees and shift weight to back foot

- Drop racket head down to center of back, with elbow pointing upward (loose drop of racket and arm)

- Shift weight forward and upward (spring forward toward the ball) (see photo *c*)

- Swing up with racket to contact the ball in a throwing-like motion

- Snap wrist at end of contact

Follow-Through

- Bring racket down toward opposite foot

- Follow-through should carry body into court (see photo *d*)

- Move to center of baseline

Scoring Rubric for Tennis Overhand Serve, Level 1

INDICATOR	DEVELOPING	COMPETENT	PROFICIENT
Critical Elements Stance	One or more critical elements not present: • Faces net in forward position • Both feet pointing toward net	Demonstrates all critical elements : • Sideways to net • Points lead foot toward opposite net post • Back foot parallel to baseline	Demonstrates all critical elements: • Knees bend allowing increased range of motion
Critical Elements Grip	One or more critical elements not present: • Baseball or other grip used	Demonstrates all critical elements: • "V" formed with thumb and forefinger • Racket edge perpendicular to surface • Spread fingers in loose grip	Demonstrates all critical elements: • Loose grip with wrist snap
Critical Elements Toss	One or more critical elements not present: • Toss at eye level or lower • Toss inconsistent • Throws ball up instead of tossing	Demonstrates all critical elements: • Toss gentle and slightly in front of body • Straight arm, released at eye level • High toss allowing full extension of arm and racket	Demonstrates all critical elements • Toss consistently in same plane with little or no variation • Toss well-timed with backswing • Full extension upon contact
Critical Elements Backswing and Contact	One or more critical elements not present: • Elbow down as racket head dropped back • Weight remains on front foot throughout motion • Racket head points down upon contact	Demonstrates all critical elements: • Racket back behind body with elbow pointing upward • Loose drop of racket and arm as weight shifts to back foot • Swing upward to contact ball with a forward weight shift • Head of racket moves to ball with a throwing motion • Snaps wrist upon contact	Demonstrates all critical elements: • Times contact with uncoiling of body, resulting in additional power on serve • Wrist snap well-timed
Critical Elements Follow-Through	One or more critical elements not present: • No or limited follow-through resulting in a "punch of the ball" • Falls away from court	Demonstrates all critical elements: • Follow-through downward toward opposite foot • Carries body into court • Moves to center of baseline	Demonstrates all critical elements • Places topspin on serve • Moves to center of baseline into ready position

✍ Sample Formative Assessment: Peer Checklist for Tennis Overhand Serve

Name of performer: _____

Name of observer: _____

For each line on the checklist use one of the following codes:

A = the movement is absent or some part of the criteria is poorly executed

P = the movement is present and meets all criteria

Checklist for Tennis Overhand Serve

- Stance – on baseline, front foot points to net post and back foot is parallel to baseline _____

- Proper grip – forms "V" with thumb and forefinger _____

- Tosses the ball and brings racket up and behind body with a fluid motion while shifting weight to back foot _____

- Tosses ball with straight arm and slightly higher than full extension of racket _____

- Bends knees with weight on back foot to spring forward upon contact with ball _____

- Rotates shoulders in a throwing motion _____

- Hits through the ball (throws the racket face at the ball) _____

- Follows through by bringing racket down toward opposite foot _____

- Moves to center of baseline in ready position _____

Lifetime Activity – Golf   Level 1

Grade-Level Outcome

Demonstrates competency and/or refines activity-specific movement skills in 2 or more lifetime activities (outdoor pursuits, individual-performance activities, aquatics, net/wall games or target games). (S1.H1.L1)

Assessment Task

Demonstrate the basic golf swing with a 4, 5 or 6 iron.

Pre-Assessment

A number of options are available as pre-assessments for the basic golf swing and students' prior knowledge of the game. Students can complete a survey specific to their experiences with golf, which would provide you with baseline data. Another option would be a written pre-test specific to golf rules and etiquette. This type of knowledge test would give you some indication of students' exposure and knowledge of the game. Another common approach is to evaluate students' swing using a checklist of key attributes. Students would hit 10 balls using a short iron (7, 8 or 9) and you would evaluate each of their swings based on the checklist. The focus of the checklist is the smooth transfer of weight and a balanced finish. A sample of a process-based checklist for the basic golf swing is provided below:

✍ Checklist for Basic Golf Swing Using a Short Iron

Name of performer: _____

For each line on the checklist use one of the following codes:

A = the movement is absent or some part of the criteria is poorly executed

P = the movement is present and meets all criteria

Pre-Assessment Checklist for Basic Golf Swing

- Weight balanced on both feet in stance   _____
- Knee flexed   _____
- Slow takeaway of club on backswing   _____
- Weight shifts to front foot starting on downswing   _____
- Swing through the ball with weight moving to front foot   _____
- Follow through and finish high   _____
- Weight on front foot in balanced position   _____

The use of this checklist is specific to pre-assessing skill levels for the class. It is not used to measure competency for the basic golf swing.

Guidelines

- Offer units of instruction 15 to 16 classes in length
- Assess skill competency through practice tasks

- Assess skill competency over time with both formative and summative assessments
- Evaluate skills based on the critical elements

Setup

- Outdoor
    - » Provide a designated target area or flag stick
    - » Use regulation clubs and golf balls
- Indoor
    - » Provide a designated target area marked by cones/hula hoops OR
    - » Hit into a net
    - » Use golf-size Wiffle balls or other appropriate indoor equipment
    - » Hit off of mats
    - » Use regulations clubs
- Access to at least 10 balls for each student
- Adequate space for a full swing

Critical Elements for Basic Golf Swing

Grip (right hand preferred – reverse for left hand preferred)

- Place left hand on club
    - » Left thumb and left index finger on shaft
    - » V formed between thumb and index finger points to right ear
    - » Side of grip against fingers
- Place right hand on club
    - » Place right hand on club with middle joints of your middle two fingers touching grip
    - » Use one of the following grips:
        - Vardon grip (overlapping)—Place little finger of right hand between the index and middle fingers of left hand. Fingers overlap, with the thumb of the left hand fit in life-line of right hand. The "V" formed by the thumb and forefinger points to the right ear.
        - Interlocking grip—Same hand placement as Vardon grip except the little finger of left hand and the index finger of right hand hook together, and the right finger dovetails around the forefinger of left hand.

Stance (right hand preferred – reverse for left hand preferred)

- Position of feet
    - » Left foot pointed at 10 o'clock
    - » Right foot at 1 o'clock
    - » Feet shoulder-width apart
    - » Feet parallel and left of target line
- Knees flexed, but not bent
- Weight balanced on both feet
- Ball position in stance
    - » Ball aligned to left heel with driver

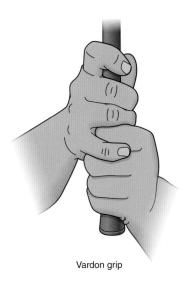

Vardon grip

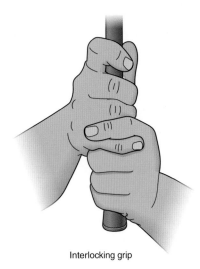

Interlocking grip

» Ball moves backward from left heel as length of club shortens (more loft on club the farther back the ball in stance)

» Wedge or 9 iron ball in middle of stance

Club Takeaway (right hand preferred – reverse for left hand preferred)

- Club starts back in this order: clubhead, arms, shoulders, hips

- Right arm stays close to right side

- Hands pass right leg, weight shifts to back leg

- Clubface pointing toe up

Halfway Back on Takeaway

- As club passes the parallel-to-ground point on backswing

  » Right elbow bends next to body and hinge the club at 90-degree angle with left arm

  » Shaft begins to move around body

  » Body coils around center

- Shoulders rotate – pulling hips into swing

Top of Backswing

- Wrist fully cocked at top of backswing

- Left arm remains straight, right elbow pointing to ground

- Hands at 11 o' clock with hands and arms under club

- Club shaft almost parallel to ground

- Weight on back foot, but balanced

Downswing

- Begins with moving left knee and hip over left foot

- Arms drop with right elbow into a position in front of right hip

- Belt buckle should point at ball, but shoulders remain closed

- Forward weight shift with lower body – head behind ball

- Retain wrist hinge as swing starts down

Impact

- Hips continue turn with left hip cleared by impact
- Hips should pull shoulders
- Body uncoils
- Keep head behind ball
- Left side straightens as right side moves forward
- Hands slightly ahead of clubhead on impact

Follow-Through

- Extend both arms
- Right shoulder lower than left shoulder
- Arms start to swing back to inside
- Right knee turns inward toward left knee
- Left leg straight
- Weight on left foot with right foot up and on its toes
- Body weight fully transferred to left heel
- Belt buckle points at or slightly left of target

Ball Flight

- Ball trajectory upward
- Ball flies straight to target

Note: *The golf swing is a closed loop skill in that once it begins there is little time to make any adjustment during the swing. Feedback on the swing occurs after its completion and is provided by an observer, review of a video, or knowledge of results (how close the ball landed in relationship to the target). Because the golf swing is one complete sequential motion, it must be evaluated more holistically. The assessment sample provided below is an example of a holistic rubric that could be used with the golf swing.*

Scoring Rubric for Basic Golf Swing, Level 1

LEVEL	CRITICAL ELEMENTS FOR BASIC GOLF SWING
Proficient **Critical Elements**	Demonstrates correct stance, ball position and posture for selected **club with bend at the waist at 45 degrees**; Grip correct (Vardon or interlocking) **with relaxed hand position**; Takeaway smooth, well-controlled with weight shift to back foot **well-timed; Hands and arms move as one unit**; Wrist fully cocked at top of backswing; Downswing begins with knee and hip over left foot **with well-coordinated forward weight shift with lower body**; Head behind ball upon contact; Upon impact hips pull shoulders through swing with hands slightly ahead of clubhead **as body uncoils**; Follow-through with weight transferred to front foot on toes in balanced position **with clubhead dropped behind head**; ball trajectory **high and straight.**
Competent **Critical Elements**	Demonstrates correct stance, ball position and posture for selected club; Grip correct (Vardon or interlocking); Takeaway smooth, well-controlled with weight shift to back foot; Wrist fully cocked at top of backswing; Downswing begins with knee and hip over left foot; Forward weight shift with lower body; Head behind ball upon contact; Upon impact hips pull shoulders through swing with hands slightly ahead of clubhead; Follow-through with weight transferred to front foot on toes in balanced position; ball trajectory straight.
Developing **Critical Elements**	Stance, ball position, posture and target path **lack alignment; Grip incorrect**; Takeaway **segmented, lacking continuity** with **no visible weight shift; fails to maintain balance; No cocking of wrist** on backswing and limited extension, reducing range of motion; Downswing **poorly timed with hands and arms leading the way**; Shoulders and hip lag behind contact; **Head position moves** throughout swing; **Weight fails to transfer** to front foot or **hitter fails to maintain balance** on front foot; Ball **trajectory along ground or right or left of target line.**

Lifetime Activity – 2 v 2 or 3 v 3 Volleyball

Level 1

Grade-Level Outcome

Demonstrates competency and/or refines activity-specific movement skills in 2 or more lifetime activities (outdoor pursuits, individual-performance activities, aquatics, net/wall games or target games). (S1.H1.L1)

Assessment Task

- Demonstrate competency for the forearm pass during 2 v 2 or 3 v 3 game play. OR

- Demonstrate competency for the forearm pass through continuous self-passing (see pre-assessment below).

Pre-Assessment

Player stands between regulation net and the 10-foot line. Using the forearm pass, the player self-passes to her or himself while a scorer counts the number of successful passes completed without the ball touching the floor or the net. For a pass to be successful, the ball must be passed higher than the net. If the ball is below the height of the net, the scorer does not count the pass, but the player can continue. If the next pass is higher than the net, then the count continues. Once a pass is missed (e.g., hits the floor or net, loss of control, etc.) the count stops. The player has three total trials and the trials alternate with the scorer until both have completed their three trials. The trial with the highest total of consecutive passes becomes the player's pre-assessment score. This assessment was modified from USAVolleyball.

This assessment can be repeated at the mid- and end-point of the unit. This will give you comparison data that can be part of your analysis specific to student's progress and instructional effectiveness.

Guidelines

- Offer units of instruction 15 to 16 classes in length

- Assess skill competency through modified game play

- Assess skill competency over time with both formative and summative assessments

- Evaluate skills based on the critical elements

Setup for Game Play Assessment

- Badminton or modified volleyball court

- Net height of 7 feet 4 inches for women; 7 feet 11 inches for men and coed

- 2 v 2 and 3 v 3 game play

- Regulation volleyball

- Analytical rubric

Setup for Continuous Forearm Pass Assessment

See pre-assessment setup and guidelines.

Critical Elements for Volleyball Forearm Pass

Stance

- Ready position with weight on balls of feet

- Straight arms away from body

- Maintain 90-degree angle between arms and upper body

- Bend at waist with shoulders forward and hips back

- Knees flexed

- Feet shoulder-width apart with one foot slightly in front of the other

Hand Position

- Form platform with thumbs and heels of palms together

- Wrist turned down so thumbs point to floor

- Keep a consistent flat platform

Passing Motion

- Hips open in direction of flight of ball

- Track ball onto platform

- Keep body behind ball

- Contact ball on lower forearm

- Maintain straight-arm position to allow ball to rebound off lower forearms

- Contact ball at hip level

- Knees extended to raise arms forward on contact (not a swing)

- Straighten legs to complete pass

- Weight transferred in direction of pass

Redirect

- Forearm pass used to redirect flight of ball

- Move to ball without crossing feet (shuffle steps)

- Always face the ball when passing

Note: *Assessment of the forearm pass occurs during 2 v 2 or 3 v 3 play to ensure students have the opportunity to demonstrate their competency during game conditions. This will provide you with a more "authentic" assessment of their skill levels. You also can evaluate competency by using the pre-assessment of self-passing. This assessment will allow you to compare entry and exit competency points based on skill level.*

Scoring Rubric for Forearm Pass, Level 1

INDICATOR	DEVELOPING	COMPETENT	PROFICIENT
Critical Elements Stance	One or more critical elements not present: • Flat footed with arms down • Arms bent and too close to body • Knees straight • Feet too close together or too wide apart	Demonstrates all critical elements: • Ready position with weight on balls of feet • Arms straight and away from body • 90-degree angle between arms and upper body • Knees flexed • Feet shoulder-width apart with one foot slightly ahead	Demonstrates all critical elements: • Feet consistently face intended ball flight direction
Critical Elements Hand Position	One or more critical elements not present: • Arms separated and hands apart • Platform uneven	Demonstrates all critical elements: • Thumbs and heels of palms together • Wrist turned down • Flat platform	Demonstrates all critical elements: • Consistent flat platform • Thumbs and heels of palms tightly together
Critical Elements Passing Motion	One or more critical elements not present: • Swings at ball • Ball contacted above hip level • Knee and leg extension disjointed and ill-timed • No weight transfer	Demonstrates all critical elements: • Hips open in direction of ball flight • Body behind ball • Ball contacted on lower forearms • Ball contacted at hip level • Ball rebounds off of flat platform • Knees extend and straighten legs to complete pass • Weight transfers in direction of pass	Demonstrates all critical elements: • Knee and leg extension well-timed • Shoulders shrugged upon contact • Platform absorbs and redirects flight path
Critical Elements Redirection	One or more critical elements not present: • Lack of control and outside boundaries • Ball below net height	Demonstrates all critical elements: • Pass redirected • Faces ball when passing • Ball travels above net height • Uses shuffle steps	Demonstrates all critical elements: • Controlled redirection of pass • Ball travels above net height and to intended target

217

Grade-Level Outcome

Demonstrates competency in dance forms used in cultural and social occasions (e.g., weddings, parties), or demonstrates competency in 1 form of dance (e.g., ballet, modern, hip hop, tap). (S1.H2.L1)

Assessment Task

Students execute creative/modern dance technique, line, timing, memorization and performance.

Pre-Assessment

Students complete a survey on their previous experience in dance to provide pre-assessment data. Upload survey results to your school's data system, or gather data in an online database (e.g., SurveyMonkey) by having students respond to the survey using their phones during class.

Guidelines

- Assess skill competency during rehearsals or performance

- Assess skill competency over time with both formative and summative assessments

- Base skill evaluations on critical elements

- Allow students to opt out of "live" performance

Setup

- Allow enough space to move freely

- Allow enough space for both individual and group practice or rehearsal

- Allow all students access to equipment and rehearsal time

Use critical elements that follow when assessing students' dance technique and execution. You may add criteria to the rubric that follows, including specifying the number of steps, shapes, or other requirements. The rubric facilitates the evaluation of specific dance techniques and skills, but you can easily include other criteria for a longer dance project or for performance specific to choreography, music selection, terminology, or creativity.

Critical Elements for Creative or Modern Dance

Technique and Line

- Uses correct posture

- Demonstrates vertical body alignment (still and moving)

- Maintains body alignment during transitions

- Turns, head spot

- Jumps, with knee bent during takeoff and landing

- Demonstrates flexibility of spine, legs, and shoulders

- Demonstrates agility and coordination in executing combinations

- Extends body parts fully

- Creates clear body shapes with correct orientation and alignment

- Occupies space – including direction, size, pathways, levels, and shapes

- Demonstrates relationships – one movement to another including pulse, tempo, rhythm and phrases

- Demonstrates force by degree of muscular tension and energy (strong/light; sharp/smooth; tension/relaxation; bound/flowing)

Timing and Memorization

- Maintains correct count

- Accurate movements in beat and tempo

- Musical phrasing evident

- Executes changes in tempo and pacing

- Memorizes steps and sequences, and executes them with precision

Performance:

- Explores formal relationship in space and time

- Uses entire dance area

- Communicates emotions and ideas through movement

- Demonstrates creativity by using prop(s) and/or costuming, unique combinations/shapes/transitions

- Demonstrates focus, projection, and energy

- Choice of music enhances performance

- Demonstrates a variety of motion/body movements such as percussive, sustained, swinging, collapse, suspend, and/or vibratory

Scoring Rubric for Dance and Rhythm – Creative or Modern Dance, Level 1

INDICATOR	DEVELOPING	COMPETENT	PROFICIENT

Critical Elements
 	
Technique and Line
	One or more critical elements not present:
	
	• Vertical alignment and posture weak with loss of control
	• Difficulty remaining in balance while moving and holding poses (still movements)
	• Limited flexibility demonstrated with reductions in extensions with spine, legs, and/or shoulders
	• Movements lack flow and coordination with hesitations or missteps throughout
	• Multiple and evident technique mistakes
		Demonstrates the following critical elements:
		
		• Maintains posture with occasional lapses (less than 20% of the time)
		• Vertical alignment maintained while still and/or moving
		• Technique on two of the four:
		  » Turns – head spot
		  » Jumps – bent knee takeoff/landing
		  » Still – balance and control maintained for two seconds
		  » Full extension
		• Demonstrates flexibility
		  » Spine
		  » Legs
		  » Shoulders
		• Shapes clear with correct orientation/alignment
		• Agility and coordination with combinations
			Demonstrates all critical elements:
			
			• Maintains posture throughout
			• Vertical alignment maintained while still and moving
			• Technique on three of the four:
			  » Turns – head spot
			  » Jumps – bent knee takeoff/landing
			  » Still – balance and control maintained for two seconds
			  » Full extension
			• Agility and coordination with combinations, transitions, beginning and ending of phases

(continued)

Scoring Rubric for Dance and Rhythm – Creative or Modern Dance, Level 1 *(continued)*

INDICATOR	DEVELOPING	COMPETENT	PROFICIENT
Critical Elements Timing and Memorization	One or more critical elements not present: • Difficulty with maintaining count, beat, and/or tempo • Seems lost with evident missteps • No changes in tempo and pace • Obvious sequence mistakes and reliance on following others • Little or no precision in movements	Demonstrates all critical elements: • Correct count with accurate beat/tempo with only minor variations (less than 20% of the time) • Changes in tempo and pace evident • Steps and sequence memorized with only minor hesitations evident • Steps and movements executed with precision	Demonstrates all critical elements: • Correct count with accurate beat/tempo • Unique changes in tempo and pace evident • Steps and sequence executed with confidence and no hesitations • Steps and movements executed with precision and full extensions

Critical Elements
 	
Performance
	One or more critical elements not present:
	
	• Limited use of dance area, which restricts the exploration of space and time
	• Lacks creativity with limited variety of motions/body movements
	• Same motions/body movements/steps repeated throughout
	• Low energy, limited projection and focus
		Demonstrates all critical elements:
		
		• Explores relationships of space and time
		• Uses all four corners of dance area
		• Demonstrates creativity by using at least two of the following:
		  » Props or costumes
		  » Unique combinations
		  » Unique shapes
		  » Unique transitions
		  » Choice of music
		• Communicates emotions/ideas
		• Demonstrates focus, projection, and energy
		• Demonstrates at least three of the following motions/body movements:
		  » Percussive
		  » Sustained
		  » Swinging
		  » Collapse
		  » Suspend
		  » Vibratory
			Demonstrates all critical elements
			
			• Demonstrates unique exploration of space and time
			• Uses entire dance area
			• Demonstrates creativity using at least three of the following:
			  » Props or costumes
			  » Unique combinations
			  » Unique shapes
			  » Unique transitions
			  » Choice of music
			• Demonstrates at least four of the following motions/body movements:
			  » Percussive
			  » Sustained
			  » Swinging
			  » Collapse
			  » Suspend
			  » Vibratory

Note: *Dance lends itself to collaboration and group work. If the assignment is a group presentation, you can modify the rubric to include indicators for measuring group performance, including group choreography and collaboration. You could use the existing rubric to evaluate individual students on technique, timing and memorization, then add a performance section on how well the group performed as a unit. These additions would address Grade-Level Outcomes under Standard 4. See Part IV, Standard 4 for an example of an assessment for evaluating how well individual students work within a group.*

Dance and Rhythms – Folk, Square, and Line Dance

Level 1

Grade-Level Outcome

Demonstrates competency in dance forms used in cultural and social occasions (e.g., weddings, parties), or demonstrates competency in 1 form of dance (e.g., ballet, modern, hip hop, tap). (S1.H2.L1)

Assessment Task

Students execute folk, square or line dance steps and sequences.

Pre-Assessment

Administrate a short quiz on dance terminology or a quiz that has students match steps to their descriptions.

Guidelines

- Offer units of instruction lasting 15 to 16 classes so that students can develop competency

- Assess skill competency during rehearsals or performance

- Assess skill over time with both formative and summative assessments

- Evaluate skill based on critical elements

- Allows students to opt out of "live" performances

Setup

- Ensure enough space to move freely

- Allocate space for both individual and group practice and/or rehearsal

- Ensure all students have access to equipment and rehearsal time

Folk, square and line dances allow students to learn formations, steps and sequences to music. While each form is unique, they all have some common elements that you can assess using similar rubric indicators. In the section that follows, you will find a list of critical elements and indicators that you can apply to all three dance forms. See the rubric that follows for indicators that are specific to each of the dance forms. The most common steps for each dance form are identified under critical elements, but they are not described. You can find descriptions of the steps and instructional videos on numerous websites.

Critical Elements Common to Folk, Square and Line Dances

Formations

- Assumes correct positions to begin and end dance

- Maintains correct posture and hand positions

- Remains in formation

Steps and Sequences

- Maintains beat of dance

- Maintains composure and control from beginning to end

- Synchronizes movements with a partner or group

- Maintains rhythm and flow

- Differentiates between slow and quick steps

- Transitions from step to step or sequence to sequence seamlessly, with no hesitation

Performance

- Performs dance steps with ease

- Performs sequences from memory

- Shows personality and authenticity through dance

- Follows dance etiquette and protocol

Steps That Are Unique to Each Dance Form

FOLK DANCE STEPS	SQUARE DANCE STEPS	LINE DANCE STEPS
Allemande	Allemande	Ankle rock
Balance	Balance	Ball change
Bounce	Box the gnat	Brush/scuff
Brush	Circle (left and right or line)	Cha-cha
Cabriole	Courtesy turn	Charleston
Cha-cha	Do paso	Chasse
Chasse	Do-si-do	Close
Close	Down center and back	Coaster
Crossover	Forward and back	Fan
Gallop	Grand right and left (weave ring)	Grapevine
Grapevine	Grand square	Heel-and-toe splits
Heel-and-toe	Honor	Heel twist
Hop	Hub back out – rim in	Heel swivels (2 and 4 counts)
Jump	Ladies chain (1 and 2)	Hitch
Kick	Pass through	Hook
Pivot	Promenade (single and couple)	Jazz box
Polka	Roll away with a half sashay	Kick-ball change
Point	Seesaw your pretty little taw	Lindy
Reel	Split the ring	Lock
Rock	Star (right/promenade)	Mambo
Slide	Swing (elbow and waist)	Monterey turn
Schottische		Pivot
Skip		Rumba box
Stomp		Sailor
Touch		Shuffle
Waltz		Slide
		Sugarfoot
		Touch/Point
		Waltz
		Weave

Note: This table is not all-inclusive and represents only some of the most common steps. The steps that you teach will depend on dance selections and unit objectives. You will note some overlap in steps across the three dance forms, which means that you could teach folk, square, and line dance as one unit if the unit comprises 15 or 16 classes.

Scoring Rubric for Folk, Square and Line Dance, Level 1

INDICATOR	DEVELOPING	COMPETENT	PROFICIENT
Critical Elements Formation	One or more critical elements not present: • Assumes incorrect position beginning or end of dance • Incorrect posture and hand positions the majority of time (51% or more) • Falls out of formation or faces wrong direction/wall	Demonstrates all critical elements: • Assumes correct positions to begin and end dance • Maintains correct posture and hand positions at least 70% of time • Remains in formation • Starting and ending on correct wall (line dance) at least 70% of time	Demonstrates all critical elements: • Correction positions to begin/end dance • Correct posture and hand positions 90% of the time or more • Remains in formation • Starting and ending on correct wall (line dance) at least 90% of time or more
Critical Elements Steps and Sequence	One or more critical elements not present: • Consistently off beat (over 51%) • Falls out of balance or loss of body control • Fails to synchronize with partner or group • Transitions lack continuity with missteps and hesitations • Does not differentiate between slow and quick steps	Demonstrates all critical elements: • Maintains beat of dance at least 70% of the time • Maintains composure and body control from beginning to end • Synchronizes movements with partner or group at least 70% of the time • Differentiates between slow and quick steps • Transitions from step to step and sequence to sequence with no hesitation at least 70% of the time	Demonstrates all critical elements: • Maintains beat throughout dance • Synchronizes movements with partner or group at least 90% of the time • Smooth/flowing transitions from step to step and sequence to sequence with no hesitation at least 90% of the time
Critical Elements Performance	One or two critical elements not present: • Struggles with dance steps throughout the performance • Watches others to determine next steps in sequence • Struggles with dance etiquette and protocol • Can only concentrate on steps • Does not recognize or respond to cues by caller (square dance)	Demonstrates all critical elements: • Performs dance steps with ease at least 70% of the time • Only minor missteps are evident in dance sequence (no more than four) • Adds personality and authenticity through dance • Follows dance etiquette and protocol • At least 70% of time steps on cue with caller (square dance)	Demonstrates all critical elements: • Performs all dance steps with ease • Adds personality, authenticity, and style throughout dance • Steps on cue with caller (square dance) at least 90% of the time • Serves as a caller for a square dance

Note: *Dance lends itself to collaboration and group work. If the assignment is for the group to create a square or line dance using various steps or even movements associated with hip hop or other dance form, the above rubric could be modified to include indicators dedicated to the group choreography and collaboration. Individuals in the dance are evaluated using the above rubric specific to formations, steps and sequences, but the performance section would include indicators specific to how well individuals in the group work together, which would address Grade-Level Outcomes under Standard 4. See the section on Standard 4 for an example of an assessment for evaluating how well individuals work within a group.*

Other assessments appropriate for dance and rhythm units include peer checklists; integration of written assignments on multicultural dances from various countries; students mapping out dance sequences or steps, video-recording dances and analyzing the movement patterns, reflecting on their experiences, and/or compiling graphic organizers. You also could have students wear pedometers or heart rate monitors to determine their activity levels during a dance unit.

Grade-Level Outcome

Demonstrates competency in 1 or more specialized skills in health-related fitness activities. (S1.H3.L1)

Assessment Task

Students perform yoga as fitness training to improve flexibility, resilience, and strength.

Pre-Assessment

You can use scores from a fitness assessment including flexibility (e.g., sit-and-reach, shoulder flex test, goniometer tests, etc.), balance (e.g., stork test, beam walk, balance board, etc.), strength (e.g., push-ups, sit-ups, handgrip strength, etc.), and resilience (e.g., rating of perceived exertion, PAR-Q, etc.) to determine individual starting points.

Guidelines

- Offer units of instruction 15 to 16 classes in length

- Assess skill competency through practice tasks

- Assess skill competency over time with both formative and summative assessments

- Evaluate skills based on the critical elements

Setup

- Enough space to move freely

- Space available for both individual and group practice

- Access to equipment (towel, blanket, or mat) and practice time

Here are critical elements for various yoga techniques, including elements specific to posture, relaxation, and breathing that are used with all poses.

Critical Elements for Yoga

Posture

- Hold steady posture for 6 to 8 breaths

- Control wobble and/or muscle trembling by lengthening breath

- Move slowly and surely

- Focus on breath and postural movement

Relaxation/Breathing Techniques

- Use active or dynamic relaxation techniques
    - » Breath as a conscious endeavor
    - » Close eyes and take deep breaths, lengthening exhalation
    - » Consciously contract and relax muscles from feet up
    - » Focus on body sensations
- Use these breathing techniques
    - » Breathe through the nose
    - » Controlled breathing

- Inhalation
- Retention or holding after inhalation
- Exhalation
- Retention or holding after exhalation

» Breathe deeply, expanding chest and abdomen

» Hold poses for 6 to 8 breaths (as long as 30 seconds)

Directions

- Flexion: Bending forward
- Extension: Bending backward
- Lateral flexion: Bending sideways
- Rotation: Twisting

Yoga Poses

POSTURE	ABS, STRENGTH, AND INVERSIONS	BALANCING AND BENDS
Posture (sitting): • Sukhasana (Easy pose) • Vajrasana (Thunderbolt pose) • Svastikasana (Auspicious pose) • Balasana (Child's pose)	**Abs:** • Paripurna navasana (Boat pose) • Utkatasana (Chair pose) • Setu bandha (Bridge pose) • Marjaryasana (Cat pose) • Ananda balasana (Happy baby pose)	**Balancing:** • Virabhadrasana III variation (Warrior at the wall pose) • Vrikshasana (Tree pose) • Ardha chandrasana (Half moon pose) • Virabhadrasana III (Warrior III pose)
Posture (standing): • Tadasana (Mountain pose) • Uttanasana (Standing forward pose) • Ardha uttanasana (Standing half forward bend pose) • Parsva uttanasana (Asymmetrical forward bend pose) • Utthita trikonasana (Triangle pose) • Virabhadrasana I (Warrior I pose) • Virabhadrasana II (Warrior II pose) • Prasarita pada uttanasana (Standing spread-legged forward bend pose) • Ardha utkatasana (Half chair pose)	**Strength:** • Urdhva mukha svanasana (Upward-facing dog pose) • Plank pose • Dolphin pose • Dolphin plank pose • Vasisthasana (Side plank pose)	**Bends:** • Bhujanga (Cobra I pose) • Bhujangasana (Cobra II pose) • Shalabhasana (Locust I pose) • Trikonasana (Triangle pose) • Utthita parsvakonasana (Extended side angle pose) • Parighasana (Gate pose) • Padangusthasana (Big toe pose) • Parsvottanasana (Intense side stretch pose)
	Inversions • Ardha sarvangasana (Half shoulder stand pose) • Adho mukha svanasana (Downward-facing dog pose) • Uttana shishosana (Extended puppy pose) • Halasana (Plow pose) • Viparita karani (Legs-up-the-wall pose)	**Twists:** • Ardha matsyendrasana (Half lord of the fishes pose) • Marichyasana III (Marichi's pose) • Parivrtta parsvakonasana (Revolved side angle pose) • Parivrtta trikonasana (Reverse or revolved triangle pose)

Note: This table is not all-inclusive and represents only some of the most common poses taught at the beginning-yoga level with a focus on increasing flexibility, strength and resilience. Choose which poses to teach based on your unit objectives. Offering a yoga unit of 15 or 16 classes gives you ample time to teach the poses in each category. If you are uncomfortable with using the Hindi terms for the various positions, use the English translations. You can find complete descriptions of all poses in instructional videos, books, and articles online.

The rubric that follows is for measuring students' skill competency in various categories of yoga poses. You could modify the rubric to measure students' ability to plan and develop a yoga sequence to share with a partner or the class, which would address Grade-Level Outcomes under Standard 2.

Scoring Rubric for Yoga Poses, Level 1

INDICATOR	DEVELOPING	COMPETENT	PROFICIENT
Critical Elements Posture	Demonstrates one or more critical elements: • Poses held for 2 breaths or less • Wobbles and out of alignment • Transitions uneven with hesitations • Movements rushed and unsure	Demonstrates all critical elements: • Poses held for 6-8 breaths • Poses correct • Smoothly transitions from pose to pose • Movements slow and sure	Demonstrates all critical elements: • Poses held for 6-8 breaths • Poses correct with ability to self-correct • Wobble and/or tremble corrected by lengthening of breath • Smoothly transitions from pose to counter pose • Movements slow and sure with correct alignment
Critical Elements Relaxation and Breathing	One or more critical elements not present: • Remains tense • Fails to achieve relaxed state • Breathes through mouth • Shallow breaths	Demonstrates all critical elements: • Dynamic relaxation technique from feet to head • Breathes through nose • Deep breathing through expansion of chest and abdomen	Demonstrates all critical elements: • Demonstrates dynamic relaxation though identified muscle groups • Breathes through nose with expansion of chest and abdomen
Critical Elements Poses	• Demonstrates three or less of the following: » Flexion » Extension » Lateral flexion » Rotation poses • Less than two poses demonstrated in each category • A category skipped • Poses lack alignment resulting in a lack of control with shortening of spine	Demonstrates all critical elements: • Demonstrates flexion, extension, lateral flexion, and rotation poses • At least two poses demonstrated from each category • Proper alignment, lengthening of spine, and breath control	Demonstrates all critical elements: • Demonstrates flexion, extension, lateral flexion, rotation, and strength poses • At least three poses demonstrated from each category • Poses demonstrate proper alignment, lengthening of spine, and breath control

Note: For all fitness activities, two types of assessments are required. Students are assessed on technique and how well they demonstrate competency in the fitness activity under Standard 1. Under Standard 3, students are assessed on improvements in their fitness levels based on the baseline assessments taken at the beginning of the unit and their personal fitness goals.

Standard 2 Sample Assessments

Standard 2: The physically literate individual applies knowledge of concepts, principles, strategies and tactics related to movement and performance.

The Grade-Level Outcomes under Standard 2 focus on applying knowledge in physical activities that students can use over a lifetime. Students should leave high school knowing the terminology, rules and etiquette of the activities that they are likely to pursue over their lifetimes. They also should be able to use biomechanical principles to analyze their skills and techniques, and demonstrate the ability to devise and implement practice plans for improving their performance in those activities. Those skills are essential if students are to maintain and improve long-term personal health and realize longer life expectancies. As the teacher, you will need to teach related lifetime career- and college-readiness skills such as problem solving, analyzing resources critically, and demonstrating effective written and oral communication skills. The sample assessments provided here will help you measure those transferable skills, in addition to students' knowledge and understanding of selected lifetime activities.

Research conducted over the past two decades is clear: the best indicator of continued participation in a movement activity over a lifetime is the perception of competency (Barnett et al., 2008; Stodden et al., 2009; Stuart et al., 2005). By high school, students recognize which activities they enjoy and want to become better at through practice and continued instruction. Student choice, then, is an essential component of any high school physical education curriculum. Not only do students need the freedom to choose the activities in which they want to improve their competency, but they also should be able to choose how they wish to demonstrate their competency.

Assessments intended to measure high school students' progress toward the Grade-Level Outcomes under Standard 2 require students to apply their knowledge of concepts, principles, strategies and tactics to demonstrate their command of a self-selected lifetime activity, dance or fitness activity. The sample assessments for Standard 2 are comprehensive, requiring students to solve problems and think critically, and some involve others in group assignments and/or projects. You also can employ more traditional assessment tasks such as quizzes, end-of-unit examinations, worksheets, activity logs, and student reflections or journals. All are appropriate assessments and can provide valuable insights about what your students are learning and are able to apply to the activities they pursue after leaving high school.

We suggest providing students with a list of options for demonstrating competency and allowing students to select the assessment that they believe would best demonstrate their competency. The suggested assessments include group projects as well as individual projects, providing students with a range of choices. Research (Assor et al., 2002; Deci & Ryan, 2000; Fisher et al., 1975; Ryan & Deci, 2000) has shown that providing some student choice increases student engagement and sense of autonomy.

Pre-Assessment

We recommend that you conduct pre-assessments for all lifetime, dance and rhythm, and fitness activities. This will provide you and the students with baseline levels of competency and allow for differentiation of instruction, communication of student progress over time, and instructional decision-making. Students can use the baseline data to determine their progress, determine areas of strengths and weaknesses, and set performance goals for each unit of instruction.

- You can use surveys or other forms of written pre-assessments. Gathering data before beginning the unit will guide instructional decision-making specific to scope and sequence, determining ability groupings, and designing differentiated practice tasks. You can survey students on their experience with the activity or their foundational knowledge of it. For example, students who have participated in weight-training activities through competitive sport will have a higher baseline of performance than students who have not participated in weight training. Likewise, students who have aquatics certifications through American Red Cross, Boy Scouts or Girl Scouts, or the YMCA will have a higher baseline of performance than those students who don't pursue those certifications. You can use written pre-assessments to determine students' knowledge in the upcoming unit. For example, you could ask students to match dance steps or yoga positions to the names of the steps or positions. For a weight-training unit, you could ask students to match weight-lifting techniques to the muscle groups that they target. That will provide you with valuable information on students' baseline knowledge.

- Examples of skill pre-assessments are provided under Standard 1.

Formative Assessments

- Quizzes allow you to have checks for understanding throughout the unit. Quizzes cover topics such as rules and etiquette for the activity, terminology, and/or concepts and principles related to the activity.

- Checklists are valuable as formative assessments. Checklists allow students to self-evaluate their performance by identifying essential criteria for movement competency. Checklists are also constructive in identifying key elements to be included in a summative project or assignment. This allows students to "check" that they have included key parts of a comprehensive project or assignment. In addition, peers can provide specific, corrective feedback based on identified criteria on a peer evaluation checklist. This allows students to provide each other feedback on performance using objective criteria based on critical elements of the skill or technique. Examples of peer checklists are found under Standard 1.

- Checks for understanding should occur during each class. These are quick checks on the students' comprehension and provide students with the opportunity to ask questions and seek clarifications. The advantage of using checks for understanding is that it takes place in real time, allowing you to adjust or modify practice tasks or instruction based on student needs.

- Worksheets are another type of formative assessment and can take many forms. Worksheets can be used to assess students' understanding of scoring in tennis, identify poses in yoga, or calculate target heart rate, to name just a few. An example of how to calculate target heart rate can be found under Standard 3. Additional examples can be found in Appendix U specific to target heart rate and FitnessGram results.

- Logs are useful to students for tracking such things as amount and length of time spent in physical activity, food intake, number of repetitions and lifts during a fitness unit, scores over time in target activities such as archery and bowling. Logs provide both you and your students a record of their progress over time. A sample nutrition log is provided in Appendix V.

Note: Units at the high school level will involve many combinations of formative assessments. Developing competency in a specific lifetime, dance, or fitness activity is a complex process crossing all learning domains. Using just one type of formative assessment provides you with a limited picture of student progress; therefore, a variety of assessments should be used. This requires multiple assessments that include all learning domains.

Individual Summative Assessments

- Portfolio: This is a comprehensive assessment that has multiple parts. Students can select examples of their work and include them in their portfolio specific to their self-selected lifetime, dance and rhythm, or fitness activity. Each section of the portfolio is assessed and aligned to goals or objectives of the overall unit. Formative assessments (listed above) could be included in the portfolio as evidence. Assessment rubrics for a portfolio assignment align with a complete description of the assignment. It is essential that students have a clear outline of specific requirements for their portfolio. An example of a fitness portfolio is provided under Standard 3.

- Develop and implement an improvement plan: For Standards 2 or 3, students develop and implement an improvement plan specific to their self-selected activity. All improvement plans should have goals, pre-, mid- and post-measures, and specific practice tasks. Students create a plan based on their pre-assessment data. This includes any of the lifetime activities or the development of a fitness plan for a specific sport based on the demands of the activity. A description of the assignment provides specific requirements and a rubric would align with the requirements identified in the description of the assignment. A sample of a description of the assignment along with the assessment rubric are found under Standard 2. For an example of a fitness plan format see Appendix W.

- Journals provide you with insight on how students are feeling about their participation in the unit, specific challenges they are facing, and their social interactions within the context of the unit. Journals provide you with a deeper understanding of the social and emotional context of the student's experiences in the unit. Guidance on the use of journals is provided under Standard 4.

- Final examination: Students take a comprehensive written final examination specific to terminology, rules and etiquette, application of concepts and movement principles, and tactics and strategies. See Appendix X for sample written examination questions.

- Research paper or biomechanical analysis: Students select a movement skill or sequence to analyze using principles from biomechanics and physics. In a research paper, students present their findings. This assignment requires students to investigate research findings and apply this research to human movement. Specific parameters identified on the description of the assignment are aligned with the rubric used to assess the project. A sample description of assignment and rubric are provided under Standard 2.

Group Summative Assessments

- Flipped classroom: One way students can demonstrate their understanding and competency in self-selected activities is through a flipped classroom assignment. Students in small groups (no more than 3 students) would create instructional videos on selected skills and/or techniques for self-selected activities. These videos are posted on the physical education website and used by other students to refine their skills. An example of a flipped classroom assignment and assessment rubric are provided under Standard 2.

- Creation of dance, yoga, or fitness routines: Based on a description of the assignment, students in small groups (no more than four) create a routine. The created routine follows the parameters established in the description of the assignment. For example, students could demonstrate their competency in square dance by creating a square dance using hip hop or break dance movements in combination with more traditional steps such as do-si-do and promenade. The parameters for the dance would be set based on traditional squares (eight in a set, everyone must start and end with the same partner, everyone must switch partners at least twice, etc.). This will require students to apply their knowledge in the creation of the dance. Students could either create a video demonstrating the dance or teach the dance to classmates. The same type of assignment could be used in the creation of routines for step aerobics, kickboxing, yoga, etc.

At the high school level, students should have a choice of how they demonstrate their competency regarding the Grade-Level Outcomes under Standard 2. You can provide them with two or three choices and let them select the assessment that works best for them. For example, you might have a group of students who want to flip a classroom, while others are more interested in completing a research paper and biomechanical analysis. As you provide students with choice, ensure the projects are equal in rigor. You also can have one required assessment and a second assessment that provides choice. For example, all students might take the written examination, but the second assessment can be one of three choices.

Movement Concepts, Principles and Knowledge

Level 1

Grade-Level Outcome

Creates a practice plan to improve performance for a self-selected skill. (S2.H3.L1)

Assessment Task

Students develop and implement a self-improvement plan. (Option 1)

Guidelines

- Select a specific lifetime, dance and rhythm, or fitness activity for which to plan a program of improvement
    - » Set goals for improvement plan based on pre-assessment(s)
    - » Select assessments to be used to determine if goals are met
- Research the fitness, lifetime, or dance and rhythm activity identified for improvement
- Develop and implement the plan for improvement
- Complete mid- and post-assessments to determine whether you have met goals
- Write a weekly reflection

Setup

- Access to computers or library resources
- Access to pre-assessment data
- Access to school physical education website

Critical Components for Self-Improvement Plan Project

Pre-Assessments

- Include at least two of the following:
    - » Fitness attribute(s)
    - » Skills or techniques
    - » Knowledge
- Pre-assessments are appropriate

Goals

- Set at least three goals for the improvement plans
    - » Goals follow the SMART format (specific, measurable, achievable, realistic, and time-bound)
    - » Goals are set in at least two of the following:
        - Fitness attribute(s)
        - Skills or techniques
        - Knowledge
- Identify assessments (pre- and post-) for each goal

Research

- At least 3 different credible sources cited in improvement plan
  - » Citations use APA style
- Research should include at least two of the following:
  - » Fitness attribute(s)
  - » Skills or techniques
  - » Knowledge
- Research is appropriate for:
  - » Fitness attribute(s)
  - » Skills or techniques
  - » Knowledge

Plan

- List drills, practice tasks, or fitness activities designed to improve performance
  - » Align selected skills/practice/fitness tasks with goals and support by research
  - » Drills/practice/fitness tasks sequential and progressive
  - » Determine how often and how long you will participate in each drill/practice/fitness task
- Develop a month-long calendar as part of your plan for improvement
  - » Plan includes 5 days with 2 days for rest
  - » Each day identify the drills/practice/fitness tasks for the day
    - Number of repetitions or length of time for each
    - One warm-up/cool-down activity for each day
    - Sample calendar available on the school's physical education website

Implementation

- Maintain a daily activity log
  - » Activity log must include the following:
    - Date
    - For each drill/practice/fitness task, number of repetitions OR amount of time
    - Perceived exertion identified
    - Location/other participants
  - » Activity log is turned in at the end of each week

Reflection

- Complete a weekly reflection that includes
  - » What were your successes?
  - » What were your challenges?
  - » What would you change in your plan moving forward?
- Each of the above questions supported with specific examples or data
- Progress or lack of progress based on pre-, mid-, and post-assessments
- Reflection due at the end of each week

Scoring Rubric for Self-Improvement Plan Project, Level 1

INDICATOR	DEVELOPING	COMPETENT	PROFICIENT

Analyzes and Uses Data to Make Decisions	One or more critical components not present:
	
	• Completes only 2 of required assessments
	• Assessments completed, but not analyzed
	• Assessments inappropriate for selected lifetime/rhythm or dance/fitness activity
	• Only 1 of these 3 assessed
	  » Fitness
	  » Skills or technique
	  » Knowledge
		Demonstrates all critical components:
		
		• Collects and analyzes pre-, mid-, and post-assessments to determine entry point, midway progress, and exit point
		• Assessments appropriate for selected lifetime/rhythm or dance/fitness activity
		• Data supports improvement plan and reflection
		• Assessments conducted on 2 of these 3 listed below:
		  » Fitness
		  » Skills or technique
		  » Knowledge
			Demonstrates all critical components:
			
			• Collects, analyzes and triangulates data from pre-, mid-, and post-assessments
			• Direct alignment of assessments to lifetime/rhythm or dance/fitness activity
			• Data supports improvement plan and reflection
			• Assessments conducted on fitness, skill/technique, and knowledge

Demonstrates Ability to Set, Track Progress, and Achieve Goals	One or more critical components not present:
	
	• 2 or fewer goals set
	• Goals set for only 1 of the following:
	  » Fitness
	  » Skills or technique
	  » Knowledge
	• Goals set missing at least 1 of the following criteria:
	  » Specific
	  » Measurable
	  » Achievable
	  » Realistic
	  » Time bound
	• Assessments misaligned with goals
		Demonstrates all critical components:
		
		• Minimum of 3 goals set in at least 2 of the following:
		  » Fitness
		  » Skills or technique
		  » Knowledge
		• Goals set meet the SMART criteria:
		  » Specific
		  » Measurable
		  » Achievable
		  » Realistic
		  » Time bound
		• Appropriate assessment identified for each goal
			Demonstrates all critical components:
			
			• 4 or more goals set in all 3 of the following:
			  » Fitness
			  » Skills or technique
			  » Knowledge
			• Goals meet SMART criteria:
			  » Specific
			  » Measurable
			  » Achievable
			  » Realistic
			  » Time bound
			• More than 1 assessment for each goal

Demonstrates Ability to Synthesize and Apply Research	One or more critical components not present:
	
	• Less than 3 credible sources cited
	• Sources cited not credible
	• Cited research misaligned with lifetime/rhythm or dance/fitness activity
	• Cited research is limited to 1 of the following:
	  » Fitness
	  » Skills or technique
	  » Knowledge
		Demonstrates all critical components:
		
		• At least 3 credible sources cited using APA style
		• Cited research appropriate for selected lifetime/rhythm or dance/fitness activity
		• Cited research specific to 2 of the following:
		  » Fitness
		  » Skills or technique
		  » Knowledge
			Demonstrates all critical components:
			
			• 4 or more credible sources cited using APA style
			• Cited research directly aligns with selected lifetime/rhythm or dance/fitness activity
			• Cited research specific to all of the following:
			  » Fitness
			  » Skills or technique
			  » Knowledge

(continued)

Scoring Rubric for Self-Improvement Plan Project, Level 1 *(continued)*

INDICATOR	DEVELOPING	COMPETENT	PROFICIENT

Demonstrates Ability to Create a Performance-Based Self-Improvement	One or more critical components not present:
	
	• Selected drills/practice/fitness tasks inappropriate for goals or not supported by research
	• No assessments identified
	• Fails to identify specific drills/practice/fitness tasks
	• Plan not daily
	• Number of repetitions or length of time not identified
	• No warm-up/cool-down activity
		Demonstrates all critical components:
		
		• Selected drills/practice/fitness tasks:
		  » Appropriate for goals
		  » Sequential and progressive
		  » Supported by research
		• Identifies assessments to evaluate success of plan
		• Develops a month-long plan to include
		  » Daily plans consisting of specific drills/practice/fitness tasks
		  » Number of repetitions or length of time for each
		  » 1 warm-up/cool-down activity identified for each day
			Demonstrates all critical components:
			
			• Selected drills/practice/fitness tasks:
			  » Appropriate for goals
			  » Sequential and progressive
			  » Supported by research
			• Identifies assessments to evaluate success of plan
			• Develops a month-long plan to include
			  » Daily plans consisting of specific drills/practice/fitness tasks
			  » Number of repetitions or length of time for each
			  » 1 warm-up/cool-down activity identified for each day
			  » 1 assessment each day

Demonstrates the Ability to Implement a Plan and Track Progress	One or more critical components not present:
	
	• Daily activity incomplete
	  » No data for some days
	  » Number of repetitions or length not identified
	  » Perceived exertion not identified
	  » Location/other participants missing
		Demonstrates all critical components:
		
		• Maintains a daily activity log to include
		  » Date
		  » Number of repetitions or length of time
		  » Perception of intensity level
		  » Location/other participants
			Demonstrates all critical components:
			
			• Maintains a daily activity log to include
			  » Date
			  » Number of repetitions or length of time
			  » Perception of intensity level
			  » Location/other participants
			  » Includes daily formative assessments

Demonstrate Ability to Reflect on and Analyze Progress Toward Goals	One or more critical components not present:
	
	• Reflections lack specificity with only general observations included
	• Reflections not supported by data or examples
		Demonstrates all critical components:
		
		• Reflects on the following:
		  » Successes
		  » Challenges
		• Reflections supported by data
		• Reflections include examples
		• Analysis of pre-, mid- and post-assessments
			Demonstrates all critical components:
			
			• Reflects on the following:
			  » Successes
			  » Challenges
			  » Modifications
			• Reflections supported by data and examples
			• Analysis of pre-, mid- and post-assessments

Note: *This assignment allows students to apply their knowledge and research to improve their performance on a self-selected lifetime/rhythm or dance/fitness activity. These are important skills for high school students moving forward into adulthood. In addition, students demonstrate data literacy, ability to apply research, and adjust the plan based on data. All students should develop the ability to be knowledgeable consumers.*

Movement Concepts, Principles and Knowledge

Level 1

Grade-Level Outcome

Uses movement concepts and principles (e.g., force, motion, rotation) to analyze and improve performance of self and/or others in a selected skill. (S2.H2.L1)

Assessment Task

Students develop a slide presentation on the analysis of a selected skill/dance and rhythm/fitness activity. (Option 2).

Guidelines

- Select a specific skill or sequence of movements and provide an analysis of the movement or sequence. This can include such things as:
  - » Applying topspin to a ball in racket sports and the effect
  - » Correct alignment and technique for a specific lift in weight training
  - » A specific dance technique such as a leap or a turn
- Complete research on the skill or sequence
- Create a narrated PowerPoint slideshow based on your research. The final slideshow will be posted on the physical education website for others to view or use.
- Include a hyperlink to at least one instructional site

Setup

- Access to presentation software
- Audio for presentation software (sound card, microphone, and speakers)

Critical Components for Presentation on Analysis of Selected Skill, Dance and Rhythm, or Fitness Activity

Research

- At least 5 different credible sources cited
  - » APA style used for each citing
- At least 3 of the following discussed and applied to the movement or sequence
  - » Balance
  - » Alignment
  - » Application of force
  - » Velocity
  - » Torque
  - » Range of motion
- Cited research appropriate to the topic

Content Requirements

- Principles cited in presentation include diagrams and/or pictures of the technique being analyzed
- Diagrams and/or pictures include both correct and incorrect techniques
- Movements broken down into stages
- Analysis of general biomechanical principles (e.g., balance, application of force, alignment, etc.) included

- Key technique points identified and illustrated
- Biomechanical principles accurately applied and presented with clarity

Presentation

- A least 12-15 slides, with audio
- Presentation includes:
  - » Pictures or diagrams that illustrate the analysis and add interest
  - » Slides sequential and well-organized
  - » Each slide illustrates a single point
  - » Letters legible
  - » Contrast between lettering and background on slide adds clarity
  - » Use no more than 2 font styles
  - » Avoid complete sentences – use outline format
  - » Design basic and simple
  - » Uses at least one hyperlink
- Audio with slides
  - » Submit audio recording with slides
  - » Audio supplements the information on slides (do not read slides)
  - » Audio recording clear and seamless

Note: *This assessment allows students to apply movement concepts and principles to their performance. Just as important, students are required to demonstrate the career and college readiness skills of communication (written and oral), application of knowledge (analysis of performance), and application of research to solve real work problems (improved performance). This is a comprehensive assessment that could be submitted in parts over time, avoiding a grading backlog at the end of the term.*

Scoring Rubric for Presentation on Analysis of Selected Skill, Dance and Rhythm, or Fitness Activity, Level 1

INDICATOR	DEVELOPING	COMPETENT	PROFICIENT
Demonstrates Ability to Synthesize Research on Self-Selected Movement Activity	One or more critical components not present: • Less than 5 different credible sources • Mistakes in APA citing conventions • Cited 5 credible sources but sources not aligned with self-selected movement activity • Less than 3 of the following included or some of the principles incorrectly applied: » Balance » Alignment » Application of force » Velocity » Torque » Range of motion	Demonstrates all critical components: • Includes at least 5 different credible sources • APA citing conventions followed • Cited research aligns with self-selected movement activity • At least 3 of the following included: » Balance » Alignment » Application of force » Velocity » Torque » Range of motion	Demonstrates all critical components: • Cited more than 5 credible sources • APA citing conventions followed • Cited research aligns with critical components of self-selected movement activity • At least 4 of the following included: » Balance » Alignment » Application of force » Velocity » Torque » Range of motion
Demonstrates Ability to Apply Biomechanical Principles to a Self-Selected Movement Activity	One or more critical components not present: • Biomechanical principles applied incorrectly • Biomechanical principles only marginally aligned with self-selected movement activity • Only correct or incorrect techniques identified • Missing analysis of key technique points	Demonstrates all critical components: • Biomechanical principles applied correctly » Diagrams and pictures included » Correct and incorrect technique identified » Key technique points identified and illustrated » Analysis broken into stages	Demonstrates all critical components: • Biomechanical principles applied correctly and suggestions for change included » Diagrams and pictures include analysis » Titles and symbols on illustrations or pictures to denote key positions or points • Analysis broken into key stages with illustrations for each stage
Demonstrates Competency in Oral Communication	One or more critical components not present: • Slides random making it difficult to determine accuracy of analysis • Slides crowded with text presenting multiple points • 3 or more fonts used • No hyperlink • Audio unclear with multiple stops • Audio simply repeats content of slides	Demonstrates all critical components: • Slides sequential and well-organized • Each slide presents a single point • Text legible with contrast between text and background • No more than 2 fonts in presentation • Pictures, illustrations, and/or diagrams add clarity • At least 1 hyperlink • Audio clear and synchronized with slides • Audio supplements information on slides	Demonstrates all critical components: • Slides sequential, well-organized with multiple pictures, diagrams and/or illustrations • Each slide presents a single point with pictures, illustrations or diagrams • Text legible with contrast between text and background • No more than 2 fonts in presentation • At least 2 hyperlinks • Audio clear and synchronized with slides • Audio supplements information on slides and adds clarity

Grade-Level Outcomes

- Uses movement concepts and principles (e.g., force, motion, rotation) to analyze and improve performance of self and/or others in a selected skill. (S2.H2.L1)

- Creates a practice plan to improve performance for a self-selected skill. (S2.H3.L1)

Assessment Task

Students complete research and biomechanical analysis. (Option 3)

Guidelines

- Select a specific skill or sequence of movements and provide a biomechanical analysis of the movement or sequence. This can include such things as:

  » Applying topspin to a ball in racket sports and the effect

  » Correct alignment and technique for a specific lift in weight training

  » Or a specific dance technique such as a leap or a turn

- Complete a research paper on the skill or sequence

- Analyze a peer performance of the skill or sequence using a peer assessment you created based on your research. You will use the created peer assessment with a partner to analyze her/his performance.

- Based on this analysis, write a summary of the performance and make recommendations for future practice tasks designed to improve performance.

Setup

- Access to free software such as Coach's Eye

- Peer assessment

Description of the Assignment With Critical Components for Research and Biomechanical Analysis Project

Research

- Cites at least 5 different credible sources

  » Sources cited include a 500 word or less abstract of the research articled to be submitted in the appendix – abstract and article both included

  » APA style

- At least 5 of the following applied to the movement or sequence:

  » Acceleration

  » Aerodynamics

  » Alignment

  » Center of gravity

  » Centripetal force

  » Coefficient of restitution

  » Energy

  » Force

- » Friction
- » Impulse
- » Magnus force
- » Momentum
- » Projectile motion
- » Torque
- » Range of motion
- » Rotation
- » Velocity
- Uses free biomechanical software such as Coach's Eye
- Cites research appropriate to the topic
- Abstracts along with research articles submitted in appendix

Content Requirements

- Principles cited include diagrams and/or pictures of the technique analyzed
- Diagrams and/or pictures include both correct and incorrect techniques
- Movements broken down into stages
- Analysis of general biomechanical principles (e.g., balance, application of force, alignment, etc.) included
- Key technique points identified and illustrated
- Biomechanical principles accurately applied and presented with clarity

Writing and Grammar

- Paper well-organized, focused, and clearly outlines major points
- Concepts logically arranged to present sound argument
- Correct APA citing
- Pictures and/or illustrations support written documentation
- Normal conventions of spelling and grammar followed with only minor errors
- Minor errors in spelling and grammar do not interfere with the readability of paper
- Transitions effectively used to ensure comprehension

Application of Knowledge

- Peer checklist aligns with analysis
- Checklist provides feedback specific to performance
- Summary of performance aligns with checklist and research analysis of skill/sequence
- Recommendations for practice tasks align with analysis of performance

Note: *Students apply movement concepts and principles to their performance and to a peer's performance. Just as important, students are required to demonstrate the career and college readiness skills of communication (written), application of knowledge (analysis of performance), and application of research to solve real work problems (improved performance). This is a comprehensive assessment that could be submitted in parts over time, avoiding a grading backlog at the end of the semester.*

Scoring Rubric for Research and Biomechanical Analysis Project, Level 1

INDICATOR	DEVELOPING	COMPETENT	PROFICIENT

Demonstrates Ability to Synthesize Research to a Movement Skill or Sequence	One or more critical components not present:
	
	• Less than 5 research articles reviewed and submitted
	  » Written abstracts included, but no articles accompany submission or vice versa
	  » Some articles do not align with appropriate concepts/principles
	• 4 or fewer concepts included
	• No use of free software
		Demonstrates all critical components:
		
		• At least 5 research articles reviewed and submitted
		  » Written abstracts align with submitted articles
		  » Concepts/principles appropriate
		• At least 5 concepts/principles included
		• Software package adds clarity and specificity to analysis
			Demonstrates all critical components:
			
			• 6 or more articles reviewed and submitted
			  » Written abstracts align with submitted articles
			  » Concepts/principles appropriate
			• 6 or more concepts/principles included
			• Software package adds clarity and specificity to the analysis – angles and directions measured

Demonstrates Ability to Apply Concepts and/or Principles to a Movement Skill or Sequence	One or more critical components not present: • Concepts/principles inappropriate • Provides only a holistic analysis • No pictures, illustrations, or diagrams • Only correct technique included	Demonstrates all critical components: • Identifies concepts/principles appropriate to the skill/sequence • Movement/sequence broken into stages with pictures or illustrations for some major stages • Key techniques identified and illustrated • At least 5 diagrams and illustrations including both correct and incorrect technique • Analysis includes general principles • Biomechanical principles accurately applied and presented with clarity	Demonstrates all critical components: • Identifies most important concepts/principles for skill/sequence • Movement/sequence appropriately broken into stages with pictures or illustrations for all major stages • Key technique points identified and illustrated • 6 or more diagrams and illustrations including both correct and incorrect technique • Analysis includes general principles • Biomechanical principles accurately applied and presented with clarity
Demonstrates Competency in Written Communication	One or more critical components not present: • Poorly organized analysis with gaps • Errors in spelling and grammar negatively impact readability • Lacks transitions from paragraph to paragraph and sentence to sentence • Includes no pictures or illustrations supporting text/analysis	Demonstrates all critical components: • Analysis well-organized, logically arranged • Only minor errors in grammar and/or spelling and do not interfere with readability • Transitions effectively ensure comprehension • Pictures and/or illustrations support analysis	Demonstrates all critical components: • Analysis well-organized, logically arranged, and directly supports analysis • Errors in grammar and/or spelling rare and do not impact readability • Transitions effective and aid in comprehension • Multiple pictures, illustrations, and/or diagrams support analysis
Demonstrates Ability to Create a Performance-Based Improvement Plan using Biomechanical Concepts	One or more critical components not present: • Performance checklist misaligned with analysis • No summary of performance • Recommendations for practice tasks inappropriate	Demonstrates all critical components: • Peer performance checklist aligns with analysis and provides feedback to partner • Summary of performance based on analysis and peer checklist • Recommendations for practice tasks align with performance analysis and checklist	Demonstrates all critical components: • Peer performance checklist aligns with analysis and provides specific feedback to partner • Summary of performance based on analysis, peer checklist, and observation • Innovative recommendations for practice tasks that align with performance analysis and checklist

Movement Concepts, Principles and Knowledge   Level 1

Grade-Level Outcomes

- Uses movement concepts and principles (e.g., force, motion, rotation) to analyze and improve performance of self and/or others in a selected skill. (S2.H2.L1)

- Applies the terminology associated with exercise and participation in selected individual-performance activities, dance, net/wall games, target games, aquatics and/or other outdoor pursuits appropriately. (S2.H1.L1)

Assessment Task

Students complete a flipped classroom analysis. (Option 4)

Guidelines

- Select 1 or 2 individuals to collaborate with for project
    - » Groups no larger than 3 individuals
- Select a specific skill or sequence of movements
    - » Create a flipped classroom instructional video
    - » Include instructional slide presentation
- Post final project on the school's physical education website
- Create a storyboard for project
    - » Include specific citing for each source of instructional tips and analysis
    - » Storyboard approved before filming
- Video cameras with microphones provided beyond class hours
- Editing tools available in computer lab
    - » Video sequences demonstrate each phase of skill
    - » Still pictures from the videos in presentation
- Slide presentation supports instructional video

Setup

- Video recording devices to film demonstrations of skill or sequence
- Audio for slide presentation (sound card, microphone, and speakers)
- Access to slide presentation software
- Quiet space for filming

Critical Components for Flipped Classroom Project

Content/Organization

- At least 3 different credible sources cited
    - » APA style
- Each citing included on slide presentation
- Cited resources appropriate to topic

- Correct terminology used throughout project

- Critical components identified and demonstrated correctly

- Whole and part demonstrations included

- Diagrams and skill pictures illustrative of skill/technique

- Video demonstrates a progressive sequence

Script/Storyboard

- Illustrates video structure with notes

- Provides information on transitions, special effects (e.g., zooming in/out), titles to be used, placement of graphics, notes on major talking points

- Script for every scene

- Script well-written with critical skill elements identified

- Shows a progressive sequence

Creativity, Design, and Quality

- Video well-edited

- Camera stable, subject in frame and in focus

- Sound clear and understandable

- Variable from scene to scene (e.g., changes in camera perspective, focus on key elements)

- Titles used effectively

- Transitions timed and seamless

- Creativity enhances video

Slide Presentation

- Prepare slide presentation of at least 10-12 slides, with audio

- Presentation includes:
  - » Pictures or diagrams to illustrate analysis, add interest
  - » Slides sequential and well-organized
  - » Each slide illustrates just a single point
  - » Letters legible
  - » Contrast between lettering and background adds clarity
  - » Use no more than 2 font styles
  - » Avoid complete sentences – use outline format
  - » Keep design basic and simple
  - » Use at least one still shot from video
  - » One hyperlink

- Audio with slides
  - » Submit audio recording with slides
  - » Audio supplements the information on slide (do not read slides)
  - » Audio recording clear and seamless

Note: *Students apply movement concepts and principles through the development of an instructional video specific to a self-selected skill or technique. In addition, students demonstrate competency in the language and terminology of the selected lifetime activities through this creative project. Just as important, students are required to demonstrate the career and college readiness skills of communication (written and oral), application of knowledge (development of an instructional sequence), and use of technology (video editing, slide presentation). This is a comprehensive assessment that could be submitted in parts over time, avoiding a grading backlog at the end of the semester. It is also possible to make the video and slide presentation two separate projects.*

Scoring Rubric for Flipped Classroom, Level 1

INDICATOR	DEVELOPING	COMPETENT	PROFICIENT
Demonstrates Ability to Apply Concepts and/or Principles in the Development of an Instructional Video	One or more critical components not present: • 2 or fewer resources cited • Cited resources inappropriate or marginal • Performance errors in demonstrated critical components • Incorrect terminology used or mispronounced • Demonstration only of whole skill/technique or only of parts of skill/technique • No citing for each resource	Demonstrates all critical components: • At least 3 different credible resources cited • Cited resources appropriate • Critical components specific to movement skill or sequence identified • Critical components demonstrated correctly • Correct terminology used • Diagram or drawings illustrative of skill or sequence • Whole and part demonstrations included • Citing included on presentation slides	Demonstrates all critical components: • 4 or more credible resources cited • Most important critical components cited • Demonstrations correct and filmed from more than one angle • Correct terminology with no jargon • Diagrams and drawings aligned directly with critical components • Multiple whole and part demonstrations
Demonstrates Competency in Written Communication Through the Production of a Storyboard	One or more critical components not present: • Outline lacks specificity • Narration incomplete • No script submitted • No clear sequence of instruction identified or documented	Demonstrates all critical components: • Plans video structure with notes and cues • Information on transitions, special effects (e.g., zooming in/out), titles, placement of graphics, notes on major talking points • Narration for every scene • Script well-written with critical components • Progressive sequence of instruction	Demonstrates all critical components: • Specific and detailed plan with notes and cues • Specific detail on transitions, special effects (e.g., zooming in/out), titles, placement of graphics, notes on major talking points • Narration for every scene including details on inflection and tone • Script well-written with critical components • Instruction progressive and sequential

(continued)

Scoring Rubric for Flipped Classroom, Level 1 *(continued)*

INDICATOR	DEVELOPING	COMPETENT	PROFICIENT
Demonstrate Competency in the Effective Use of Technology (Creativity, Design, Quality)	One or more critical components not present: • Video poorly edited with gaps and hesitations • Part of video out of focus or frame • Sound uneven (too loud or too soft) • Only one camera angle used • No transitions • Titles not present or do not enhance instruction • Lacks creativity with no changes in graphics, camera angles, and/or titles	Demonstrates all critical components: • Video well-edited with no hesitations or gaps • Camera stable and frames in focus • Sound clear and understandable • Multiple angles and perspectives • Titles enhance instruction • Transitions well-timed and smooth • Creativity enhances video (unique use of graphics, camera angles, illustrations, etc.)	Demonstrates all critical components: • Video well-edited with creative use of music, graphics, etc. • Camera stable, frames in focus, and multiple angles and perspectives • Titles along with symbols enhance instruction • Transitions well-timed and smooth with creative use of music, graphics, etc.
Demonstrates Competency in Oral Communication	One or more critical components not present: • Slides random making it difficult to determine accuracy of content • Slides crowded with text presenting multiple points • 3 or more fonts used • No hyperlink • Audio unclear with multiple stops • Audio simply repeats content of slides	Demonstrates all critical components: • Slides sequential and well-organized • Each slide presents a single point • Text legible with contrast between text and background • No more than 2 fonts in presentation • Pictures, illustrations, and/or diagrams add clarity • Uses at least one still shot from video • One hyperlink • Audio clear and synchronized • Audio supplements information on slides	Demonstrates all critical components: • Slides sequential, well-organized with multiple pictures, diagrams and/or illustrations • Each slide presents a single point with pictures, illustrations or diagrams • Text legible with contrast between text and background • No more than 2 fonts used • At least 2 hyperlinks • Audio clear and synchronized • Audio supplements information on slides and adds clarity

Standard 3 Sample Assessments

Standard 3: The physically literate individual demonstrates the knowledge and skills to achieve and maintain a health-enhancing level of physical activity and fitness.

Students' ability to develop a comprehensive and individualized physical activity plan that prepares them for a lifetime of wellness and regular physical activity is central to the high school Grade-Level Outcomes. Outcomes for Standard 3 include areas such as injury prevention, nutrition, stress management, behavior modification, consumer awareness, and fitness knowledge related to physiological responses to exercise, strength and conditioning, and fitness program development. In addition, students are expected to document their physical activity levels in and outside of class. The intent at the high school level is for students to demonstrate their ability to apply knowledge in the area of health and fitness to their own wellness. The evaluation of their ability to apply fitness and wellness knowledge requires an assortment of assessments.

One method of assessment frequently used by schools and school systems is to require students to create a "portfolio" that includes a range of evidence or artifacts specific to fitness and physical activity. Requirements for portfolios span an array of worksheets, logs, journals, assignments, and reflections. The number of required evidence/artifacts you select for a portfolio is based on the length of the unit, number of meeting days, and course content. Some school districts or individual schools have a standardized assignment completed by all students in the system. Excellent examples of district-wide fitness plans or portfolios are readily available using any number of web search engines such as Google, Bing, Yahoo, or others. Simply search using key words "fitness plan" or "fitness portfolio" and you will find multiple examples and approaches.

The approach taken for the Standard 3 sample assessments is to break down individual elements of the fitness plan/portfolio and provide specific recommendations for assessing those elements. This will allow you to select the elements that are "best fits" for your program and simply include them in your assessment package for the unit. An example of a complete plan, including selected elements, can be found in Appendix E. Guidance on skills that are specific to fitness, such as yoga or strength training, can be found under the Standard 1 sample assessments.

When students embark on creating a fitness plan, they will have many challenges, including their own lifelong habits and behaviors. No fitness plan is complete without addressing these barriers to their fitness goals. To address these barriers, a sample behavior modification plan is included. Students not only apply knowledge to develop a plan but also need to reflect on habits and behaviors that interfere with their goal of regular physical activity and wellness. For many student this will require some modification in behaviors and making different choices.

Grade-Level Outcome

Develops and maintains a fitness portfolio (e.g., assessment scores, goals for improvement, plan of activities for improvement, log of activities being done to reach goals, timeline for improvement). (S3.H11.L2)

Assessment Task

Assessing student performance against this outcome requires multiple measures and involves an array of skills on the part of students. Creating a fitness portfolio is a multipart process in which students complete a series of required elements. In the text that follows, we've listed the elements that are used most frequently, with suggested assessments for each element. The number of elements for your fitness portfolio will be determined by the length of the unit, number of class days and staff capacity. Creating and maintaining an electronic portfolio makes submitting artifacts easier for students than a paper portfolio would and facilitates the feedback process for you.

Element 1: Pre-Assessment Data

Before students begin to develop a fitness portfolio, they first must collect some baseline data on their current fitness and nutrition habits. Using heart rate monitors, pedometers and other fitness measures provides formative assessment data on students' exertion during participation (heart rate), on how many steps taken during the activity, or beginning levels of flexibility, for example. These tools provide students with a measure of how much physical benefit they might be building by participating in the activity.

All students should complete a FitnessGram or other fitness assessment to determine the current fitness levels. This allows students to set achievable fitness goals based on data and compare their data to established Healthy Fitness Zones. Students should also complete surveys specific to their current activity levels and nutrition knowledge and habits. See the sample Pre-Assessment Activity Level Survey.

If you are requiring students to rate their perceived exertion, you need to include instruction on the Perceived Exertion Scale (Borg Rating of Perceived Exertion Scale - RPE) that is available on the Centers for Disease Control and Prevention website. Students should practice using the scale during class. The scale is from 6-20 with 6 being no exertion at all and 20 being maximal exertion.

Element 2: Personal Contract

Many fitness portfolios begin with students signing a contract making a commitment to improve their fitness and nutrition habits. In most contracts, the student also pledges to set goals for both fitness and nutrition, keep up-to-date activity and nutrition logs, reflect on progress, and follow the guidelines for submitting the portfolio. Most of the contracts end with a statement that students understand the content of the contract and agree to commit to improving their health and wellness. Students sign the contract as well as you. Some programs will have parents sign the contract as well. Samples of contracts for fitness portfolios can be found on the web.

Assessment of the contract is simply a check (yes or no) that it has been signed by you and the student. For an example of a personal fitness contract for the secondary level see Appendix Y.

Element 3: Setting SMART Goals for Personal Fitness Portfolio

For the fitness portfolio, students set goals they wish to achieve during the unit. The number of goals should be specific to requirements identified for the portfolio and determined by you. Goals in a portfolio may address health-related fitness components, nutrition, behavior modification, and/or skill proficiency. Students should reflect on the progress toward meeting their goals at least twice during the unit. In addition to setting long-term goals for the unit, students should also set short-term goals that allow them to measure their progress relative to their long-term goals.

As the teacher, you can set guidelines for the number and type of individual goals that students are to set. Examples of guidelines include:

- One goal must be cardiorespiratory

- All five components of health-related fitness must be included

- At least one nutritional goal must be set

- At least one high-risk behavior goal must be set

✍ *Pre-Assessment Activity Level Survey*

Rating Scale Key

0 = Not active – no participation in physical activity on a weekly basis

1 = Occasionally active – once or twice a week

2 = Somewhat active – twice a week on a regular basis

3 = Regularly active – at least three or four times a week on a regular basis

4 = Daily active – five or more days a week on a regular basis

Based on the scale above, how often to you participate in activities designed to increase your cardiorespiratory endurance?

0   1   2   3   4

Based on the scale above, how often to you participate in activities designed to increase your flexibility?

0   1   2   3   4

Based on the scale above, how often to you participate in activities designed to increase your muscular strength and endurance?

0   1   2   3   4

Based on the scale above, how often to you participate in recreational activities such as tennis, basketball, walking, yoga, etc.?

0   1   2   3   4

Based on the scale above, how often do you currently participate in any organized physical activity and/or sport such as soccer, dance classes, swimming, etc.?

0   1   2   3   4

Note: *Collecting data allows students to compare their current levels of activity at the beginning of the unit to levels at the end of the unit. Students who are very active should not be penalized if their activity levels do not increase during the unit. Their focus may be on improving one aspect of their current participation. The survey provides some baseline data for comparisons later.*

- All goals must be based on pre-assessment data

Students set goals (long- and short-term) based on the SMART principles:

- **S**pecific = Specify what you are to accomplish.

- **M**easurable = Identify exactly what criteria you will use to measure success.

- **A**chievable = Make goals realistic and attainable within the time frame.

- **R**ealistic = State the final desired results in quantifiable terms.

- **T**ime-bound = Identify the target date for achieving the goal.

For example: By May 1 I will improve my cardiorespiratory fitness as measured by the mile run by 10 percent. (Current 9-minute mile lowered to 8.1 minutes)

- **S**pecific = What is to be accomplished? Improve cardiorespiratory fitness

- **M**easurable = How is it to be measured? Time on mile run

- **A**chievable = Is it achievable? Is 10 percent realistic or should it be 5 percent?

- **R**ealistic = Goal is 8.1 minutes

- **T**ime-bound = by May 1

For an example of goal setting format see Appendix Z.

Note: *All goals set for the fitness portfolio must be based on pre-assessment data. Students should review their pre-assessment results before determining their goals. For example, if a student scores in the Healthy Fitness Zone for muscular strength and endurance, but low on flexibility, a goal related to improving flexibility would be expected.*

Scoring Rubric for Goal Setting, Level 1

INDICATOR	DEVELOPING	COMPETENT	PROFICIENT
Goals meet the SMART criteria.	• One or two of the SMART criteria missing for each goal • Some goals missing one or more of the SMART criteria • Lack specificity within SMART criteria	• All SMART criteria included for each goal • Each SMART criterion addressed with specificity	• All SMART criteria included for each goal • Each SMART criterion addressed with specificity • SMART goals align with important fitness or behavior changes
Goals are based on pre-assessment data.	• General statements of change unrelated to pre-assessment data • Inconsistent alignment with pre-assessment data (some goals align and others do not align)	Consistent and direct alignment with pre-assessment data	• Consistent and direct alignment with pre-assessment data • Based on pre-assessment data, the most important fitness or behavior changes addressed

Assessment and Program Planning   Level 1

Grade-Level Outcome

Designs a fitness program, including all components of health-related fitness, for a college student and an employee in the learner's chosen field of work. (S3.H12.L1)

Pre-Assessment

FitnessGram or a similar fitness assessment

Assessment Task*

A fitness plan is based on identified goals and addresses any of the health-related fitness components (cardiorespiratory, muscular strength and endurance, flexibility, and body composition) that may need attention based on pre-assessment data. Fitness plans may also include nutrition and/or high-risk behaviors (e.g., smoking) that impact overall health. The fitness plan should be at least four weeks and include the three elements: a contract, pre-assessment data, and goals. The fitness plan could be part of an overall wellness portfolio.

> *Note: The assessment task is specific to students planning and implementing a personal fitness plan. Outcome S3.H12.L1 requires students to develop a fitness plan for another student. You can modify the assignment to require students to serve as a fitness coach for another classmate and develop a fitness plan for that individual. Their role would include working with another student in the implementation of the plan.

Element 4: Developing a Fitness Plan

For Element 4, students create and design at least a four-week 7-day plan of activities that will allow them to reach their self-selected fitness/wellness goals. The plan should include the following:

- At least 60 minutes of activity at the planned level of exertion

- Warm-up and cool-down activities

- Rest days among the 7 days

- Spending at least 20 minutes at least 3 times per week in the target heart rate zone (see Appendix U for target heart rate worksheet)

- For each day identify the FITT factors (frequency, intensity, type, and time)

Students would track their progress through a provided calendar format that allows them to plan each day's activities for the month or length of the fitness plan. These plans are reviewed and modified each week based on the previous week's performance. This should be an active document that allows students to adjust their plan based on their experience in the previous week.

An example of a typical planning document for students to use as they develop their plan for the required elements of the fitness portfolio is presented here. You can create documents like this through Google Docs and students can store plans in the cloud.

✑ Fitness Plan Format

DAY/DATE	FITNESS COMP.	PLANNED AC- TIVITY (TYPE)	METRIC USED	INTENSITY (BORG)	TIME	GOAL FROM PLAN
Monday **May 1**	Cardio					
	Strength					
	Endurance					
	Flexibility					
	Warm-up					
	Cool-down					
Tuesday **May 2**	Cardio					
	Strength					
	Endurance					
	Flexibility					
	Warm-up					
	Cool-down					
Wednesday **May 3**	Cardio					
	Strength					
	Endurance					
	Flexibility					
	Warm-up					
	Cool-down					
You will provide this document in an electronic format with all 7 days of the week completed. Identify the specific goal that is being met with your planned activities in the goal column.						

Note: *If the unit is for 8 weeks, students could plan the first 4 weeks and after assessing their progress over the first 4 weeks, they could plan the last 4 weeks.*

You also can include items on the rubric specific to the parameters set for the fitness plan. Using the example from above, additional indicators are added specific to the required 60 minutes per day, identified rest days with lower levels of activity, and spending at least 30 minutes in the target heart rate zone:

- At least 60 minutes of activity at the planned level of exertion

- Warm-up and cool-down activities

- Rest days among the 7 days

- Spending at least 20 minutes at least 3 times per week in the target heart rate zone (see Appendix U for target heart rate worksheet)

- FITT factors (frequency, intensity, type, and time) identified for each day

Scoring Rubric for Developing a Fitness Plan, Level 1

INDICATOR	DEVELOPING	COMPETENT	PROFICIENT
Activities align with and are realistic for identified fitness component and self-selected goals.	• Misalignment of activities with specific fitness components • Activities misaligned with goals • Activities either too hard or too easy based on pre-assessment data	• Activities align with identified fitness component • Activities align with self-selected goals • Activities selected realistic and based on pre-assessment data	• Activities align with identified fitness component • Activities align with self-selected goals • Activity levels progressive and lead to improved performance
Intensity levels align and are realistic for activity choice.	• Intensity levels misaligned with activity choice • Intensity levels either too high or too low for activity • Intensity levels either too high or too low based on pre-assessment data	• Intensity levels align with activity choice • Intensity levels realistic and based on pre-assessment data	• Intensity levels align with activity choice • Intensity levels realistic and based on pre-assessment data • Intensity levels challenging • Intensity levels lead to improved performance
Warm-up and cool-downs appropriate for activity.	• Warm-up or cool-downs insufficient for the activity and intensity level • Warm-up or cool-downs unrelated to activity choice	• Warm-up/cool-downs align with activity • Warm-up/cool-downs realistic and based on activity and intensity level	• Warm-up/cool-downs align with activity • Warm-up/cool-downs realistic and based on activity and intensity level • Warm-up/cool-downs address specific muscle groups essential to the activity

Scoring Rubric for Developing a Fitness Plan, Level 1

INDICATOR	DEVELOPING	COMPETENT	PROFICIENT
Plan includes daily activity with at least three days specific to cardiorespiratory fitness.	• Activity minutes less than 60 minutes per day • Less than 3 days devoted to cardiorespiratory fitness (less than 20 minutes in target heart rate zone) • Rest days identified with no activity	• Each day at least 60 minutes of activity • At least 3 days include 20 minutes in target heart rate zone • Days of greater intensity mixed with lighter intensity • Rest days identified with at least 30 minutes of lower intensity activities	• Each day at least 60 minutes of activity • At least 3 days include 20 minutes in target heart rate zone • Days of greater intensity mixed with lighter intensity • Rest days identified with 60 minutes of light activity • Plan is sequential and progressive

Grade-Level Outcome

Participates several times a week in a self-selected lifetime activity, dance or fitness activity outside of the school day. (S3.H6.L1)

Assessment Task

Element 5: Implement the Plan

The assessment for this outcome is a participation log that students maintain for a predetermined length of time. The log contains at least some of the following criteria: Date of activity, location of activity, length of participation, perceived exertion level, warm-up/cool-down activity, and a space for a weekly reflection on how they are feeling about their participation. Students participate in self-selected activities at least 5 times in a 7-day period. Their participation in class counts toward the achievement of the 5 times a week goal. The assessment of the log can be a simple checklist (yes or no) stating that the log was submitted and all parts were completed. If the activities they have selected are inappropriate or data provided in the log seem suspect, you should provide feedback specific to the log. An example of a general rubric is provided below:

Quality of Log Items

1 = Log is incomplete with missing data and few or no details provided. Selected activities do not align with fitness goals.

2 = Log is complete, but limited detail is provided. No supporting documentation to support perceived exertion score (step count, heart rate monitor, Fitbit, weight and number of repetitions, etc.).

3 = Log is complete with specific detail and supporting documentation on perceived exertion (step count, heart rate monitor, Fitbit, weight and number of repetitions, etc.).

If you require a weekly or biweekly reflection, you should provide feedback and encouragement based on students' reflection. For specific details on assessing reflections, see Standard 4. You could also use a rating scale from 1-3 that makes some determination on the quality of the log and reflection. An example is provided below:

Quality of Reflection

1 = Reflection only describes the activity without a personal response to the experience. Does not make connection to participation and personal health and wellness.

2 = Reflection describes the activity and includes some general comments on personal response to the experience. Indirect connections made to personal health and wellness.

3 = Reflection describes the activity, includes detailed and insightful statements on personal response to the experience. Direct connections made to personal health and wellness.

A sample of a participation log is provided here including a category specific to metrics used to document time and/or intensity. This could be such things as step counts, heart rate, Fitbit data, number of laps with times, and number of repetitions with weight. Students identify the metric they are going to use during the planning stage.

In addition, students reflect on their week of activity at the bottom of the form. Each week you provide a writing prompt they reference in their reflection or students simply follow guidelines you have established for reflections as part of the unit. A sample rubric for a participation log with a reflection is provided after the sample log.

The following example is for three days, but the form would continue through a seven-day cycle.

✍ *Physical Activity Participation Log*

Directions

Fill out the activity log based on your level of activity for the 7-day cycle. Remember to include any of the planned activities from your fitness plan. The form is available online, and you should complete the form within 24 hours after the activity. At the end of the form, reflect on your week of activity by answering the provided prompts.

DAY/DATE	FITNESS COMP.	ACTIVITY(IES) PARTICIPATED IN (TYPE)	INTENSITY (BORG)	TIME	METRIC USED	THR ZONE
Monday **May 1**	Cardio					
	Strength					
	Endurance					
	Flexibility					
	Warm-up					
	Cool-down					
Tuesday **May 2**	Cardio					
	Strength					
	Endurance					
	Flexibility					
	Warm-up					
	Cool-down					
Wednesday **May 3**	Cardio					
	Strength					
	Endurance					
	Flexibility					
	Warm-up					
	Cool-down					
Reflection Prompt 1: My biggest challenges this week were …						
Reflection Prompt 2: My biggest successes this week were …						

You provide this document in an electronic format with all 7 days of the week.

Scoring Rubric for a Participation Log With Reflection, Level 1

INDICATOR	DEVELOPING	COMPETENT	PROFICIENT
Documents participation in a timely manner using activity, time, intensity, metric used, and target heart rate.	• Components missing in log or not reported • Workouts logged at one time or in bunches outside of 48 hours • Some days skipped or not reported • No metrics reported supporting log	• Online log completed for all components for the week • Workout posted within 48 hours on site • Metrics support participation data • All days included	• Online log completed for all components for the week • Workout posted within 24 hours on site • Multiple metrics support participation data • All days included
Reflections demonstrate a growing insight on the role of physical activity in wellness.	• Only one of the prompts addressed • Simple description of the activity • No connection to wellness or fitness made	• Prompts answered with specific examples • Analysis of impact on fitness level • Connects participation to fitness level	• Prompts answered with specific examples • Analysis of impact referenced specific metrics • Connects participation to own wellness

Nutrition   Level 1

Grade-Level Outcome

Designs and implements a nutrition plan to maintain an appropriate energy balance for a healthy, active lifestyle. (S3.H13.L1)

Pre-Assessments

There are a number of different methods for collecting baseline data on eating habits. Students could answer short statements and determine if that behavior is true for them "always, usually, sometimes, or never". For example, the statement would be: "I avoid eating sugary cereals" and they would select one of the four options based on the frequency of their behavior. Using this method allows you to collect more data per student. Examples of this type of nutrition rating scale can be found on the web.

Another method is to simply ask questions specific to their eating habits such as "Do you know how many calories you eat each day?" or "How often do you read food labels?" or "How would you rate your overall eating habits?" If you are gathering baseline data on their nutritional knowledge, students complete a multiple-choice test specific to nutrition. This will provide them with data on their current knowledge specific to nutrition. Later the same test could be given as a post-measure of their knowledge after participating in the unit of instruction.

One of the most common methods of collecting baseline data on nutrition is for students to complete a short survey. These surveys simply ask for how frequently behaviors occur related to eating and nutrition. Below are some survey questions specific to nutrition knowledge and habits that might be included in this pre-assessment.

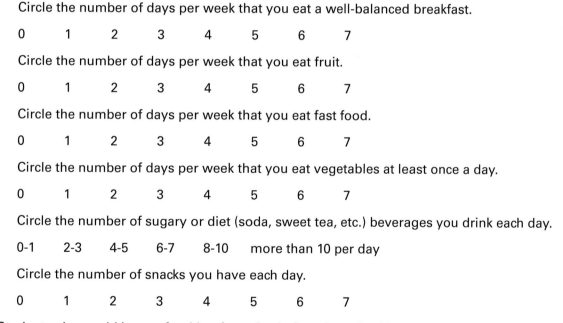

Circle the number of days per week that you eat a well-balanced breakfast.

0   1   2   3   4   5   6   7

Circle the number of days per week that you eat fruit.

0   1   2   3   4   5   6   7

Circle the number of days per week that you eat fast food.

0   1   2   3   4   5   6   7

Circle the number of days per week that you eat vegetables at least once a day.

0   1   2   3   4   5   6   7

Circle the number of sugary or diet (soda, sweet tea, etc.) beverages you drink each day.

0-1   2-3   4-5   6-7   8-10   more than 10 per day

Circle the number of snacks you have each day.

0   1   2   3   4   5   6   7

Students also could keep a food log for a day before the unit of instruction starts. This will provide them with baseline data specific to their eating habits. Once the unit begins, they would complete a food log over a 5-day period at the mid-point and at the end of the unit. The analysis of the nutrition data would be part of their reflection on their experience.

Assessment Task

Element 6: Food Log

As part of the portfolio students can complete a food log for a specific length of time. The length of time will vary based on the length of the unit and time devoted to nutrition instruction. After gathering information on their eating habits, students reflect on how their eating habits impact their health and wellness. If you are including a unit on nutrition in conjunction with a fitness plan, you might consider a separate assignment specific to nutrition. A nutrition plan is an extensive assignment with multiple elements similar to the fitness plan. Most plans include instruction on setting goals specific to nutrition, reading and evaluating food labels, planning balance meals, analyzing influences specific to eating habits, accessing information, and determining what triggers unhealthy eating. For the purpose of this example, students are simply keeping a food log for a week and reflecting on their eating habits and the possible impact of those habits on their fitness levels.

An example is provided of a 5-day food log:

✍ Food Log

Directions

Complete the food log for a five-day period. Remember to include everything you ate and drank during the day. Complete each column. At the end of the week, complete a reflection on your eating habits and compare your current eating habits to your one-day food log pre-assessment. Access the MyPyramid website and compare your calorie count and food choices to the recommendations for daily consumption. Data should be submitted with 48 hours.

DAY/DATE	MEAL/SNACK	WHAT DID YOU EAT?	WHERE DID YOU EAT AND WHO DID YOU EAT WITH?	HOW MANY CALORIES DID YOU CONSUME?
Monday **May 1**	Snacks			
	Breakfast			
	Lunch			
	Dinner			
Tuesday **May 2**	Snacks			
	Breakfast			
	Lunch			
	Dinner			
Wednesday **May 3**	Snacks			
	Breakfast			
	Lunch			
	Dinner			
Thursday **May 4**	Snacks			
	Breakfast			
	Lunch			
	Dinner			
Friday **May 5**	Snacks			
	Breakfast			
	Lunch			
	Dinner			
Reflection:				

Note: *Provide specific guidance to students on their reflections on their food log. You could ask them to compare their current data with their pre-assessment data or have them compare their food intake for the week with recommended nutritional guidelines from a website such as MyPyramid. Students could also identify what changes they would like to make or changes they need to make in their diet. They also could identify eating patterns or what might trigger overeating or food binges. Providing writing prompts facilitates more detailed reflections. Whatever parameters you set, they should appear in the rubric as indicators.*

Scoring Rubric for Food Log With Reflection, Level 1

INDICATOR	DEVELOPING	COMPETENT	PROFICIENT
Documents eating patterns over a five-day period including type of meal, where, who with, and a calorie count.	• Components missing in log or not reported • Some days skipped or not reported • No calorie count provided or calorie count is incorrect • Data submitted all at once in a cluster more than 48 hours after the date	• Online log completed for all components for the week • Food log for the day completed within 48 hours on site • Calorie count correct • All days included	• Online log completed for all components for the week • Food log posted within 24 hours on site • Calorie count correct with comparison to recommended amounts • All days included
Reflections demonstrate a growing insight on the role of nutrition in a healthy, active lifestyle.	• No comparisons to either pre-assessment or recommended daily intake of calories and categories • Recommended changes inappropriate based on analysis • No eating patterns or triggers identified	• Current data compared to pre-assessment data • Calorie count compared to recommended daily intake and categories (fruits, vegetables, meat, etc.) • Eating patterns or triggers identified • At least two appropriate changes identified and based on analysis	• Current data compared to pre-assessment data with specific examples • Calorie count compared and contrasted to recommended daily intake and categories (fruits, vegetables, meat, etc.) • Eating patterns or triggers identified • Three or more appropriate changes identified and based on analysis

Note: *A nutrition portfolio can have more than the six elements listed above and can include worksheets along the way. Many portfolios include brainstorming activities with partners as students begin setting goals or have a worksheet specifically developing the plan. The examples above are the most common elements found in most nutrition plans. When assigning a nutrition portfolio, you need to select and include the activities most appropriate for your teaching environment, student outcomes for your program, and the needs and interests of your students.*

Grade-Level Outcome

Creates and implements a behavior-modification plan that enhances a healthy, active lifestyle in college or career settings. (S3.H11.L1)

Pre-Assessment

To begin the unit, students complete a survey specific to risk-taking behaviors common to high school students. The CDC had developed a survey that is available online entitled the Youth Risk Behavior Survey (YRBS), which has 89 questions specific to common risk-taking behaviors of high school students. The survey is free from the CDC. You could review the survey and select questions that you think are most relevant to your teaching environment. Students complete the survey and based on the results, select a behavior they would like to modify. You can also take a more informal approach and simply allow students to select a behavior they would like to change.

Assessment Task

High school students are risk takers and often do not think of consequences of their actions. To facilitate their decision-making and the development of behavior change strategies, high school students develop and implement a behavior-modification plan that enhances a healthy, active lifestyle. For this assignment, high school students reflect on their risk-taking behaviors and develop a plan to modify their behavior. Students select the behavior they seek to modify, develop a plan, and implement the plan.

Description of the Assignment

This project is designed to have you reflect on behaviors or habits that negatively impact your wellness and develop a plan for change. Based on your survey results or your personal reflection select a behavior that needs to change to enhance a healthy, active lifestyle. You make the selection and provide a justification for your choice. Listed below are the parameters for the assignment.

- Choose one behavior (target behavior) that you would like to change related to a healthy, active lifestyle. You must provide a justification for your choice. After selecting your target behavior, write a behavior-change goal using the SMART criteria for goal setting.

- Define your goal statement in terms of the desired outcome resulting from the behavior change. State the goal in objective terms and make it measurable and specific. Avoid making a general statement such as "I want to be more active." A goal statement should define a behavior and should delineate a timeline for achieving the change. For example, replace the statement "I want to be more active" with "I want to complete 10,000 steps per day at least four days a week over a two-week period."

- After stating your goal, describe why you want to change the behavior (justification for selection). It is important to connect the "what" you would like to change to the "why" you believe you need to make the change. Identify at least three benefits associated with the behavior change.

- Decide how you are going to measure and collect data on your identified target behavior. That will require you to collect baseline data for a week before implementing the plan for change. For the goal above, you would track how may steps you take over a seven-day period, and that would establish your baseline. If you average 3,986 steps a day, you then either can make some decisions about how to increase your step count to 10,000 or modify the goal. If the current baseline step count is low, you might need to revise the goal to 8,000 steps. At the end of the week, you will graph your baseline data onto a chart and calculate an average for the week.

- Identify at least three triggers that might facilitate the behavior change or barriers that might inhibit it. For example, weather or friends who would rather play video games might present a barrier to reaching your 10,000-step target. Once you've identified those triggers or barriers, develop a plan for how to deal with them. Use effective self-management skills to implement the plan.

- Design and implement a plan for changing the behavior. Using your baseline data, develop a two-week behavior plan that includes a timeline for change. For the example above, you might create a plan to walk a specific number of steps on Monday, Wednesday, Friday, and Sunday of the first week to build to the 10,000-step goal.

- Over the two weeks of the program, collect data on your progress toward meeting the goal. At the end of the two weeks, graph the data and compare final data results with baseline data.

- Write a two-page reflection on the success of your behavior-change plan. Analyze the data to support any conclusions you have reached about meeting or not meeting your goal. Support all conclusions with examples. Answer the following questions as part of your reflection:

  » Did you meet your goal? Why or why not? Use examples to support your conclusions.

  » What barriers did you encounter and how did you overcome them?

  » What skills or knowledge did you use to change your behavior?

  » How would you improve your behavior plan? Be specific.

  » How has your outlook changed based on this experience?

- Assessment of the final project will be based on the attached rubric. The submitted paper should follow all writing conventions and demonstrate competency in written communication skills. Your ability to collect and analyze data is an important part of completing this assignment.

- On the next page is the rubric that will be used for the assessment of the project.

Adapted by permission from SHAPE America, *National Standards & Grade-Level Outcomes for K-12 Physical Education* (Champaign, IL: Human Kinetics, 2014), 99.

Scoring Rubric for Behavior-Change Plan, Level 1

INDICATOR	DEVELOPING	COMPETENT	PROFICIENT
Target behavior is identified with a goal.	• Target behavior inappropriate • General statement that does not meet SMART criteria	• Target behavior appropriate • Goal statement meets SMART criteria	• Target behavior appropriate and represents a challenge • Goal statement meets SMART criteria • Specific metrics identified
Justification and benefits identified.	• Fewer than 3 benefits identified • Benefits identified lack specificity • Benefits identified misaligned with target behavior/goal	• Three benefits identified • Specific benefits identified • All identified benefits align with target/goal	• More than 3 benefits identified • Specific benefits identified • All identified benefits align with target/goal • Supports each benefit with source information
Data are collected and analyzed.	• No metrics included • Metrics do not align with target behavior/goal	• Selected metrics align with goal • Baseline and final data graphed correctly • Data analysis appropriate	• Selected metrics align with goal • Baseline and final data represented correctly on comparison graph • Analysis correct with supporting documentation
Triggers or barriers identified and self-management.	• Identifies fewer than 3 triggers or barriers • No self-management plan OR • Self-management plan misaligned with triggers or barriers	• Identifies at least 3 triggers or barriers • Develops a self-management plan that aligns with triggers or barriers • Provides strategies for change	• Identifies four or more triggers or barriers • Develops a self-management plan that aligns with triggers or barriers • Provides specific strategies for each trigger or barrier

(continued)

Scoring Rubric for Behavior-Change Plan, Level 1 *(continued)*

INDICATOR	DEVELOPING	COMPETENT	PROFICIENT
Design and implement a behavior management plan.	• Plan not aligned with baseline data and/or goal • Plan does not support target behavior change • No steps identified in plan with only general or vague statements • No strategies for data collection identified	• Plan aligns with baseline data and goal • Plan appropriate to target behavior • Identifies appropriate steps for behavior change • Identifies strategies for data collection	• Plan directly aligns with baseline data and/or goals • Plan directly aligns with target behavior • Identifies appropriate and progressive steps for behavior change • Identifies strategies and specific metrics to be collected
Reflection is insightful and supported by data.	• Not all questions addressed in reflection • Reflection consists of generalized statements without support or data	• All questions at least partially addressed • Reflection supported by cited data or examples • Conclusions supported by data and/or examples	• All questions answered in detail • Reflection supported by cited data and specific examples • Conclusions supported by data and/or examples and directly aligned with goal
Demonstrate a command of written communication skills.	• More than 10 grammar or spelling errors • Lacks transition sentences between paragraphs or within paragraphs • Technical language not used or used inappropriately	• Fewer than 10 grammar or spelling errors • Written with clarity and effective transitions • Technical language specific to health and wellness used appropriately	• Fewer than 5 grammar or spelling errors • Written with clarity with effective transitions directly supporting conclusions • Technical language specific to health and wellness used appropriately
Demonstrate the ability to analyze and present data.	• Data assigned incorrectly on X and Y axes • Conclusions not supported by data • No comparisons made between pre and post data	• Data represented correctly on X and Y axes • Analysis of data appropriate • Pre and post data comparison made and appropriate	• Data represented correctly on X and Y axes • Analysis of data appropriate and supports conclusions • Pre and post data compared with logical conclusions reached

Adapted by permission from SHAPE America, *National Standards & Grade-Level Outcomes for K-12 Physical Education* (Champaign, IL: Human Kineticss, 2014), 100-101.

Standard 4 Sample Assessments

Standard 4: The physically literate individual exhibits responsible personal and social behavior that respects self and others.

Assessments for Standard 4 at the high school level require students to demonstrate self-management skills, demonstrate the ability to collaborate with others, use communication skills to solve problems and think critically, and apply best practices to ensure safe participation in self-selected activities. The assessment of affective domain behaviors provides unique challenges to all educators, but they are important transferable and lifelong skills. Physical education provides a laboratory where students have opportunities to "practice" these skills with their peers. In addition, participation in physical activity usually involves working with others or at least beside others. Movement is inherently a social activity.

Comprehensive assessments identified under previous standards provide you with opportunities to teach and assess outcomes specific to Standard 4. For example, sample assessments for Standards 1, 2, and 3 provide opportunities for groups or individual students to solve problems (e.g., practice plan), think critically (e.g., biomechanics research project), and demonstrate self-management skills (e.g., behavior management plan). Any of these rubrics also can assess personal and social behaviors by simply adding an indicator or two specific to Standard 4. The use of peer assessments, though typically focused on Standard 1, also provides opportunities for assessing Standard 4 outcomes. Peer assessments require students to give and receive feedback in an atmosphere of trust and mutual support. Students are taught to provide and receive feedback through responsible social behavior and respect for self and others. As a teacher, you cannot assume that students come to your classroom with these skills in place. Like all skills, they must be practiced, modified, and assessed in a supportive learning environment.

While Standard 4 outcomes are often embedded in movement activities, there also are opportunities to teach directly to these outcomes. For example, experiential education focuses on collaborative and team-building skills through movement activities. These activities require students to work together to solve a movement problem or to achieve a group goal. The movement activity is a conduit for improving interpersonal and communication skills. The focus is not on the outcome of the activity but on debriefing about the process. Students share feelings about their participation, reflect on their role, and learn to communicate with each other in appropriate ways.

In a movement environment, there are many opportunities for students to demonstrate responsible personal and social behavior. Students share space as well as equipment daily, which requires diligence on their part to ensure safety. However, just as important as physical safety is psychological safety for all students. Students must be aware of both words and actions to ensure a supportive environment is created and maintained. Your responsibility is to hold students accountable for outcomes under Standard 4. Physical education class must be both a physically and psychologically safe space for all students.

Grade-Level Outcomes

- Exhibits proper etiquette, respect for others and teamwork while engaging in physical activity and/or social dance. (S4.H2.L1)

- Uses communication skills and strategies that promote team or group dynamics. (S4.H3.L1)

Assessment Tasks

One of the major prerequisites to creating a safe and supportive environment, where learning can occur, is the development of interpersonal skills in students. You will need to teach and reinforce skill development specific to communicating effectively, collaborating to find solutions or increase competency, and respecting and accepting others. Students must be accountable for their words and actions, and it is your responsibility to hold them accountable through assessing Standard 4 outcomes. One method is to have students self-evaluate their behaviors each class period based on a rubric. You would then complete the same evaluation instrument. If there are discrepancies in the two scores, you and the student discuss the differences.

Guidelines

- Using the provided rubric, students self-evaluate their interpersonal skills in the following categories:
    - » Communications
    - » Teamwork
    - » Etiquette/Respect
- Evaluation completed each class period
    - » Submit as exit slip OR
    - » Submit to the school's physical education website

Setup

- Provide 5 minutes at the end of class for self-evaluation completion
- Exit slips available with pencils
- Deposit box for exit slips

Critical Components for Interpersonal Skills

Communications

- Facilitates discussion
- Engages in feedback process
- Willingness to share thoughts and ideas
- Effectively reflects on the meaning, values, and intentions of actions and words
- Uses positive vocal tone, facial expressions and/or body language to convey positive attitude
- Provides assistance and/or encouragement to others

Teamwork/Collaboration

- Adaptability to changing circumstances
- Accepting differing ideas and diverse opinions
- Building consensus
- Compromises to accomplish a common goal

- Deals positively with praise, setbacks, and criticism

- Reflects critically on learning experiences and processes

Etiquette/Respect

- Empathy – see situation from another's viewpoint

- Gives credit to others

- Demonstrates active listening

- Follows behavioral norms and policies

- Commits to fairness

- Uses respectful language

Scoring Rubric for Interpersonal Skills, Level 1

INDICATOR	DEVELOPING	COMPETENT	PROFICIENT
Demonstrates effective communication skills that promote teamwork and collaboration.	• Dominates discussion and interrupts others • Feedback given 　» as a judgment on ability and not based on criteria 　» only identifies challenges 　» argues or disagrees with feedback • Unaware of intentions and meanings of words and actions • Tone, facial expression, and body language negative	• Facilitates discussions by including others • Provides and/or accepts feedback to/from peers 　» Uses criteria provided 　» Provides feedback both on strengths and challenges 　» Feedback statements non-judgmental and supportive of change 　» Accepts feedback without being defensive • Willing to share ideas and thoughts by volunteering comments, thoughts, and ideas • Reflects on meaning, values, and intentions of words and actions • Uses positive tone, facial expression, and body language with few lapses	• Facilitates discussions by active listening and ensuring all individuals have opportunity to participate • Provides and/or accepts feedback to/from peers 　» Uses criteria provided 　» Provides feedback both on strengths and challenges 　» Feedback statements non-judgmental and supportive of change 　» Uses feedback sandwich (positive, challenge, positive) 　» Actively seeks feedback • Uses positive tone, facial expression, and body language • Reflects on meaning, values, and intentions of words and actions and accepts consequences
Demonstrates teamwork and collaboration skills in a movement environment.	• Inflexible with any changes or suggestions from others • Disengages from group if idea or suggestion not accepted • Unable to compromise • Often argumentative • Non-reflective specific to own behavior • Negatively impacts the group/class	• Demonstrates flexibility based on changing dynamics 　» Accepts other suggestions/ideas 　» Works for consensus 　» Provides ideas, but never argumentative 　» Able to compromise • Deals positively with setbacks and criticism • Reflects critically on learning experience and processes 　» Provides insights on the group process 　» Identifies personal behaviors that may interfere and/or support group success • Positively impacts group	• Demonstrates flexibility and leadership based on changing dynamics 　» Actively seeks suggestions/ideas from others 　» Builds consensus 　» Inclusive behaviors to ensure equity (making sure everyone is heard, etc.) 　» Supports and contributes to compromise • Deals positively with setbacks and criticisms

(continued)

Scoring Rubric for Interpersonal Skills, Level 1 *(continued)*

INDICATOR	DEVELOPING	COMPETENT	PROFICIENT

Demonstrates respect for others in a movement environment.	• Demonstrates impatience with others
	• Uses sarcasm with peers
	• Demonstrates exclusive behaviors (stays in cliques; makes fun of others)
	• Lapses in language with put downs such as "losers walk"
	• Tolerates disrespectful behaviors of others
	• Lacks commitment to fairness
	  » Cannot be trusted to self-officiate
	  » Difficulty sharing equipment or space
	  » Intentionally unfair or unkind to classmates
		• Demonstrates empathy
		  » Active listening
		  » Supportive of others
		  » Demonstrates inclusive behaviors (inviting others to share; acknowledge assumptions and bias; check facts)
		• Gives credit to others
		• Respectful language at all times
		• Commitment to fairness
		  » Accepting line calls without questioning
		  » Sharing space and equipment without rancor
		  » Giving classmates the benefit of the doubt
		  » Not tolerating unfairness/ unkindness to others by classmates
			• Demonstrates and models empathy
			  » Active listening
			  » Supportive of others
			  » Demonstrates inclusive behaviors (inviting others to share; acknowledge assumptions and bias; check facts)
			• Acknowledges all contributions of others
			• Respectful language at all times
			• Commits to and models fairness
			  » Accepting line calls without questioning
			  » Sharing space and equipment without rancor
			  » Giving classmates the benefit of the doubt
			  » Not tolerating unfairness/ unkindness to others by classmates
			  » Advocates for others to ensure equity

✍ Sample Exit Slip for Interpersonal Skills

Name: _____ Class period: _____

Based on your participation in today's class, self-assess your interpersonal skills. **Please use the Interpersonal Skills rubric to guide your assessment.** Just circle one of the three terms listed under the indicator and provide a rationale for each score. Include one specific example with your rationale for your score. At the bottom of the exit slip, cite one specific behavior you might change moving forward.

1. Effective communication skills that promote teamwork and collaboration.

   Developing   Competent   Proficient

   Rationale for score:

2. Teamwork and collaboration skills in a movement environment.

   Developing   Competent   Proficient

   Rationale for score:

3. Respect for others in a movement environment.

   Developing   Competent   Proficient

   Rationale for score:

4. Behavior change:

Working With Others   Level 1

Grade-Level Outcomes

- Uses communication skills and strategies that promote team or group dynamics. (S4.H3.L1)

- Solves problems and thinks critically in physical activity or dance settings, both as an individual and in groups. (S4.H4.L1)

Assessment Task

With experiential education focusing on team building, collaboration, communication, and group problem solving, it provides an ideal opportunity to teach to outcomes under Standard 4. A unit could be developed that utilizes an experiential education approach with Standard 4 outcomes, or one or two lessons with a focus on experiential education could be incorporated into an existing unit. In a dance or fitness unit, where groups of students create a dance or a fitness routine as the summative assessment, it would be advantageous to students to have opportunities to practice their interpersonal skills before beginning their group project. Planning learning experiences that allow students to develop and practice communication, collaboration, and problem-solving skills will give them the foundation they need to complete the summative project. For these assessments, students would complete a reflection on their experience in the group problem-solving activity (e.g., Helium Stick).

Pre-Assessment

Many of the learning activities under the experiential education umbrella can be used as pre-assessments for units requiring students to collaborate with a partner or be in groups for the completion of a summative assessment. Team-building activities such as Minefield or Helium Stick can provide teachers with guidance on which students may struggle with social interactions or participating with a group or even a partner. The pre-assessment will help you determine if the class will first need to improve their interpersonal and social skills before participating in a required group project. These skills must be practiced in a safe and supportive environment.

Listed below are guidelines for debriefing an experiential education learning activity. The focus of the debriefing process is to lead students through a discussion of their experience with a problem-solving activity with a group of peers. The actual "solution" of the problem is secondary to the group debriefing, which focuses on communication skills, various roles individuals played in the group, how challenges were approached within the group process, and how each individual "felt" about their experience within the group.

Guidelines

Experiential education activities must present a challenge to the group and require group problem solving. The example provided is called Helium Stick. This activity requires a group of students (8-12 students per group) to lower a long lightweight rod or pole to the ground using only their index fingers. Students are divided into two equal rows facing each other with their index finger remaining in constant contact with the pole that is between the two rows. They start with the stick at chest height in horizontally level position. The task is to lower the stick to the ground with each individual's finger staying in constant contact with the stick. This requires students to work together. The task is deceptively simple, but it is difficult for groups to accomplish. For complete details on the activity, search online for "Helium Stick."

Setup

Long lightweight pole or rod

Possible Debriefing Questions

- How did your group approach the task?

- What were the challenges? How did your group approach the challenges?

- How did the group handle suggestions or ideas offered by members of the group?

- Did any conflict arise during the activity? How did the group handle conflicts?

- What were the major discussion points during the activity?

- What type of communication skills were needed to make the group successful?

- What did you learn about yourself during the activity?

- What other situations in your life give you some of the same feelings you had during Helium Stick?

- What can you apply from the Helium Stick experience to these other situations?

Critical Components for Reflection

Self-Disclosure

- Openly examines the experience

- Non-defensive in responses

- Includes examples of both personal growth and challenges

- Answers questions or probes with honesty and insight

- Reflects on their role in the group

Communication

- Reflects on the types of communications occurring in the group

- Identifies any conflicts and how group handled conflicts

- Reflects on how communication could be improved

- Reflects on how suggestions and ideas were offered and accepted/rejected by group

- Describes how the group organized itself for the task

Applications

- Relates the experience to other experiences

- Focuses on solving the problem through
  - » Innovation
  - » Discussing and accepting/rejecting possible approaches/ideas
  - » Attempting alternative solutions and modifying based on results

- Reflects on personal role in the group (leader, follower, arbitrator, etc.)

- Critically analyzes the final results
  - » Challenges to succeeding
  - » Conjecturing why or why not group succeeded
  - » Analyzing other points of view during the group process

- Based on analysis, draws a logical conclusion supported by specific examples

Scoring Rubric for Self-Reflection on Communication and Problem Solving, Level 1

INDICATOR	DEVELOPING	COMPETENT	PROFICIENT

Reflects accurately on their role within the group.	• Lacks specific examples
	• Generalized statements without supports
	• Makes excuses or blames others
	• Questions unanswered or answers lack clarity
	• Provides no supporting evidence for insights
		• Openly and accurately examines their experience providing specific examples
		  » Personal growth
		  » Personal challenges
		• No excuses or blame to others
		• Answers probing or leading questions with insight and honesty
		• Discusses their role within the group
		  » Provides examples to support their role choice
		  » Provides supporting evidence on why they selected or were assigned the role
			• Multiple examples provided for both growth and challenges
			• Takes personal responsibility for choices
			• Answers probing/leading questions with insight, honesty, and addresses the "why"
			• Examines role within group in context of the challenge
			  » Notes how role changed OR
			  » Examines "why" role was taken

Demonstrates effective communication skills.	• Makes general statements that lack specificity and examples
	• Identifies conflicts without describing how conflicts were handled
	• Offers no suggestions on how communication could be improved
		• Reflects on how communication occurred in the group
		  » How did the group organize itself to hear ideas?
		  » Were all voices heard?
		  » How inclusive was the process?
		• Identifies how conflicts and disagreements were handled
		  » Specific examples support conclusion
		• Provides suggestions on how communication could be improved:
		  » Provides the "why" on how the suggestion would improve communication
			• Provides specific details supported by examples on communication within the group
			• Identifies specific examples supporting observations
			• Makes multiple (at least 3) specific suggestions on improving communication within group

Reflects critically on the group process specific to outcome.	• Reflections shallow and lack examples • No specific details provided on alternatives or innovations by group • Discusses group process, but does not identify role within group • Makes no comment on barriers encountered • Makes no suggestions for improvement	• Reflects on "how" ideas were accepted/rejected by group • Identifies any innovations or insights discovered during problem-solving activity • Reflects on how the group explored alternatives or modified approach based on achieving outcome • Reflects on role within group and provides examples supporting conclusion • Analyzes barriers group encountered • Identifies how the process could be more productive	• Reflects on "how" and "why" ideas were accepted or rejected by group • Provides specific examples of innovations or insights • Reflects on the "how" and "why" alternatives or modifications were explored • Explores the "why" roles were taken and supports with specific examples • Analyzes barriers group encountered and makes specific suggestions for improving process

Grade-Level Outcomes

- Uses communication skills and strategies that promote team or group dynamics. (S4.H3.L1)

- Solves problems and thinks critically in physical activity or dance settings, both as an individual and in groups. (S4.H4.L1)

Assessment Task

As a student begins to work with a partner or in a group to complete projects, it is important for the partner or other members of the group to provide feedback on the student's contribution to the group. These types of peer assessments provide an additional data point for you to consider when evaluating the final partnership or group project. The assessment can take the form of open-ended questions, checklists, rating scales, or writing prompts.

Listed below are samples of various peer evaluations that could be used to gather information on personal and social behaviors of students while they participate in partner or group problem-solving or creative activities. Many of the suggested assignments require students to work together, communicate with clarity, and reflect on their personal and social behaviors.

Guidelines

- Students' privacy must be protected as they evaluate peers on

  » Communication skills

  » Teamwork

  » Empathy

  » Inclusive behaviors

- Complete at the end of the project

Setup

- Responses submitted to a protected website

- Responses submitted directly to the teacher

✍ Peer Evaluation Checklist on Personal and Social Responsibility

*Name of student submitting evaluation: _____

For each member in your group, submit the following checklist based on your experience during the project. Your answers will not be shared and are part of the overall evaluation of the experience and the final project.

Group Member #1:_____

Offered suggestions and ideas	Yes	No
Listened to others and accepted change	Yes	No
Provided assistance and/or encouragement	Yes	No
Treated others with respect and kindness	Yes	No
Worked cooperatively with others	Yes	No
Was a major contributor to the group's success	Yes	No

After students have completed the checklist, you could ask them to evaluate each member's contribution to the group on a scale from 1 to 4.

Overall rank from 1 to 4 based on scale listed below: ____

1 = Had to be prompted to participate and contributed no ideas or suggestions to the group

2 = Participated without prompting but contributed few ideas or suggestions to the group

3 = Actively participated and contributed ideas and suggestions

4 = Actively participated while contributing multiple ideas and suggestions

*The same form is completed for each member in the group. All members evaluate each other using the checklist. Checklist items can be specific to the project. For example, if the assignment is to create a square dance with three others, the indicator might be "Contributed innovative movements and sequences to the dance". The focus of the checklist is on those individual and social behaviors that can contribute to the success of the group.

Another approach to determine individual's contribution to the group is to have each member of the group answer prompts specific to each of the group members. Examples are below.

1. _____ major contributions to the group were ------
2. _____ attitude during the project was ------
3. _____ helped create an environment of --------

Students would answer each prompt for each of the group members. This provides you with a rich narrative specific to the group project.

Standard 5 Sample Assessments

Standard 5: The physically literate individual recognizes the value of physical activity for health, enjoyment, challenge, self-expression and/or social interaction.

Standard 5 requires students to reflect on the value of physical activity for their overall wellness. Students are expected to demonstrate a cognitive understanding of health benefits associated with their self-selected activities along with the enjoyment, self-expression, and challenge the activity provides. While students' cognitive understanding can be assessed using traditional measures such as tests, quizzes, or worksheets, the assessment of how students value physical activity requires other types of measures, which may be more indirect. These measures include tools such as journals, logs, reflections, or possibly allowing students to select other types of assessments that allow them to creatively express the value they find in movement. Students may choose to create a dance or movement sequence that expresses the joy or challenge they find in movement, maybe a poem or essay will work for some, a drawing or bulletin board for others, some may prefer to rap or sing, others may create a video, or an interactive movement activity they share with classmates. The important thing is not the product that is produced but allowing students to use their creativity to showcase the values they find in movement.

As students are improving their movement competency, there are multiple opportunities to remind students to "think about" and "reflect on" the joy and fun associated with movement. These values are difficult to quantify but should not be ignored. Students should reflect on their progress and how they "feel" while participating, as well as identify challenges they are facing. This is an opportunity for students to share with you what they are feeling without fear of judgment or a grade assigned to their reflections. Your focus should be on responding to these feelings and providing guidance.

Grade-Level Outcome

Analyzes the health benefits of a self-selected physical activity. (S5.H1.L1)

Assessment Tasks

The assessment of this outcome can be accomplished using a number of traditional assessment methods including quizzes, examinations, worksheets, and/or written analysis on health benefits related to their self-selected physical activity. The sample provided below is specific to a written analysis of health benefits of physical activity.

Pre-Assessments

Pre-assessments need to include measures of flexibility, cardiorespiratory endurance, body composition, muscular endurance, and muscular strength. These pre-assessments will give students baseline data to make comparisons on the impact of their participation in a self-selected activity to these attributes of fitness.

Guidelines

- Pre-assessment data provided

- Description of assignment provided with rubric

Setup

No specific setup needed since this is an on-going project

Description of the Assignment With Critical Components

- Identify and analyze the fitness attributes most closely related to self-selected activity
  - » Report pre- and post-assessment scores on these measures
  - » Describe how those attributes were or were not improved by participation in self-selected activity
  - » Describe what you learned about the fitness benefits from regular participation in self-selected activity
  - » Analyze how improving these attributes improved or did not improve your performance in self-selected activities
- Using the CDC benefits of physical activity, describe how the self-selected activity provides at least three of these benefits:
  - » Builds and maintains healthy bones and muscles
  - » Reduces the risk of obesity and chronic diseases such as diabetes, cardiorespiratory disease and colon cancer
  - » Aids in reduction of depression and anxiety
  - » Promotes psychological well-being
  - » Improves academic performance
  - » Improves concentration
- Reflect on participation
  - » Responses are based on your perceptions
    - What challenges did you face?
    - What was the best part of the experience?

- What was the worst part of the experience?
- How did you feel about any set-backs or accomplishments?
  - » What benefits do you believe you gained? Be honest.
  - » Support your responses with examples
  - » Provide insight on the experience
- Writing and grammar
  - » Only minor errors in grammar and/or spelling
  - » Written with clarity and readability
  - » Effective use of transitions

Scoring Rubric for Analysis of Health Benefits, Level 1

INDICATOR	DEVELOPING	COMPETENT	PROFICIENT

Analyze the relationship of fitness attributes to self-selected physical activity.	• Only pre- or only post-assessments analyzed
	• Analysis provided, but no specific examples support analysis
	• Data inappropriately used or not included
	• General statements made on fitness benefits with no supporting documentation
	• No analysis or inappropriate analysis of fitness attributes' effect on performance
		• Both pre- and post-assessments analyzed
		• Analyzes how attributes were or were not impacted
		  » Provides specific examples supporting analysis
		  » Data cited from pre- and post-assessment that supports analysis
		• Reflects on fitness benefits from regular participation
		• Analyzes effect of fitness attributes on performance
			• Pre- and post-assessments included with analysis of attributes specific to selected activity
			• Specifically aligns attributes to improved performance with multiple examples
			• Reflection on regular participation is insightful and accurate
			• Aligns fitness attributes to specific personal performance gains with data or examples

Analyze and reflect on impact regular physical activity has on overall health and wellness.	• Less than 3 CDC benefits identified and described OR
	• Identified benefits do not align with selected activity
	• No examples in support of analysis provided
	• Only reflects on one or two of the following:
	  » Challenges
	  » Best experience
	  » Worst experience
	  » Personal feelings about participation
		• At least 3 CDC benefits identified and described
		  » Benefits align with identified physical activity
		  » Examples support analysis
		  » Personal experiences support description
		• Reflects on the following:
		  » Challenges
		  » Best experience
		  » Worst experience
		  » Personal feelings about participation
		• Examples provided for at least two of the above
		• Honest insights
			• More than 3 CDC benefits identified and described
			  » Benefits directly align with physical activity
			  » Multiple examples provided in support
			• Reflects on the following and provides specific examples for each:
			  » Challenges
			  » Best experience
			  » Worst experience
			  » Personal feelings about participation
			• Insights honest and thoughtful

Demonstrate competency in written communication.	• Errors in spelling and grammar interfere with readability • Lack of transitions impact clarity • No logical sequence	• Only minor errors in spelling and grammar that do not interfere with readability • Transitions from sentence to sentence and paragraph to paragraph • Clarity in writing (logical sequence)	• One or two errors in spelling and grammar that do not interfere with readability • Transitions increase readability and clarity • Logically sequenced with connections between analysis

Grade-Level Outcome

Selects and participates in physical activities or dance that meet the need for self-expression and enjoyment. (S5.H3.L1)

Assessment Tasks

One method of determining how students are feeling about their participation is to require them to complete a weekly or biweekly journal. The assessment of the journal is simply a checklist on the submission of the journal. There should be no judgment on the contents of the journal. You can provide a weekly prompt that facilitates the reflection, but no grade should be assigned based on the prompt. The prompt is simply something for them to think about as they participate in the activity.

Guidelines for Journal Writing

- Protect privacy of students
- Only you and the student should have access to the journal
- Your comments are limited to how students are feeling
    - » Can offer suggestions
    - » Provide encouragement
- Think of the journal as a private conversation between you and the student
- Biweekly journals require students to comment at least four times over the four-week period
- Weekly journals require students to comment at least once a week

Setup

Electronic journal format provided on school's physical education website

Critical Components for Journal Writing

- Describe the objective part of the experience
    - » Who, what, when, where, and how of experience
- Describe subjective part of the experience
    - » Feelings, perceptions, and thoughts during the experience
- Reflect on the experience by thinking about "why" you felt the way you did
    - » What challenges did you face?
    - » What frustrations occurred?
    - » What changes might have made the experience more positive?
- Summarize practical lessons learned
    - » What changes will you make moving forward?
    - » What barriers can you remove?
    - » What would you do differently?

- Write quickly and naturally
  - » Just write what you are feeling and avoid self-editing
  - » Let yourself enjoy the process and just write
  - » Do not be concerned with grammar, spelling or rules – let it flow
- Tell yourself the truth
  - » Don't talk yourself out of what you are feeling
  - » Give yourself permission to tell the truth
- Date each entry

Your role is to track that students have submitted their journals the required number of times.

Sample Checklist for Journal Entries

Journals submitted on time	Yes	No
All entries dated	Yes	No
Parameters are met	Yes	No

Grade-Level Outcome

Selects and participates in physical activities or dance that meet the need for self-expression and enjoyment. (S5.H3.L1)

Assessment Task

Offer a "self-expression and/or enjoyment" day on the last lesson of the unit. On this day, students present their selected method of demonstrating the self-expression and/or enjoyment they gain from being physically active. Students can work in groups or as individuals to select a specific option. Some possible options are listed below, but this is not an inclusive list. Students can suggest alternatives and upon your approval, use the approved alternatives.

In a group or as an individual, select one of the options listed below to demonstrate the "self-expression or enjoyment" gained from their selected physical activity.

- Create a dance as an individual or with a group that celebrates the self-expression or enjoyment found in movement
    - » Groups can be no larger than six individuals
    - » Dances are limited to no more than 3 minutes
    - » Music must be pre-approved
- Write a poem or essay that expresses the self-expression or enjoyment you found in movement
    - » Poems and essays will be posted on the website
    - » Individual project only
- Create a work of art that celebrates the self-expression or enjoyment found in movement
    - » Art work can be a drawing, sculpture, or other art form
    - » Written interpretation submitted with art work
        - Submit with a 500-word abstract on the art work
        - Abstract posted with art work
    - » Individual project only
- Create a bulletin board that illustrates the self-expression and enjoyment found in movement
    - » Can be a partner project
    - » Can include use of poems, essays, art work, etc. submitted by other students
    - » Identifies health benefits associated with regular physical activity
- Create a rap or parody song celebrating the self-expression and enjoyment found in movement
    - » Can be an individual or partner project
    - » Lyrics and parody pre-approved
- Create a video documenting multiple physical activities that provide opportunities for self-expression and enjoyment
    - » Group project limited to four individuals
    - » Audio to accompany video product
    - » Identifies various benefits related to regular physical activity

- Create an activity that focuses on fun and enjoyment of participants as a goal
  - » Group project limited to four individuals
  - » Activity taught to class
  - » Facilitate debriefing after activity
- Other
  - » Other alternatives can be suggested
  - » Prior approval required of suggested alternatives
  - » Can be an individual or group project
    - Groups limited to four members

✍ *Sample Rating Scale for Self-Expression and Enjoyment*

Creativity   1   2   3

1 = Lacks creativity and innovation

2 = Demonstrates some creative elements and innovations

3 = Highly creative with multiple innovations

Parameters   1   2   3

1 = Missing at least two parameters for the selected option

2 = Missing only one parameter for the selected option

3 = All parameters are met

Self-Expression and Enjoyment   1   2   3

1 = Fails to address self-expression and/or enjoyment

2 = Addresses only self-expression or enjoyment, but not both

3 = Addresses both self-expression and enjoyment

Students selecting to work in groups would complete an evaluation on group members. For a specific example of group evaluation, see Standard 4.

Appendixes

Appendix A: National Standards and Grade-Level Outcomes

Elementary School Outcomes (K-Grade 5)

Standard 1. Demonstrates competency in a variety of motor skills and movement patterns.

STANDARD 1	KINDERGARTEN	GRADE 1	GRADE 2	GRADE 3	GRADE 4	GRADE 5
Locomotor						
S1.E1 Hopping, galloping, running, sliding, skipping, leaping	Performs locomotor skills (hopping, galloping, running, sliding, skipping) while maintaining balance. (S1.E1.K)	Hops, gallops, jogs and slides using a mature pattern. (S1.E1.1)	Skips using a mature pattern. (S1.E1.2)	Leaps using a mature pattern. (S1.E1.3)	Uses various locomotor skills in a variety of small-sided practice tasks, dance and educational gymnastics experiences. (S1.E1.4)	Demonstrates mature patterns of locomotor skills in dynamic small-sided practice tasks, gymnastics and dance. (S1.E1.5a) Combines locomotor and manipulative skills in a variety of small-sided practice tasks in game environments. (S1.E1.5b) Combines traveling with manipulative skills for execution to a target (e.g., scoring in soccer, hockey and basketball). (S1.E1.5c)
S1.E2 Jogging, running	*Developmentally appropriate/emerging outcomes first appear in Grade 2.*	*Developmentally appropriate/emerging outcomes first appear in Grade 2.*	Runs with a mature pattern. (S1.E2.2a) Travels showing differentiation between jogging and sprinting. (S1.E2.2b)	Travels showing differentiation between sprinting and running. (S1.E2.3)	Runs for distance using a mature pattern. (S1.E2.4)	Uses appropriate pacing for a variety of running distances. (S1.E2.5)
S1.E3 Jumping & landing, horizontal	Performs jumping & landing actions with balance. (S1.E3.K)	Demonstrates 2 of the 5 critical elements for jumping & landing in a horizontal plane using 2-foot take-offs and landings. (S1.E3.1)	Demonstrates 4 of the 5 critical elements for jumping & landing in a horizontal plane using a variety of 1- and 2-foot take-offs and landings. (S1.E3.2)	Jumps and lands in the horizontal plane using a mature pattern. (S1.E3.3)	Uses spring-and-step takeoffs and landings specific to gymnastics. (S1.E3.4)	Combines jumping and landing patterns with locomotor and manipulative skills in dance, gymnastics and small-sided practice tasks in game environments. (S1.E3.5)

(continued)

Elementary School Outcomes (K-Grade 5) *(continued)*

STANDARD 1	KINDERGARTEN	GRADE 1	GRADE 2	GRADE 3	GRADE 4	GRADE 5
Locomotor *(continued)*						
S1.E4 Jumping & landing, vertical	Refer to S1.E3.K.	Demonstrates 2 of the 5 critical elements for jumping & landing in a vertical plane. (S1.E4.1)	Demonstrates 4 of the 5 critical elements for jumping & landing in a vertical plane. (S1.E4.2)	Jumps and lands in the vertical plane using a mature pattern. (S1.E4.3)	Refer to S1.E3.4.	Refer to S1.E3.5.
S1.E5 Dance	Performs locomotor skills in response to teacher-led creative dance. (S1.E5.K)	Combines locomotor and nonlocomotor skills in a teacher-designed dance. (S1.E5.1)	Performs a teacher- and/or student-designed rhythmic activity with correct response to simple rhythms. (S1.E5.2)	Performs teacher-selected and developmentally appropriate dance steps and movement patterns. (S1.E5.3)	Combines locomotor movement patterns and dance steps to create and perform an original dance. (S1.E5.4)	Combines locomotor skills in cultural as well as creative dances (self and group) with correct rhythm and pattern. (S1.E5.5)
S1.E6 Combinations	*Developmentally appropriate/emerging outcomes first appear in Grade 3.*	*Developmentally appropriate/emerging outcomes first appear in Grade 3.*	*Developmentally appropriate/emerging outcomes first appear in Grade 3.*	Performs a sequence of locomotor skills, transitioning from one skill to another smoothly and without hesitation. (S1.E6.3)	Combines traveling with manipulative skills of dribbling, throwing, catching and striking in teacher- and/or student-designed small-sided practice tasks. (S1.E6.4)	*Applies skill.*
Nonlocomotor (stability)[1]						
S1.E7 Balance	Maintains momentary stillness on different bases of support. (S1.E7.Ka) Forms wide, narrow, curled, and twisted body shapes. (S1.E7.Kb)	Maintains stillness on different bases of support with different body shapes. (S1.E7.1)	Balances on different bases of support, combining levels and shapes. (S1.E7.2a) Balances in an inverted position[1] with stillness and supportive base. (S1.E7.2b)	Balances on different bases of support, demonstrating muscular tension and extensions of free body parts. (S1.E7.3)	Balances on different bases of support on apparatus, demonstrating levels and shapes. (S1.E7.4)	Combines balance and transferring weight in a gymnastics sequence or dance with a partner. (S1.E7.5)
S1.E8 Weight transfer	*Developmentally appropriate/emerging outcomes first appear in Grade 1.*	Transfers weight from one body part to another in self-space in dance and gymnastics environments. (S1.E8.1)	Transfers weight from feet to different body parts/bases of support for balance and/or travel.[1] (S1.E8.2)	Transfers weight from feet to hands for momentary weight support. (S1.E8.3)	Transfers weight from feet to hands, varying speed and using large extensions (e.g., mule kick, handstand, cartwheel).[i] (S1.E8.4)	Transfers weight in gymnastics and dance environments. (S1.E8.5)
S1.E9 Weight transfer, rolling	Rolls sideways in a narrow body shape. (S1.E9.K)	Rolls with either a narrow or curled body shape. (S1.E9.1)	Rolls in different directions with either a narrow or curled body shape. (S1.E9.2)	*Applies skill.*	*Applies skill.*	*Applies skill.*

Elementary School Outcomes (K-Grade 5) *(continued)*

STANDARD 1	KINDERGARTEN	GRADE 1	GRADE 2	GRADE 3	GRADE 4	GRADE 5
Nonlocomotor (stability)¹ *(continued)*						
S1.E10 Curling & stretching; twisting & bending	Contrasts the actions of curling & stretching. (S1.E10.K)	Demonstrates twisting, curling, bending & stretching actions. (S1.E10.1)	Differentiates among twisting, curling, bending & stretching actions. (S1.E10.2)	Moves into and out of gymnastics balances with curling, twisting & stretching actions. (S1.E10.3)	Moves into and out of balances on apparatus with curling, twisting & stretching actions. (S1.E10.4)	Performs curling, twisting & stretching actions with correct application in dance, gymnastics and small-sided practice tasks in game environments. (S1.E10.5)
S1.E11 Combinations	*Developmentally appropriate/emerging outcomes first appear in Grade 2.*	*Developmentally appropriate/emerging outcomes first appear in Grade 2.*	Combines balances and transfers into a 3-part sequence (i.e., dance, gymnastics). (S1.E11.2)	Combines locomotor skills and movement concepts (levels, shapes, extensions, pathways, force, time, flow) to create and perform a dance. (S1.E11.3)	Combines locomotor skills and movement concepts (levels, shapes, extensions, pathways, force, time, flow) to create and perform a dance with a partner. (S1.E11.4)	Combines locomotor skills and movement concepts (levels, shapes, extensions, pathways, force, time, flow) to create and perform a dance with a group. (S1.E11.5)
S1.E12 Balance & weight transfers	*Developmentally appropriate/emerging outcomes first appear in Grade 3.*	*Developmentally appropriate/emerging outcomes first appear in Grade 3.*	*Developmentally appropriate/emerging outcomes first appear in Grade 3.*	Combines balance and weight transfers with movement concepts to create and perform a dance. (S1.E12.3)	Combines traveling with balance and weight transfers to create a gymnastics sequence with and without equipment or apparatus. (S1.E12.4)	Combines actions, balances and weight transfers to create a gymnastics sequence with a partner on equipment or apparatus. (S1.E12.5)
Manipulative						
S1.E13 Throwing underhand	Throws underhand with opposite foot forward. (S1.E13.K)	Throws underhand, demonstrating 2 of the 5 critical elements of a mature pattern. (S1.E13.1)	Throws underhand using a mature pattern. (S1.E13.2)	Throws underhand to a partner or target with reasonable accuracy. (S1.E13.3)	*Applies skill.*	Throws underhand using a mature pattern in nondynamic environments (closed skills), with different sizes and types of objects. (S1.E13.5a) Throws underhand to a large target with accuracy. (S1.E13.5b)
S1.E14 Throwing overhand	*Developmentally appropriate/emerging outcomes first appear in Grade 2.*	*Developmentally appropriate/emerging outcomes first appear in Grade 2.*	Throws overhand demonstrating 2 of the 5 critical elements of a mature pattern. (S1.E14.2)	Throws overhand, demonstrating 3 of the 5 critical elements of a mature pattern, in nondynamic environments (closed skills), for distance and/or force. (S1.E14.3)	Throws overhand using a mature pattern in a nondynamic environments (closed skills). (S1.E14.4a) Throws overhand to a partner or at a target with accuracy at a reasonable distance. (S1.E14.4b)	Throws overhand using a mature pattern in nondynamic environments (closed skills), with different sizes and types of balls (S1.E14.5a) Throws overhand to large target with accuracy (S1.E14.5b)

(continued)

Elementary School Outcomes (K-Grade 5) *(continued)*

STANDARD 1	KINDERGARTEN	GRADE 1	GRADE 2	GRADE 3	GRADE 4	GRADE 5
Manipulative *(continued)*						
S1.E15 Passing with hands	*Developmentally appropriate/emerging outcomes first appear in Grade 4.*	*Developmentally appropriate/emerging outcomes first appear in Grade 4.*	*Developmentally appropriate/emerging outcomes first appear in Grade 4.*	*Developmentally appropriate/emerging outcomes first appear in Grade 4.*	Throws to a moving partner with reasonable accuracy in a nondynamic environment (closed skills). (S1.E15.4)	Throws with accuracy, both partners moving. (S1.E15.5a) Throws with reasonable accuracy in dynamic, small-sided practice tasks (S1.E15.5b)
S1.E16 Catching	Drops a ball and catches it before it bounces twice. (S1.E16.Ka) Catches a large ball tossed by a skilled thrower. (S1.E16.Kb)	Catches a soft object from a self-toss before it bounces. (S1.E16.1a) Catches various sizes of balls self-tossed or tossed by a skilled thrower. (S1.E16.1b)	Catches a self-tossed or well-thrown large ball with hands, not trapping or cradling against the body. (S1.E16.2)	Catches a gently tossed hand-size ball from a partner, demonstrating 4 of the 5 critical elements of a mature pattern. (S1.E16.3)	Catches a thrown ball above the head, at chest or waist level, and below the waist using a mature pattern in a nondynamic environment (closed skills). (S1.E16.4)	Catches a batted ball above the head, at chest or waist level, and along the ground using a mature pattern in a nondynamic environment (closed skills). (S1.E16.5a) Catches with accuracy, both partners moving. (S1.E16.5b) Catches with reasonable accuracy in dynamic, small-sided practice tasks. (S1.E16.5c)
S1.E17 Dribbling/ball control with hands	Dribbles a ball with 1 hand, attempting the second contact. (S1.E17.K)	Dribbles continuously in self-space using the preferred hand. (S1.E17.1)	Dribbles in self-space with preferred hand demonstrating a mature pattern. (S1.E17.2a) Dribbles using the preferred hand while walking in general space. (S1.E17.2b)	Dribbles and travels in general space at slow to moderate jogging speed with control of ball and body. (S1.E17.3)	Dribbles in self-space with both the preferred and the nonpreferred hands using a mature pattern. (S1.E17.4a) Dribbles in general space with control of ball and body while increasing and decreasing speed. (S1.E17.4b)	Combines hand dribbling with other skills during 1v1 practice tasks. (S1.E17.5)
S1.E18 Dribbling or ball control with feet	Taps a ball using the inside of the foot, sending it forward. (S1.E18.K)	Taps or dribbles a ball using the inside of the foot while walking in general space. (S1.E18.1)	Dribbles with the feet in general space with control of ball and body. (S1.E18.2)	Dribbles with the feet in general space at slow to moderate jogging speed with control of ball and body. (S1.E18.3)	Dribbles with the feet in general space with control of ball and body while increasing and decreasing speed. (S1.E18.4)	Combines foot dribbling with other skills in 1v1 practice tasks. (S1.E18.5)

STANDARD 1	KINDERGARTEN	GRADE 1	GRADE 2	GRADE 3	GRADE 4	GRADE 5
Manipulative *(continued)*						
S1.E19 Passing & receiving with feet	*Developmentally appropriate/emerging outcomes first appear in Grade 3.*	*Developmentally appropriate/emerging outcomes first appear in Grade 3.*	*Developmentally appropriate/emerging outcomes first appear in Grade 3.*	Passes & receives ball with the insides of the feet to a stationary partner, "giving" on reception before returning the pass. (S1.E19.3)	Passes & receives ball with the insides of the feet to a moving partner in a nondynamic environment (closed skills). (S1.E19.4a) Receives and passes a ball with the outsides and insides of the feet to a stationary partner, "giving" on reception before returning the pass. (S1.E19.4b)	Passes with the feet using a mature pattern as both partners travel. (S1.E19.5a) Receives a pass with the feet using a mature pattern as both partners travel. (S1.E19.5b)
S1.E20 Dribbling in combination	*Developmentally appropriate/emerging outcomes first appear in Grade 4.*	*Developmentally appropriate/emerging outcomes first appear in Grade 4.*	*Developmentally appropriate/emerging outcomes first appear in Grade 4.*	*Developmentally appropriate/emerging outcomes first appear in Grade 4.*	Dribbles with hands or feet in combination with other skills (e.g., passing, receiving, shooting). (S1.E20.4)	Dribbles with hands or feet with mature patterns in a variety of small-sided game forms. (S1.E20.5)
S1.E21 Kicking	Kicks a stationary ball from a stationary position, demonstrating 2 of the 5 elements of a mature kicking pattern. (S1.E21.K)	Approaches a stationary ball and kicks it forward, demonstrating 2 of the 5 critical elements of a mature pattern. (S1.E21.1)	Uses a continuous running approach and kicks a moving ball, demonstrating 3 of the 5 critical elements of a mature pattern. (S1.E21.2)	Uses a continuous running approach and intentionally performs a kick along the ground and a kick in the air, demonstrating 4 of the 5 critical elements of a mature pattern for each. (S1.E21.3a) Uses a continuous running approach and kicks a stationary ball for accuracy. (S1.E21.3b)	Kicks along the ground and in the air, and punts using mature patterns. (S1.E21.4)	Demonstrates mature patterns of kicking and punting in small-sided practice task environments. (S1.E21.5)
S1.E22 Volleying underhand	Volleys a lightweight object (balloon), sending it upward. (S1.E22.K)	Volleys an object with an open palm, sending it upward. (S1.E22.1)	Volleys an object upward with consecutive hits. (S1.E22.2)	Volleys an object with an underhand or sidearm striking pattern, sending it forward over a net, to the wall or over a line to a partner, while demonstrating 4 of the 5 critical elements of a mature pattern. (S1.E22.3)	Volleys underhand using a mature pattern in a dynamic environment (e.g., 2 square, 4 square, handball). (S1.E22.4)	*Applies skill.*

(continued)

Elementary School Outcomes (K-Grade 5) *(continued)*

STANDARD 1	KINDERGARTEN	GRADE 1	GRADE 2	GRADE 3	GRADE 4	GRADE 5
Manipulative *(continued)*						
S1.E23 Volleying over-head	*Developmentally appropriate/emerging outcomes first appear in Grade 4.*	*Developmentally appropriate/emerging outcomes first appear in Grade 4.*	*Developmentally appropriate/emerging outcomes first appear in Grade 4.*	*Developmentally appropriate/emerging outcomes first appear in Grade 4.*	Volleys a ball with a two-hand overhead pattern, sending it upward, demonstrating 4 of the 5 critical elements of a mature pattern. (S1.E23.4)	Volleys a ball using a two-hand pattern, sending it upward to a target. (S1.E23.5)
S1.E24 Striking, short implement	Strikes a lightweight object with a paddle or short-handled racket. (S1.E24.K)	Strikes a ball with a short-handled implement, sending it upward. (S1.E24.1)	Strikes an object upward with a short-handled implement, using consecutive hits. (S1.E24.2)	Strikes an object with a short-handled implement, sending it forward over a low net or to a wall. (S1.E24.3a) Strikes an object with a short-handled implement while demonstrating 3 of the 5 critical elements of a mature pattern. (S1.E24.3b)	Strikes an object with a short-handled implement while demonstrating a mature pattern. (S1.E24.4a) Strikes an object with a short-handled implement, alternating hits with a partner over a low net or against a wall. (S1.E24.4b)	Strikes an object consecutively, with a partner, using a short-handled implement, over a net or against a wall, in either a competitive or cooperative game environment. (S1.E24.5)
S1.E25 Striking, long implement	*Developmentally appropriate/emerging outcomes first appear in Grade 2.*	*Developmentally appropriate/emerging outcomes first appear in Grade 2.*	Strikes a ball off a tee or cone with a bat using correct grip and side orientation/proper body orientation. (S1.E25.2)	Strikes a ball with a long-handled implement (e.g., hockey stick, bat, golf club), sending it forward, while using proper grip for the implement. *Note: Use batting tee or ball tossed by teacher for batting.* (S1.E25.3)	Strikes an object with a long-handled implement (e.g., hockey stick, golf club, bat, tennis or badminton racket) while demonstrating 3 of the 5 critical elements of a mature pattern for the implement (grip, stance, body orientation, swing plane, and follow-through). (S1.E25.4)	Strikes a pitched ball with a bat using a mature pattern. (S1.E25.5a) Combines striking with a long implement (e.g., bat, hockey stick) with receiving and traveling skills in a small-sided game. (S1.E25.5b)
S1.E26 In combination with locomotor	*Developmentally appropriate/emerging outcomes first appear in Grade 4.*	*Developmentally appropriate/emerging outcomes first appear in Grade 4.*	*Developmentally appropriate/emerging outcomes first appear in Grade 4.*	*Developmentally appropriate/emerging outcomes first appear in Grade 4.*	Combines traveling with the manipulative skills of dribbling, throwing, catching and striking in teacher- and/or student-designed small-sided practice-task environments. (S1.E26.4)	Combines manipulative skills and traveling for execution to a target (e.g., scoring in soccer, hockey, and basketball). (S1.E26.5)

Elementary School Outcomes (K-Grade 5) *(continued)*

STANDARD 1	KINDERGARTEN	GRADE 1	GRADE 2	GRADE 3	GRADE 4	GRADE 5
Manipulative *(continued)*						
S1.E27 Jumping rope	Executes a single jump with self-turned rope. (S1.E27.Ka) Jumps a long rope with teacher-assisted turning. (S1.E27.Kb)	Jumps forward or backward consecutively using a self-turned rope. (S1.E27.1a) Jumps a long rope up to 5 times consecutively with teacher-assisted turning. (S1.E27.1b)	Jumps a self-turned rope consecutively forward and backward with a mature pattern. (S1.E27.2a) Jumps a long rope 5 times consecutively with student turners. (S1.E27.2b)	Performs intermediate jump-rope skills (e.g., a variety of tricks, running in & out of long rope) for both long and short ropes. (S1.E27.3)	Creates a jump-rope routine with either a short or long rope. (S1.E27.4)	Creates a jump-rope routine with a partner using either a short or long rope. (S1.E27.5)

[1]Teachers must use differentiated instruction and developmentally appropriate practice tasks for individual learners when presenting transfers of weight from feet to other body parts.

Standard 2. Applies knowledge of concepts, principles, strategies and tactics related to movement and performance.

STANDARD 2	KINDERGARTEN	GRADE 1	GRADE 2	GRADE 3	GRADE 4	GRADE 5
Movement concepts, principles & knowledge						
S2.E1 Space	Differentiates between movement in personal (self-space) and general space. (S2.E1.Ka) Moves in personal space to a rhythm. (S2.E1.Kb)	Moves in self-space and general space in response to designated beats/rhythms. (S2.E1.1)	Combines locomotor skills in general space to a rhythm. (S2.E1.2)	Recognizes the concept of open spaces in a movement context. (S2.E1.3)	Applies the concept of open spaces to combination skills involving traveling (e.g., dribbling and traveling). (S2.E1.4a) Applies the concept of closing spaces in small-sided practice tasks. (S2.E1.4b) Dribbles in general space with changes in direction and speed. (S2.E1.4c)	Combines spatial concepts with locomotor and nonlocomotor movements for small groups in gymnastics, dance and games environments. (S2.E1.5)
S2.E2 Pathways, shapes, levels	Travels in 3 different pathways. (S2.E2.K)	Travels demonstrating low, middle and high levels. (S2.E2.1a) Travels demonstrating a variety of relationships with objects (e.g., over, under, around, through). (S2.E2.1b)	Combines shapes, levels and pathways into simple travel, dance and gymnastics sequences.[ii] (S2.E2.2)	Recognizes locomotor skills specific to a wide variety of physical activities. (S2.E2.3)	Combines movement concepts with skills in small-sided practice tasks, gymnastics and dance environments. (S2.E2.4)	Combines movement concepts with skills in small-sided practice tasks in game environments, gymnastics and dance with self-direction. (S2.E2.5)

Elementary School Outcomes (K-Grade 5) *(continued)*

STANDARD 2	KINDERGARTEN	GRADE 1	GRADE 2	GRADE 3	GRADE 4	GRADE 5
Movement concepts, principles & knowledge *(continued)*						
S2.E3 Speed, direction, force	Travels in general space with different speeds. (S2.E3.K)	Differentiates between fast and slow speeds. (S2.E3.1a) Differentiates between strong and light force. (S2.E3.1b)	Varies time and force with gradual increases and decreases. (S2.E3.2)	Combines movement concepts (direction, levels, force, time) with skills as directed by the teacher. (S2.E3.3)	Applies the movement concepts of speed, endurance and pacing for running. (S2.E3.4a) Applies the concepts of direction and force when striking an object with a short-handled implement, sending it toward a designated target. (S2.E3.4b)	Applies movement concepts to strategy in game situations. (S2.E3.5a) Applies the concepts of direction and force to strike an object with a long-handled implement. (S2.E3.5b) Analyzes movement situations and applies movement concepts (e.g., force, direction, speed, pathways, extensions) in small-sided practice tasks in game environments, dance and gymnastics. (S2.E3.5c)
S2.E4 Alignment & muscular tension	*Developmentally appropriate/emerging outcomes first appear in Grade 3.*	*Developmentally appropriate/emerging outcomes first appear in Grade 3.*	*Developmentally appropriate/emerging outcomes first appear in Grade 3.*	Employs the concept of alignment in gymnastics and dance. (S2.E4.3a) Employs the concept of muscular tension with balance in gymnastics and dance. (S2.E4.3b)	*Applies skill.*	*Applies skill.*
S2.E5 Strategies & tactics	*Developmentally appropriate/emerging outcomes first appear in Grade 3.*	*Developmentally appropriate/emerging outcomes first appear in Grade 3.*	*Developmentally appropriate/emerging outcomes first appear in Grade 3.*	Applies simple strategies & tactics in chasing activities. (S2.E5.3a) Applies simple strategies in fleeing activities. (S2.E5.3b)	Applies simple offensive strategies & tactics in chasing & fleeing activities. (S2.E5.4a) Applies simple defensive strategies & tactics in chasing and fleeing activities. (S2.E5.4b) Recognizes the types of kicks needed for different games & sports situations. (S2.E5.4c)	Applies basic offensive and defensive strategies & tactics in invasion small-sided practice tasks. (S2.E5.5a) Applies basic offensive and defensive strategies & tactics in net/wall small-sided practice tasks. (S2.E5.5b) Recognizes the type of throw, volley or striking action needed for different games & sports situations. (S2.E5.5c)

Standard 3. Demonstrates the knowledge and skills to achieve and maintain a health-enhancing level of physical activity and fitness.

STANDARD 3	KINDERGARTEN	GRADE 1	GRADE 2	GRADE 3	GRADE 4	GRADE 5
Physical activity knowledge						
S3.E1	Identifies active-play opportunities outside physical education class. (S3.E1.K)	Discusses the benefits of being active and exercising and/or playing. (S3.E1.1)	Describes large-motor and/or manipulative physical activities for participation outside physical education class (e.g., before and after school, at home, at the park, with friends, with the family). (S3.E1.2)	Charts participation in physical activities outside physical education class. (S3.E1.3a) Identifies physical activity benefits as a way to become healthier. (S3.E1.3b)	Analyzes opportunities for participating in physical activity outside physical education class. (S3.E1.4)	Charts and analyzes physical activity outside physical education class for fitness benefits of activities. (S3.E1.5)
Engages in physical activity						
S3.E2	Actively participates in physical education class. (S3.E2.K)	Actively engages in physical education class. (S3.E2.1)	Actively engages in physical education class in response to instruction and practice. (S3.E2.2)	Engages in the activities of physical education class without teacher prompting. (S3.E2.3)	Actively engages in the activities of physical education class, both teacher-directed and independent. (S3.E2.4)	Actively engages in all the activities of physical education. (S3.E2.5)
Fitness knowledge						
S3.E3	Recognizes that when you move fast, your heart beats faster and you breathe faster.[iii] (S3.E3.K)	Identifies the heart as a muscle that grows stronger with exercise, play, and physical activity. (S3.E3.1)	Recognizes the use of the body as resistance (e.g., holds body in plank position, animal walks)[iv] for developing strength. (S3.E3.2a) Identifies physical activities that contribute to fitness. (S3.E3.2b)	Describes the concept of fitness and provides examples of physical activity to enhance fitness. (S3.E3.3)	Identifies the components of health-related fitness.[v] (S3.E3.4)	Differentiates between skill-related and health-related fitness.[vi] (S3.E3.5)
S3.E4	*Developmentally appropriate/emerging outcomes first appear in Grade 3.*	*Developmentally appropriate/emerging outcomes first appear in Grade 3.*	*Developmentally appropriate/emerging outcomes first appear in Grade 3.*	Recognizes the importance of warm-up & cool-down relative to vigorous physical activity. (S3.E4.3)	Demonstrates warm-up & cool-down relative to the cardiorespiratory fitness assessment. (S3.E4.4)	Identifies the need for warm-up & cool-down relative to various physical activities. (S3.E4.5)

Elementary School Outcomes (K-Grade 5) *(continued)*

STANDARD 3	KINDERGARTEN	GRADE 1	GRADE 2	GRADE 3	GRADE 4	GRADE 5
Assessment & program planning						
S3.E5	*Developmentally appropriate/emerging outcomes first appear in Grade 3.*	*Developmentally appropriate/emerging outcomes first appear in Grade 3.*	*Developmentally appropriate/ emerging outcomes first appear in Grade 3.*	Demonstrates, with teacher direction, the health-related fitness components. (S3.E5.3)	Completes fitness assessments (pre- & post-). (S3.E5.4a) Identifies areas of needed remediation from personal test and, with teacher assistance, identifies strategies for progress in those areas. (S3.E5.4b)	Analyzes results of fitness assessment (pre- & post-), comparing results with fitness components for good health. (S3.E5.5a) Designs a fitness plan to address ways to use physical activity to enhance fitness. (S3.E5.5b)
S3.E6 Nutrition	Recognizes that food provides energy for physical activity. (S3.E6.K)	Differentiates between healthy and unhealthy foods. (S3.E6.1)	Recognizes the "good health balance" of nutrition and physical activity. (S3.E6.2)	Identifies foods that are beneficial for before and after physical activity. (S3.E6.3)	Discusses the importance of hydration and hydration choices relative to physical activities. (S3.E6.4)	Analyzes the impact of food choices relative to physical activity, youth sports & personal health. (S3.E6.5)

Standard 4. Exhibits responsible personal and social behavior that respects self and others.

STANDARD 4	KINDERGARTEN	GRADE 1	GRADE 2	GRADE 3	GRADE 4	GRADE 5
Personal responsibility						
S4.E1	Follows directions in group settings (e.g., safe behaviors, following rules, taking turns). (S4.E1.K)	Accepts personal responsibility by using equipment and space appropriately. (S4.E1.1)	Practices skills with minimal teacher prompting. (S4.E1.2)	Exhibits personal responsibility in teacher-directed activities. (S4.E1.3)	Exhibits responsible behavior in independent group situations. (S4.E1.4)	Engages in physical activity with responsible interpersonal behavior (e.g., peer to peer, student to teacher, student to referee). (S4.E1.5)
S4.E2	Acknowledges responsibility for behavior when prompted. (S4.E2.K)	Follows the rules & parameters of the learning environment. (S4.E2.1)	Accepts responsibility for class protocols with behavior and performance actions. (S4.E2.2)	Works independently for extended periods of time. (S4.E2.3)	Reflects on personal social behavior in physical activity. (S4.E2.4)	Participates with responsible personal behavior in a variety of physical activity contexts, environments, and facilities. (S4.E2.5a) Exhibits respect for self with appropriate behavior while engaging in physical activity. (S4.E2.5b)
Accepting feedback						
S4.E3	Follows instruction/directions when prompted. (S4.E3.K)	Responds appropriately to general feedback from the teacher. (S4.E3.1)	Accepts specific corrective feedback from the teacher. (S4.E3.2)	Accepts and implements specific corrective feedback from the teacher. (S4.E3.3)	Listens respectfully to corrective feedback from others (e.g., peers, adults). (S4.E3.4)	Gives corrective feedback respectfully to peers. (S4.E3.5)
Working with others						
S4.E4	Shares equipment and space with others. (S4.E4.K)	Works independently with others in a variety of class environments (e.g., small & large groups). (S4.E4.1)	Works independently with others in partner environments. (S4.E4.2)	Works cooperatively with others. (S4.E4.3a) Praises others for their success in movement performance. (S4.E4.3b)	Praises the movement performance of others both more- and less-skilled. (S4.E4.4a) Accepts players of all skill levels into the physical activity. (S4.E4.4b)	Accepts, recognizes, and actively involves others with both higher and lower skill abilities into physical activities and group projects. (S4.E4.5)
Rules & etiquette						
S4.E5	Recognizes the established protocols for class activities. (S4.E5.K)	Exhibits the established protocols for class activities. (S4.E5.1)	Recognizes the role of rules and etiquette in teacher-designed physical activities. (S4.E5.2)	Recognizes the role of rules and etiquette in physical activity with peers. (S4.E5.3)	Exhibits etiquette and adherence to rules in a variety of physical activities. (S4.E5.4)	Critiques the etiquette involved in rules of various game activities. (S4.E5.5)

Elementary School Outcomes (K-Grade 5) *(continued)*

STANDARD 4	KINDERGARTEN	GRADE 1	GRADE 2	GRADE 3	GRADE 4	GRADE 5
Safety						
S4.E6	Follows teacher directions for safe participation and proper use of equipment with minimal reminders. (S4.E6.K)	Follows teacher directions for safe participation and proper use of equipment without teacher reminders. (S4.E6.1)	Works independently and safely in physical education. (S4.E6.2a) Works safely with physical education equipment. (S4.E6.2b)	Works independently and safely in physical activity settings. (S4.E6.3)	Works safely with peers and equipment in physical activity settings. (S4.E6.4)	Applies safety principles with age-appropriate physical activities. (S4.E6.5)

Standard 5. Recognizes the value of physical activity for health, enjoyment, challenge, self-expression and/or social interaction.

STANDARD 5	KINDERGARTEN	GRADE 1	GRADE 2	GRADE 3	GRADE 4	GRADE 5
Health						
S5.E1	Recognizes that physical activity is important for good health. (S5.E1.K)	Identifies physical activity as a component of good health. (S5.E1.1)	Recognizes the value of "good health balance." (Refer to S3.E6.2)	Discusses the relationship between physical activity and good health. (S5.E1.3)	Examines the health benefits of participating in physical activity. (S5.E1.4)	Compares the health benefits of participating in selected physical activities. (S5.E1.5)
Challenge						
S5.E2	Acknowledges that some physical activities are challenging/difficult. (S5.E2.K)	Recognizes that challenge in physical activities can lead to success. (S5.E2.1)	Compares physical activities that bring confidence and challenge. (S5.E2.2)	Discusses the challenge that comes from learning a new physical activity. (S5.E2.3)	Rates the enjoyment of participating in challenging and mastered physical activities. (S5.E2.4)	Expresses (via written essay, visual art, creative dance) the enjoyment and/or challenge of participating in a favorite physical activity. (S5.E2.5)
Self-expression & enjoyment						
S5.E3	Identifies physical activities that are enjoyable.vii (S5.E3.Ka) Discusses the enjoyment of playing with friends. (S5.E3.Kb)	Describes positive feelings that result from participating in physical activities. (S5.E3.1a) Discusses personal reasons (i.e., the "why") for enjoying physical activities. (S5.E3.1b)	Identifies physical activities that provide self-expression (e.g., dance, gymnastics routines, practice tasks in game environments). (S5.E3.2)	Reflects on the reasons for enjoying selected physical activities. (S5.E3.3)	Ranks the enjoyment of participating in different physical activities. (S5.E3.4)	Analyzes different physical activities for enjoyment and challenge, identifying reasons for a positive or negative response. (S5.E3.5)
S5.E4 Social interaction	*Developmentally appropriate/emerging outcomes first appear in Grade 3.*	*Developmentally appropriate/emerging outcomes first appear in Grade 3.*	*Developmentally appropriate/emerging outcomes first appear in Grade 3.*	Describes the positive social interactions that come when engaged with others in physical activity. (S5.E4.3)	Describes & compares the positive social interactions when engaged in partner, small-group and large-group physical activities. (S5.E4.4)	Describes the social benefits gained from participating in physical activity (e.g., recess, youth sport). (S5.E4.5)

iNASPE, 1992, p. 12.
iiIbid., p. 11.
iiiNASPE, 2012, p. 14.
ivIbid., p. 6.
vIbid., p. 16.
viIbid., p 17.
viiIbid., p. 19.

Reprinted by permission from SHAPE America, *National Standards & Grade-Level Outcomes for K-12 Physical Education* (Champaign, IL: Human Kinetics, 2014), 26.

Middle School Outcomes (Grades 6-8)

Standard 1. Demonstrates competency in a variety of motor skills and movement patterns.

STANDARD 1	GRADE 6	GRADE 7	GRADE 8
Dance & rhythms			
S1.M1	Demonstrates correct rhythm and pattern for 1 of the following dance forms: folk, social, creative, line or world dance. (S1.M1.6)	Demonstrates correct rhythm and pattern for a different dance form from among folk, social, creative, line and world dance. (S1.M1.7)	Exhibits command of rhythm and timing by creating a movement sequence to music as an individual or in a group. (S1.M1.8)
Games & sports: Invasion & field games			
S1.M2 Throwing	Throws with a mature pattern for distance or power appropriate to the practice task (e.g., distance = outfield to home plate; power = 2nd base to 1st base). (S1.M2.6)	Throws with a mature pattern for distance or power appropriate to the activity in a dynamic environment. (S1.M2.7)	Throws with a mature pattern for distance or power appropriate to the activity during small-sided game play. (S1.M2.8)
S1.M3 Catching	Catches with a mature pattern from a variety of trajectories using different objects in varying practice tasks. (S1.M3.6)	Catches with a mature pattern from a variety of trajectories using different objects in small-sided game play. (S1.M3.7)	Catches using an implement in a dynamic environment or modified game play. (S1.M3.8)
Games & sports: Invasion games			
S1.M4 Passing & receiving	Passes and receives with hands in combination with locomotor patterns of running and change of direction & speed with competency in modified invasion games such as basketball, flag football, speedball, or team handball. (S1.M4.6)	Passes and receives with feet in combination with locomotor patterns of running and change of direction and speed with competency in modified invasion games such as soccer or speedball. (S1.M4.7)	Passes and receives with an implement in combination with locomotor patterns of running and change of direction, speed and/or level with competency in modified invasion games such as lacrosse or hockey (floor, field, ice). (S1.M4.8)
S1.M5 Passing & receiving	Throws, while stationary, a leading pass to a moving receiver. (S1.M5.6)	Throws, while moving, a leading pass to a moving receiver. (S1.M5.7)	Throws a lead pass to a moving partner off a dribble or pass. (S1.M5.8)
S1.M6 Offensive skills	Performs pivots, fakes and jab steps designed to create open space during practice tasks. (S1.M6.6)	Executes at least 1 of the following designed to create open space during small-sided game play: pivots, fakes, jab steps. (S1.M6.7)	Executes at least 2 of the following to create open space during modified game play: pivots, fakes, jab steps, screens. (S1.M6.8)
S1.M7 Offensive skills	Performs the following offensive skills without defensive pressure: pivot, give & go, and fakes. (S1.M7.6)	Performs the following offensive skills with defensive pressure: pivot, give & go, and fakes. (S1.M7.7)	Executes the following offensive skills during small-sided game play: pivot, give & go, and fakes. (S1.M7.8)
S1.M8 Dribbling/ball control	Dribbles with dominant hand using a change of speed and direction in a variety of practice tasks. (S1.M8.6)	Dribbles with dominant and nondominant hands using a change of speed and direction in a variety of practice tasks. (S1.M8.7)	Dribbles with dominant and nondominant hands using a change of speed and direction in small-sided game play. (S1.M8.8)
S1.M9 Dribbling/ball control	Foot-dribbles or dribbles with an implement with control, changing speed and direction in a variety of practice tasks. (S1.M9.6)	Foot-dribbles or dribbles with an implement combined with passing in a variety of practice tasks. (S1.M9.7)	Foot-dribbles or dribbles with an implement with control, changing speed and direction during small-sided game play. (S1.M9.8)
S1.M10 Shooting on goal	Shoots on goal with power in a dynamic environment as appropriate to the activity. (S1.M10.6)	Shoots on goal with power and accuracy in small-sided game play. (S1.M10.7)	Shoots on goal with a long-handled implement for power and accuracy in modified invasion games such as hockey (floor, field, ice) or lacrosse. (S1.M10.8)
S1.M11 Defensive skills	Maintains defensive ready position with weight on balls of feet, arms extended, and eyes on midsection of the offensive player. (S1.M11.6)	Slides in all directions while on defense without crossing feet. (S1.M11.7)	Drop-steps in the direction of the pass during player-to-player defense. (S1.M11.8)

(continued)

STANDARD 1	GRADE 6	GRADE 7	GRADE 8
Games & sports: Net/wall games			
S1.M12 Serving	Performs a legal underhand serve with control for net/wall games such as badminton, volleyball or pickleball. (S1.M12.6)	Executes consistently (at least 70% of the time) a legal underhand serve to a predetermined target for net/wall games such as badminton, volleyball or pickleball. (S1.M12.7)	Executes consistently (at least 70% of the time) a legal underhand serve for distance and accuracy for net/wall games such as badminton, volleyball or pickleball. (S1.M12.8)
S1.M13 Striking	Strikes with a mature overhand pattern in a nondynamic environment (closed skills) for net/wall games such as volleyball, handball, badminton or tennis. (S1.M13.6)	Strikes with a mature overhand pattern in a dynamic environment for net/wall games such as volleyball, handball, badminton or tennis. (S1.M13.7)	Strikes with a mature overhand pattern in a modified game for net/wall games such as volleyball, handball, badminton or tennis. (S1.M13.8)
S1.M14 Forehand & backhand	Demonstrates the mature form of the forehand and backhand strokes with a short-handled implement in net games such as paddleball, pickleball or short-handled racket tennis. (S1.M14.6)	Demonstrates the mature form of forehand and backhand strokes with a long-handled implement in net games such as badminton or tennis. (S1.M14.7)	Demonstrates the mature form of forehand and backhand strokes with a short- or long-handled implement with power and accuracy in net games such as pickleball, tennis, badminton or paddleball. (S1.M14.8)
S1.M15 Weight transfer	Transfers weight with correct timing for the striking pattern. (S1.M15.6)	Transfers weight with correct timing using low-to-high striking pattern with a short-handled implement on the forehand side. (S1.M15.7)	Transfers weight with correct timing using low-to-high striking pattern with a long-handled implement on the forehand and backhand sides. (S1.M15.8)
S1.M16 Volley	Forehand volleys with a mature form and control using a short-handled implement. (S1.M16.6)	Forehand and backhand volleys with a mature form and control using a short-handled implement. (S1.M16.7)	Forehand and backhand volleys with a mature form and control using a short-handled implement during modified game play. (S1.M16.8)
S1.M17 Two-hand volley	Two-hand volleys with control in a variety of practice tasks. (S1.M17.6)	Two-hand-volleys with control in a dynamic environment. (S1.M17.7)	Two-hand-volleys with control in a small-sided game. (S1.M17.8)
Games & sports: Target games			
S1.M18 Throwing	Demonstrates a mature pattern for a modified target game such as bowling, bocce or horseshoes. (S1.M18.6)	Executes consistently (70% of the time) a mature pattern for target games such as bowling, bocce, or horseshoes. (S1.M18.7)	Performs consistently (70% of the time) a mature pattern with accuracy and control for 1 target game such as bowling or bocce. (S1.M18.8)
S1.M19 Striking	Strikes, with an implement, a stationary object for accuracy in activities such as croquet, shuffleboard or golf. (S1.M19.6)	Strikes, with an implement, a stationary object for accuracy and distance in activities such as croquet, shuffleboard or golf. (S1.M19.7)	Strikes, with an implement, a stationary object for accuracy and power in such activities as croquet, shuffleboard or golf. (S1.M19.8)
Games & sports: Fielding/striking games			
S1.M20 Striking	Strikes a pitched ball with an implement with force in a variety of practice tasks. (S1.M20.6)	Strikes a pitched ball with an implement to open space in a variety of practice tasks. (S1.M20.7)	Strikes a pitched ball with an implement for power to open space in a variety of small-sided games. (S1.M20.8)
S1.M21 Catching	Catches, with a mature pattern, from different trajectories using a variety of objects in a varying practice tasks. (S1.M21.6)	Catches, with a mature pattern, from different trajectories using a variety of objects in small-sided game play. (S1.M21.7)	Catches, using an implement, from different trajectories and speeds in a dynamic environment or modified game play. (S1.M21.8)

Middle School Outcomes (Grades 6-8)   *(continued)*

STANDARD 1	GRADE 6	GRADE 7	GRADE 8
Outdoor pursuits			
S1.M22 Activities might include but are not limited to recreational boating (e.g., kayaking, canoeing, sailing, rowing); hiking; backpacking; fishing; orienteering or geocaching; ice skating; skateboarding; snow or water skiing; snowboarding; snowshoeing; surfing; bouldering, traversing, or climbing; mountain biking; adventure activities; and ropes courses.	Demonstrates correct technique for basic skills in 1 self-selected outdoor activity. (S1.M22.6)	Demonstrates correct technique for a variety of skills in 1 self-selected outdoor activity. (S1.M22.7)	Demonstrates correct technique for basic skills in at least 2 self-selected outdoor activities. (S1.M22.8)
Aquatics			
S1.M23	*Preferably taught at elementary or secondary levels. However, availability of facilities might dictate when swimming and water safety are offered in the curriculum.*		
Individual-performance activities			
S1.M24 Activities might include but are not limited to gymnastics, figure skating, track and field, multisport events, in-line skating, wrestling, self-defense and skateboarding.	Demonstrates correct technique for *basic skills* in 1 self-selected individual-performance activity. (S1.M24.6)	Demonstrates correct technique for a *variety of skills* in 1 self-selected individual-performance activity. (S1.M24.7)	Demonstrates correct technique for basic skills in *at least 2* self-selected individual-performance activities. (S1.M24.8)

Standard 2. Applies knowledge of concepts, principles, strategies and tactics related to movement and performance.

STANDARD 2	GRADE 6	GRADE 7	GRADE 8
Games & sports*: Invasion games			
S2.M1 Creating space with movement	Creates open space by using locomotor movements (e.g., walking, running, jumping & landing) in combination with movement (e.g., varying pathways; change of speed, direction or pace). (S2.M1.6)	Reduces open space by using locomotor movements (e.g., walking, running, jumping & landing, changing size and shape of the body) in combination with movement concepts (e.g., reducing the angle in the space, reducing distance between player and goal). (S2.M1.7)	Opens and closes space during small-sided game play by combining locomotor movements with movement concepts. (S2.M1.8)
S2.M2 Creating space with offensive tactics	Executes at least 1 of the following offensive tactics to create open space: moves to open space without the ball; uses a variety of passes, pivots and fakes; give & go. (S2.M2.6)	Executes at least 2 of the following offensive tactics to create open space: uses a variety of passes, pivots and fakes; give & go. (S2.M2.7)	Executes at least 3 of the following offensive tactics to create open space: moves to create open space on and off the ball; uses a variety of passes, fakes and pathways; give & go. (S2.M2.8)
S2.M3 Creating space using width & length	Creates open space by using the width and length of the field/court on offense. (S2.M3.6)	Creates open space by staying spread on offense, and cutting and passing quickly. (S2.M3.7)	Creates open space by staying spread on offense, cutting and passing quickly, and using fakes off the ball. (S2.M3.8)
S2.M4 Reducing space by changing size & shape	Reduces open space on defense by making the body larger and reducing passing angles. (S2.M4.6)	Reduces open space on defense by staying close to the opponent as he/she nears the goal. (S2.M4.7)	Reduces open space on defense by staying on the goal side of the offensive player and reducing the distance to him/her (third-party perspective). (S2.M4.8)
S2.M5 Reducing space using denial	Reduces open space by not allowing the catch (denial) or by allowing the catch but not the return pass. (S2.M5.6)	Reduces open space by not allowing the catch (denial) or anticipating the speed of the object or person for the purpose of interception or deflection. (S2.M5.7)	Reduces open space by not allowing the catch (denial) and anticipating the speed of the object and person for the purpose of interception or deflection. (S2.M5.8)
S2.M6 Transitions	Transitions from offense to defense or defense to offense by recovering quickly. (S2.M6.6)	Transitions from offense to defense or defense to offense by recovering quickly and communicating with teammates. (S2.M6.7)	Transitions from offense to defense or defense to offense by recovering quickly, communicating with teammates and capitalizing on an advantage. (S2.M6.8)
Games & sports: Net/wall games			
S2.M7 Creating space through variation	Creates open space in net/wall games with a short-handled implement by varying force and direction. (S2.M7.6)	Creates open space in net/wall games with a long-handled implement by varying force and direction, and moving opponent from side to side. (S2.M7.7)	Creates open space in net/wall games with either a long- or short-handled implement by varying force or direction or by moving opponent side to side and/or forward and back. (S2.M7.8)
S2.M8 Using tactics & shots	Reduces offensive options for opponents by returning to home position. (S2.M8.6)	Selects offensive shot based on opponent's location (hit where opponent is not). (S2.M8.7)	Varies placement, force and timing of return to prevent anticipation by opponent. (S2.M8.8)
Games & sports: Target games			
S2.M9 Shot selection	Selects appropriate shot and/or club based on location of the object in relation to the target. (S2.M9.6)	Varies the speed and/or trajectory of the shot based on location of the object in relation to the target. (S2.M9.7)	Varies the speed, force and trajectory of the shot based on location of the object in relation to the target. (S2.M9.8)

Middle School Outcomes (Grades 6-8) *(continued)*

STANDARD 2	GRADE 6	GRADE 7	GRADE 8
Games & sports: Fielding/striking games			
S2.M10 Offensive strategies	Identifies open spaces and attempts to strike object into that space. (S2.M10.6)	Uses a variety of shots (e.g., line drive, high arc) to hit to open space. (S2.M10.7)	Identifies sacrifice situations and attempt to advance a teammate. (S2.M10.8)
S2.M11 Reducing space	Identifies the correct defensive play based on the situation (e.g., number of outs). (S2.M11.6)	Selects the correct defensive play based on the situation (e.g., number of outs). (S2.M11.7)	Reduces open spaces in the field by working with teammates to maximize coverage. (S2.M11.8)
Individual-performance activities, dance & rhythms			
S2.M12 Movement concepts	Varies application of force during dance or gymnastic activities. (S2.M12.6)	Identifies and applies Newton's laws of motion to various dance or movement activities. (S2.M12.7)	Describes and applies mechanical advantage(s) for a variety of movement patterns. (S2.M12.8)
Outdoor pursuits			
S2.M13 Movement concepts	Makes appropriate decisions based on the weather, level of difficulty due to conditions or ability to ensure safety of self and others. (S2.M13.6)	Analyzes the situation and makes adjustments to ensure the safety of self and others. (S2.M13.7)	Implements safe protocols in self-selected outdoor activities. (S2.M13.8)

Standard 3. Demonstrates the knowledge and skills to achieve and maintain a health-enhancing level of physical activity and fitness.

STANDARD 3	GRADE 6	GRADE 7	GRADE 8
Physical activity knowledge			
S3.M1	Describes how being physically active leads to a healthy body. (S3.M1.6)	Identifies barriers related to maintaining a physically active lifestyle and seeks solutions for eliminating those barriers. (S3.M1.7)	Develops a plan to address 1 of the barriers within one's family, school, or community to maintaining a physically active lifestyle. (S3.M1.8)
Engages in physical activity			
S3.M2	Participates in self-selected physical activity outside of physical education class. (S3.M2.6)	Participates in a physical activity twice a week outside of physical education class. (S3.M2.7)	Participates in physical activity 3 times a week outside of physical education class. (S3.M2.8)
S3.M3	Participates in a variety of aerobic-fitness activities such as cardio–kick, step aerobics and aerobic dance. (S3.M3.6)	Participates in a variety of strength- and endurance-fitness activities such as Pilates, resistance training, bodyweight training and light free-weight training. (S3.M3.7)	Participates in a variety of self-selected aerobic-fitness activities outside of school such as walking, jogging, biking, skating, dancing and swimming. (S3.M3.8)
S3.M4	Participates in a variety of aerobic-fitness activities using technology such as Dance Dance Revolution or Wii Fit. (S3.M4.6)	Participates in a variety of strength- and endurance-fitness activities such as weight or resistance training. (S3.M4.7)	Plans and implements a program of cross-training to include aerobic, strength & endurance and flexibility training. (S3.M4.8)
S3.M5	Participates in a variety of lifetime recreational team sports, outdoor pursuits or dance activities. (S3.M5.6)	Participates in a variety of lifetime dual and individual sports, martial arts or aquatic activities. (S3.M5.7)	Participates in a self-selected lifetime sport, dance, aquatic or outdoor activity outside of the school day. (S3.M5.8)
Fitness knowledge			
S3.M6	Participates in moderate to vigorous aerobic physical activity that includes intermittent or continuous aerobic physical activity of both moderate and vigorous intensity for at least 60 minutes per day. (S3.M6.6)	Participates in moderate to vigorous muscle- and bone-strengthening physical activity at least 3 times a week. (S3.M6.7)	Participates in moderate to vigorous aerobic and/or muscle- and bone-strengthening physical activity for at least 60 minutes per day at least 5 times a week. (S3.M6.8)
S3.M7	Identifies the components of skill-related fitness. (S3.M7.6)	Distinguishes between health-related and skill-related fitness.[i] (S3.M7.7)	Compares and contrasts health-related fitness components.[ii] (S3.M7.8)
S3.M8	Sets and monitors a self-selected physical-activity goal for aerobic and/or muscle- and bone-strengthening activity based on current fitness level. (S3.M8.6)	Adjusts physical activity based on quantity of exercise needed for a minimal health standard and/or optimal functioning based on current fitness level. (S3.M8.7)	Uses available technology to self-monitor quantity of exercise needed for a minimal health standard and/or optimal functioning based on current fitness level. (S3.M8.8)
S3.M9	Employs correct techniques and methods of stretching.[iii] (S3.M9.6)	Describes and demonstrates the difference between dynamic and static stretches.[iv] (S3.M9.7)	Employs a variety of appropriate static-stretching techniques for all major muscle groups. (S3.M9.8)
S3.M10	Differentiates between aerobic and anaerobic capacity and between muscular strength and endurance. (S3.M10.6)	Describes the role of exercise and nutrition in weight management. (S3.M10.7)	Describes the role of flexibility in injury prevention. (S3.M10.8)
S3.M11	Identifies each of the components of the overload principle (FITT formula: frequency, intensity, time & type) for different types of physical activity (aerobic, muscular fitness, and flexibility). (S3.M11.6)	Describes the overload principle (FITT formula)) for different types of physical activity, the training principles on which the formula is based and how the formula and principles affect fitness.[v] (S3.M11.7)	Uses the overload principle (FITT formula) in preparing a personal workout.[vi] (S3.M11.8)

STANDARD 3	GRADE 6	GRADE 7	GRADE 8
Fitness knowledge *(continued)*			
S3.M12	Describes the role of warm-ups and cool-downs before and after physical activity. (S3.M12.6)	Designs a warm-up/ cool-down regimen for a self-selected physical activity. (S3.M12.7)	Designs and implements a warm-up/ cool-down regimen for a self-selected physical activity. (S3.M12.8)
S3.M13	Defines resting heart rate and describes its relationship to aerobic fitness and the Borg Rating of Perceived Exertion (RPE) Scale.[vii] (S3.M13.6)	Defines how the RPE Scale can be used to determine the perception of the work effort or intensity of exercise. (S3.M13.7)	Defines how the RPE Scale can be used to adjust workout intensity during physical activity. (S3.M13.8)
S3.M14	Identifies major muscles used in selected physical activities.[viii] (S3.M14.6)	Describes how muscles pull on bones to create movement in pairs by relaxing and contracting.[ix] (S3.M14.7)	Explains how body systems interact with one another (e.g., blood transports nutrients from the digestive system, oxygen from the respiratory system) during physical activity.[x] (S3.M14.8)
Assessment & program planning			
S3.M15	Designs and implements a program of remediation for any areas of weakness based on the results of health-related fitness assessment. (S3.M15.6)	Designs and implements a program of remediation for 2 areas of weakness based on the results of health-related fitness assessment. (S3.M15.7)	Designs and implements a program of remediation for 3 areas of weakness based on the results of health-related fitness assessment. (S3.M15.8)
S3.M16	Maintains a physical activity log for at least 2 weeks and reflects on activity levels as documented in the log. (S3.M16.6)	Maintains a physical activity and nutrition log for at least 2 weeks and reflects on activity levels and nutrition as documented in the log. (S3.M16.7)	Designs and implements a program to improve levels of health-related fitness and nutrition. (S3.M16.8)
Nutrition			
S3.M17	Identifies foods within each of the basic food groups and selects appropriate servings and portions for his/ her age and physical activity levels.[xi] (S3.M17.6)	Develops strategies for balancing healthy food, snacks and water intake, along with daily physical activity.[xii] (S3.M17.7)	Describes the relationship between poor nutrition and health risk factors.[xiii] (S3.M17.8)
Stress management			
S3.M18	Identifies positive and negative results of stress and appropriate ways of dealing with each.[xiv] (S3.M18.6)	Practices strategies for dealing with stress, such as deep breathing, guided visualization, and aerobic exercise.[xv] (S3.M18.7)	Demonstrates basic movements used in other stress-reducing activities, such as yoga and tai chi. (S3.M18.8)

Standard 4. Exhibits responsible personal and social behavior that respects self and others.

STANDARD 4	GRADE 6	GRADE 7	GRADE 8
Personal responsibility			
S4.M1	Exhibits personal responsibility by using appropriate etiquette, demonstrating respect for facilities, and exhibiting safe behaviors. (S4.M1.6)	Exhibits responsible social behaviors by cooperating with classmates, demonstrating inclusive behaviors, and supporting classmates. (S4.M1.7)	Accepts responsibility for improving one's own levels of physical activity and fitness. (S4.M1.8)
S4.M2	Identifies and uses appropriate strategies to self-reinforce positive fitness behaviors, such as positive self-talk. (S4.M2.6)	Demonstrates both intrinsic and extrinsic motivation by selecting opportunities to participate in physical activity outside of class. (S4.M2.7)	Uses effective self-monitoring skills to incorporate opportunities for physical activity in and outside of school. (S4.M2.8)
Accepting feedback			
S4.M3	Demonstrates self-responsibility by implementing specific corrective feedback to improve performance. (S4.M3.6)	Provides corrective feedback to a peer using teacher-generated guidelines and incorporating appropriate tone and other communication skills. (S4.M3.7)	Provides encouragement and feedback to peers without prompting from the teacher. (S4.M3.8)
Working with others			
S4.M4	Accepts differences among classmates in physical development, maturation, and varying skill levels by providing encouragement and positive feedback. (S4.M4.6)	Demonstrates cooperation skills by establishing rules and guidelines for resolving conflicts. (S4.M4.7)	Responds appropriately to participants' ethical and unethical behavior during physical activity by using rules and guidelines for resolving conflicts. (S4.M4.8)
S4.M5	Cooperates with a small group of classmates during adventure activities, game play, or team-building activities. (S4.M5.6)	Problem solves with a small group of classmates during adventure activities, small-group initiatives, or game play. (S4.M5.7)	Cooperates with multiple classmates on problem-solving initiatives, including adventure activities, large-group initiatives, and game play. (S4.M5.8)
Rules & etiquette			
S4.M6	Identifies the rules and etiquette for physical activities, games and dance activities. (S4.M6.6)	Demonstrates knowledge of rules and etiquette by self-officiating modified physical activities and games or following parameters to create or modify a dance. (S4.M6.7)	Applies rules and etiquette by acting as an official for modified physical activities and games and creating dance routines within a given set of parameters. (S4.M6.8)
Safety			
S4.M7	Uses physical activity and fitness equipment appropriately and safely, with the teacher's guidance. (S4.M7.6)	Independently uses physical activity and exercise equipment appropriately and safely. (S4.M7.7)	Independently uses physical activity and fitness equipment appropriately, and identifies specific safety concerns associated with the activity. (S4.M7.8)

Standard 5. Recognizes the value of physical activity for health, enjoyment, challenge, self-expression and/or social interaction.

STANDARD 5	GRADE 6	GRADE 7	GRADE 8
Health			
S5.M1	Describes how being physically active leads to a healthy body. (S5.M1.6)	Identifies different types of physical activities and describes how each exerts a positive impact on health. (S5.M1.7)	Identifies the 5 components of health-related fitness (muscular strength, muscular endurance, flexibility, cardiorespiratory endurance and body composition) and explains the connections between fitness and overall physical and mental health. (S5.M1.8)
S5.M2	Identifies components of physical activity that provide opportunities for reducing stress and for social interaction. (S5.M2.6)	Identifies positive mental and emotional aspects of participating in a variety of physical activities. (S5.M2.7)	Analyzes the empowering consequences of being physical active. (S5.M2.8)
Challenge			
S5.M3	Recognizes individual challenges and copes in a positive way, such as extending effort, asking for help or feedback, or modifying the tasks. (S5.M3.6)	Generates positive strategies such as offering suggestions or assistance, leading or following others and providing possible solutions when faced with a group challenge. (S5.M3.7)	Develops a plan of action and makes appropriate decisions based on that plan when faced with an individual challenge. (S5.M3.8)
Self-expression & enjoyment			
S5.M4	Describes how moving competently in a physical activity setting creates enjoyment. (S5.M4.6)	Identifies why self-selected physical activities create enjoyment. (S5.M4.7)	Discusses how enjoyment could be increased in self-selected physical activities. (S5.M4.8)
S5.M5	Identifies how self-expression and physical activity are related. (S5.M5.6)	Explains the relationship between self-expression and lifelong enjoyment through physical activity. (S5.M5.7)	Identifies and participates in an enjoyable activity that prompts individual self-expression. (S5.M5.8)
Social interaction			
S5.M6	Demonstrates respect for self and others in activities and games by following the rules, encouraging others and playing in the spirit of the game or activity. (S5.M6.6)	Demonstrates the importance of social interaction by helping and encouraging others, avoiding trash talk and providing support to classmates. (S5.M6.7)	Demonstrates respect for self by asking for help and helping others in various physical activities. (S5.M6.8)

*The foundation for this section comes from Griffin and Butler, 2005; Griffin, Mitchell, and Oslin, 2006; and Rovegno and Bandauer, 2013.

[i]NASPE, 2012, p. 16.
[ii]Ibid.
[iii]Ibid., p. 7.
[iv]Ibid.
[v]Ibid., p. 17.
[vi]Ibid.
[vii]Ibid., p. 14.
[viii]Ibid., p. 13.
[ix]Ibid.
[x]Ibid.
[xi]Ibid., p. 42.
[xii]Ibid., p. 45.
[xiii]Ibid., p. 40.
[xiv]Ibid., p. 35.
[xv]Ibid.

Reprinted by permission from SHAPE America, *National Standards & Grade-Level Outcomes for K-12 Physical Education* (Champaign, IL: Human Kinetics, 2014), 42.

High School Outcomes (Grades 9-12)

Standard 1. Demonstrates competency in a variety of motor skills and movement patterns.

STANDARD 1	LEVEL 1	LEVEL 2
Lifetime activities		
S1.H1	Demonstrates competency and/or refines activity-specific movement skills in 2 or more lifetime activities (outdoor pursuits, individual-performance activities, aquatics, net/wall games or target games).i (S1.H1.L1)	Refines activity-specific movement skills in 1 or more lifetime activities (outdoor pursuits, individual-performance activities, aquatics, net/wall games or target games).ii (S1.H1.L2)
Dance & rhythms		
S1.H2	Demonstrates competency in dance forms used in cultural and social occasions (e.g., weddings, parties), or demonstrates competency in 1 form of dance (e.g., ballet, modern, hip hop, tap). (S1.H2.L1)	Demonstrates competency in a form of dance by choreographing a dance or by giving a performance. (S1.H2.L2)
Fitness activities		
S1.H3	Demonstrates competency in 1 or more specialized skills in health-related fitness activities. (S1.H3.L1)	Demonstrates competency in 2 or more specialized skills in health-related fitness activities. (S1.H3.L2)

Standard 2. Applies knowledge of concepts, principles, strategies and tactics related to movement and performance.

STANDARD 2	LEVEL 1	LEVEL 2
Movement concepts, principles & knowledge		
S2.H1	Applies the terminology associated with exercise and participation in selected individual-performance activities, dance, net/wall games, target games, aquatics and/or outdoor pursuits appropriately. (S2.H1.L1)	Identifies and discusses the historical and cultural roles of games, sports and dance in a society.[iii] (S2.H1.L2)
S2.H2	Uses movement concepts and principles (e.g., force, motion, rotation) to analyze and improve performance of self and/or others in a selected skill.[iv] (S2.H2.L1)	Describes the speed/accuracy trade-off in throwing and striking skills.[v] (S2.H2.L2)
S2.H3	Creates a practice plan to improve performance for a self-selected skill. (S2.H3.L1)	Identifies the stages of learning a motor skill. (S2.H3.L2)
S2.H4	Identifies examples of social and technical dance forms. (S2.H4.L1)	Compares similarities and differences in various dance forms. (S2.H4.L2)
S2.H5	Uses strategies and tactics effectively during game play in net/wall and/or target games. (S2.H5.L1)	Applies strategies and tactics when analyzing errors in game play in net/wall and/or target games. (S2.H5.L2)

Standard 3. Demonstrates the knowledge and skills to achieve and maintain a health-enhancing level of physical activity and fitness.

STANDARD 3	LEVEL 1	LEVEL 2
Physical activity knowledge		
S3.H1	Discusses the benefits of a physically active lifestyle as it relates to college or career productivity. (S3.H1.L1)	Investigates the relationships among physical activity, nutrition, and body composition. (S3.H1.L2)
S3.H2	Evaluates the validity of claims made by commercial products and programs pertaining to fitness and a healthy, active lifestyle.[vi] (S3.H2.L1)	Analyzes and applies technology and social media as tools for supporting a healthy, active lifestyle.[vii] (S3.H2.L2)
S3.H3	Identifies issues associated with exercising in heat, humidity, and cold.[viii] (S3.H3.L1)	Applies rates of perceived exertion and pacing.[ix] (S3.H3.L2)
S3.H4	Evaluates—according to their benefits, social support network, and participation requirements—activities that can be pursued in the local environment.[x] (S3.H4.L1)	*If the outcome was not achieved in Level 1, it should be a focus in Level 2.*
S3.H5	Evaluates risks and safety factors that might affect physical activity preferences throughout the life cycle.[xi] (S3.H5.L1)	Analyzes the impact of life choices, economics, motivation, and accessibility on exercise adherence and participation in physical activity in college or career settings. (S3.H5.L2)
Engages in physical activity		
S3.H6	Participates several times a week in a self-selected lifetime activity, dance or fitness activity outside of the school day. (S3.H6.L1)	Creates a plan, trains for and participates in a community event with a focus on physical activity (e.g., 5K, triathlon, tournament, dance performance, cycling event).[xii] (S3.H6.L2)
Fitness knowledge		
S3.H7	Demonstrates appropriate technique in resistance-training machines and free weights.[xiii] (S3.H7.L1)	Designs and implements a strength and conditioning program that develops balance in opposing muscle groups (agonist–antagonist) and supports a healthy, active lifestyle.[xiv] (S3.H7.L2)
S3.H8	Relates physiological responses to individual levels of fitness and nutritional balance.[xv] (S3.H8.L1)	Identifies the different energy systems used in a selected physical activity (e.g., adenosine triphosphate and phosphocreatine, anaerobic glycolysis, aerobic).[xvi] (S3.H8.L2)
S3.H9	Identifies types of strength exercises (isometric, concentric, eccentric) and stretching exercises (static, proprioceptive neuromuscular facilitation (PNF), dynamic) for personal fitness development (e.g., strength, endurance, range of motion).[xvii] (S3.H9.L1)	Identifies the structure of skeletal muscle and fiber types as they relate to muscle development.[xviii] (S3.H9.L2)
S3.H10	Calculates target heart rate and applies that information to personal fitness plan. (S3.H10.L1)	Adjusts pacing to keep heart rate in the target zone, using available technology (e.g., heart rate monitor), to self-monitor aerobic intensity. (S3.H10.L2)[xix]

STANDARD 3	LEVEL 1	LEVEL 2
Assessment & program planning		
S3.H11	Creates and implements a behavior-modification plan that enhances a healthy, active lifestyle in college or career settings. (S3.H11.L1)	Develops and maintains a fitness portfolio (e.g., assessment scores, goals for improvement, plan of activities for improvement, log of activities being done to reach goals, timeline for improvement).[xx] (S3.H11.L2)
S3.H12	Designs a fitness program, including all components of health-related fitness, for a college student and an employee in the learner's chosen field of work. (S3.H12.L1)	Analyzes the components of skill-related fitness in relation to life and career goals and designs an appropriate fitness program for those goals.[xxi] (S3.H12.L2)
Nutrition		
S3.H13	Designs and implements a nutrition plan to maintain an appropriate energy balance for a healthy, active lifestyle. (S3.H13.L1)	Creates a snack plan for before, during, and after exercise that addresses nutrition needs for each phase. (S3.H13.L2)
Stress management		
S3.H14	Identifies stress-management strategies (e.g., mental imagery, relaxation techniques, deep breathing, aerobic exercise, meditation) to reduce stress.[xxii] (S3.H14.L1)	Applies stress-management strategies (e.g., mental imagery, relaxation techniques, deep breathing, aerobic exercise, meditation) to reduce stress.[xxiii] (S3.H14.L2)

Standard 4. Exhibits responsible personal and social behavior that respects self and others.

STANDARD 4	LEVEL 1	LEVEL 2
Personal responsibility		
S4.H1	Employs effective self-management skills to analyze barriers and modify physical activity patterns appropriately as needed.[xxiv] (S4.H1.L1)	Accepts differences between personal characteristics and the idealized body images and elite performance levels portrayed in various media.[xxv] (S4.H1.L2)
Rules & etiquette		
S4.H2	Exhibits proper etiquette, respect for others and teamwork while engaging in physical activity and/or social dance. (S4.H2.L1)	Examines moral and ethical conduct in specific competitive situations (e.g., intentional fouls, performance-enhancing substances, gambling, current events in sport).[xxvi] (S4.H2.L2)
Working with others		
S4.H3	Uses communication skills and strategies that promote team or group dynamics.[xxvii] (S4.H3.L1)	Assumes a leadership role (e.g., task or group leader, referee, coach) in a physical activity setting. (S4.H3.L2)
S4.H4	Solves problems and thinks critically in physical activity or dance settings, both as an individual and in groups. (S4.H4.L1)	Accepts others' ideas, cultural diversity, and body types by engaging in cooperative and collaborative movement projects. (S4.H4.L2)
Safety		
S4.H5	Applies best practices for participating safely in physical activity, exercise and dance (e.g., injury prevention, proper alignment, hydration, use of equipment, implementation of rules, sun protection). (S4.H5.L1)	*If the outcome was not achieved in Level 1, it should be a focus in Level 2.*

Standard 5. Recognizes the value of physical activity for health, enjoyment, challenge, self-expression and/ or social interaction.

STANDARD 5	LEVEL 1	LEVEL 2
Health		
S5.H1	Analyzes the health benefits of a self-selected physical activity. (S5.H1.L1)	*If the outcome was not achieved in Level 1, it should be a focus in Level 2.*
Challenge		
S5.H2	*Challenge is a focus in Level 2.*	Chooses an appropriate level of challenge to experience success and desire to participate in a self-selected physical activity.[xxviii] (S5.H2.L2)
Self-expression & enjoyment		
S5.H3	Selects and participates in physical activities or dance that meet the need for self-expression and enjoyment. (S5.H3.L1)	Identifies the uniqueness of creative dance as a means of self-expression. (S5.H3.L2)
Social interaction		
S5.H4	Identifies the opportunity for social support in a self-selected physical activity or dance. (S5.H4.L1)	Evaluates the opportunity for social interaction and social support in a self-selected physical activity or dance.[xxix] (S5.H4.L2)

[i]Manitoba Education and Training, School Programs Division, 2000, www.edu.gov.mb.ca/k12/cur/physhlth/index.html
[ii]Ibid.
[iii]NASPE, 1992, p. 15.
[iv]Ibid.
[v]Mohnsen, 2010.
[vi]NASPE, 1992, p. 16.
[vii]NASPE, 2012, p. 20.
[viii]Ibid., p. 9.
[ix]Ibid., p. 5.
[x]NASPE, 1992, p. 15.
[xi]Ibid.
[xii]NASPE, 2012, p. 27.
[xiii]Ibid., p. 6.
[xiv]Manitoba Education and Training, School Programs Division, 2000, www.edu.gov.mb.ca/k12/cur/physhlth/index.html
[xv]NASPE, 2012, p. 15.
[xvi]Ibid., p. 16.
[xvii]Manitoba Education and Training, School Programs Division, 2000, www.edu.gov.mb.ca/k12/cur/physhlth/index.html
[xviii]Ibid.
[xix]NASPE, 2012, p. 23.
[xx]Ohio State Board of Education, 2009, p. 113.
[xxi]Superintendent of Public Instruction, Washington, 2008, p. 101.
[xxii]Manitoba Education and Training, School Programs Division, 2000, www.edu.gov.mb.ca/k12/cur/physhlth/index.html
[xxiii]Ibid.
[xxiv]NASPE, 2012, p. 25.
[xxv]NASPE, 1992, p. 16.
[xxvi]Manitoba Education and Training, School Programs Division, 2000, www.edu.gov.mb.ca/k12/cur/physhlth/index.html
[xxvii]Ibid.
[xxviii]Ohio State Board of Education, 2009, p. 115.
[xxix]Ibid.

Appendix B: Rubric With Weighted Values by Level

✍ *Sample of a Weighted Rubric With Constant Range of Point Values for Each Level*

Below is a sample of a rubric where a range of point values (weights) are assigned for each of the three levels. In this sample the range of point values are constant for each indicator on the rubric (developing = 0 to 3 points; competent = 4 to 7 points; proficient = 8 to 10 points). This makes the maximum value of the assignment 40 points. Assigning point values using a range allows you to differentiate the scoring within each level. Using this method, you can convert the final score into a percentage. If a student scores a total of 32 points out of a possible 40 points, the student's percentage is 80%. You can increase or decrease the point values for the levels depending on the value you place on the assignment.

Scoring Rubric for Flipped Classroom, Level 1

INDICATOR	DEVELOPING (WEIGHT = 0 TO 3 PTS)	COMPETENT (WEIGHT = 4 TO 7 PTS)	PROFICIENT (WEIGHT = 8 TO 10 PTS)
Demonstrates Ability to Apply Concepts and/or Principles in the Development of an Instructional Video	One or more critical components not present: • 2 or fewer resources cited • Cited resources inappropriate or marginal • Performance errors in demonstrated critical elements • Incorrect terminology used or mispronounced • Demonstration only of whole skill/technique or only of parts of skill/technique • No citing for each resource	Demonstrates all critical components: • At least 3 different credible resources cited • Cited resources appropriate • Critical elements specific to movement skill or sequence identified • Critical elements demonstrated correctly • Correct terminology used • Diagram or drawings illustrative of skill or sequence • Whole and part demonstrations included • Citing included on presentation slides	Demonstrates all critical components: • 4 or more credible resources cited • Most important critical elements cited • Demonstrations correct and filmed from more than one angle • Correct terminology with no jargon • Diagrams and drawings aligned directly with critical elements • Multiple whole and part demonstrations
Demonstrates Competency in Written Communication Through the Production of a Storyboard	One or more critical components not present: • Outline lacks specificity • Narration incomplete • No script submitted • No clear sequence of instruction identified or documented	Demonstrates all critical components: • Plans video structure with notes and cues • Information on transitions, special effects (e.g., zooming in/out), titles, placement of graphics, notes on major talking points • Narration for every scene • Script well-written with critical components • Progressive sequence of instruction	Demonstrates all critical components: • Specific and detailed plan with notes and cues • Specific detail on transitions, special effects (e.g., zooming in/out), titles, placement of graphics, notes on major talking points • Narration for every scene including details on inflection and tone • Script well-written with critical components • Instruction progressive and sequential

From SHAPE America, *PE Metrics*, 3rd ed. (Champaign, IL: Human Kinetics, 2019).

INDICATOR	DEVELOPING (WEIGHT = 0 TO 3 PTS)	COMPETENT (WEIGHT = 4 TO 7 PTS)	PROFICIENT (WEIGHT = 8 TO 10 PTS)
Demonstrates Competency in the Effective Use of Technology (Creativity, Design, Quality)	One or more critical components not present: • Video poorly edited with gaps and hesitations • Part of video out of focus or frame • Sound uneven (too loud or too soft) • Only one camera angle used • No transitions • Titles not present or do not enhance instruction • Lacks creativity with no changes in graphics, camera angles, and/or titles	Demonstrates all critical components: • Video well-edited with no hesitations or gaps • Camera stable and frames in focus • Sound clear and understandable • Multiple angles and perspectives • Titles enhance instruction • Transitions well-timed and smooth • Creativity enhances video (unique use of graphics, camera angles, illustrations, etc.)	Demonstrates all critical components: • Video well-edited with creative use of music, graphics, etc. • Camera stable, frames in focus, and multiple angles and perspectives • Titles along with symbols enhance instruction • Transitions well-timed and smooth with creative use of music, graphics, etc.
Demonstrates Competency in Oral Communication	One or more critical components not present: • Slides random making it difficult to determine accuracy of content • Slides crowded with text presenting multiple points • 3 or more fonts used • No hyperlink • Audio unclear with multiple stops • Audio simply repeats content of slides	Demonstrates all critical components: • Slides sequential and well-organized • Each slide presents a single point • Text legible with contrast between text and background • No more than 2 fonts in presentation • Pictures, illustrations, and/or diagrams add clarity • Uses at least one still shot from video • One hyperlink • Audio clear and synchronized • Audio supplements information on slides	Demonstrates all critical components: • Slides sequential, well-organized with multiple pictures, diagrams, and/or illustrations • Each slide presents a single point with pictures, illustrations or diagrams • Text legible with contrast between text and background • No more than 2 fonts used • At least 2 hyperlinks • Audio clear and synchronized • Audio supplements information on slides and adds clarity

From SHAPE America, *PE Metrics*, 3rd ed. (Champaign, IL: Human Kinetics, 2019).

Appendix C: Rubric With Weighted Values by Indicator

✍ *Sample of a Weighted Rubric With Range of Point Values Changing for Each Indicator*

Below is a sample of a rubric where a range of point values (weights) are assigned for each of the indicators. In this sample the range of point values varies for each indicator on the rubric. This allows you to designate specific indicators as more valued on the assignment. This method is often used with complex assessments where the amount of "work" required for each indicator may vary. For example, maintaining a participation log for a fitness portfolio would have a lesser value than analyzing and reflecting on final results. This allows you to weight the various components within an assignment by using a rubric. The maximum value of the assignment presented below is 24 points. Assigning point values using a range allows you to differentiate the scoring within each level for each individual indicator. Using this method, you can convert the final score into a percentage. If a student scores a total of 18 points out of a possible 24 points, the student's percentage is 75%. You can increase or decrease the point values for each indicator depending on the value you place on the assignment.

Scoring Rubric for Developing a Fitness Plan, Level 1

INDICATOR	DEVELOPING	COMPETENT	PROFICIENT
WEIGHT FOR EACH INDICATOR	**WEIGHT = 0 TO 3 POINTS**	**WEIGHT = 4 TO 7 POINTS**	**WEIGHT = 8 TO 10 POINTS**
Activities align with and are realistic for identified fitness component and self-selected goals.	• Misalignment of activities with specific fitness components • Activities misaligned with goals • Activities either too hard or too easy based on pre-assessment data	• Activities align with identified fitness component • Activities aligned with self-selected goals • Activities selected realistic based on pre-assessment data	• Activities align with identified fitness component • Activities aligned with self-selected goals • Activity levels progressive and lead to improved performance
WEIGHT	**DEVELOPING** **WEIGHT = 1 TO 2 POINTS**	**COMPETENT** **WEIGHT = 3 TO 4 POINTS**	**PROFICIENT** **WEIGHT = 5 TO 6 POINTS**
Intensity levels align and are realistic for activity choice.	• Intensity levels misaligned with activity choice • Intensity levels either too high or too low for activity • Intensity levels either too high or too low based on pre-assessment data	• Intensity levels align with activity choice • Intensity levels realistic and based on pre-assessment data	• Intensity levels align with activity choice • Intensity levels realistic and based on pre-assessment data • Intensity levels challenging • Intensity levels lead to improved performance
WEIGHT	**DEVELOPING** **WEIGHT = 0 TO 2 POINTS**	**COMPETENT** **WEIGHT = 3 TO 5 POINTS**	**PROFICIENT** **WEIGHT = 6 TO 8 POINTS**
Warm-up and cool-downs appropriate for activity.	• Warm-up or cool-downs insufficient for the activity and intensity level • Warm-up or cool-downs unrelated to activity choice	• Warm-up/cool-downs align with activity • Warm-up/cool-downs realistic based on activity and intensity level	• Warm-up/cool-downs align with activity • Warm-up/cool-downs realistic based on activity and intensity level • Warm-up/cool-downs address specific muscle groups essential to the activity

Appendix D: Analytic Rubric With More Than One Standard (Embedded Assessment)

Analytic Rubric for Galloping (Standard 1) and Pathways (Standard 2)

INDICATOR	DEVELOPING	COMPETENT	PROFICIENT
Critical Elements Galloping (S1.E1.1)	Demonstrates fewer than 5 of the critical elements for galloping	Demonstrates all critical elements for galloping • Trunk faces in forward direction • Lead leg lifts and moves forward • Rear foot closes quickly • Lead leg lifts • Arms in front, slightly bent	Demonstrates all critical elements for galloping using both the preferred and nonpreferred foot as lead
Rhythm for Galloping	Movement has erratic rhythm	Movement has steady rhythm	Movement has steady rhythm
Continuity for Galloping	Cannot maintain mature pattern in a continuous sequence (at least 5 times in a row)	Maintains mature pattern in a continuous sequence (at least 5 times in a row) with preferred lead foot	Maintains mature pattern in a continuous sequence (at least 10 times in a row) with both the preferred and nonpreferred foot as lead
Identifying Pathways (S2.E2.1a)	Unable to identify pathways in illustrations or when demonstrated by another student/teacher or performance	Identifies pathways correctly in 2 of the 3 venues—diagram, observation of others, performance	Demonstrates a functional understanding of pathways: diagram, observation, performance

From SHAPE America, *PE Metrics*, 3rd ed. (Champaign, IL: Human Kinetics, 2019).

Appendix E: Suite of Assessments for Fitness Portfolio

✍ *Sample Description of Assignment With Assessments for*
Multiple-Part Project or Portfolio

Fitness Portfolio

A fitness portfolio is a multiple-part assignment that is completed in phases. Each phase of the assignment has specific required elements that are assessed as the element is completed. Below is a sample description of the assignment for a fitness portfolio with identified elements to be assessed using various types of assessments.

Phase 1 of Fitness Portfolio

Element 1:

Task 1: Pre-assessment: Record your FitnessGram results on form provided on the PE website entitled Worksheet on FitnessGram Results.

Task 2: Complete the short Activity Survey on the website and determine your current activity level. Place both worksheets in your Fitness Portfolio.

Assessments for Phase 1: Check *sheet* noting that both pre-assessments have been completed and submitted electronically.

Phase 2 of Fitness Portfolio

Element 2:

Task 3: Based on both of your pre-assessments, set SMART goals for yourself for the fitness unit. Your SMART goals should reference your pre-assessment data and meet all SMART goal criteria.

Task 4: Submit signed Personal Contract and place it into your electronic portfolio.

Assessment for Phase 2: Check *sheet* for signed Personal Contract and *rubric* for SMART goals.

INDICATOR	DEVELOPING	COMPETENCY	PROFICIENCY
Goals meet the SMART criteria	• One or two of the SMART criteria are missing for each goal • Some goals are missing one or more of the SMART criteria • Lack specificity within SMART criteria	• All SMART criteria included for each goal • Each SMART criteria addressed with specificity	• All SMART criteria included for each goal • Each SMART criteria addressed with specificity • SMART goals align with important fitness or behavior changes
Goals are based on pre-assessment data	• General statements of change unrelated to pre-assessment data • Inconsistent alignment with pre-assessment data (some goals align and others do not align)	Consistent and direct alignment with pre-assessment data	• Consistent and direct alignment with pre-assessment data • Based on pre-assessment data, the most important fitness or behavior changes addressed

From SHAPE America, *PE Metrics*, 3rd ed. (Champaign, IL: Human Kinetics, 2019).

Students cannot move into the next phase until SMART goals are assessed and approved.

Phase 3 of Fitness Portfolio

Element 3:

Task 5: Develop a fitness plan following the guidelines and in the format provided. Plan should align with your SMART goals, identify intensity levels, and align with your activity choices. Remember to include the following: 1) at least 60 minutes of activity at the planned level of exertion; 2) warm-up and cool-down activities; 3) planned rest days; 4) 20 minutes at least 3 times a week in the target heart rate zone; and 5) each day must identify the FITT factors (frequency, intensity, type and time).

Assessment for Phase 3: *Analytic rubric* is used to evaluate your submitted plan. You cannot begin Phase 4 until your plan is approved.

INDICATOR	DEVELOPING	COMPETENCY	PROFICIENCY
Activities align with and are realistic for identified fitness component and self-selected goals	• Misalignment of activities with specific fitness components • Activities misaligned with goals • Activities are either too hard or too easy based on pre-assessment data	• Activities align with identified fitness component • Activities align with self-selected goals • Activities selected are realistic based on pre-assessment data	• Activities align with identified fitness component • Activities align with self-selected goals • Activity levels are progressive and should lead to improved performance
Intensity levels align and are realistic with activity choice	• Intensity levels misaligned with activity choice • Intensity levels are either too high or too low for activity • Intensity levels are either too high or too low based on pre-assessment data	• Intensity levels align with activity choice • Intensity levels are realistic based on pre-assessment data	• Intensity levels align with activity choice • Intensity levels are realistic based on pre-assessment data • Intensity levels are challenging and should lead to improved performance
Warm-up and cool-downs appropriate for activity	• Warm-up or cool-downs are insufficient for the activity and intensity level • Warm-up or cool-downs unrelated to activity choice	• Warm-up/cool-downs align with activity • Warm-up/cool-downs are realistic based on activity and intensity level	• Warm-up/cool-downs align with activity • Warm-up/cool-downs are realistic based on activity and intensity level • Warm-up/cool-downs address specific muscle groups that are essential to the activity
Plan includes daily activity with at least three days specific to cardiovascular fitness	• Activity minutes less than 60 minutes per day • Less than 3 days devoted to cardiovascular fitness (less than 20 minutes in target heart rate zone) • Rest days are identified with no activity	• Each day has at least 60 minutes of activity • At least 3 days include 20 minutes in target heart rate zone • Days of greater intensity mixed with lighter intensity • Rest days identified with at least 30 minutes of lower intensity activities	• Each day has at least 60 minutes of activity • At least 3 days include 20 minutes in target heart rate zone • Days of greater intensity mixed with lighter intensity • Rest days identified with 60 minutes of light activity • Plan is sequential and progressive

From SHAPE America, *PE Metrics*, 3rd ed. (Champaign, IL: Human Kinetics, 2019).

Phase 4 of Fitness Portfolio

Element 4: Implement Plan

Task 6: Track your progress by submitting your weekly participation log in the format provided on the website.

Task 7: At the end of the participation log is a space for you to complete a reflection on your progress each week. Each week there will be a different set of prompts to help guide your reflection. A completed reflection is required along with the weekly participation log.

Assessment for Phase 4: A *rating scale* will be used to assess your participation log and your reflections. You will be assessed on a 1-3 scale. The definitions for each level are provided below for both your participation log and reflections.

Quality of Participation Log Items

1 = Log is incomplete with missing data and few or no details provided. Selected activities do not align with fitness goals.

2 = Log is complete, but limited detail is provided. No supporting documentation to support perceived exertion score (step count, heart rate monitor, Fitbit, weight and number of repetitions, etc.).

3 = Log is complete with specific detail and supporting documentation on perceived exertion (step count, heart rate monitor, Fitbit, weight and number of repetitions, etc.).

Quality of Reflection

1 = Reflection only describes the activity without a personal response to the experience. Does not make connection of participation and personal health and wellness.

2 = Reflection describes the activity and includes some general comments on personal response to the experience. Indirect connections made to personal health and wellness.

3 = Reflection describes the activity, includes detailed and insightful statements on personal response to the experience. Direct connections made to personal health and wellness.

Phase 5 of Fitness Portfolio

Element 5: Final Reflection

Task 8: At the end of the unit, you will compare your pre and post scores on FitnessGram using the FitnessGram worksheet provided at the beginning of the unit.

Task 9: Analyze your results based on your FitnessGram scores and determine which of your goals you met or failed to meet by the end of the fitness unit. Describe your successes and challenges during the unit and support each with specific examples. Finally, reflect on what you learned about yourself during the unit and how you might use this information in the future.

Assessment for Phase 5: *Analytic rubric* will be used for the final reflection. The final reflection is limited to two or three pages double spaced.

From SHAPE America, *PE Metrics*, 3rd ed. (Champaign, IL: Human Kinetics, 2019).

INDICATOR	DEVELOPING	COMPETENCY	PROFICIENCY
FitnessGram data are analyzed correctly	• Data are incomplete • Conclusions reached are not supported by data • No specific examples supporting conclusions provided • Only vague or incomplete analysis provided	• Both pre and post data provided and complete • Data support conclusions • At least one specific example is provided for each conclusion	• Both pre and post data provided and complete • Data support conclusions • At least two or more specific examples are provided for each conclusion
Goals analysis is based on data and supported	• Only some goals are addressed • Vague excuses for lack of achievement of goals • Only successes or only challenges are addressed	• All goals are addressed • Data used to support insights based on goal achievement • Both successes and challenges are addressed with at least one specific example	• All goals are addressed • Data used to support insights based on goal achievement • Both successes and challenges are addressed with at least two or more examples • Insights are specific and demonstrate self-awareness
Next steps align with analysis and appropriate	• No next steps are identified • Next steps do not align with data or analysis • No insight on personal growth provided	• Next steps are identified • Identified next steps are aligned with data and analysis • At least one personal growth insight provided with a specific example	• Next steps are identified • Identified next steps are aligned with data and analysis • Two or more personal growth insights provided with at least one specific example • Next steps are concrete and aligned with personal goals

From SHAPE America, *PE Metrics*, 3rd ed. (Champaign, IL: Human Kinetics, 2019).

Appendix F: Sample Score Sheets

✍ *Sample Score Sheet for Locomotor Skills at Elementary Level*

Based on the rubric for each of the locomotor skills, record the levels attained by each student on the score sheet below. Level 1 = Developing; Level 2 = Competent; Level 3 = Proficient. Record "NO" for no opportunity to observe.

NAME OF STUDENT	HOPPING	SLIDING	GALLOPING	SKIPPING	NOTES
Jeremy Linn	2	3	3	NO	Absent for skipping
Steph Curry	3	3	2	1	
Candace Parker	3	3	1	2	
Diana Taurasi	2	3	3	2	

✍ *Sample Score Sheet for Analytic Rubric for Backhand Stroke in Badminton, Middle or High School*

Based on the rubric for the backhand clear in badminton, record the levels attained by each student on the various components of the backhand stroke. The components are identified in the columns of the score sheet below. Score each student using this scale: Level 1 = Developing; Level 2 = Competent; Level 3 = Proficient. Record "NO" for no opportunity to observe.

NAME OF STUDENT	GRIP	BACK-SWING	FORWARD SWING	FINISH	POWER AND ACCURACY	COMMENTS
Sloane Stephens	3	3	2	2	3	
Madison Keys	3	2	3	3	2	
Taylor Fritz	3	2	2	3	2	
Frances Tiafoe	NO	NO	NO	NO	NO	Absent

From SHAPE America, *PE Metrics*, 3rd ed. (Champaign, IL: Human Kinetics, 2019).

Appendix G: Pre-Assessment With Wordle

✍ *Sample Wordle Worksheet*

You can use wordles (word clouds) as a form of pre-assessment, giving you a quick read on students' attitudes toward and knowledge of fitness portfolios. You can repeat this activity at the end of the lesson or unit to determine whether students have changed their attitudes and/or gained knowledge.

Instructions to Students

Using a tablet, or other electronic device, write a one-paragraph (three to five sentences) message stating what you believe should be included in a fitness portfolio. Once you have completed your paragraph, email the paragraph to _____. Be sure to include your first name.

At the end of the session, we will share the results of what the group believes about fitness portfolios.

Example of a Completed Wordle

From SHAPE America, *PE Metrics*, 3rd ed. (Champaign, IL: Human Kinetics, 2019).

Appendix H: Exit Slip Examples

✍ *Collaboration Exit Slip*

Exit Slip: During class today, you worked with classmates on a series of group problem-solving activities. Based on this experience, please provide insight on what you learned about collaboration and working within a group by reflecting on the prompts provided below.

1. What was the most challenging aspect for you in working with your group on the problem-solving activities? Provide at least one example.

2. What behaviors by group members contributed to the group's success in the various activities? Support your statement with an example.

3. What behaviors by group members inhibited the group's success in the various activities? Support your statement with examples.

4. If you could change one thing about your experience, what would it be and why?

Name: _____   Date: _____

✍ *Exit Slip: Overhand Throw*

Exit Slip: During class today, you worked with a classmate on the overhand throw. Below, list three critical elements for the overhand throw.

1.
2.
3.

Name: _____   Date: _____

From SHAPE America, *PE Metrics*, 3rd ed. (Champaign, IL: Human Kinetics, 2019).

Appendix I: Identifying Locomotors in Physical Activities

✍ **Worksheet on Identifying Locomotors in Physical Activities (S2.E2.3)**

Name: _____   Homeroom: _____

Locomotors	**Movement Concepts**
walk	general and self-space
hop	levels: high, medium, low
gallop	pathways: straight, curved, zigzag
slide	force: strong, light
run	directions: 6 + 2
skip	time: fast, slow
leap	shapes: wide, narrow, curled, twisted

NAME OF PHYSICAL ACTIVITY	LOCOMOTORS	MOVEMENT CONCEPTS

For the activities listed above, identify all the locomotors used in the activity. Then list any movement concepts you studied with that locomotor.

Appendix J: Embedded Analytic Rubric With Passing and Receiving and Game Strategy

Analytic Sample Combination Rubric: Games Strategy

INDICATOR	DEVELOPING	COMPETENT	PROFICIENT
Critical Elements Passing and Receiving (S1.E19.5a)	Does not demonstrate all the critical elements of passing and receiving • Stops to pass and/or stops to receive pass • Fails to execute a lead pass to receiver	Demonstrates all the critical elements of passing and receiving • Tap/dribble with inside and outside of feet • Maintains 2- to 3-foot distance of ball and body • Checks momentum before passing • Passes ahead of partner • Gives to receive pass • Receives the pass without stopping	Demonstrates all the critical elements of passing and receiving • Successful assessment without and with cones
Force and Accuracy	• Insufficient force to send ball to partner • Inaccurate passes to partner	Matches force of pass to distance of partner	Adjusts pathways, force, directions without cones, with cones, against defense
Success (S2.E3.5c)	Completes less than 4 successful attempts of passing and receiving, moving the ball down the field (with or without cones)	Successfully completes all 4 assessment attempts without cones	Successfully completes passing and receiving with partner against 2 v 2 defense
Movement Concepts (S2.E3.5c)	No application of movement concepts when passing and receiving with feet, partners traveling	Applies movement concepts when passing and receiving with reasonable success in moving the ball the length of the field • pathways • force • direction • speed	• Adjusts pathways, force, directions, and speed against passive and active defense • Successfully completes passing and receiving with partner against 2 v 2 defense, applying a variety of movement concepts

From SHAPE America, *PE Metrics*, 3rd ed. (Champaign, IL: Human Kinetics, 2019).

Appendix K: Peer Assessment for Striking With Force and Direction

✍ *Peer Assessment for Striking With Force and Direction*
Using a Long-Handled Implement (S2.E3.5b)

Batter: _____   Recorder: _____

Strike 3 balls so that they travel beyond the bases (to the outfield). Record a plus or minus for each attempt.

Strike 3 balls so that they land inside the bases (in the infield). Record a plus or minus for each attempt.

DISTANCE/FORCE	#1	#2	#3	DATE
Outfield				
Infield				

Tell the recorder if you are striking to the left or to the right, then strike the ball to that target zone: 3 balls to the right, 3 balls to the left target zone. Record a plus or a minus for each correct response, that is, the ball traveled to the zone that you designated.

DIRECTION	#1	#2	#3	DATE
To the left				
To the right				

From SHAPE America, *PE Metrics*, 3rd ed. (Champaign, IL: Human Kinetics, 2019).

Appendix L: Exit Slip

✍ *Exit Slip Example for S3.E3.K: Healthy Heart*

Name: _____

Couch potato   Jumping rope   Playing video games

Which activity helps the heart grow stronger? Circle your answer.

Appendix M: Self-Assessment of Physical Activity Patterns

✍ *Self-Assessment of Physical Activity Patterns Outside of Physical Education Class*

Directions: Review your physical activity log and observe your physical activity patterns. Focus on the physical activity in which you participated outside of physical education class.

1. Did you participate in physical activity three or more times during the week (not physical education class)? Circle: Yes   No

2. What surprised you after viewing the physical activity log?

3. List the types of physical activity you performed and describe the decisions of choosing them or not.

4. In what ways can you increase the number of times you participate in physical activity outside of physical education class?

Appendix N: Elementary Personal Fitness Plan

✍ *My Personal Fitness Plan (S3.E5.5b)*

Name: _____ Homeroom: _____

For each health-related fitness component below, compare your score with the score needed for the Healthy Fitness Zone. Are you in the "Zone" or below the level needed for the healthy zone? Record your zone score: below, at, or above.

For each fitness component, record a strategy or physical activity of your choice for improving or maintaining your level of fitness: below = strategy for improvement; at or above = strategy for maintenance. Record whether your activity will be at home, neighborhood park, school recess, swimming, gymnastics, dance, sports practice.

FITNESS COMPONENT	HEALTHY ZONE (BELOW, AT OR ABOVE)	STRATEGY FOR IMPROVEMENT OR MAINTENANCE LOCATION
Cardiorespiratory (PACER)		
Abdominal strength (curl-ups)		
Flexibility (sit-and-reach)		
Upper body strength (push-ups, etc.)		

Personal Goal for One Fitness Area

By the end of the school year, I hope to be:

_____ _____
My signature   Parent or teacher signature

From SHAPE America, *PE Metrics*, 3rd ed. (Champaign, IL: Human Kinetics, 2019).

Appendix O: Self-Assessment of Physical Activity Rating Scale

✍ *Self-Assessment of Physical Activity Rating Scale for Elementary School*

Letterhead for Your School (S5.E4.5)

Vision Statement for Physical Education at Your School

Student name: _____   Homeroom: _____

Physical education is about developing the skills to remain active for a lifetime: at middle school, high school and beyond school. It is about being healthy, being physically fit. It also is about having fun, playing with friends and moving, moving, moving.

Some of our physical education activities require you to practice a skill by yourself. At other times, you work with a partner, in a small group and occasionally, in a large group. Think about those times and use this chart to rate your enjoyment and social interaction in each of those settings.

Circle your rating (5 is high):

Physical activities by myself   1 2 3 4 5

Physical activities with a partner   1 2 3 4 5

Physical activities in a small group   1 2 3 4 5

Physical activities in a large group   1 2 3 4 5

My favorite physical activity is:

It is my favorite because

Appendix P: Analysis of Physical Activity at the Elementary Level (S5.E3.5)

✎ *Analysis of Physical Activities (S5.E3.5)*

Name: _____ Homeroom: _____

Column 1 is a listing of the physical education activities for this school year.

Column 2 is your response to the activity: negative or positive. Place a "plus" or a "minus" sign in the column beside the activity.

In Column 3, identify the reasons for your positive or negative response to the activity. You may write your reasons in a sentence or in a one- to three-word description, such as "Fun," "Not fun," "Difficult," "Fun with friends," "Challenge" or "Challenge with mastery".

There are no right or wrong answers; just record your feelings about each activity.

The bottom of the worksheet provides space for you to list "out of school" physical activities in which you participate, such as sports, gymnastics or dance. You may add those to your critique of physical activities.

Include the directions above when you present the assessment task to students. You may choose to include the written instructions above or eliminate them to provide more space for student responses.

PHYSICAL EDUCATION ACTIVITIES	RESPONSE: +, -	REASONS FOR LIKE OR DISLIKE
After-school activities		

From SHAPE America, *PE Metrics*, 3rd ed. (Champaign, IL: Human Kinetics, 2019).

Appendix Q: Frequency Count for Striking – Middle School

Sample Scoring Rubric for Striking a Pitched Ball to Open Space With Power

INDICATOR	ATTEMPT 1	ATTEMPT 2	ATTEMPT 3	ATTEMPT 4	ATTEMPT 5
Strikes a pitched ball • Proper weight transfer during swing • Contacts ball with sweet spot (top third of bat)					
Power Hits ball so that it travels quickly past the pitcher					
Open Space Hits ball so that it travels to open space					

Check (√) to indicate whether all critical elements of performance were met.

Comments:

INDICATOR	ATTEMPT 6	ATTEMPT 7	ATTEMPT 8	ATTEMPT 9	ATTEMPT 10
Strikes a pitched ball • Proper weight transfer during swing • Contacts ball with sweet spot (top third of bat)					
Power Hits ball so that it travels quickly past the pitcher					
Open Space Hits ball so that it travels to open space					

Check (√) to indicate whether all critical elements of performance were met.

Comments:

From SHAPE America, *PE Metrics*, 3rd ed. (Champaign, IL: Human Kinetics, 2019).

Appendix R: Peer Assessment for Shot Selection and Location – Middle School

✍ *Peer Assessment: Sample of Frequency Count for Shot Selection and Location in Net/Wall Games*

Frequency Count for Shot Selection and Location (drop, high clear, smash, drive, cross court, down the line, middle, short or deep)

Observe your partner during a badminton game against an opponent. Track your partner's shot selection and location on the form below. Mark the shot used and the location of the shot. At the end of an 11-point game, provide feedback to your partner on the effectiveness of his or her shot selection and location. Use the codes below to denote location.

Name of performer: _____ Date: _____

Name of observer: _____

Location Codes:

CC = Cross court   AP = At opponent with power

DL = Down the line   NN = Near net

MC = Middle of court   DC = Deep into court

SHOT SELECTION	COUNT	LOCATION						
Offensive clear								
Defensive clear								
Drop shot								
Drive								
Smash								
Other								

Peer Feedback

Provide two examples of how the performer used shot selection to gain a competitive advantage.

Provide two examples of how the performer used shot location to gain a competitive advantage.

From SHAPE America, *PE Metrics*, 3rd ed. (Champaign, IL: Human Kinetics, 2019).

Appendix S: Physical Activity Log Time Recording – Middle School

Physical Activity Log – Time Recordings

For one week, you are to track your physical activity, the level of effort (light, moderate or vigorous) for that activity and the amount of time you spent on each activity. Base your level of effort on the definitions provided in class, with strolling and talking with friends as light, walking briskly as moderate and running as vigorous. Decide the level of perceived exertion based on your experience. For a continuous seven-day period, complete the chart below.

Name: _____

NAME OF ACTIVITY	PERCEIVED EFFORT	AMOUNT OF TIME BY MINUTES							
		Mon.	Tue.	Wed.	Thur.	Fri.	Sat.	Sun.	Total

From SHAPE America, *PE Metrics*, 3rd ed. (Champaign, IL: Human Kinetics, 2019).

Appendix T: Physical Activity Log for Step Count – Middle School

---

✍ Physical Activity Log – Step Counts

Name: _____

Over the next three days, you are to wear your pedometer to determine the average number of steps you take each day. Before going to bed each night, use the chart below to record the total number of steps taken that day. Also, record any physical activities in which you participated that day. For example, if you participated in physical education class, attended a practice for a team or dance group, played tag at recess, walked home from school or undertook any other activity that affected your step count, record it. Once you complete the log, answer the questions at the bottom of the sheet.

DAY	TOTAL NUMBER OF STEPS TAKEN	ACTIVITIES DURING THE DAY
#1		
#2		
#3		
Totals		

Questions:

1. What was the average number of steps taken for each day?

2. On what day were you most active? Why were you most active on that day?

3. Based on your three days, should you increase or decrease your activity level? Justify your answer.

From SHAPE America, *PE Metrics*, 3rd ed. (Champaign, IL: Human Kinetics, 2019).

Appendix U: Worksheets on Fitness – High School

✍ *Calculating Target Heart Rate*

Assessment Task

Give students the following instructions:

Complete the following calculations to identify your target heart rate zone (THR). This information is important when engaging in aerobic fitness and/or cardiorespiratory endurance activities.

Note: *Calculations of THR range percentages taken from Target Heart Rate and Estimated Maximum Heart Rate, Centers for Disease Control and Prevention, found at www.cdc.gov/physicalactivity/basics/measuring/heartrate.htm*

Maximum Heart Rate (MHR)   220 – your age   =

_____

Resting Heart Rate (RHR)   HR at rest =

_____

Target Heart Rate (THR)   50%-70% of MHR

_____

Moderate Intensity

Lower THR range (50% of MHR)   MHR x 50% =

_____

Upper THR range (70% of MHR)   MHR x 70% =

_____

Target Heart Rate (THR)   70%-85% of MHR

_____

Vigorous Intensity

Lower THR range (70% of MHR)   MHR x 70% =

_____

Upper THR range (85% of MHR)   MHR x 85% =

_____

Scoring Guide

PERFORMANCE LEVEL	CALCULATION OF MAXIMUM HEART RATE & TARGET HEART RATE ZONES
3	Student calculates maximum heart rate and both target heart rate zones accurately.
2	Student calculates maximum heart rate and one of the target heart rate zones accurately.
1	Student does not calculate maximum heart rate or target heart rate zones accurately.

From SHAPE America, *PE Metrics*, 3rd ed. (Champaign, IL: Human Kinetics, 2019).

✍ *Worksheet on FitnessGram Results*

Name: _____ Class/Day: _____ Teacher: _____

Using the charts provided on the website and wall, report which of the areas (NI = Health risk; HFZ = Healthy Fitness Zone) you scored in each of the five health-related fitness components based on your age and gender.

FITNESS COMPONENT	ACTUAL SCORE (PRE)	ACTUAL SCORE (POST)	ZONE (PRE)	ZONE (POST)
Aerobic Capacity				
Body Composition				
Abdominal Strength and Endurance				
Trunk Extensor Strength and Flexibility				
Flexibility				

FITNESS COMPONENT FOR UPPER BODY STRENGTH AND ENDURANCE (SELECT ONE OF THE THREE BELOW)	ACTUAL SCORE (PRE)	ACTUAL SCORE (POST)	ZONE (PRE)	ZONE (POST)
90-degree push-up				
Modified pull-up				
Flexed-arm hang				

Based on my data, my two strongest fitness areas are:

1. _____   2. _____

Based on my data, my two weakest fitness areas are:

1. _____   2. _____

Looking forward, these will be the biggest challenges or obstacles that I face in improving my health-related fitness:

1. _____   2. _____

I would like to participate in these activities during class to improve my health-related fitness:

1. _____   2. _____

From SHAPE America, *PE Metrics*, 3rd ed. (Champaign, IL: Human Kinetics, 2019).

Appendix V: Nutrition Log – High School

✎ *Sample Nutrition Log*

Nutrition Log

DAY/DATE	MEAL/SNACK	WHAT DID YOU EAT?	WHERE DID YOU EAT AND WITH WHOM DID YOU EAT?	HOW MANY CALORIES DID YOU CONSUME?
Monday **May 1**	Snacks			
	Breakfast			
	Lunch			
	Dinner			
Tuesday **May 2**	Snacks			
	Breakfast			
	Lunch			
	Dinner			
Wednesday **May 3**	Snacks			
	Breakfast			
	Lunch			
	Dinner			
Thursday **May 4**	Snacks			
	Breakfast			
	Lunch			
	Dinner			
Friday **May 5**	Snacks			
	Breakfast			
	Lunch			
	Dinner			
Reflection:				

From SHAPE America, *PE Metrics*, 3rd ed. (Champaign, IL: Human Kinetics, 2019).

Appendix W: Fitness Plan Template – High School

Name: _____ Class/Day: _____ Teacher: _____

DAY/DATE	FITNESS COMPONENT	PLANNED ACTIVITY (TYPE)	METRIC USED	INTENSITY (BORG)	TIME	GOAL FROM PLAN
Monday May 1	Cardio					
	Strength Endurance					
	Flexibility					
	Warm-up					
	Cool-down					
Tuesday May 2	Cardio					
	Strength Endurance					
	Flexibility					
	Warm-up					
	Cool-down					
Wednesday May 3	Cardio					
	Strength Endurance					
	Flexibility					
	Warm-up					
	Cool-down					
Thursday May 4	Cardio					
	Strength Endurance					
	Flexibility					
	Warm-up					
	Cool-down					
Friday May 5	Cardio					
	Strength Endurance					
	Flexibility					
	Warm-up					
	Cool-down					
Saturday May 6	Cardio					
	Strength Endurance					
	Flexibility					
	Warm-up					
	Cool-down					
Sunday May 7	Cardio					
	Strength Endurance					
	Flexibility					
	Warm-up					
	Cool-down					

Note: *You can use this fitness plan at the middle school or high school level. To use it at the middle school level, remove the last four columns on the right to better align the form with the relevant Grade-Level Outcomes for middle school.*

From SHAPE America, *PE Metrics*, 3rd ed. (Champaign, IL: Human Kinetics, 2019).

Appendix X: Written Examination Sample – High School

✍ *Short-Answer Questions Related to Exercise Physiology and Stress Management*

Grade-Level Outcomes

Relates physiological responses to individual levels of fitness and nutritional balance. (S3.H8.L1)

Identifies the structure of skeletal muscle and fiber types as they relate to muscular development. (S3.H9.L2)

Identifies stress-management strategies (e.g., mental imagery, relaxation techniques, deep breathing, aerobic exercise, meditation) to reduce stress. (S3.H14.L1)

Applies stress-management strategies (e.g., mental imagery, relaxation techniques, deep breathing, aerobic exercise, meditation) to reduce stress. (S3.H14.L2)

Respond to the following questions in detail to demonstrate your knowledge of how physical activity can affect the body, one's stress level.

1. Explain how a person's physiological responses relate to his or her level of fitness and nutritional balance (i.e., how your body responds to or changes from exercising). Examples:
   - You might grow short of breath quickly when walking or jogging up a hill if your fitness level is low or your nutrition is poor.
   - You might not be able to carry on a conversation with your friend while cycling at a fast pace.
   - Your muscles might become very sore after completing strength-training exercises.

2. Identify the structure of skeletal muscle and fiber types as they relate to muscular development.
3. Identify three stress-management strategies an individual can use to reduce stress.
4. Apply two of the three stress-management strategies identified in question 3 to reduce your stress. Reflect upon and describe the process for adopting these strategies and what outcomes occurred when you implemented them.

Question 1

PERFORMANCE LEVEL	PHYSIOLOGICAL RESPONSES– FITNESS	PHYSIOLOGICAL RESPONSES – NUTRITIONAL BALANCE
3	Student relates physiological responses to individual levels of fitness specific to a targeted population (e.g., athlete training in pre-season, person beginning to exercise).	Student relates physiological responses to individual levels of nutrition balance specific to a targeted population (e.g., athlete training in pre-season, person beginning to exercise).
2	Student relates physiological responses to individual levels of fitness.	Student relates physiological responses to individual levels of nutrition balance.
1	Student does not relate physiological responses to individual levels of fitness.	Student does not relate physiological responses to individual levels of nutrition balance.

From SHAPE America, *PE Metrics*, 3rd ed. (Champaign, IL: Human Kinetics, 2019).

Question 2

PERFORMANCE LEVEL	SCORING CRITERIA
3	Student correctly identifies the structure of skeletal muscle and fiber types as they relate to muscular development and describes the physiological responses that occur to muscle and fibers based on the health fitness component.
2	Student correctly identifies the structure of skeletal muscle and fiber types as they relate to muscular development.
1	Student does not correctly identify the structure of skeletal muscle and fiber types as they relate to muscular development.

Question 3

PERFORMANCE LEVEL	SCORING CRITERIA
3	Student identifies stress-management strategies (e.g., mental imagery, relaxation techniques, deep breathing, aerobic exercise, meditation) to reduce stress in a particular situation.
2	Student identifies stress-management strategies (e.g., mental imagery, relaxation techniques, deep breathing, aerobic exercise, meditation) to reduce stress.
1	Student does not identify stress-management strategies (e.g., mental imagery, relaxation techniques, deep breathing, aerobic exercise, meditation) to reduce stress.

Question 4

PERFORMANCE LEVEL	SCORING CRITERIA
3	Student applies stress-management strategies (e.g., mental imagery, relaxation techniques, deep breathing, aerobic exercise, meditation) to reduce stress in different situations.
2	Student applies stress-management strategies (e.g., mental imagery, relaxation techniques, deep breathing, aerobic exercise, meditation) to reduce stress.
1	Student does not apply stress-management strategies (e.g., mental imagery, relaxation techniques, deep breathing, aerobic exercise, meditation) to reduce stress.

From SHAPE America, *PE Metrics*, 3rd ed. (Champaign, IL: Human Kinetics, 2019).

Appendix Y: Fitness Contract – High School

✍ *Sample Fitness Plan Contract*

Name: _____ Date: _____

Soon, you will implement your personal fitness plan. The plan that you developed is based on your fitness assessments, your personal activity interest and the areas for improvement that you selected. This contract is to document your commitment to implementing and completing your fitness plan over the course of the health and fitness unit. This will require you to maintain your weekly activity log, track your progress over time and modify your plan as needed. At the end of the unit, you will reflect on your progress based on the SMART goals you set at the beginning.

Your SMART goals:

By signing this contract, you commit to making the changes necessary for improving your current fitness levels and meeting your goals. This includes committing to working out at least three times a week for 60 minutes, tracking your progress by recording the appropriate metrics and reflecting on your progress once a week.

_____

My signature

_____

Parent or teacher signature

Appendix Z: Goal Setting – High School

✎ *Goal Setting Based on a Fitness Scenario*

Name: _____   Class/Day: _____   Teacher: _____

Karen is a 16-year-old sophomore. While she is in the Healthy Fitness Zone (HFZ) for her age group in body composition, based on her body mass index score, she would like to lose 5 pounds for appearance and improve her core body strength. Karen is proud of the fact that she does not exercise regularly and is still able to maintain her weight. She never walks when she can ride and does not like to get sweaty. The only time she is active is in a twice-weekly physical education class and during the daily marching band practices, which contributes to her step counts on most days. She does not participate in any recreational sport or dance activities outside of school. She spends much of her spare time reading, playing video games and practicing her flute. The two activities in which she would like to participate for fitness are any type of aerobic activity that involves music (e.g., step aerobics, cardio kick) and Pilates of some type.

She usually eats breakfast at home, consisting of cereal on most days. Karen buys her lunch at school from the a la carte menu and usually has dinner at home with her family. She does not drink soda but does drink 20 ounces of low-calorie Gatorade on most days. Her favorite snacks are potato chips, chocolate of any kind and anything sweet.

FitnessGram Scores for Karen

Body mass index: 22.3   Flexed-arm hang: 2

Aerobic capacity based on PACER: 37.5   Sit-and-reach: 14

Curl-up: 16   Trunk lift: 11

Based on the scenario above, what fitness or wellness goals would you set for Karen using the SMART criteria, and what activities would you select for her in which to participate during the six-week fitness unit? You may work with a partner in setting the goals and determining activities that Karen might enjoy during the fitness unit. At least one of the goals must be specific to cardiorespiratory endurance and one other must be specific to another selected component of health-related fitness. The two remaining goals may be specific to other fitness components, nutrition or the development of healthy habits. Provide a rationale for your selections based on the data provided. The SMART criteria are listed below as a reminder.

S = Specific: Goals should be written with clarity and define specifically what is to be accomplished.

M = Measurable: Goals should identify exactly what criteria are to be used to measure success.

A = Achievable: Goals should be realistic and attainable given the timeframe.

R = Realistic: Goals should state the final desired results in quantifiable terms.

T = Time-bound: Goals should identify the target date for attaining the goal.

For example: By May 1, 2018, I will improve my cardiorespiratory endurance as measured by the mile run by 10 percent over the next six weeks. (Reduce current 9-minute mile to 8.1 minutes)

Complete the worksheet for Karen on the next page.

From SHAPE America, *PE Metrics*, 3rd ed. (Champaign, IL: Human Kinetics, 2019).

Goal #1 (cardiorespiratory)

Plan of Action: List activities and strategies used to assess progress toward the goal.

Evidence: Identify the type of evidence or metrics collected to determine whether the activities and strategies are effective in meeting the goal or determining progress toward the goal.

Provide a rationale for selecting the goal.

Goal #2

Plan of Action: List activities and strategies used to assess progress toward the goal.

Evidence: Identify the type of evidence or metrics collected to determine whether the activities and strategies are effective in meeting the goal or determining progress toward the goal.

Provide a rationale for selecting the goal.

Goal #3

Plan of Action: List activities and strategies used to assess progress toward the goal.

Evidence: Identify the type of evidence or metrics collected to determine whether the activities and strategies are effective in meeting the goal or determining progress toward the goal.

Provide a rationale for selecting the goal.

Goal #4

Plan of Action: List activities and strategies used to assess progress toward the goal.

Evidence: Identify the type of evidence or metrics collected to determine whether the activities and strategies are effective in meeting the goal or determining progress toward the goal.

Provide a rationale for selecting the goal.

Glossary

21st century skills—"Essential skills, knowledge and dispositions that children need to succeed as citizens and workers in today's world, as well as the necessary support systems needed to create learning environments that support that kind of learning." (Partnership for 21st Century Learning, www.p21.org/index.php?option=com_content&task=view&id=195&Itemid=183, retrieved 11/24/17).

analytic rubric—An assessment and instructional tool that divides assignments/tasks into independent component parts with criterion behaviors defined for each part and across levels of the rubric. Each part is evaluated separately across levels and learners receive feedback for each component part of the assignment/task. The assessment occurs on a continuum defined by criterion behaviors unique to each component (Society of Health and Physical Educators, 2014, p. 115).

applying—Learners can demonstrate the critical elements of the motor skills/knowledge components of the Grade-Level Outcomes within a variety of physical activity environments (Society of Health and Physical Educators, 2014, p. 115).

assessment—The gathering of evidence about student learning and making inferences on student progress and growth based on that evidence (Society of Health and Physical Educators, 2014, p. 90).

authentic assessment—Assessment that takes place under real-world conditions.

blended learning—A combination of classroom, online, and self-directed learning.

checklist—An assessment and instructional tool that evaluates whether individual performance criteria are present or absent. It consists of a list of criterion behaviors and evaluators simply determine "yes" the criterion behavior is present or "no" the criterion behavior is not present. This type of assessment does not attempt to determine the quality of the response (Society of Health and Physical Educators, 2014, p. 115).

Competent level—At the Competent level, students demonstrate all of the identified criteria, exhibiting mastery of the indicator. The Competent level defines the minimal level of performance required for meeting the indicator.

critical components—The equivalent of critical elements for the knowledge and skills in the cognitive and affective domains.

critical elements—The key components of a motor skill that can be observed, the sum of which result in movement efficiency (Society of Health and Physical Educators, 2014, pp. 115-116).

Developing level—At the Developing level, students are moving toward competency and mastery of the identified criteria. At this level competency is "emerging," but further development is needed. With deliberate practice students can move from the Developing level to the Competent level.

differentiated instruction—Teachers vary instruction to address the needs of students and their varying levels of skill/knowledge. Teachers differentiate instruction by modifying the learning environment (e.g., tiered learning activities); providing choices on equipment (e.g., increasing or decreasing the length of a racket); providing choices on the process (e.g., participate in modified game play or continue to practice); modifying practice (e.g., work alone or in a group); and facilitating self-directed activities (e.g., developing and implementing an individualized physical activity program) (Society of Health and Physical Educators, 2014, pp. 115-116).

embedded outcomes—Grade-Level Outcomes that are related to the primary content of a lesson and that give students opportunities to meet more than one outcome during the learning or practice task (Holt/Hale & Hall, 2016, p. 18; Society of Health and Physical Educators, 2014, p. 116).

emerging—Learners participate in deliberate practice tasks that will lead to skill and knowledge acquisition. Learners are in the beginning stages of acquiring motor skills/knowledge. Mastery of the skills/knowledge is emerging through deliberate practice tasks, and at this stage learners are developing competency (Society of Health and Physical Educators, 2014, p. 116).

flipped classroom—Switches conventional lesson content such as lectures or readings to homework, typically online. Class time is then spent on application and active learning experiences.

formal assessment—Involves evaluating a learner's performance with a written or standardized instrument that may have predetermined criteria.

formative assessment—Assessments that are ongoing during instruction, allowing teachers to track student progress and adapt instruction accordingly (Society of Health and Physical Educators, 2014, p. 90).

functional understanding—A combination of cognitive and performance understanding, where the student has a cognitive understanding of the skill or concept and can demonstrate that understanding through movement.

fundamental motor skills—The locomotor, nonlocomotor/stability and manipulative skills that provide the foundation for the more complex and sport-specific movement patterns used in games and sports (Society of Health and Physical Educators, 2014, p. 116).

general rubric—A rubric with indicators that can be used across a variety of activities. For example, a rubric for tactics in an invasion game can be applied to multiple sports within that category, such as soccer, hockey and lacrosse.

grid activities—Grids are squares or rectangles where learners participate in modified game play using predetermined tactics or skills. For example, learners could practice such skills as give & go with a partner within a grid. The passer passes (gives) to a receiver and moves to another portion of the grid (goes) to receive a return pass. The sequence of passing (give), moving to a new space in the grid (go) would be repeated for a predetermined amount of time (e.g., 45 seconds) with partners tracking the number of completed passes. Grids can vary in many ways, including size and shape, number of players within the grid, and with or without defensive pressure (Society of Health and Physical Educators, 2014, p. 116).

holistic rubric—An assessment and instructional tool that assigns a level of performance based on multiple criteria and evaluates the performance as a whole. Learners must demonstrate all the identified criterion behaviors at the level for evaluators to determine the level has been achieved. Like all rubrics, at least two levels must be defined (Society of Health and Physical Educators, 2014, p. 116).

indicator—Indicators identify what is to be specifically assessed using the three rubric levels. For example, an indicator for goal setting at the high school level is "Goals meet the SMART criteria." In other words, the ability of students to write goals that meet the SMART criteria specific to their fitness plan is being assessed. For Standard 1 at the elementary level, indicators are specific to the critical elements for the skill. The indicator column simply states "critical elements" and students must demonstrate the identified critical elements to be scored at the Competent level for the skill. The indicators are similar to student learning outcomes and you can think of them as an "indication" of students demonstrating their mastery of a student outcome.

informal assessment—Involves evaluating a learner's performance without a formal or written instrument.

mature pattern—Learners can execute with efficiency the critical elements of the motor skills pattern in authentic environments (Society of Health and Physical Educators, 2014, p. 117).

maturing—Learners can demonstrate the critical elements of the motor skills/knowledge components of the Grade-Level Outcomes, which will continue to be refined with practice. As the environmental context varies, a maturing pattern may fluctuate, reflecting more maturity in familiar contexts and less maturity in unfamiliar (new) contexts (Society of Health and Physical Educators, 2014, p. 117).

modified games—Small-sided games in which the rules have been modified to emphasize the skills taught in class (e.g., creating a penalty for dribbling to emphasize teaching students to pass rather than dribble) (Society of Health and Physical Educators, 2014, p. 117).

physical literacy—The ability to move with competence and confidence in a wide variety of physical activities in multiple environments that benefits the healthy development of the whole person (Mandigo, Francis, Lodewyk, & Lopez, 2012, p. 28; Whitehead, 2001).

portfolio—A collection of artifacts or assignments used by students to demonstrate their competencies.

post-assessment—Assessment that measures student learning at the end of a unit of instruction.

pre-assessment—Assessment that occurs prior to the start of a unit of instruction. Pre-assessment helps the teacher determine what the students already know and can do.

Proficient level—At the Proficient level, students have not only demonstrated all the required criteria at the Competent level, but demonstrated additional criteria or qualitatively demonstrated a more advanced level of performance. For example, a student could demonstrate all the criteria for the overarm throw and be a competent thrower, while another student adds the wrist snap at the end or lengthens the stride length allowing for more power. The first student has demonstrated competency while the second student has demonstrated proficiency by showing a more advanced level of performance.

project-based learning—"A teaching method in which students gain knowledge and skills by working for an extended period of time to investigate and respond to an authentic, engaging and complex question, problem, or challenge" (BIE, www.bie.org/about/what_pbl, retrieved 11/24/17).

range of motion—The full degree of movement around a joint in any direction.

rating scale—This assessment and instructional tool is similar to a checklist but provides added information on the extent to which criterion behaviors are met. This is accomplished by a gradation of criterion across levels. Gradation of performance can be differentiated by the number of times the behavior occurs (frequency) or by descriptions of performance at each level (quality) (Society of Health and Physical Educators, 2014, p. 117).

rubric—An assessment and instructional tool that identifies criterion behaviors for at least two levels of performance. Each level of the rubric identifies and describes criterion behaviors that contain essential elements of the tasks along a range or continuum of performance expectations (Society of Health and Physical Educators, 2014, p. 117).

small-sided games—Organized games in which the number of players involved is reduced from the conventional competitive version of the sport (e.g., 2v2 basketball, 3v3 volleyball, 6v6 lacrosse) (Society of Health and Physical Educators, 2014, pp. 117-118).

strategy—The overall (long-term) game plan that can lead to success (Mitchell & Walton-Fisette, 2016, p. 231).

summative assessment—Assessment that occurs at the close of a unit of instructional sequence, providing teachers with a comprehensive summary of each student's progress and growth (Society of Health and Physical Educators, 2014, p. 90).

tactics—Moment-to-moment (short-term) adaptations made to address the problems that arise during game play (Mitchell & Walton-Fisette, 2016, p. 231).

wordle—An application for creating a word cloud where the frequency of a particular word determines its size in the cloud.

References

Assor, A., Kaplan, H., & Roth, G. (2002). Choice is good, but relevance is excellent: Autonomy-enhancing and suppressing teacher behaviours predicting students' engagement in schoolwork. *British Journal of Educational Psychology, 72*(2), 261-278.

Barnett, L.M., van Beurden, E., Morgan, P.J., Brooks, L.O., & Beard, J.R. (2008). Does childhood motor skill proficiency predict adolescent fitness? *Medicine & Science in Sports & Exercise, 40*, 2137-2144.

Bryan, C., Sims, S., Hester, D., & Dunaway, D. (2013). Fifteen years after the Surgeon General's Report: Challenges, changes and future directions in physical education. *Quest, 65*, 139-150.

The Cooper Institute. (2017). *FitnessGram administration manual* (5th ed.). Champaign, IL: Human Kinetics.

Corbin, C.B. (2001). The 'untracking' of sedentary living: A call for action. *Pediatric Exercise Science, 13*, 347-356.

Deci, E., & Ryan, R. (2000). The "what" and "why" of goal pursuits: Human needs and the self-determination of behavior. *Psychological Inquiry: An International Journal for the Advancement of Psychological Theory, 11*(4), 227-268. https://doi.org/10.1207/S15327965PLI1104_01

Fisher, M.D., Blackwell, L.R., Garcia, A.B., & Greene, J.C. (1975). Effects of student control and choice on engagement in a CAI arithmetic task in a low-income school. *Journal of Educational Psychology, 67*(6), 776-783. http://dx.doi.org/10.1037/0022-0663.67.6.776

Griffin, L.L., & Butler, J.I. (2005). *Teaching games for understanding: Theory, research and practice.* Champaign, IL: Human Kinetics.

Griffin, L.L., Mitchell, S.A., & Oslin, J.L. (2006). *Teaching sport concepts and skills: A tactical games approach.* Champaign, IL: Human Kinetics.

Hannon, J.C., & Ratcliffe, T. (2005). Physical activity levels in coeducational and single-gender high school physical education settings. *Journal of Teaching in Physical Education, 24*, 149-164.

Hellison, D. (2011). *Teaching personal and social responsibility through physical activity* (3rd ed.). Champaign, IL: Human Kinetics.

Holt/Hale, S.A., & Hall, T. (2016). *Lesson planning for elementary physical education.* Champaign, IL: Human Kinetics.

Lieberman, L., Kowalski, E., et al. (2011). *Assessment for everyone: Modifying NASPE assessments to include all elementary school children.* Reston, VA: National Association for Sport and Physical Education.

Mandigo, J., Francis, N., Lodewyk, K., & Lopez, R. (2012). Physical literacy for educators. *Physical Education and Health Journal, 75*(3), 27-30.

Manitoba Education and Training, School Programs Division. (2000). *Physical education/health education: Manitoba curriculum framework of outcomes for active healthy lifestyles.* Available: www.edu.gov.mb.ca/k12/cur/physhlth/index.html.

Marzano, R.J., & Pickering, D.J. (2011). *The highly engaged classroom.* Bloomington, IN: Marzano Research.

Miller, A., Imrie, B., & Cox, K. (1998). *Student assessment in higher education: A handbook for assessing performance.* London: Kogan Page.

Mitchell, S., & Walton-Fisette, J. (2016). *The essentials of teaching physical education: Curriculum, instruction, and assessment.* Champaign, IL: Human Kinetics.

Mohnsen, B. (Ed.). (2010). *Concepts and principles of physical education: What every student needs to know.* Reston, VA: NASPE.

NASPE. (1992). *Outcomes of quality physical education programs.* Reston, VA: Author.

NASPE. (1995). *Moving into the future: National standards for physical education.* Reston, VA: Author.

NASPE. (2004). *Moving into the future: National standards for physical education* (2nd ed.). Reston, VA: Author.

NASPE. (2009). *PE Metrics: Assessing the national standards: Elementary Standard 1.* Reston, VA: American Alliance for Health, Physical Education, Recreation and Dance.

NASPE. (2010). *PE Metrics: Assessing national standards 1–6 in elementary school.* Champaign, IL: Human Kinetics.

NASPE. (2011). *PE Metrics: Assessing national standards 1–6 in secondary school.* Champaign, IL: Human Kinetics.

NASPE. (2012). *Instructional framework for fitness education in physical education.* Reston, VA: Author.

National Education Association. (2014). *Preparing 21st century students for a global society: An educator's guide to the 'Four Cs'.* Retrieved from www.nea.org/assets/docs/A-Guide-to-Four-Cs.pdf.

Ohio State Board of Education. (2009). *Physical education standards.* Available: http://education.ohio.gov/GD/Templates/Pages/ODE/ODEDetail.aspx?Page=3&TopicRelationID=1793&Content=132142.

Rovegno, I., & Bandauer, D. (2013). *Elementary physical education: Curriculum and instruction.* Burlington, MA: Jones & Bartlett Publishing.

Ryan, R.M., & Deci, E.L. (2000). Self-determination theory and the facilitation of intrinsic motivation, social development, and well-being. *American Psychologist, 55*(1), 68-78. http://dx.doi.org/10.1037/0003-066X.55.1.68

SHAPE America – Society of Health and Physical Educators. (2014). *National standards & grade-level outcomes for K-12 physical education.* Champaign, IL: Human Kinetics.

SHAPE America – Society of Health and Physical Educators. (2015). *The essential components of physical education.* Retrieved October 17, 2017, from www.shapeamerica.org/publications/resources/teachingtools/teachertoolbox/studentassessment.aspx

Stodden, D., Langendorfer, S., & Roberton, M. (2009). The association between motor skill competence and physical fitness in young adults. *Research Quarterly for Exercise and Sport, 80*(2), 223-229.

Stuart, J.H., Biddle, S.H., O'Donovan, T.M., & Nevill, M.E. (2005). Correlates of participation in physical activity for adolescent girls: A systematic review of recent literature. *Journal of Physical Activity and Health, 2*, 423-434.

Superintendent of Public Instruction, Washington. (2008). *Washington State K–12 health and fitness learning standards.* Olympia, WA: Author.

Ward, J., Wilkinson, C., Graser, S.V., & Prusak, K.A. (2008). Effects of choice on student motivation and physical activity behavior in physical education. *Journal of Teaching in Physical Education, 27*, 385-398.

Whitehead, M. (2001). The concept of physical literacy. *European Journal of Physical Education, 6*, 127-138.

Zhang, T., Solmon, M., Kosma, M., Carson, R.L., & Gu, X. (2011). Need support, need satisfaction, intrinsic motivation and physical activity participation among middle school students. *Journal of Teaching in Physical Education, 30*, 51-68.

About the Principal Authors

Stevie Chepko, EdD, is assistant dean in the College of Education at the University of Nebraska at Omaha. She is a well-respected authority on performance-based standards, teaching for mastery and assessment. A hallmark of Dr. Chepko's professional service has been the development of materials that engage practitioners and reflect best practices in the field. She served as chair of the task force that revised the National Standards for Initial Physical Education Teacher Education and served on the AAHPERD Curriculum Framework Task Force for the National Standards & Grade-Level Outcomes for K-12 Physical Education. Dr. Chepko's commitment to the profession has been recognized with many honors including the AAHPERD Honor Award, Eastern District Association, Vermont, Massachusetts and South Carolina Honor Awards; NASPE's Joy of Effort award; selection as an inaugural fellow in the North American Society of Health, Physical Education, Recreation, and Dance; and EDA Memorial Lecturer. She is a member of the West Virginia University Physical Education Hall of Fame and the Castleton State University Athletic Hall of Fame. Dr. Chepko has made hundreds of presentations nationally on performance-based standards and assessment. She earned her undergraduate degree in physical education from West Virginia University and her EdD in curriculum and instruction and sport history at Temple University. Photo courtesy of Winthrop University.

Shirley Holt/Hale, PhD, is a retired physical educator from Linden Elementary School in Oak Ridge, Tennessee, where she taught physical education for 38 years. Dr. Holt/Hale is a former National Elementary Physical Education Teacher of the Year and served as president of the American Alliance for Health, Physical Education, Recreation and Dance (now SHAPE America). She is the coauthor of *Children Moving: A Reflective Approach to Teaching Physical Education* and a coauthor of *Lesson Planning for Elementary Physical Education*. She served as a member of the task force for the revision of the *National Standards & Grade-Level Outcomes for K-12 Physical Education* and was a member of the task force for the first edition of *PE Metrics*. Dr. Holt/Hale is a consultant in elementary physical education curriculum, assessment, and curriculum mapping throughout the United States. Photo courtesy of Oak Ridge Portraits.

Dr. Robert Doan is an assistant professor of Physical Education in the School of Kinesiology at the University of Southern Mississippi. He previously taught elementary physical education before moving into higher education. He currently serves as a board member for the Mississippi SHAPE organization. He is a teacher-education program reviewer for SHAPE America and an article reviewer for two of SHAPE America's professional journals: *Strategies* and *Journal of Physical Education, Recreation and Dance.* Dr. Doan has conducted research studies in a variety of physical education and sports officiating topics. Dr. Doan is an editor of two lesson plan books: *Planning Lessons for Middle School* (2nd book *High School*) *Physical Education: Meeting the National Standards and Grade-Level Outcomes*. He has presented at multiple conferences at the state, district, and national level. Dr. Doan earned his undergraduate degree from Grand Valley State University, attended Winthrop University for his master's degree, and completed his PhD in physical education with an emphasis in curriculum and assessment at the University of South Carolina. Dr. Doan enjoys officiating baseball and volleyball, exploring the outdoors, and spending time with his wife and four kids. Photo courtesy of University of Southern Mississippi.

Dr. Lynn Couturier MacDonald, DPE, is professor and former chair of the Physical Education Department at SUNY Cortland. She is a past president of the National Association for Sport and Physical Education (NASPE) and chaired NASPE's Curriculum Framework & K-12 Standards Revision Task Force, which revised the standards and developed Grade-Level Outcomes. Dr. MacDonald also served as a member of SHAPE America's Physical Education Teacher Education Initial Standards Revision Committee and has served in numerous capacities for AAHPERD, NASPE, and the National Council for the Accreditation of Coaching Education. She has published in numerous peer-reviewed journals in the areas of physical education pedagogy and women's sport history. Dr. MacDonald earned her BS and DPE degrees in physical education from Springfield College and her MS in biomechanics from the University of Illinois at Champaign–Urbana. Her postdoctoral study includes earning a graduate certificate in Advanced Feminist Studies from the University of Massachusetts – Amherst and a MA in American Studies from Trinity College. She was inducted as a fellow in the North American Society for Health, Physical Education, Recreation, Sport and Dance (2016) and recognized for her service to the profession with the AAHPERD Honor Award (2014). Photo courtesy of SUNY.

About SHAPE America

SHAPE America – Society of Health and Physical Educators is committed to ensuring that all children have the opportunity to lead healthy, physically active lives. As the nation's largest membership organization of health and physical education professionals, SHAPE America works with its 50 state affiliates and is a founding partner of national initiatives including the Presidential Youth Fitness Program, Active Schools, and the Jump Rope For Heart and Hoops For Heart programs.

Since its founding in 1885, the organization has defined excellence in physical education, most recently creating *National Standards & Grade-Level Outcomes for K-12 Physical Education* (2014), National Standards for Initial Physical Education Teacher Education (2016), National Standards for Health Education Teacher Education (2017) and *National Standards for Sport Coaches* (2006). Also, SHAPE America participated as a member of the Joint Committee on National Health Education Standards, which published *National Health Education Standards, Second Edition: Achieving Excellence* (2007). Our programs, products and services provide the leadership, professional development and advocacy that support health and physical educators at every level, from preschool through university graduate programs.

The SHAPE America website, www.shapeamerica.org, holds a treasure trove of free resources for health and physical educators, adapted physical education teachers, teacher trainers and coaches, including activity calendars, curriculum resources, tools and templates, assessments and more. Visit www.shapeamerica.org and search for Teacher's Toolbox.

Every spring, SHAPE America hosts its National Convention & Expo, the premier national professional-development event for health and physical educators.

Advocacy is an essential element in the fulfillment of our mission. By speaking out for the school health and physical education professions, SHAPE America strives to make an impact on the national policy landscape.

Our Vision: A nation where all children are prepared to lead healthy, physically active lives.

Our Mission: To advance professional practice and promote research related to health and physical education, physical activity, dance and sport.

Our Commitment: 50 Million Strong by 2029

50 Million Strong by 2029 is SHAPE America's commitment to put all children on the path to health and physical literacy through effective health and physical education programs. We believe that through effective teaching, health and physical educators can help students develop the ability and confidence to be physically active and make healthy choices. As educators, our guidance can also help foster their desire to maintain an active and healthy lifestyle in the years to come. To learn more visit www. shapeamerica.org/50Million.